'Cosgrove weaves a compelling web of circumstance that maps a city struggling with the loss of its youth to the Vietnam War, the hard edge of the civil rights movement and ferocious inner-city rioting. His prose is dense, not the kind that readers looking for a quick tale about singers they know and love might take to, but a proper music journalist's tome redolent of the field research that he carried out in Detroit's public and academic libraries. It is rich in titbits gathered from news reports. It is to be consumed rather than to be dipped into, a whole-hearted evocation of people and places filled with the confidence that it is telling a tale set at a fulcrum of American social and cultural history'

The Independent

'Broadcaster Stuart Cosgrove lifts the lid on the time when the fight for civil rights and clash of cultures and generations came together in an incendiary mix'

Daily Record

'The set-up sparks like the finest pulp thriller. A harsh winter has brought the city to its knees. The car factories are closed and Motown major domo Berry Gordy is fighting to keep his empire afloat.
Stuart Cosgrove's immaculately researched account of a year in the life of the Motor City manages a delicate balancing act. While his love for the era – particularly the music, best exemplified by the dominance of Motown, whose turbulent twelve months are examined in depth – is clear, he maintains a dispassionate, journalistic distance that gives his epic narrative authority and depth . . . History is quick to romanticise Hitsville USA but Cosgrove is not quite so credulous, choosing to focus instead on the dark shadows at the heart of his gripping story. *****'

The Skinny

'A thoroughly researched and fascinating insight into the music and the times of a city which came to epitomise the turmoil of a nation divided by race and class, while at the same time offering it an unforgettable, and increasingly poignant, soundtrack. With his follow-up, *Memphis 68*, on the way, Cosgrove is well set to add yet another string to his already well-strung bow, becoming a reliable chronicler of a neglected area of American culture, telling those stories which are still unknown to most'
Alistair Braidwood

'The story is unbelievably rich. Motown, the radical hippie underground, a trigger-happy police force, Vietnam, a disaffected young black community, inclement weather, The Supremes, the army, strikes, fiscal austerity, murders – all these elements coalesced, as Cosgrove noted, to create a remarkable year. In fact, as the book gathers pace, one can't help think how the hell did this city survive it all? In fact such is the depth and breadth of his research, and the skill of his pen, at times you actually feel like you are in Berry Gordy's office watching events unfurl like an unstoppable James Jamerson bass line. I was going to call this a great music book. Certainly, it contains some of the best ever writing and insight about Motown. Ever. But its huge canvas and backdrop, its rich social detail, negate against such a description. *Detroit 67* is a great and a unique book, full stop.'
Paolo Hewitt, *Caught by the River*

'The subhead for Stuart Cosgrove's *Detroit 67* is "the year that changed soul". But this thing contains multitudes, and digs in deep, well beyond just the city's music industry in that fateful year . . . All of this is written about with precision, empathy, and a great, deep love for the city of Detroit'
Detroit Metro Times

'Big daddy of soul books . . . Over twelve month-by-month chapters, the author – a TV executive and northern soul fanatic – weaves a thoroughly researched, epic tale of musical intrigues and escalating social violence'
TeamRock

'*Detroit 67* is full of detailed information about music, politics and society that engages you from beginning to end. You finish the book with a real sense of a city in crisis and of how some artists reflected events. It is also the first in a trilogy by Cosgrove (*Memphis 68* and *Harlem 69*). By the time you finish this, you'll be eagerly awaiting the next book'
Socialist Review

'A gritty portrait of the year Motown unravelled . . . a wonderful book and a welcome contribution to both the history of soul music and the history of Detroit'
Spiked

'*A* fine telling of a pivotal year in soul music'
Words and Guitars

DETROIT 67

The Year That Changed Soul

STUART COSGROVE

First published in Great Britain by the author in 2015.
This revised edition published in Great Britain in 2016 by Polygon,
an imprint of Birlinn Ltd.

Birlinn Ltd
West Newington House
10 Newington Road
Edinburgh
EH9 1QS

www.polygonbooks.co.uk

3

ISBN 978 1 84697 366 6
eBook ISBN 978 0 85790 334 1

British Library Cataloguing-in-Publication Data
A catalogue record for this book is available on request from the British Library.

Typeset by 3btype.com
Printed by Clays Ltd, Bungay, Suffolk

CONTENTS

HEART AND SOUL

I want to acknowledge the help of those people who influenced *Detroit 67* knowingly or otherwise: most of all my gratitude to the singers, songwriters, musicians and activists who shaped the high-point of sixties soul. Over many years as a journalist frequently writing about soul music, I have met and interviewed many of the central characters in this book but would like to single out two. Mary Wilson of the Supremes, who I had the pleasure to interview at length live on stage at the Victorian and Albert Museum in London, and the late Jimmy Ruffin who shared with me his personal family perspectives about his father and brother; his accounts of his early life in the Deep South were moving in the extreme. I have tried to be as objective as possible about an era of music that has been the subject of wild myth-making and have tried throughout to see the complex events of 1967 in their context, rather than as a battle of good versus evil. Strange as it may seem there are very few books that touch on the story of Motown that have not tried to take sides in the premature death of Florence Ballard. I have resisted taking sides and try wherever possible to see merit in all the key characters, even when their young emotions were driving them forward.

In researching this book, I have been able to mine a wealth of primary resources. I acknowledge several academic institutions, including the Walter P. Reuther Library at Wayne State University in Detroit, which has a world reputation for labour affairs and industrial history. My thanks to the staff of my local library at the University of Glasgow in Scotland, who always made me warmly welcome. I drew heavily on the support of the staff and the primary sources of the Hatcher Graduate Library who provided most of the newspapers of the time and the Bentley Historical Library at the University of Michigan campus in Ann Arbor, Michigan, a specialist historical library which holds the Gordy Family papers, the personal papers of Motown publicist Al Abrams, and the private papers of Detroit radical John Sinclair. It also holds an inestimable collection of Detroit police files and photographs covering the riots of 1967.

I'd also like to acknowledge the influence and support of those underground 'seats of learning' that have formed such an important part of my life – my friends and contacts within the northern rare soul scene. I have had the lifetime privilege to be attached to a subculture which is not only engaged in a passionate love affair with black American music but has defied every attempt to tame that passion over several decades. My thanks therefore to the Universities of Soul that have helped me along the way: Perth City Soul Club, Wigan Casino, Blackpool Mecca, Top of the World, Stafford, and the 100 Club, London. It is impossible to convey to people outwith the scene how informed and analytical collectors on the northern scene are – they are the popular historians of soul music. This imprint of the book is what is known in the rare soul scene as the issue copy. In 2015, to test the potential for the book, it was self-published, or as record collectors would say it was released as a 'private pressing'. But it had its faults, and by contrast, the quality of the book you have in your hand is more professional and the global distribution is of a different class to its predecessor. So, my sincere thanks to the phenomenal team at Polygon who made this version happen, including publisher Neville Moir, the passionate and relentless editor Alison Rae, and designer Chris Hannah.

Finally, I'd like to thank my colleagues at Channel 4 in London and Glasgow, and my colleagues at BBC Scotland for their support. Most of all I want to thank my close friends and family for their encouragement, their good humour and the hope that drives our lives.

The Whole World in His Hands. Berry Gordy, the owner of
the Motown Corporation, poses in his Detroit home in 1966. At the time
he was one of the richest African-Americans in the USA and the
entrepreneurial figurehead of sixties soul. The photo was taken by a
visiting French soul collector Gilles Petard.

JANUARY

Snow

Berry Gordy's townhouse on the exposed corner of Outer Drive and Monica was trapped in a furious wind tunnel. A steep porcelain wall of drifting snow blocked the road outside, and two frozen trees hung heavy like sentries over the doorway. Gordy was reduced to the routine of a prisoner: pacing the room, speaking solemnly to himself, and looking out through the frosted windows at the white prison yards of his hometown.

A deathly silence had descended on the Motor City. Snow had fallen for three consecutive days, and it came with such fury that it smothered the life out of America's busiest city. Suddenly, a city synonymous with the clamour of industry had grown eerily quiet. Most people hid indoors, guarding themselves from the cold and unable to dig a path to their cars, and those few brave souls who did try to get to work were left stranded on street corners, shrouded in military-surplus overcoats and blowing into woollen mittens. Others smoked to stay warm and huddled together, waiting for buses that never came. Cars were left abandoned in side streets, and the scene on Highland Park looked like something from a different decade, where wandering ghosts from the Great Depression stumbled across intersections to the old Ford assembly plant. Over 100,000 automobile workers reported absent from work, Dodge Main in Hamtramck was closed, Chrysler's Eldon Avenue Gear and Axle Plant ground to a halt, and Ford's giant River Rouge plant was on short time. A layer of dense smog hung over the stranded trains at Dequindre Cut, where rusting freight containers lay half hidden beneath the drifts. The newly installed furnaces at Huber Avenue Foundry had more than enough power to smelt steel, but the temperature stayed stubbornly below zero, and nothing could melt the snow. Schools were closed, flights disrupted, and the few reckless freighters that tried to navigate the frozen waters of the Detroit River or made only glacial progress to the lakes were impacted in ice.

Already a teenager when the Second World War broke out, Gordy had grown up in a restless and self-confident city driven by arms manufacturing and the automobile industry. In the years between 1940 and 1943, half a million people migrated to Detroit, and like the Gordy clan over 350,000 of those were African-Americans, mostly from the southern states. But all of that was history now.

Berry Gordy Jr was cut off from his world. He was thirty-eight years old, with a closely cropped afro that had infinitesimal specks of grey settling on the hairline, as if he had been momentarily caught in the blizzards outside. In January 1967 he was one of the richest black entrepreneurs in America and the driving force behind the Motown Record Corporation, the black-owned company that had defied the rules of the recording industry to become the powerhouse of sixties soul from an unfashionable base in the heart of the Rust Belt. In the previous fiscal year alone, over seventy-five per cent of the company's releases had been hits, and Motown's major acts – the Supremes, the Four Tops, the Temptations and Marvin Gaye – were international household names. It seemed to those who had watched his success that Gordy had discovered a modern form of alchemy on turning gospel into gold. By the time the Motown Corporation was incorporated on 12 January 1959, Detroit's image as a boomtown was wearing thin, and the first corrosive signs of decline were beginning to show. Unemployment was rising, particularly among unskilled black males, many of whom were dependent on irregular shifts and low-paid labour in the car plants and armament factories. The underlying realities were plain to see, but the powerful myth of Detroit as 'the arsenal of democracy' overshadowed everything, and immigrants from the South still flocked northward to the city, believing that it was a placed paved with limitless opportunity.

Gordy had just returned home from Miami Beach, where the Supremes were in residency at the Deauville Hotel; he'd caught one of the last flights to land at a bitterly cold Metro Airport. The central heating in his Outer Drive home was turned up full blast, but it had next to no impact, and the cold was so fierce he had draped himself in layers of clothes: a poplin shirt, neat slacks with hip slit pockets, and a scruffy hooded sweater over his suit jacket. Two paintings of exotic palm trees hung on the wall above his piano. He had put them there to bring a touch of exotica to his home, but they looked forlorn and out of place.

Gordy was unaccustomed to silence. He had worked on the Detroit assembly lines, upholstering new cars, and had grown up with the endless percussion of the automobile plants. He had even trained himself to beat out tunes in his head, scribbling them in his mind and then recording them on paper when his shift ended. Gordy tried to fight the snowy silence at first by playing the piano, listening to acetate copies of newly recorded Motown songs, and flipping through the latest release sheets. His life had been shaped by vinyl. Records were stacked casually in the backseat of his car, piles of them lay scattered around his office, and those he really liked were stored in alcoves in his home. He had grown up surrounded by the sounds of the Motor City – the atonal journeys of jazz, the wholesome divinity of gospel, the hard-drinking coarseness of R&B, and the sweet choral repetitions of sixties soul.

To his friends and family, Gordy was a difficult man to fathom.

He hid behind a contradictory personality, preferring the thrill of creativity to the managerial machinations of his wealthy business. He was a proud family man yet he played fast and loose with family values, playing poker, chasing other women and drinking hard liquor. From a young age he had come to romanticise the word 'family' – and used it promiscuously to describe Motown as if it were a timeless and impregnable virtue – but as 1967 unfolded it was a term that was shattered under the weight of over-use. He had grown up in a bustling post-war home, the second youngest child in a family of ten. He had been married three times, had four children, and racked up numerous love affairs. Those who knew of his past as a local boxer described him as at times pugnacious, a man who jabbed at problems, but when the fight hardened and the gloves came off, he often weaved away from direct confrontation. Despite his skill in the ring, Gordy spent most of 1967 trying to avoid fights and when Motown's most talented stars reached a point where they wanted to know more about his business and its worth, Gordy often withdrew and took animosity like a punch-bag.

In the freezing early hours of the new year, Detroit had claimed its first victim. Kenneth Biel, a fourteen-year-old boy from Oak Park, lay dead in the snow, his face resting on a pillow of solid ice beneath a row of elm trees. When his body was first examined at the Wayne County morgue, his death was attributed to intentional carbon monoxide poisoning, but his parents reacted badly to the news and resisted any suggestion of suicide. A subsequent investigation determined that the teenager had been drinking cheap whisky and then slumped down drunk by a tree not far from his home. Still hunting for dignity in his death, the family denied that their son had ever drunk alcohol, but the police confirmed that buried beer bottles had been found nestled in the snow and patches of spilled liquor had burned into the rock-hard Michigan soil below. Biel was from Detroit's Motown generation, a young white teenager discovering girls, music and cheap thrills, and growing up in a city witnessing change on a massive scale. But like most of the events that were to unfold in 1967, his death was shrouded in doubt and his funeral mired in dispute. His friends disagreed with his parents, who disagreed with the police, who in turn were not wholly convinced of their own version of events. It was a tragedy that proved to be prescient of the twelve months ahead – a year that was destined to become one of unexplained deaths and conflicting narratives, a time in which friendships would fracture into ugly and irreconcilable shapes. Even the morgue where Biel's body was taken was destined to become an unlikely character in the year ahead, embroiled in cases of missing bodies as Detroit's death toll mounted and the city's budget came under unprecedented pressure.

The only good news was soul music. Detroit's conveyor belt of black music had triggered a creative Klondike and small four-track recording studios were crammed into suburban homes and basement cellars. More than 400 independent music labels had sprung up in the city in less than five years. The vast majority of these local enterprises were undercapitalised and destined for obscurity, but it proved to be one of the most creative moments in the history of pop music, and for those who found success, it was the era that defined their lives. The sudden influx of cash into predominantly poor households overturned the natural order: rivalries were intense, egos went unchecked, and the city crackled with the energetic sound of black America. 'The stream of hits was endless,' Gordy said in his autobiography *To Be Loved*. 'The whole world was fast becoming aware of our artists, our songs, our sound. I was being called a star-maker, the magic man.' Gordy's magic was in many respects predicated on a compromise. He had softened the rough edges of rhythm and blues, draped the music in the familiar cadences of teenage love, and his girl groups – borrowing from predecessors like the Ronettes and the Crystals – pioneered a highly addictive form of 'bubblegum soul' that lent itself perfectly to the still-segregated radio stations of America. Phil Spector, a major influence on the Motown Sound, described it as 'little symphonies for the kids'. It was in every respect an art of repetition: familiar backing tracks were refashioned, everyday phrases repackaged and the anxieties of young love were played out as memorable drama.

Gordy's sorcery was founded on talent and circumstance. Detroit had an enlightened public-school system that brought classical music, choral training and jazz into ghetto classrooms. The city had hundreds of churches dotted along its main boulevards, and the gospel choirs were among the most competitive in black America. More importantly, Detroit had a magnetic force that drew talent towards it. It had been a hub of inward migration for over 200 years dating back to the Underground Railroad network that helped fugitive slaves escape north to Detroit and then over the river to freedom in Canada. For decades it was the southern states that provided Detroit's human capital. All three members of the Supremes could trace their family's roots back to the Deep South; Eddie Kendricks and Paul Williams of the Temptations had been part of a more recent migration and came north from Birmingham, Alabama; Marvin Gaye had relocated from his native Washington DC, via jazz and doo-wop; and an eccentric barber named George Clinton had moved from New Jersey to join the local Revilot label and to lead yet another emergent group, the Parliaments. Most came prospecting for gold discs and found themselves in a city of unrestrained rivalry, vocal brilliance and bitter feuding.

Motown was based in a converted house at 2648 West Grand Boulevard on Detroit's West Side. It was an unremarkable shambles of a place with only the most basic facilities. Situated on a street that had only recently been reclassified to allow commercial businesses, it sat among local homes and other hopeful businesses, including a doctor's office, a funeral parlour, the Your Fair Lady Boutique and Wig Room, and Mr Sykes's Hernia Clinic. The Motown neighbourhood near General Motors headquarters had once been prosperous, but the shingled walls, polite porches and wooden window frames had all decayed with the passage of time. Mary Wilson, in her book *My Life as a Supreme*, described it as 'a small nondescript two-storey house that had been converted to a photography studio'. Stevie Wonder's mother, Lula Hardaway, remembered an office that was 'brimming with people and noise – the entire house was teeming, chaotic, always, as if in the middle of an air raid'. Smokey Robinson's staccato description painted a picture of cramped efficiency: 'Downstairs became headquarters. Kitchen became the control room. Garage became the studio. The living room was bookkeeping. The dining room [was] sales. Berry stuck a funky sign in the front window – "Hitsville USA" – and we were in business.'

America was changing, too slowly for some, but nonetheless this small row of unremarkable houses had become the fulcrum of the most dynamic music business in the world. Soul had made Gordy phenomenally rich. Although he dressed fashionably in slick suits, he was always one of the more understated members of the family. His sisters Anna and Gwen, who had preceded him as label owners in the local independent music scene, were among Detroit's black demi-monde and stepped out at night in ermine and mink. Gordy's second wife, Raynoma, described the sisters as being bigger than the music itself. 'Show business was Gwen Gordy's middle name . . . She was exquisite from head to toe, with an assortment of gorgeous black wigs and dyed shoes to match all her outfits. Her face was flawless, and her figure was so stunning that later she would become a fashion model.' By contrast, Gordy's suits were off the rack. He had a half-hearted moustache and close-cropped hair in a vaguely military style that had changed little since he had served in the Korean War. And while the big stars of Motown travelled with monogrammed luggage, Gordy's bags usually carried the imprimatur of BOAC-Cunard, the airline that ran weekly flights from Detroit to Europe.

Diana Ross, the regal lead singer of the Supremes, once described Gordy as 'a genius open to abundant possibilities'. 'He never thought small,' Ross claimed. 'No matter how difficult the challenge, he could envision and hold on to the big picture, and he had little time or patience for anyone who wouldn't go there with him.' Ross first fell in love with him in 1965 as they travelled together from venue to venue, and she soon began to speak of him as both a father figure and a lover, 'an incomparable visionary, a dynamite character'. Even in the face of hostile criticism, she remained devoted to Gordy. She reorganised his virtues as a leader while others denounced him as a control freak, womaniser and a reckless gambler.

Gordy was years ahead of his time. He was obsessed with sales charts and publishing data, and how music was perceived by the different ages and demographics across America. His curiosity was instinctive and it anticipated major changes yet to come in the recording industry. At times his passion for music tipped into an autistic-like control. He was able to identify faults in a recording within seconds, and he worried away at recording takes as if he were counting on an abacus. Although he was wealthy enough to own the most up-to-date sound systems in America, he preferred to listen to his songs the way real people did – on box record players, on transistor radios, and in cars. Gordy often went against the acoustic grain of his studio engineers and turned the volume down, reckoning that many people listened to music in the background, not at its highest volume. He would sometimes drive around the block to listen to a song on his car radio rather than at the studio desk and he preferred voices that were pleasing but distinctive: singers like Tammi Terrell, Levi Stubbs of the Four Tops, and the tempestuous David Ruffin of the Temptations. One of his favourite voices belonged to his eccentric and emotionally unpredictable brother-in-law Marvin Gaye, who had married Gordy's sister, Anna, in 1963. But Gordy was also deeply judgemental and often consigned new songs to the scrap heap on the basis of the first few incriminating beats. Careers had been cut short in those few decisive opening bars, and so artists across Detroit had come to respect and resent him in equal measure.

In the previous few days Gordy had experienced extremes of weather – the dry heat of Miami and the brutal cold of Detroit. The Supremes were performing at the Casanova Room at the fashionable Deauville Hotel on Miami Beach and had been contracted to do two shows daily using a local pick-up band, the Les Rohde Orchestra. They sang 'Baby Love' in Santa hats and posed for photographs on the bench beneath the sweltering Christmas sun. The stick-thin lead singer, Diane Ross, had by now glamorised her name to Diana Ross. Her friend, the stockier Florence Ballard, had shortened her name to Flo, while the third Supreme, the coquettish and fashionable Mary Wilson, was content just to be Mary. They sang happy holiday songs, signed autographs, flirted with the cameras, blew kisses to high-rollers, and smiled at staff in the hotel lobby. Fans gave them the 'stop' sign wherever they went. It had become the trademark opening of their worldwide hit 'Stop In The Name of Love', a rush of adrenaline that the rock magazine *Rolling Stone* described as quixotic: 'The sound mixes with your bloodstream and heartbeat even before you begin to listen to it.' By 1967, the Supremes had sung the song so often and performed the actions so many times, onstage, at industry conventions, and for fans' photographs, that it had become an everyday obligation they all in different ways had come to resent.

In reality, the Supremes' outwardly cheery and enthusiastic personas had become a carefully controlled deceit. Their friendship was under severe strain, they had travelled extensively for three years without a break, and they were exhausted – to the point of breakdown – by damaging disputes over workload and hierarchy. Although Christmas had thrown superficial glitter across the surfaces of their lives, back in their Miami hotel rooms the girls brooded alone, often phoning home for advice and emotional support. It was an unholy and unpleasant mess, poisonous venom had bored into the heart of the group, and friendships that had been forged during excited teenage years were cracking.

Gordy had made a short round trip to Florida in the last days of December 1966, ostensibly to choreograph the Deauville residency and supervise network television coverage of the annual King Orange Jamboree Parade. But his real motive was to act as a peacemaker and try yet again to bring a semblance of harmony back to the group. He had spent the last six months calming disputes and had become anxious that the in-fighting and bitching were about to go public. Hostile journalists were hovering around looking for a story, and although Motown had always counselled the girls to behave in public that too brought pressure. Gordy was not naive about the dynamics within the Supremes and had frequently chastised his girlfriend, Diana, about her role in provoking disputes. He instructed the road crew to enforce corporation policy at all times, reminding the Supremes that Motown had a family image and the last thing he needed was bad press, tantrums or empty bottles of alcohol in hotel bedrooms. He told them things would improve and that within a few days they would be on a flight back to Metro Airport, and then they could take a short break, hand out gifts to their families back in Detroit, and bicker in the comfort of their own homes. For now they were to look happy, wave to the crowds, and blow kisses to the cameras.

By the Christmas of 1966, American television networks were at their competitive height, and sales of colour TV sets had taken off. Gordy had been an early convert to the promotional potential of television and was convinced that the networks were the next logical phase of Motown's success. He had mapped out TV as a priority for the company in 1967 and instructed Motown staff in Detroit to make a strategic shift of focus from radio to television and from small-scale live shows to television spectaculars. Gordy's aim was to make musical history by taking black music into the living rooms of white America, which until then had been culturally resistant to soul music. Network television was by now a priority over everything, including family, friends and even concert engagements. Throughout the year, the Supremes appeared on all the major network television shows – *The Ed Sullivan Show*, *The Andy Williams Show* and *The Tonight Show* starring Johnny Carson – but their vibrancy onscreen masked a bitter, self-destructive war behind the scenes, one that would erupt into public view as the year unfolded.

The most popular girl group in the world were being pushed to the point of exhaustion, and all of them were on prescription drugs, trying to shake off a catalogue of illnesses. On the first day of the year, as Detroit lay engulfed in snow, the Supremes led a parade of marching bands and carnival floats down Biscayne Boulevard under a humid afternoon sun. They recorded two promotional shows. One was an NBC telecast from the Orange Bowl, broadcast on the morning of 2 January and presented by Lorne Green, best known as Ben Cartwright, the quintessential father figure from the TV series *Bonanza*. Lorne joked with the girls and acted as if he was the caring father of a multiracial family. The second show was a pre-recording of the *Ice Capades*, a variety show on ice starring American ice-skating champion Donald Knight and life-size characters from the cartoon series *The Flintstones*. It was scheduled for broadcast in February.

On the third day of January, Gordy received a series of frantic phone calls from Miami. There had been a car accident and two of the Supremes had been rushed to hospital; there were fears that one or more of them were on life-support. Information was sketchy, and neither the police nor hospital staff could give a full account of what had actually happened. An officer with the Miami police had tried to reach Gordy but failed to get through, and so Motown were forced to respond to questions from local reporters without being in full possession of the facts. Eventually it emerged that a car crash involving three vehicles had taken place at the junction of Sixty-Fifth and Collins, just south of the Deauville Hotel, and that various passengers – including two of the Supremes, Diana Ross and Florence Ballard – had been rushed to the hospital. Police had already charged a Motown security guard named Barry Don Oberg with dangerous driving. By the time the patchy news reached Detroit, the girls were in separate rooms at Miami's St Francis Hospital. Shows were hurriedly cancelled and audiences turned away disappointed. When the full picture began to emerge, however, it was significantly less dramatic than Gordy had been led to believe. The girls had been on their way to an afternoon fishing trip when the accident happened, and although they were kept in the hospital overnight, Ross and Ballard were released with only superficial wounds. Mary Wilson had stayed back at the hotel to relax by the pool – possibly an act of personal respite. She had become increasingly caught up in persistent disputes between Ross and Ballard, and rather than take sides often simply avoided their company.

Ross and Ballard cuddled and consoled each other on their way back to the hotel, and it momentarily appeared as if the trauma of the car crash had allowed peace to break out. Hearing it all second-hand, Gordy had a good feeling about the incident and told his sister Esther that it was a wake-up call that might just shake the girls out of their constant bickering. But it was wishful thinking. Back at the hotel, another argument erupted, and each of the Supremes returned to their separate rooms in rancorous silence. Divisions within Motown's biggest-selling group were already deeper than the Detroit snow.

Deep snow drifts had stacked up alongside a stretch of old converted stores by the John Lodge Freeway. Inside the ramshackle buildings were the headquarters of the Detroit Artists Workshop, the Committee to End the War in Vietnam, and the offices of a group of political subversives who were known by the mysteriously bureaucratic name 'the Steering Committee'. They had launched the year with a mission statement that threatened social unrest: 'This is truly a new year. We have been preparing for 1967 all our lives, and we are ready for it now.' Trapped by the snow, they passed their time playing jazz, planning disruption, and plotting the downfall of America. Over the next few years, they would become notorious across the city. There was John Sinclair, a jazz-obsessed journalist from Flint, Michigan, Gary Grimshaw, a graphic artist from Lincoln Park, Jim Semark, a poet and student at nearby Wayne State University, and Rob Tyner, a local singer whose real name was Robert 'Bob' Derminer but who had adopted the surname of jazz musician McCoy Tyner. Tyner was the lead singer of a then unknown Detroit guitar band, the Motor City Five, which by the end of 1967 were rechristened MC5 and destined to become the vanguard of Detroit's other great musical subculture: insurrectionary garage rock.

The Steering Committee was plotting social change, borrowing promiscuously from cool jazz, the American beat poets, and Detroit's black Muslim firebrand, Malcolm X. In one audacious manifesto, they threatened to disrupt Detroit with rock music, declaring 'a total assault on the culture by any means necessary, including rock and roll, dope, and fucking in the streets'. They had fashioned numerous half-secret identities, sometimes working under the name Trans-Love Energies, sharing office space with LEMAR (LEgalize MARijuana), and hosted fundraisers for the anti-war movement.

But unknown to the storefront radicals of the Steering Committee, they had already been infiltrated by undercover police officers working for the Detroit narcotics squad, and their lives were about to turn upside down. The Steering Committee was on a growing list of underground groups whom the FBI's counterintelligence network had identified as a threat to American security, but within a matter of a few years, despite being monitored almost daily, they delivered on their bombastic promise. MC5 became a self-styled 'guitar army' and one of the most controversial rock cadres in the kaleidoscopic history of rock counterculture.

Detroit was divided by race and social class, and although the hives of creativity that grew up around Motown and MC5 developed only a few miles apart, the racial characteristics of the city meant that they occupied profoundly different worlds. Berry Gordy was the undisputed boss of Motown; if the Steering Committee had anything as conventional as a leader, then it was affable jazz freak John Sinclair, who wrote passionate diatribes for the jazz magazine *Downbeat* and had recently been released from DeHoCo, the Detroit House of Corrections, where he had served a short sentence for possessing marijuana.

The bearded Sinclair was a giant of a man. His writings were a hybrid of gonzo journalism, revolutionary rhetoric and jazz homage, and his musical tastes shifted eclectically from day to day, jumping restlessly from free-form jazz to gutbucket R&B and onward to the nascent noise of garage rock. Music and drugs fused in his mind, and he vowed in his prison writings to change America 'by the magic eye of LSD and the pounding heartbeat of music'. Within a matter of a few months in early 1967, he became the mentor and then the manager of MC5, who were destined to become the demonic fathers of punk rock. The band's name was deliberately vague, designed to sound like a car component. Although technically short for Motor City Five, the band sometimes claimed that MC5 stood for the Morally Corrupt Five or the Much Cock Five – whatever the band members made up in the presence of gullible journalists. Sinclair added to the hyperbole, describing the group as 'a raggedy horde of holy barbarians, marching into the future'. It was not just posturing. Within two years they would be the most notorious band in America, and Sinclair would be back in jail, this time as an international cause célèbre accused of conspiring to blow up the Michigan headquarters of the CIA.

Sinclair despised Motown. He was suspicious of Gordy and the grip he had over young artists, and believed that Motown was peddling an anodyne, compromised and saccharine style of R&B that did not deserve the name soul and had fatally compromised a rougher and more honest form of black expression. Periodically, he used his *Downbeat* column to comment on Detroit's local black music scene, and he did it with unrestrained passion, often by disparaging Gordy's burgeoning empire. It was a one-way rivalry. Gordy never replied, and it is not even clear whether he knew he was under attack. Sinclair, like many others of his generation, felt that Motown had diluted the burning liquor of R&B and turned it into a soft drink. In one near libellous attack, he described Motown as an 'exploitation creep scene' and accused Gordy of ripping off naïve and impressionable young ghetto singers, or 'spade groups', as he routinely called them.

It was not the first time Gordy had been accused of exploitation. His own musicians whispered behind his back, and the term 'exploitation' was to pursue him – often unfairly – for the rest of his working life. Gordy was not a particularly litigious man, nor was he easily wounded. He tended to brush off criticism with a shrug. He had a work schedule stacked higher than the snow and precious little free time and was not about to waste time pursuing a bickering jazz critic or the half-chewed polemic of local hippies. Gordy treated the Steering Committee with the ultimate disdain: he didn't appear to even know they existed.

Motown and the Steering Committee lived in different versions of Detroit, a city where housing was still largely segregated, where communities existed incommunicado, and where suspicion had crept into everyday life. Gordy and Sinclair were both hard-core jazz fans who bought records from the same makeshift shops, but they heard radically different things in music. Sinclair was the son of a teacher, and heard a revolutionary zeal in jazz and thought it angry, disruptive and challenging. Gordy had grown up under the stewardship of an immensely aspirational black family who had already escaped the ghetto. He had come to resent the way that African-American music was marginalised. Gordy was determined to occupy the mainstream; to him anyone who wanted music to change the world through disruption was speaking a different language.

A growing number of people in Detroit did want to change the world. The war in Vietnam was escalating, and by the evening of 2 January, Detroit had lost another victim, but this time the death was far from home. In Vietnam, dense wet fog and swollen rice paddies had bogged down US patrols around the Hoa Basin in South Vietnam, and in a brief flurry of confusion, eighteen-year-old George Scanlan of the Eleventh Military Transport Battalion, an Irish-Catholic boy with twelve siblings from the northeast side of Detroit, was shot in the stomach. It was less than a week since Scanlan had landed at Da Nang Harbor, and a close friend told the local press that his death was 'a call to reality'. Scanlan was the first of several hundred young men from Detroit who would be killed or seriously injured in 1967. Unlike Scanlan, most were black and many had been recruited from the ranks of the city's unemployed. Gordy had served in Korea and was predisposed to the military effort. He viewed everything through the prism of music sales and rarely talked about politics. The Steering Committee was less reticent. It was already at the vanguard of a restless Detroit underground that was willing to mobilise against American militarism and stop the war.

Although their paths never crossed, Berry Gordy and John Sinclair both owed a debt of gratitude to the irrepressible 'Frantic' Ernie Durham. Frantic Ernie rocked Detroit. He was a famous R&B DJ on WJLB and had a custom-built studio in the Gold Room of a local nightclub called the 20 Grand, a bowling alley, jazz lounge and soul venue which sat astride a corner on Fourteenth and Warren. Ernie was just one of the formidable cast of characters drawn there. A master self-promoter, he came after bebop but before hip-hop and spoke in rhyming couplets in the demonstrative language of cool: 'Cut the chatter and roll a platter, it's "Treasure Of Love", by Clyde McPhatter.'

You had to hand it to Ernie Durham – he had never been restrained by shyness. He once sold pots and pans around the streets of Harlem, hustled a job as a news anchorman, and then moved to Detroit, where his frantic delivery style made him one the most popular DJs in the Midwest. Frantic Ernie was in such demand that he had two shows on the same night, one in the blue-collar town of Flint, where Sinclair grew up, and the other deep in the heart of the Motor City. He drove frantically from one show to the other, come rain or snow, with an entertainer's contempt for speed limits, never missing a beat and never missing a show.

Gordy owed Durham. He hand-delivered the DJ newly pressed Motown records as soon as they saw light of day. Whether it was Stevie Wonder or Hattie Littles, the stars who shone brightest or those who simply disappeared, Ernie Durham played them all, and his influence was all pervasive. John Sinclair of the Steering Committee saw him as a sort of shaman and singled him out as an influence in his memoirs: 'I just turned the radio dial one day, sitting in my little bedroom in Davison, Michigan, and *boom*! There it was – the music that would turn my whole life around and shoot all of us into a totally new future.' Sinclair had grown up smitten with R&B, and the music had left an indelible mark on him. 'It was incredible,' he once wrote in *Guitar Army*, a series of collected essays, where he paid bombastic homage to artists like Little Richard, James Brown and Detroit's Little Willie John: 'These dudes opened their mouths to sing, and a whole new race of mutants leaped out dancing and screaming into the future, driving fast cars and drinking beer and bouncing around half naked in the backseats, getting to march through the sixties and soar into the seventies like nothing else that ever existed before.'

As a sixteen-year-old high-school student, Sinclair had become so besotted by the new R&B he cast himself as Durham's acolyte. As a disc jockey at high-school hops in the Flint area, he even used the moniker 'Frantic John', playing records by Little Richard until the lights went out. By 1967 his schoolboy nickname was long gone, and the local press now dubbed him 'the high priest of Detroit's hippies'. As the winds of change circled round Detroit he remained loyal to the subversive power of R&B: 'These black singers and magic music makers were the real "freedom fighters" of America, but nobody even knew it. They walked right into the bedrooms of middle-class Euro-Amerika and took over, whispering their super sensual maniac drivel into the ears and orifices of the daughters of Amerika, turning its sons into lust-crazed madmen and fools.'

By 1967 Frantic Ernie Durham's power was in decline and the old R&B radio-station era he had come to personify was hanging on for dear life. The executive team at Motown believed that the R&B of their youth was trapped in a ghetto of its own making and was stuck in the past. They still kept the old-style DJs onside, but time was passing them by and the tastes and infrastructure of the city had changed around them. The freeways through Detroit had wiped away many of the ageing R&B haunts. Hastings Street, in the old Black Bottom ghetto on the near East Side where Gordy had grown up when his family migrated north from Georgia, had been bulldozed to make way for the Chrysler Freeway. New supper clubs were springing up, and network television was a direct route to bringing pop music into American homes. The radio personalities that had inspired Gordy as a teenager – Frantic Ernie Durham, Joltin' Joe Howard, Long Lean Larry Dean and Martha Jean 'the Queen' Steinberg – were losing their grip on power. They had been transistor gods in the late fifties and had helped out when he'd hawked his first Tamla releases around town, but with each passing year the new FM stations and the growth of television eroded their relevance. Even Frantic Ernie was slowing down.

When Mary Wilson of the Supremes first met the Gordys, they had left the Hastings Street ghetto behind and become a 'prominent middle-class Detroit family'. She witnessed Gordy's success close-up. 'There were lots of young entrepreneurs like Berry around in the fifties,' she wrote. 'In those days some of these men were looked on as hustlers, and to some degree, I guess they were. The music business was tough, unlike any other hustle. Smooth talk went only so far; sooner or later you had to deliver the goods.' Gordy had absorbed a more resilient sense of business at the Booker T. Washington store, his father's small neighbourhood grocery at Farnsworth and St Antoine. The store was named after the nineteenth-century Negro educator Booker T. Washington, whose philosophy of self-help had shaped three generations of ambitious African-Americans since slavery. Even in childhood, Gordy had been taught to challenge discrimination and seize success. His second wife, Raynoma Liles, described the early years of Motown as living in a tornado, and she felt swept along by unpredictable energy. In a score-settling book *Berry, Me and Motown*, she described Gordy as 'a born leader' with 'an unquenchable gift for infusing a group with such spirit that they'd come out of a meeting fired up and raring to go'. But those who described his success as meteoric or unbridled were only telling part of the truth. Gordy's first music venture, running a local jazz store, failed ignominiously. His fascination with jazz was not universally shared, and he naïvely invested in racks of obscure records that remained undiscovered and unsold. One periodic customer was John Sinclair but the shop was not open long enough for anything close to recognition. Pops Gordy, the family's sage, frequently recited an enduring family motto: 'A smart man profits from his mistakes.' It was a lesson his second-youngest son learned the hard way. For a period of time in 1964, Motown itself teetered on the brink of bankruptcy, and there was widespread anxiety within the family that he was staring another catastrophic failure in the face. It was Gordy's more financially savvy sister Loucye who rescued the business by implementing improved management systems and changing the terms of recoupment in order to improve liquidity and cash flow. She was of the view that raw talent was meaningless unless you could claw in revenues quickly from national distributors.

Despite these early setbacks, by January 1967 the great-grandson of a dirt-farm slave from Milledgeville, Georgia, had broken the mould of American music. He had taken the Supremes into the mainstream of America's white pop market. When it came to understanding and exploiting the music market, Gordy had few rivals. He was an instinctive entrepreneur who had absorbed business acumen around the kitchen table or behind the counter at the grocery store. He knew that the music business was different, but he was wise enough to know it wasn't that different, and that what he didn't know could be learned from his sisters or his father. Pops Gordy was a wire-thin man with a pointed grey beard that seemed to accentuate his long skinny face. A product of the Great Migration north, on his arrival in Detroit in the twenties he had been the unwitting victim of a property scam. He'd lost the family's life savings when he tried to secure a lease on a dilapidated slum from a rogue landlord. It was a humiliating setback that dented his self-esteem and left the family in dire straits, but wounded pride was to breed an even greater desire to succeed and a lifelong hatred of low-level cheats and criminals. Within a matter of another ten years, Gordy Sr owned several small businesses: a plastering company, a printing shop, and the jewel in the crown, the Booker T. Washington grocery store.

Hard work, social enterprise and lifelong learning were to become a Gordy family trait and the underlying reason that Motown ultimately succeeded. While raising her seven children, Gordy's mother, Bertha, had carved out her own career. She was an agent for Western Mutual Insurance, studied retail management at Wayne State University, and ran several local initiatives. She eventually set up one of Detroit's first mutual insurance companies aimed at low-income black families and was an activist in the Detroit chapter of the National Association for the Advancement of Colored People (NAACP). For a period of time in the early sixties, she was a branch member of the Housewives League of Detroit, a group led by the visionary community activist Fannie B. Peck. It was a social enterprise that sought to convince black housewives that they could influence the economy by targeting their household spending at stores owned by African-Americans. Under the galvanising motto 'Stabilize the economic status of the Negro through directed spending', the Housewives League turned their purses into a political force. This spirit of self-help became the Gordy family's core value, and it was in the new year of 1959 that Berry Gordy applied for a business loan to set up the Motown Record Corporation.

While many aspiring black businesses were locked out of start-up funding by discriminatory banks or by restrictive commercial contracts, Gordy had the option of applying to his family's own bank, the Ber-Berry Co-op, a family fund established by his mother. The headquarters of the Gordys' mutual fund was around the family dinner table at 5139 St Antoine. It was a tense meeting at which his usually loyal sister Esther voiced significant doubts about the music distribution industry and its inherent racial bias. Despite her interventions Gordy was loaned $800 to launch Motown. It proved to be one of the most spectacularly successful start-up investments in the corporate history of America. Gordy's sisters already ran a network of small businesses across the city, from cigarette franchises to record labels. Preeminent among them was the cautious Esther, who founded the Gordy Printing Company, and Loucye, who became the first black administrator at the Michigan Army Reserve at Fort Wayne. Both were eventually recruited to Motown in senior positions, and although they were among Gordy's most trusted allies, there was an underlying sense that they had been put there to protect the family's investment. When the company faced any major problems, it was to his sisters that Gordy instinctively turned.

Snow fell persistently throughout January. For those raised in Detroit, extremes of weather triggered personal memories of childhood long into adult life. For Motown's first solo star, Mary Wells, snow signified the crushing poverty of her early years. She was the daughter of a single mother and an absentee father, and worked punishing hours through a series of childhood illnesses cleaning apartment corridors in the fierce cold of winter. 'Day work, they called it, and it was *damn* cold on hallway linoleum,' she said many years later. 'Misery is Detroit linoleum in January with a half-froze bucket of Spic and Span.' For Florence Ballard of the Supremes, snow also provoked memories of a hand-to-mouth upbringing in ghetto neighbourhoods across the city. 'I remember singing,' she once said. 'My favourite song was "Silent Night". It seemed like every winter I was pulling up the window and singing that.' The more privileged Aretha Franklin, who was the daughter of the charismatic preacher C. L. Franklin and had grown up in a mansion not far from Motown, remembered snow creating a carpet of poetic 'beauty' with giant flakes 'falling softly across the city', so deep that 'life just stopped'. For the original members of the Temptations, it meant cold keys on a battered piano as they sat huddled in woollen winter coats in the basement of Hitsville as the snow fell relentlessly outside.

For Berry Gordy, snow was a reminder of the day he nearly died. He was driving through a blizzard in 1959 with his best friend Smokey Robinson. They were on their way to the American Record Pressing plant in Owosso, Michigan, at the height of one of the area's worst-ever winter storms. Ten inches of snow fell in a single day. Although logic said they should turn back, Gordy and Robinson continued to drive towards musical history. They were on their way to pick up a batch of newly pressed copies of Marv Johnson's 'Come To Me', the debut release on their cherished Tamla label and one of the first releases of the Motown empire. Driven on by reckless enthusiasm and desperate to lay their hands on the first box of newly minted records, they battled through the snow. The plan was to return to Detroit that night and distribute promotional copies to radio DJs across the city. Then Gordy's '57 Pontiac skidded off the state highway and into a field. An emergency tow truck was summoned to drag them from a snowbound ditch. Battered and bruised, the men were pulled out of the wreckage and escorted home in the tow truck through the snow-packed suburbs of Detroit. They survived, but Motown itself was nearly stillborn.

Gordy made several calls to Florida and spoke at length to Diana Ross. She was recuperating from the road accident and spending her time by the pool at the Deauville Hotel. The Supremes had been slow starters, and Gordy had seriously considered scrapping their contracts back in 1963. Four years before, they couldn't deliver a hit song for love nor money, but when success did come, it was sudden and transformational. By January 1967 the Supremes were bigger than any act that had ever emerged from Detroit – bigger than Jackie Wilson, bigger than Mitch Ryder and the Detroit Wheels, and significantly more profitable than Motown's leading male groups, the Four Tops and the Temptations. Their effervescent black-girl-next-door style had struck a chord in a society where attitudes towards race and segregation were evolving. But Gordy had sensed that the Supremes could go further still and that their journey to the mainstream, breaking down the invisible barriers to acceptance, was not yet complete. One-hit wonders would come and go, but a group that could achieve global success was something he strove for.

Working with his sister Esther, Gordy had mapped out a punishing schedule designed to maximise every opportunity that came the way of the Supremes. It was a gruelling plan, at times verging on sadistic, but everyone had signed up for it, knowing that global success was well within their reach. 1967 marked their third successive year of travelling during which all three of the Supremes had faced periods of exhaustion, illness and mental breakdown. The relatively relaxed residency in Miami only disguised the relentlessness of their normal workload – the public engagements, twice-nightly concerts and red-eye flight itineraries. Insiders worried that one of the Supremes might collapse onstage or be hospitalised with fatigue. It had happened before. Between 1965 and 1967, all three members of the Supremes had spent time in hospital. Gordy had been generous with gifts but showed no inclination to reduce their workloads. Nor was he willing to compromise on quality control. The Supremes were frequently sent back to the studios together or individually to re-record songs or improve on tracks; those that fell short, like the song 'Deep Inside', were simply shelved as sub-standard. Gordy knew that pop music was quixotic and to take time out or entertain a more reasonable schedule risked their place in pop history. By January of 1967, the strain on the Supremes had reached breaking point. They had begun to hate the sight of each other.

Gordy had wrestled with internal dissent before and had managed disputes within other Motown acts, but what was different about the three Supremes was that their disputes had become increasingly bitter and threatened to drive them apart. There had been several incidents on the road, mostly in private or backstage, but well known to Motown staff. On a couple of occasions, disputes between Diana Ross and Florence Ballard had spilled over onto the stage. It was not always clear what really lay behind the dispute. Jealousy, petty hierarchies and misunderstandings were part of it, but familiarity had also begun to breed a corrosive contempt. Simply being together day in and day out was the root of the problem. The mood backstage could change on the weakest of jokes or a perceived slight. None of this reflected well on Motown, which, for all its sophistication in artist management, was still viewed by many in the industry as an outsider, a black-owned company on the outer edges of American society.

Like many people facing an apparently insurmountable problem, Gordy chose to ignore it in the vain hope it would go away. But after months of agonising, he had come to the conclusion that the fights would never end. Ballard was a founding member of the Supremes and had been the lead singer and de facto leader of the group when they were known by a previous name, the Primettes, but she seemed increasingly isolated and detached. Her light reddish hair had given her the teenage nickname 'Blondie', and Motown mythology claimed that it was Ballard who had originally come up with the Supremes' name. Her attitude towards Gordy had once been flirtatious and even devoted, but by 1967 it had changed completely. She had become sullen and resentful, portraying Gordy as an uncaring boss and his girlfriend, Diana, as a self-centred and scheming manipulator. The demands of fame, extensive travel and Gordy's intimacy with Ross had exacerbated the bad feeling and turned the once loyal Ballard into someone who seemed ungrateful and insubordinate. Initially Gordy had dismissed Ballard's attitude as a passing storm and waved the problem away when others mentioned it, but time was not a healer, and her feisty insolence refused to recede. Gordy had realised that ignoring the disputes at the heart of the Supremes would risk Motown's greatest opportunity. Over a few soul-searching months, towards the end of 1966, he had made the decision to stand up to Ballard's outbursts or what he increasingly described as her 'crazy behaviour'. He had been discreet about his views and only really discussed his plans in any detail with his sister Esther.

By 1967 Motown was a fully-fledged international corporation with targets, a sales force, and a well-oiled distribution chain. Reaching the top of *Billboard* magazine's Hot 100 chart was now commonplace, and failure was no longer an option. Artists were expected to succeed or at very least pay their way; those who didn't were quickly dropped from the roster, and those who fell short of the required standards of professionalism were often sidelined. Each new year brought with it increased expectations and new measures of success. Back in 1961, when the Marvelettes recorded Motown's first significant chart success, 'Please Mr Postman', success was measured by regional yardsticks. A hit in the Midwest was good news, for it meant local radio plays and a new song reaching the cramped bedrooms of black Detroiters. In 1964 'My Guy', by Mary Wells, became Motown's first global hit, charting first in the United States and then breaking internationally when the so-called Tamla-Motown sound reached Britain. Then the trickle became a stream, and the conveyor belt of success rolled without inhibition. The Supremes released a string of consecutive number one hits, including 'Baby Love', 'Come See About Me', 'Back In My Arms Again', 'I Hear A Symphony', 'You Can't Hurry Love', 'You Keep Me Hanging On', and the iconic 'Stop In The Name Of Love'. No African-American group before or since has made such a sudden and lasting impact. Gordy frequently told those who came to interview him that the Supremes were not a black group and that their music was not about colour. It was about falling in and out of love. They outsold Elvis, rivalled the Beatles, and paved the way for successive generations of urban dance artists. According to critic Nelson George, in his definitive book on Motown *Where Did Our Love Go*, they were 'without challenge the biggest-selling female act in the history of recorded music'.

Motown's success was not only about shipping records. The

company had forged a sound, a uniquely identifiable form of up-tempo popular soul that came to be associated with Detroit and its inexhaustible fund of local talent. Beneath the charismatic hooks, infectious backing tracks and memorable lyrics was an addictive sound often delivered by the production triumvirate of Holland-Dozier-Holland – brothers Brian and Eddie Holland and their partner, Lamont Dozier. All three had long-standing associations with Gordy dating back to their teenage years. Lamont Dozier had met Gordy in 1958 when he recorded under the name Lamont Anthony, and they went on to release primitive R&B records together for Anna Records, a label named after Gordy's sister. The Anna label traded from 1959 to 1961 and was finally sold to Motown, by which time Holland-Dozier-Holland had teamed up and naturally gravitated to the ramshackle Hitsville USA studios. Relationships forged in the fifties became central to Motown's success but also stored up future problems. An undercurrent of bad blood was coursing through the veins of the writing teams too. The Holland-Dozier-Holland team had authored many global hits, but Eddie Holland in particular had come to suspect that he was not reaping the full rewards or a fair share of royalties. Gordy had not yet grasped the extent of Eddie's disenchantment, and, distracted by the warring Supremes, he allowed another damaging dispute to fester.

By January 1967 Motown had built up an unrivalled sales force under the formidable direction of their white Sicilian-American sales boss, Barney Ales, whom Gordy had met when Ales was a rising star at Warner Brothers. Ales was more than a salesman. He had been a strategic lynchpin in Motown's ability to break through racial barriers and sell its sound to a white teenage audience. He had conceived a project called *Motown Monday*, a live show from the upper deck of the Roostertail Club on the crest of Lake St Clair, broadcast on WKNR, a radio station known locally as Keener 13. Ales had built up an influential friendship with a local radio personality named Scott Regan, whose show promoted Motown more effectively than the old R&B stations by taking the Motown sound beyond the urban ghetto and into suburbia. Ales and his team spent the first part of 1967 taking pre-orders for a new greatest hits album, *The Supremes Sing Holland-Dozier-Holland*, which had phenomenal pre-sales potential and pulled together many of Motown's most recognisable songs. But it had one other distinction that Gordy had yet to comprehend: it was a brilliantly acrimonious compilation album whose feelgood veneer disguised bad blood behind the scenes. Holland-Dozier-Holland felt underpaid and undervalued, and as 1967 unfolded, their resentments would flare into a bitter legal war.

Old friendships were deteriorating. Many of Motown's senior staff members had grown up with Gordy and witnessed success close up. There was a tendency, that persists to this day, to describe Motown as a 'family'. While that was superficially true – not least because Motown had its roots in the kitchen-table entrepreneur-ialism of the Gordy family home, and brothers, sisters, cousins and neighbours would often help out and play a part in each other's records – by 1967 the metaphor was already being stretched beyond credibility. Smokey Robinson, always loyal to Gordy, once said, 'One thing I can say about the Motown acts is that we were a family. That's not a myth.' But unfortunately it was. As each month passed, it became increasingly clear that the 'family' might not last the year intact. The close-knit relationships forged in postwar Detroit were destined to be dismantled as success and dysfunction tore the surrogate family apart.

By the end of the first week of January 1967, hypothermia had claimed three more victims and, more darkly, the homicide rate was running higher than at any time since Prohibition, when Detroit was a frontier town for illegal liquor and cross-border smuggling. In 1966 there were 232 homicides: 175 of these were murders, 39 self-defence, 17 were classified as 'justifiable homicide', and one death was attributed to manslaughter by negligence. In the previous three months alone, there had been 1,757 serious crimes, 30 unsolved killings and, against the grain of public perception, nearly half of the victims were from the minority African-American population. Detroit was becoming a city traumatised by crime, but

26

elsewhere, and increasingly abroad, it had become synonymous with soul music.

For the first few frozen days of the new year, the local newspapers struggled to communicate with snowbound Detroiters. Distribution of the two main titles, the *Detroit Free Press* and the *Detroit News*, was seriously disrupted by the weather. Delivery trucks were stuck in the snow, staff failed to show for work, and newspaper vendors gave up on their pitches. Those customers who did venture out barely made it to the mailbox, let alone to local stores, so over-the-counter sales plummeted. When newspapers did make it through to customers on 3 January, the *Detroit News* carried an ad for a homecoming show starring the Supremes, which was scheduled for the following month. It proved to be an engagement that had to be hurriedly rethought as tensions within the group worsened.

Detroit's newspapers were consistent about the issues that would dominate public life in 1967: anxiety about escalating murder rates, the city's economy under Mayor Jerome Cavanagh, the Vietnam War and its toll on the city, industrial disputes in the car plants, and the new alternative counterculture sweeping the campuses of the United States. The one subject that was sidelined was civil rights. Only Detroit's major African-American title, the *Michigan Chronicle*, regularly reported on voter registration and discrimination in housing and segregation. A stack of *Chronicle*s towered in Gordy's sitting room like an end table. It was the paper he had grown up with, and it had the reassuring smell of home. One industry rumour claimed that Gordy used to stuff crumpled copies of the paper into his spare shoes when he travelled, not only to protect their fashionable shape, but so that he had something familiar to read on the road. The *Chronicle* was a sister paper to the pioneering African-American title the *Chicago Defender* and promoted the general 'advancement of colored people'. It was originally published at 1727 St Antoine, on the street where Gordy had grown up, and he had earned his first wages delivering the paper around the old Hastings Street ghetto. It was a delivery round that took him past nightclubs, brothels, illegal gambling dens and, most compelling of all, the booming doors of Joe Von Battle's record store, a landmark institution where R&B and gospel blared from public loudspeakers.

It was through the *Chronicle*'s entertainment pages that Gordy first learned about the Runyonesque characters who dominated Detroit's exotic nightlife: quixotic tap dancer Ziggy Johnson, flamboyant hustler Diamond Jim Riley, ventriloquist Willie Tyler and his incorrigible dummy Lester, exotic dancer Lottie 'the Body' Graves, and R&B matriarch Johnnie Mae Matthews, whose gritty voice and even grittier determination influenced more than fifty years of Detroit funk. Like many kids growing up in Detroit, the young Berry Gordy had an emotional soft spot for Clayton 'Peg Leg' Bates, a one-legged dancer whose leg had been crudely amputated on his mother's kitchen table after an accident in a cotton field. Pops Gordy often used to recount the story as a reminder of their modest roots in the rural South.

Gordy had remained loyal to Detroit and the *Chronicle* all his life, often giving the newspaper Motown exclusives and encouraging his artists to front promotional campaigns, but cracks had begun to show in their relationship. On 5 January Gordy was invited to a birthday party at the 20 Grand nightclub in honour of *Chronicle* staff writer Rita Griffin. She had been an enthusiastic Motown mouthpiece for many years and had promoted almost every significant act on Gordy's portfolio of labels. In more recent months, Motown had had a series of spats with the *Chronicle*, mostly over a rogue story published in their October 1966 issue that 'wrongly' claimed Gordy had secretly married Diana Ross during a tour of Japan. No marriage had ever taken place, but for many music industry insiders, it was unnervingly close to the truth: Gordy and Ross were not only in love, they had become infatuated with each other, and their close relationship was heightening distrust at the heart of Motown. For some reason, maybe connected to the inclement weather, Gordy's invitation to Griffin's party had gone missing, and he failed to show up at the club. It was an oversight, but it was interpreted by many at the newspaper as a deliberate snub.

Although Gordy was absent, Motown staffers were out in force at the 20 Grand's Driftwood Lounge. Gordy's sister Esther Edwards, by now a Motown vice-president and also an avid supporter of the *Chronicle*, led a retinue of black America's most successful performers, with tables hosted by the Temptations, Martha and the Vandellas, Edwin Starr, Tammi Terrell, Jimmy Ruffin and the Four Tops. Periodically, members of the Motown party would leap onstage to join in with lesser-known local acts like Lee Rogers, the Devotions and Ed Crook, who had been hired as the official entertainment. To cap the night, Aretha Franklin and her husband, Ted White, presented Rita Griffin with white orchids to celebrate her lifetime achievement in celebrity journalism. No other city in the world – not even Liverpool – could come close to marshalling such talent in a single room. A week later Franklin and her husband flew from Detroit's Metro Airport to join Atlantic boss Jerry Wexler at the Downtowner Motor Inn in Florence, Alabama, on a historic trip to Muscle Shoals for the first leg of a disrupted recording session which forged Franklin's reputation as the greatest female soul singer of her generation and produced the civil rights torch song 'Respect'. It was a measure of Detroit's breadth of talent that Franklin's rise to prominence as the Queen of Soul coincided with the highpoint of Motown's commercial success.

Gordy's Motown empire dominated Detroit music but a hundred smaller labels barked aggressively around him. The flamboyant James 'Diamond Jim' Riley, a boxing promoter and R&B producer, attended the party with two of his male harmony groups, the Tempos and the Rivieras. Diamond Jim hated Motown with a vengeance. He was a garrulous and indiscreet man who at the time of the *Chronicle*'s party was facing a two- to twenty-year jail sentence for living off the earnings of prostitutes, and he had only recently been released from custody on a bond of $1,500. Riley had threatened Gordy with violence on several occasions and had also made bold public threats against Motown acts. He circled the Driftwood Lounge like a prize fighter, telling anyone in earshot that Gordy's no-show was a sign of weakness. He claimed that Gordy had fallen into depression after hearing the bad news that a big shot at Motown was about to jump ship. Diamond Jim cackled like Cassius Clay, telling everyone that the news would be the beginning of the end for Motown. He shouted rather than spoke, and even through the darkness of a nightclub, one could see his trademark teeth, encrusted with sparkling diamonds. He personified the term 'ghetto fabulous' decades before it was coined, and he anticipated the gangsta-rap style by more than thirty years. Although he never came close to emulating Gordy's success, what he lacked in record sales he more than made up for in hype and high-five humour. To paraphrase a comment once made about the boxer Sonny Liston, Diamond Jim Riley was 'a blatant mother in a fucker's game'.

The news really was bad. Earlier that day, Gordy had taken a phone call from one of his closest allies, the producer and talent manager William 'Mickey' Stevenson. Gordy immediately sensed trouble. 'Mickey was a street cat, a wheeler-dealer, but I knew it was that same hustling quality that made him the superstar A&R man he was,' he wrote many years later. 'I could hear something was up in his voice.' Mickey told him that he was resigning from Motown to join MGM in Los Angeles, where he had been offered a deal that dwarfed his salary in Detroit and guaranteed greater creative freedom. He then dropped the bombshell that the new contract provided him with the resources to set up and manage a soul-music subsidiary called Venture Records, which MGM hoped could rival Motown. He had already promised a deal to his first act – his wife, the singer Agatha 'Kim' Weston.

Weston was already an established Motown singer when she married Stevenson, but that did not protect her from the increasingly incestuous world of Hitsville and the barely credible claims that Stevenson had feather-nested her career to the disadvantage of others. Weston had already performed with Marvin Gaye on soul duets and replaced Mary Wells as his partner when she left the company to pursue a solo career. Wells had sued Motown in the mid sixties to escape what her lawyers described as the 'onerous' contract she had signed at the age of seventeen amid claims that the profits from the sales of her international hit 'My Guy' were being used to promote the Supremes. It was the public fallout of that dispute – and the bad light that was shone on Motown's contracts – that provided John Sinclair of the Steering Committee with the critical ammunition he used to trash Motown in his columns in the jazz press. Gordy had shrugged off that dispute, but even then he knew more would follow. 'People used to attack me and say it was a conflict of interest: I was the manager, I was the record company, I was the publisher, and I would say, "Yes, of course, conflict of interest, but it's in their favor, you stupid fuck".'

The departure of Mary Wells had irked Gordy, and their relationship had soured on the back of legal acrimony. But her departure was nothing compared to the loss of Stevenson. Musicians had come and gone, office staff had been hired and fired, studio technicians had been hurriedly replaced, and even Mary Wells had been quickly superseded by the next generation of vocal talent, but Stevenson's departure was different. Gordy knew that losing such a formidable figure was a harbinger of organisational change. Yet Motown significantly underestimated the damaging chain of consequences that was to follow.

Like Smokey Robinson and the Holland-Dozier-Holland production team, Stevenson was in with the woodwork. He acted as the company's artists-and-repertoire (A&R) manager and had earned a substantial reputation for galvanising difficult musicians. He exercised power over the notorious and supremely talented Funk Brothers, the group of unruly studio musicians who provided the instrumental undercarriage for most of Motown's greatest hits. Stevenson was the de facto foreman of the 'Snake Pit', the reptilian nickname given to Motown's recording studio. The Funk Brothers' reputation preceded them, and among their recalcitrant ranks were bandleader Joe Hunter, keyboard virtuoso Earl Van Dyke, and bassist James Jamerson. Gordy described Jamerson as a 'wild-eyed genius' who could 'build his own bass line so intricately it was hard to duplicate'. Several Motown musicians have testified to the bassist's eccentric brilliance. Jamerson drank recklessly and answered to the nickname 'Igor'. He often pretended to be Scottish, speaking comically in a Highland accent, but in truth he had been born in

Edisto Island, South Carolina, and moved to Detroit as a child. The main studio drummer, William Benny 'Papa Zita' Benjamin, was a more paternal figure than Jamerson and more accommodating of lesser talents. Gordy claimed his steadiness was his art. 'He had a pulse, a steadiness that kept the tempo better than a metronome,' he said, adding colloquially, 'Benny was my man.'

The Funk Brothers resented authority and frequently disappeared from their place of work to moonlight behind Motown's back in local nightclubs, but they were the creative engine of Motown's success, and managing them was an all-consuming task. Stevenson once said, 'Berry used to tell me that I not only had to be father, mother, sister and brother, I had to be psychologist as well.'

Although well remunerated, Stevenson's job was not for the fainthearted. There was a dark and tragic side to the men he managed. Most drank heavily, and others, including Benny Benjamin, stared drug addiction in the face. Otis Williams of the Temptations, never a shrinking violet himself, admitted to being scared in their company: 'These guys were like a chain gang. Especially Benny and James. They could scare you. They'd make you wet your drawers just by looking at you.' They might have been virtuosos in their own right, and they unquestionably shaped the Detroit sound, but individually and collectively they were intensely difficult characters who were in thrall to heroin or hard liquor and who intimidated young, impressionable singers. Gordy tended to mythologise Benny Benjamin, having seen him dragged from local bars and virtually propped up on his drum stool. But 'once Benny had those sticks in his hand,' he claimed, 'drunk or sober, he was the best.' That respect was not always reciprocated. The Funk Brothers, like so many supporting musicians, resented their 'invisible' role, and Stevenson had a constant fight to keep them in check. A standard contract of the time paid the band $6.25 for a session and one cent for every record sold. It required them to buy their own costumes for live shows and insisted that no external management or agency could be hired to negotiate with Motown. It might have been a contractual norm, but there was much to grouse about, and the Funk Brothers became a perennial source of complaint.

Stevenson often boasted that only he could make the trains run on time; as a retaliatory strike, the Funk Brothers nicknamed him 'Il Duce' after the Italian fascist leader Benito Mussolini.

Stevenson was more than a disciplinarian. Managing the Snake Pit was a job he had trained for all his life. He had grown up on the road, spent most of his infancy in recording studios, and witnessed the skulduggery of the recording industry since childhood. He was the son of blues singer and pianist Kitty Stevenson, a vocalist with the Todd Rhodes Orchestra who recorded on the Chicago blues label Vitacoustic and whose act was the personification of the term 'moody blues'. Kitty was a multi-instrumentalist with a smouldering voice who adored her son and taught him to succeed. She died in Detroit Memorial Hospital in June 1952 when Mickey was still a youngster, and she had already been deceased five years when he eventually joined forces with Gordy.

Stevenson had the personality of a switchblade – edgy, thin and razor-sharp. He cut a significant figure around the offices at Motown, loud in his praise of talent and intolerant of those who squandered it. He was uniquely incentivised to back talent and not his own private agendas. 'I got a royalty of everything, every song, no matter what, as the A&R director,' he once said. 'I got paid on every hit, that was part of my deal. That's why if I wrote a song and you wrote a better one, I'd go with yours. 'Cause we'd both make money off it. I didn't need to fucking ego rub.' Stevenson's power within Motown had allowed him to strike deals with aspiring songwriters including session musician Ivy Jo Hunter, which meant that anything Hunter wrote was automatically co-credited to Stevenson, providing him with a royalty income from songs he played little part in composing. It was a tax on access to the system. Stevenson had Gordy's ear and convinced him to acquire a local independent rival, Ed Wingate's Ric-Tic and Golden World labels, which Motown acquired legally in the latter months of 1966. The acquisition delivered a significant roster of new artists to Motown, including male vocalists Edwin Starr and J. J. Barnes and female singer Rose Batiste, but its real value was in bricks and mortar, namely Golden World's studio on West Davidson. By 1967 Motown's own Hitsville studios were stretched to overcapacity, and expansion was long overdue.

Losing Stevenson meant the loss of an ally, and the resignation triggered three immediate problems: how to replace him as a song-writer; how to replace his wife Kim Weston; and most of all how to fill the crucial role of company foreman. Songwriting was Gordy's least concern. Stevenson had co-written some well-known hits, including 'Dancing In The Street', for Martha and the Vandellas, 'It Takes Two' for Marvin Gaye and Kim Weston, and Stevie Wonder's energetic 'Uptight (Everything's All Right)'. But he was not in the top tier of Motown writer-composers. Nor would the talented Weston be impossible to replace – the one thing Detroit did not lack was great female vocalists. Stevenson assured Gordy he was leaving Motown 'to run his own ship' and was adamant that there was no hidden agenda. He simply wanted a degree of creative freedom. But it wasn't the whole truth. Stevenson was one of a small and increasingly disgruntled group of senior Motown producers who had grown up with the company but been denied an equity share in the corporation. Motown was structured as a Subchapter S corporation, which allowed income to pass to shareholders with only a single layer of taxation. Gordy had always been reluctant to dilute ownership of Motown stock and had managed to avoid any meaningful commitment to Stevenson or indeed to the simmering and increasingly disenchanted Holland brothers. The issue of share ownership ate away at Stevenson even after he had left Motown. 'I left because I wanted a piece of the company,' he admitted. 'Berry wanted me to stay because I was a powerful force and he offered me a big raise but I wanted the power to go with the force.'

Stevenson's departure proved to be the beginning of a year of interconnected problems. A relationship that stretched back to the start-up years in the late fifties was over, and the uncomfortable question of who owned Motown and its wealth had reared its ominous head. It was a grumble that would grow into a roar in 1967 as more artists and producers stepped forward looking for greater remuneration. By now several Motown producers were well aware that the real money in music was not in performance fees but in publishing rights, and that Gordy's publishing company, Jobete, was the jewel in Motown's crown. Several years earlier, in partnership with Gordy, Stevenson had participated in a clever and diversionary music industry scam: they had registered an entirely separate publishing arm called Stein & Van Stock, leading industry insiders to believe it was a classic Brill Building enterprise run by Jewish composers. In a racially biased industry, both men felt that the colour of their skin threatened to exclude them from publishing rights. Stevenson even used the pseudonym 'Avery Vandenberg' for some of his songs to perpetuate the ruse, and if anyone called Motown looking for Vandenberg, Stevenson would take the phone and affect a Brooklyn drawl.

Stevenson had another frustration. Ever since the Supremes had enjoyed stellar success, he sensed that they were having a disadvantageous impact on his wife's career. Weston had some creditable solo hits to her name, including the frantic 'Helpless', but she was now principally known for her classic love duets with Marvin Gaye, including the towering love song 'It Takes Two'. She was guaranteed an artist's contract as part of her husband's new agreement with MGM, so while his exit from Motown was being negotiated, she astutely decided to stay away from the studios to rehearse for a concert on behalf of an organisation called the Progressive Ladies of Detroit, one of a number of black social networks that raised funds for charitable causes or for civil rights. The group was closely affiliated with Motown and had been founded earlier in the sixties by the wives of the Miracles and the Four Tops. Smokey Robinson's wife, Claudette, was the president, and Kim was vice-president. The Progressive Ladies of Detroit were at the fashion-conscious end of the civil rights movement and held monthly concerts at local supper clubs and an annual masked ball aboard a pleasure boat called the *Bob-Lo*, which ran between Detroit and Bois Blanc Island off the coast of Ontario.

Kim Weston's emotional farewell to the Progressive Ladies of Detroit was held at the Latin Quarter nightclub and attracted a well-heeled audience of performers, record executives and local business entrepreneurs. It underlined a distinctive feature of the city's public life. In the language of the times, Detroit was known across the nation as 'the Model City'. However, Detroit had a complex sociology. Although it suffered from endemic poverty, it was not a poor city by any stretch of the imagination, and in 1967 it had one of the biggest and wealthiest black middle classes in the United States. Commentators frequently argued that the size and spending power of its 'Negro bourgeoisie' insulated Detroit from the serious social unrest and that it was the least likely city to succumb to rioting and social disturbance. By the summer of 1967, this theory was proven to be hopelessly ill-judged.

The growth of Motown had broadly coincided with the rise of Mayor Jerome Cavanagh, a successful city politician whose career invited comparisons with that of President John F. Kennedy. The handsome young Irish American was in his mid thirties when he took control of the city and radiated optimistic charisma. Like JFK before him, he had the support of the African-American community. Cavanagh's appointment brought with it a resurgence of Detroit's civic fortunes. His ability to reach out across the racial divide meant that he was able to attract unprecedented levels of federal funding. Between 1962 and 1967, Detroit received $230,422,000 from a range of social and structural support programmes, many of them to alleviate inner-city poverty. Cavanagh duly honoured the debt he owed to the city's black electorate, pushing through a civic ordinance that public service employees were to be 'recruited, appointed, trained, assigned, and promoted without regard to race, color, religion, national origin, or ancestry'. As a consequence, more African-Americans were appointed to public office than under any previous mayor, and by the end of 1963, for the first time in living memory, the city of Detroit's books actually balanced. It was a fiscal miracle. The popular press dubbed him 'the mayor who woke up a city', and Cavanagh's Detroit began to represent a new kind of politics. He was vociferous in his passion for the Motor City and felt its success had much to teach sixties America.

Gordy was more than tangential to Mayor Cavanagh's rise to

power. Although they had grown up in different communities, they both believed in civil rights and self-improvement. In the summer of 1963, Cavanagh, Gordy and Aretha Franklin's father, the Reverend C. L. Franklin, played host to the Walk to Freedom, a historic civil rights march organised to raise funds for Martin Luther King Jr's Southern Christian Leadership Conference and to promote the non-violent campaign to desegregate the state of Alabama. The desegregation issue resonated in Detroit, where tens of thousands of migrants had relocated from the segregated South. To coincide with the march, Motown released a spoken-word album of King's major sermons that was frequently gifted to visiting dignitaries at Motown and used to promote the company's civil-rights credentials. Gordy's cherished photographs of himself with King and Cavanagh had greater prominence in his office than any publicity shots of Motown stars.

Mickey Stevenson gathered up his personal possessions and left. There was no party and no fuss. He took his Rolodex, a clutch of business cards from his drawer, and a list of private phone numbers, and then left Motown with an assurance that, apart from his statuesque wife, he would not poach Motown staff. Press releases were hurriedly prepared, and *Jet* magazine reported his departure in the time-honoured way, stating that Stevenson had left Motown by 'mutual consent'. It was a term that disguised a multitude of resentments and unresolved tensions. Stevenson had given up his salary but not his royalties. Within a matter of a few months, he had set up the Venture label – 'Motown in exile' – on the West Coast. But despite its early promise, Venture never came close to matching the Detroit sound or Motown's unbridled success. The only artist he signed that could have survived at Motown was the Atlanta-based soul singer Calvin Arnold. The rest disappeared without much trace.

Stevenson had barely packed his bags when Gordy announced a new partner for Marvin Gaye. This time his co-singer was to be the Philadelphia-born vocalist Tammi Montgomery, who had moved to Detroit after a turbulent period with the James Brown Revue.

Gordy had already advised Montgomery to change her name, and drawing on his passion for boxing, he proposed the surname of Chicago's heavyweight champion, Ernie Terrell. So Thomasina Montgomery was given the name 'Tammi Terrell' and returned to the Snake Pit to record her epic love duets with Marvin Gaye.

Replacing Stevenson's wife was straightforward; replacing Stevenson himself proved harder. Gordy's eventual choice made sense to everyone inside the company, though, and seemed logical to anyone who had ever bought a Motown record. Gordy promoted Eddie Holland, the older brother of the Holland-Dozier-Holland production team, to the vacant role. Eddie's brother, Brian, was also promoted to fill another vacuum when Motown staffer Billie Jean Brown took a sabbatical from the quality control department, and Brian Holland was given the more grandiose title 'vice-president of creative evaluation'. The name never stuck, however, and the department was always known as quality control. The promotion of the Holland brothers was in some respects an attempt to buy off their demands for equity or a greater stake in publishing, but it was a gesture that led to unintended consequences. Gordy's clumsy attempt to placate Eddie Holland proved to be a disastrous error in judgement and was soon to have a disruptive impact on the entire Motown Record Corporation. Gordy admitted many years later that the promotions of the two Holland brothers were 'moves I would come to regret'. That was something of an understatement. In one of the most ill-advised strategic moves that Gordy ever made, he gave positions of power and preeminence to the two men who were most aggrieved about being locked out of Motown's shareholding structure. Within less than a year, he would become embroiled in one of the most tumultuous legal disputes in the history of popular music, and his friendship with the Holland brothers, which stretched back to adolescence, would shatter.

At long last the snow stopped. On Monday, 8 January 1967, Detroit woke up to milder weather. Car plants returned to full employment, sledging at Rouge Park stopped, and the shops on Woodward reopened. For the first time in the new year, most major industrial plants were operational, and any lingering excuse for being absent from work melted with the snow. At 1300 Beaubien, the fabled headquarters of the Detroit Police Department, law and order shuffled back to life. The head of the narcotics bureau, Inspector Joseph Brown, and his assistant, Detective Lieutenant Warner Stringfellow, had returned to their desks determined to execute a hard-line policy on illegal drug abuse. One of their major priorities for the new year was to pursue prosecutions under Public Act 266, the overarching law that classified banned narcotic substances in the state of Michigan. Stringfellow had secured increased resources and had recruited a second-generation Armenian-American police officer named Vahan Kapagian to join his unit working undercover. Kapagian's role was to insinuate himself into the student neighbour-hood of Warren Forrest, track the supply of drugs, and identify the source of trafficking among Detroit's hippie community.

Detroit had a long-standing problem with narcotics, and even in the years before Prohibition the city had been a magnet for illegal trading. Since the early sixties, the police had identified new patterns of drug trafficking that they described bureaucratically as 'cross community'. Stringfellow and his fellow officers had focused on a local marijuana supply chain that emanated from the city's African-American underground jazz scene and had spread to college campuses. The narcotics bureau believed that John Sinclair and the Steering Committee were acting as a bridgehead between two apparently disconnected communities. They presumed he was buying weed in the jazz clubs and ghetto bars of the West Side to sell to white teenagers at Wayne State University, at the Artists Workshop, or at anti-war rallies across the city. Although the Detroit police were prone to fanciful conspiracies, this was not one of them. Sinclair was unusually open about his contacts. Working as a jazz critic, he often frequented some of the city's most subterranean clubs, such as Cornelius Watts' Club Mozambique and the Chit Chat Club on Fourteenth Street. Sinclair had befriended several local jazz musicians and boasted about his contacts in the underground scene. 'I had connections with some brothers on the West Side, dudes I knew through the back jazz scene,' he wrote in his prison writings. 'I had the only steady reefer supply in the campus area.'

By 1967, criminologists estimated that a million dollars' worth of property a day was stolen by junkies across the city of Detroit, mostly to fund heroin habits. Ross Ellis, district supervisor of Detroit's federal narcotics team, claimed that seizures of marijuana had doubled in Michigan in a year and that drug abuse was now epidemic. Cocaine was an open secret, too, and was more commonly abused by the younger generation, including musicians from within the city's soul scene. Despite Motown's much touted family image, many of Gordy's most popular acts snorted snow: the Contours were flagrant coke users, Martha Reeves later admitted to addiction, and the bespectacled vocalist of the Temptations, David Ruffin, was already fatally obsessed. The Detroit police had also recorded an exponential growth in the circulation of a synthetic hallucinogenic, LSD-25, a mystifying drug with a powerful locus in the student population. The point of intersection of these various forms of illegal drug transaction was the music scene and a warren of houses and communes on the fringes of Wayne State University, also the habitat of the Artists Workshop, LEMAR and the Steering Committee.

Kapagian's undercover role was to entrap John Sinclair and implicate his inner circle in drug running. He abandoned his uniform, grew his hair long, cultivated a short straggly beard, and spent most of the first few weeks of January hanging around the Steering Committee, attending poetry readings, jazz gigs and hip events. Using the undercover pseudonym 'Louis', Kapagian posed as a candlemaker from Detroit's hippie enclave on Plum Street. His first contact was an attempt to buy marijuana from Fred 'Sonic' Smith, a guitarist with the MC5, but he was unsuccessful. Kapagian persisted, and as January thawed he teamed up with another under-cover officer, a young woman named Jane Mumford, who had recently joined the Detroit police from a sales role at a Hertz car-rental office. They posed as a loved-up hippie couple and gravitated towards jazz and poetry events where Sinclair was scheduled to appear as a performance poet. Unaware of the entrapment, Sinclair befriended the pair and invited them back to his apartment on

John R, within the premises of the Detroit Artists Workshop. At the cops' request, he subsequently supplied them with marijuana. Kapagian carefully secreted the evidence in a pack of Kool cigarettes and then announced himself as an officer of Detroit police department. He introduced Mumford as his witness and arrested Sinclair.

Enraged by the sting, Sinclair took characteristic revenge. In a flamboyant gesture of defiance that was to become his belligerent trademark, he placed a mock 'Wanted' poster featuring Officer Kapagian in the *Fifth Estate*, a radical newspaper. It offered a reward of 'one pound of US grass to anyone who can drop a thousand micrograms of LSD into this man's misdirected body'. The January sting was not the first time Sinclair had been entrapped. Three years earlier he had been arrested in an undercover operation and charged with sale and possession, but he had pleaded to a reduced charge of possession. Under Michigan law, a conviction for selling marijuana was subject to a prison sentence of one to ten years, and, according to Sinclair, his lawyer told him that 'any jury in Detroit, no matter how strong and how right our case is, will automatically find you guilty no matter what you say, because it's the cop's word against yours, and they always believe the cop'. At his appearance at the Detroit Recorder's Court, Sinclair was given two years' probation and a $250 fine and was advised to keep a low profile.

This advice did not come easy to Sinclair, and he continued to be a high-profile advocate of drug use as the shifting patterns of narcotics swept the map of Detroit. On the basis of his second arrest, Sinclair was given six months in the Detroit House of Corrections (DeHoCo). The entrapment only hardened Sinclair's views and provoked a lifelong resentment of both Michigan drug law and the Detroit police.

On his release from DeHoCo, Sinclair and the Steering Committee advanced their plans to assault the city with 'noise and disruption' under the banner of a new organisation, Trans-Love Energies Unlimited, a name they had borrowed from the Scottish psychedelic folk singer Donovan. In a song called 'The Fat Angel', Donovan described finding 'happiness in a pipe' and flying by

'Translove Airways'. Sinclair wrote a short mission statement in the utopian style of the era: 'The 1967 Steering Committee exists as an agent of the sun – to bring people light and color as a natural function. To illuminate them and bring them together. One of the committee's jobs will be to produce a benefit at least once a month which will bring together artists and audience in a totally positive context, to help raise money for needy members of the community. The committee's first such event will take place Sunday, January 29, at the Grande Ballroom, a benefit for GUERRILLA. In February a benefit for the newly formed Detroit LEMAR will be held, and for March plans are being made to benefit the San Francisco Zen temple community, who have just purchased (made a down payment toward) 106 acres of land in the Sur, to be used for meditation and community living.'

Pop music was in kaleidoscopic flux, and lyrics were being stretched by LSD and Eastern mysticism. Artists like Donovan and the Beatles were already under the tutelage of the Indian guru and master of transcendental meditation Maharishi Mahesh Yogi, and the British beat scene, which had invaded America in 1964, had by now evolved into a full-blown anti-establishment counterculture. The intense three-minute pop song that had underpinned the success of both the Beatles and Motown was being torn apart by an alternative creativity. The Beatles had also recorded an impenetrable fourteen-minute album track called 'Carnival Of Light', which was deemed too obscure for general release and dismissed as 'distorted and hypnotic'. With January barely two weeks old, John Lennon sat down at a piano in his London home and improvised words he had randomly sourced from the morning edition of the London *Daily Mail*, which carried a report about a car crash and a feature on road maintenance that had discovered 'four thousand holes in Blackburn, Lancashire'. Lennon transposed the clippings into the lyrics of 'A Day In The Life', the momentous closing track of *Sgt. Pepper's Lonely Hearts Club Band*, which, on its release later in the year, was promptly banned by the BBC for its 'permissive attitude to drugs'.

These early gestures of psychedelic improvisation had no

immediate impact on Motown's assembly-line soul. Gordy was by nature cautious and reluctant to move away from teenage love songs. He was in sporadic contact with the Beatles, who had covered 'Money (That's What I Want)', one of his own compositions, which had been a fledgling hit for Barrett Strong in 1959. The bond had been strengthened in 1965, when the Motown Revue toured Britain and Motown's roster of relatively unknown artists was photographed with the Beatles; the favour was reciprocated when the Beatles toured America. Motown offered Brenda Holloway as a supporting act, and she became the only female artist to open a concert by the Beatles. But Gordy's links with the Beatles stopped far short of psychedelia. Throughout 1967 some of his most successful artists pressured him about changing direction and expanding the Motown formula into more adventurous sounds, but he proved stubbornly resistant. Gordy calculated that covert references to drugs would be counterproductive, and that coded songs about junk, coke or 'flying high in the friendly sky' would come back to haunt Motown.

Gordy was systematic about music. He had a recipe for success and was prone to repeat the same formula until the market itself moved on, but even then he had an unshakeable belief that, like Hollywood, Motown's success was predicated on storytelling. He argued vociferously that all great songs should have a central narrative and, where possible, the stories should be told in the present tense. Many great Motown songs adhere to the rules: 'My Baby Must Be A Magician', recorded by the Marvelettes, is a love song that conjures up love and magic; Smokey Robinson's 'Tears Of A Clown' uses a circus storyline to describe the mask of unhappiness; and R. Dean Taylor tells the story of a home haunted by lost love in 'There's A Ghost In My House'. Gordy had worked out that rival studios like Stax in Memphis, Chess in Chicago and Jewel Records in Shreveport reflected the blues or country sounds of their local music scene, but he was adamant that Motown did not just make sound – it told stories. Otis Williams of the Temptations claimed that Gordy often seemed more trusting of female advice, and he had gathered from his sisters that women loved songs in which men were forced to plead for love. It might have been questionable psychology, but a remarkable number of Motown hits involve emotionally desperate men pleading, begging and confessing. According to Williams, 'most Motown lyricists – Norman Whitfield, Eddie Holland and Smokey Robinson – wrote to appeal to that sensibility'. Smokey Robinson's 'Tracks Of My Tears' is a classic example.

Driven by his own deeply held values about music, Gordy was convinced that Motown would never profit from psychedelia or from copying the outer reaches of rock, and he reasserted to anyone who asked that Motown was on a journey into the mainstream of America. Being on the margins was the past, and rather than experiment on the outer fringes of culture, success for Gordy lay at the conservative heart of society, where few if any black entrepreneurs had succeeded before. His big idea for 1967 was the holy trinity of crossover: Las Vegas, network television, and ultimately Hollywood.

By 1967 there was not a single area of American nightlife that the Supremes had not conquered. They had played hotel lounges in Las Vegas, Miami and Hollywood, and could trace their mainstream appeal back to 1965, when they accepted their first 'Borscht Belt' engagement at the Concord Hotel in the Catskills, a popular resort for Jewish families from New York. The Supremes had hurriedly inserted show tunes into their act, employed nightclub informality to introduce their songs, and had even added short comic sketches into the act. It was while watching them from a table at the Concord that a light went on for Gordy, and he hatched a longer-term plan to groom Diana Ross as a lead vocalist and a major international star.

The Supremes were working simultaneously on three separate albums. One was a compilation of their greatest hits written by Holland-Dozier-Holland; the second was a tribute to Broadway, *The Supremes Sing Rodgers and Hart*; and the third was a crassly conceived album in honour of Walt Disney. The Broadway album was produced by Berry Gordy and Motown musical director Gil Askey and was recorded haphazardly over a six-month period. It featured show tunes like 'The Lady Is A Tramp' and 'My Funny Valentine' and was viewed by several Motown insiders as a vanity project. Although Motown had long since abandoned the R&B sound of the early sixties and had smoothed out the rough edges of soul, a proud heritage still pervaded Motown, and there was open disgruntlement in the Snake Pit. Many felt that a musical tribute to Walt Disney smacked of opportunism, and some of Motown's staff even threatened to boycott the project. Disney had been a heavy smoker and had died of lung cancer a month before in December 1966. Gordy was of the hopeful belief that the tribute album would take the Supremes to a new audience – children and their parents – but it was resented at Motown when the Supremes flew back from Florida and the studio schedules were cleared to make way for the recordings. Diana Ross went through the motions, learning and replicating Disney classics, but with no great personal motivation or strong support from her in-house producers. The Disney album was eventually shifted from Detroit to the Bell Sound Studios on Eighth Avenue in New York, where it was overseen by Broadway composer Michael 'Mickey' Gentile. Within a few months of Disney's funeral, the misguided venture dropped down the priority list. Some said there were problems with securing the rights, as the guarded Disney machine worried about a black-owned business in Detroit recording their songs; others said Motown simply ran out of belief in the project. Either way, it was not dead yet, and Gordy returned to it fitfully throughout the year.

In mid January 1967, Gordy had his last management meeting with the departing Stevenson. Both men behaved professionally, and whatever undercurrents of resentment had grown up between them, the meeting stuck to the script. Stevenson gave him an assurance that recording schedules would continue without disruption and that a robust studio roster was in place. Among the next batch of releases was a nod to garage rock, a song called 'Love's Gone Bad' by the Underdogs, a four-man guitar band from Grosse Pointe. Although the song was written by Holland-Dozier-Holland, it took its influences from mop-top British bands like the

Beatles and the Animals. The Underdogs were the house band at the Hideout off Eight Mile Road, an underground garage club that Motown sometimes used as a rehearsal venue. Coincidentally, the lead guitarist's father owned a catering company that serviced Motown, and he knew Gordy and Barney Ales through his part ownership of the Latin Quarter nightclub on East Grand. Calls were exchanged, a deal was struck, and the Underdogs were placed under the tutelage of Stevie Wonder's producer Clarence Paul. It was the closest Gordy ever came to embracing the Motor City's underground guitar-band scene, but sales were slow, and the Underdogs soon drifted off Motown's radar – at the very moment when Detroit's guitar underground was about to screech into significance.

Towards the end of January, the Steering Committee was preparing a series of events near Wayne State University, including a rock concert featuring the Detroit Edison White Lights followed by a happening-cum-dinner in honour of jazz musician John Coltrane, whose recent 'cosmic' recordings had been produced under the influence of LSD and who was fatally ill with liver cancer. The dinner was to be held at Sinclair's rambling apartment at 4863 John Lodge, but unknown to the guests, a police informer had communicated Sinclair's plans to the Detroit Narcotics Bureau, and plans were in place for a covert drug operation earmarked for the night of Tuesday, 25 January.

In the few hectic days before the bust, Detroit police, Michigan state police, and officers from the US Food and Drug Administration met to plan the joint operation and mapped out an area of Detroit around the Wayne State University campus. Armed with warrants signed by prior agreement by Judge Robert DeMascio, the police raid on the area began at Lower De Roy Hall on Cass Avenue, where Sinclair was a guest speaker at a pro-marijuana rally. When police were sure that most of the audience was already inside the auditorium, the exits were sealed, and local access points were blocked by arresting officers. The plan thereafter was for a second wave of police to fan outward from the campus and raid apartments in the streets around the university. The biggest catch was at a redstone apartment commune at 647 West Forest, where fourteen arrests were made and a stash of drugs seized.

The big drug bust put Detroit's hippie counterculture on the front pages of the local press and propelled John Sinclair to city-wide notoriety. In total the joint operation had seized fifty-six people, including high-school pupils, eighteen women, and, to the embarrassment of the academic establishment, two faculty members of Wayne State University. The elders of Wayne State had been taken entirely by surprise. It was days later when they finally cross-checked their records and found that only thirteen of those arrested were registered students, not the fifty-six reported. But the university's reputation was tarnished, and the disciplinary probes that dragged on for months to come did nothing to repair it.

The *Detroit News* described the operation as a startling success for the police and 'a huge raid aimed at Detroit's narcotic-using "turned-on" set'. In a retaliatory strike, Sinclair described the raids with his customary flair for melodrama: 'The raiding team started climbing through the windows and busting down the doors, guns in hand, handcuffing everybody in sight and tearing the house apart.' Jail cells were full to overflowing, and some people were released simply because there was nowhere to keep them. The following morning the Detroit Recorder's Court was swarming with journalists, and the bullpen was crowded with a bleary-eyed gathering of musicians, writers and artists. Under the disdainful eye of presiding judge Geraldine B. Ford, they faced arraignment on charges of using and selling marijuana and LSD. The man facing the biggest sentence was a twenty-five-year-old 'head' named Thomas Medina, who was on parole for previous offences and whose bond was set at $4,500. Other defendants among the motley gathering included Sanford Weinstock, vice-chair of the Detroit Committee to End the War in Vietnam, Michael Knight, an artist from the Plum Street hippie community, and, inevitably, John Sinclair. To the annoyance of the judge, Sinclair was caught briefing journalists through the bars of the courtroom cell, ever the showman. He had a remarkable knack for turning any event into a countercultural spectacle, and he told the press that, far from being efficient, the police had been entranced by Coltrane's music. 'They pushed their way in and stood around at a loss,' he said. 'We just went ahead playing. We were playing "A Love Supreme".'

For Sinclair, the Wayne State drug bust was the latest chapter in a long and convoluted dispute with Michigan's marijuana laws. It was his third arrest and the final straw for Detroit's irritated legal system. Sinclair was jailed overnight and released on bond, but as a consequence of the raids he was ultimately sentenced to nine-and-a-half to ten years for 'possessing two cigarettes containing 11.5 grains of *Cannabis sativa* contrary to Sections 2 and 3 of the Public Act 266 of 1952'. With the support of his attorney and the LEMAR organisation, Sinclair triggered a legal counterattack and became a cause célèbre in the process. A few years later, still protesting his incarceration, his friends staged a landmark rally at Crisler Arena in Ann Arbor under the banner 'Free John Now', starring John Lennon, Yoko Ono and Stevie Wonder.

Members of local rock band the MC5 were clad in woollen scarves, fingerless gloves and army jackets as they rehearsed in the freezing cold of a cavernous ballroom-cum-mattress warehouse known as the Grande Ballroom. The dank old ballroom on Grand River had recently been bought by a teacher turned music promoter, Russ Gibb, and was fast asserting itself as the gathering place of underground rock. MC5 were rehearsing for a Steering Committee benefit show, the 'Guerrilla Love Fair', scheduled for the last Sunday of the month. Colourful posters featured the cream of Detroit's rock underground: the Spike Drivers, MC5, Livonia Tool & Die Company, Detroit Edison White Light Band and a psychedelic light show by High Society and the Bulging Eyeballs of Guatama. At Sinclair's insistence, a smattering of jazz groups, including the Lyman Woodard Ensemble and the English Spangler Jazz Unit, were also on the bill.

With Sinclair in jail, however, the organisational side was collapsing, momentum was lost, and the Guerrilla Love Fair was eventually cancelled. Unperturbed, Sinclair began to fantasise about a much bigger idea, and from his jail cell in Jackson State Penitentiary, he began to plan the biggest countercultural demonstration in the history of Detroit. In the spirit of the times, it came to be called a 'love-in', and in feverish correspondence from behind bars Sinclair secured the services of New York beat freaks the Fugs as headliners. The love-in was pencilled in for the spring, but despite its peaceful intent it was an event that would eventually descend into violence and unleash three months of urban disturbances across Detroit.

Berry Gordy was in Los Angeles when police raided Wayne State. He returned to Detroit in the last week of January with the embattled Supremes, who had vacated their Hollywood hotel in disarray and driven to the airport in separate limousines. The rifts within the group appeared to be irreparable. Gordy was struggling to control events. With Stevenson gone, the Motown studios were under a less cooperative regime, and his most successful group was tearing itself apart.

On the surface at least, Gordy's return to Detroit coincided with a time of remarkable creative output. Gladys Knight and the Pips recorded the Barrett Strong song 'Take Me In Your Arms And Love Me', produced by the increasingly influential producer Norman Whitfield. Three days later, the Four Tops were in the Snake Pit, accompanied by the formidable Holland-Dozier-Holland production team, to record 'Bernadette', having laid the vocals of another hit, 'Walk Away Renée', earlier in the month. By 29 January Marvin Gaye and his new vocal partner, Tammi Terrell, were listed on the studio roster and scheduled to complete an Ashford and Simpson song, 'Ain't No Mountain High Enough', produced by Gordy's brother-in-law Harvey Fuqua. Nothing about the session stood out as significant at the time, and for those who were there that day the recording was overshadowed by the release of Smokey Robinson's elegiac 'The Love I Saw In You Was Just A Mirage', the second in his great 'mirage trilogy', which included the soul masterpieces 'Tracks Of My Tears' and 'The Tears Of A Clown'. As the days passed, it became clear that a special chemistry had emerged in Gaye and Terrell's recordings, something akin to love. But in the coming months, the fates of Gaye and Terrell were also to become scarred by the thundering pace of 1967.

In the final days of January, Motown recorded some of the most joyous soul music ever. But beneath the surface, the label was showing signs of strain, and the pressure to represent Detroit to the world was increasing daily. Journalists flocked to the city to profile Motown or to pronounce that Mayor Cavanagh had overseen an economic miracle and was leading a thriving city. But this was gross oversimplification; reporters were missing a more complex story. Superficially Detroit had come to be represented by the shimmering hopefulness of the Supremes and the formulaic brilliance of the Motown machine, but dark clouds were gathering, and they pointed to a very different story, one of profound social problems.

Detroit's economic miracle was by now largely illusory. The city's image as a boomtown had for many decades disguised underlying patterns of industrial decline. Between 1953 and 1960, seven major manufacturing plants closed on the East Side, resulting in the loss of over 70,000 jobs, mostly for black workers, and dozens of ancillary businesses had shut down. The umbilical cord that linked Motown to Mayor Cavanagh's 'model city' was being cut, and if the city and its most famous musical corporation were bound together, then it was not through success but in adversity. The year 1967 marked a turning point. Detroit's budget was in the red for the first time in years, and events seemed to be conspiring against the Mayor. The escalating cost of the snowstorms crippled the city – more than 25,000 tons of salt had been scattered on the roads, double that of the previous winter, and Detroit was facing a budget shortfall of $11 million. It was the first time in his career that Cavanagh had been forced to use the leprous word 'deficit'.

And Detroit was changing physically. The freeways had slashed through the city, destroying old neighbourhoods and tree-lined avenues alike. A ten-year battle against Dutch elm disease had been lost after a strain of beetle imported in untreated antique furniture from Holland had spread virulently. Despite a city-wide programme of chemical spraying, Detroit had lost more than

120,000 trees, and once-shaded avenues were now marked by deformed rows of rotten timber. Those who could remember the city in its magisterial postwar days mourned the passing of the elms, and many clung to a widespread myth that dying elms could be cured by pure alcohol. Entomologists had long dismissed the idea as erroneous, but housewives could periodically be seen in side streets pouring liquor onto the roots of neighbourhood trees in an act of caring desperation.

When the snow returned again in the last few days of January, it came with an unforgiving fierceness. The whole of the Midwest was engulfed. Chicago experienced the worst snowstorms in its history and spent weeks beneath twenty-four million tons of snow. Detroit was experiencing its worst winter in fourteen years. Forty-five inches of snow had fallen since November 1966. Stalled cars were stuck bumper to bumper on main avenues or were abandoned to rust in the freezing air. There was pressure on the mayor to hire a 'snow czar', a city official who could lead the battle to reclaim the city streets, but Cavanagh held his ground, knowing that soon the weather had to change.

Detroit had most to lose from the snow, and more obliquely from the war in Vietnam too. The federal budget had increasingly diverted resources away from inner-city poverty programmes to fund the expensive and unpopular foreign war in Vietnam. When President Johnson inherited the war upon his succession to the presidency in 1963, he had said prophetically, 'If you think there have been problems so far, I can only suggest you hold on for the next round.' It was one of the most fateful remarks he would ever make. The president had made the optimistic calculation that the war would be over by June 1967, but it was a misguided prediction that in time forced his administration to renege on grander promises to fund his ambitions for his Great Society programmes. As his personal ratings plummeted, the influential news magazine *Time* wrote, 'Lyndon Johnson, the supreme cultivator of consensus, pondered a bitter paradox . . . The only audible consensus in the nation is the one building against him . . . On the farms and in the cities, in the suburbs and the slums, among intellectuals and businessmen, a consuming sense of unease has gripped America.'

The Johnson administration tried to manage the impact of the war with a policy of 'guns and butter' spending on the military and domestic projects, but it was an equilibrium that could never be maintained. As the war escalated, domestic investment was slashed, and the impact disproportionately hit the city of Detroit. Young African-American men – the Motown generation – were among the most vulnerable. Many faced unemployment or being conscripted into military service. Demographically, Detroit's young soul rebels were more likely to die in combat than almost any other subset of society. Of the 4,557 Americans killed in Vietnam during the first eleven months of 1966, the Department of Defense reported that 16.3 per cent were Negroes. In the Marines the rate was even higher, at 20.6 per cent, and dead bodies were returning to Detroit in steady streams. Funeral parlours were among the only businesses showing growth.

It was against this backdrop of angry frustration that a local Detroit clergyman, a black nationalist Christian leader by the name of Reverend Albert Cleage, invited the chairman of the Student Nonviolent Coordinating Committee (SNCC), Stokely Carmichael, to speak in the city at a meeting of a recently formed Black Power coalition, the Organization of Afro-American Unity. On the evening of the speech, a cadre of Marxist-revolutionary auto workers drove in a flotilla of cars along Kercheval to attend the rally. A crowd of 700 gathered at the Methodist church on East Grand, due east of Motown's Hitsville studios. It was here on a cold dry night that Carmichael made his most inflammatory speech, ending with words that provoked fearful editorials across America. Martha and the Vandellas were in the Snake Pit recording, Sinclair was in jail, and Gordy had flown back to Hollywood, where he was working in Motown's West Coast offices. Carmichael's speech was a strident piece of oratory. He raged against racism on the streets of Detroit and in the paddy fields of Vietnam, but the words that fuelled the headlines were full of righteous anger: 'People tell me I should be proud to fight for my country,' Carmichael shouted. 'I'll burn it down first!' This ignited a flame in the minds of many that, as the pace of 1967 grew more intense, proved impossible to extinguish.

Opposition to the war in Vietnam had gone from a whisper to a scream. By the summer of 1967 it would reach a deafening crescendo. America had been in Vietnam for thirteen years, and with each passing day the city of Detroit paid a price. The *New York Times* published a damning report claiming that American bombing raids were deliberately targeting civilian villages, lending dismal weight to an increasing tally of atrocities and war crimes. In Da Nang in mid January, two US Marines were convicted by court-martial of acts of murder and mutilation in a village near Chu Lai. Bigger atrocities were yet to come. Detroit-based war reporter Jo Ann Hardie filed disturbing copy from Winh An, a South Vietnamese village violated by a Viet Cong raiding party: 'What appeared to be a mud-covered log was an old man, his back ripped open by rifle fire.'

The year was not yet a month old, but the pace of events was already relentless. At 5.15 p.m. on 27 January, in the East Room of the White House, President Johnson signed a treaty preventing nuclear weapons from being deployed in outer space. It proved to be one of the most inopportune moments of his beleaguered presidency. The next day, three Apollo astronauts – Gus Grissom, Roger Chaffee and Edward White – died in a test mission at Cape Kennedy when an electrical spark ignited in the area that stored oxygen supplies and fire ripped through their capsule. Watching the tragedy at Cape Kennedy was back-up astronaut James McDivitt, a University of Michigan aeronautics graduate and a passionate Motown fan. Two years previously McDivitt had talked mission control in Houston into playing the Supremes' 'Where Did Our Love Go' to the astronauts aboard *Gemini 5*. This has often been cited as a turning point for Motown, taking the Supremes into every home in America and securing their status as the most famous black girls in the world. The Supremes were travelling through the Windsor Tunnel after a four-day residency at the Elmwood Casino in Windsor, Ontario, when they first heard about the Apollo disaster over a crackling car radio. NASA had released an ambiguous press statement to buy time to allow the management team in Houston to inform the next of kin.

On the last day of January 1967, Marvin Gaye ambled out of Hitsville into the cold dry wind of West Grand Boulevard. He was already a heavy user of marijuana but not yet cocaine, and he had just laid down the male vocal tracks of the stratospheric love duet 'Ain't No Mountain High Enough', featuring Tammi Terrell. She had recorded her vocals two weeks earlier. Gaye and Terrell barely knew each other. They had met casually once or twice but had not yet sung together on the same stage. The song was not finished, the vocals had yet to be mixed, and there was no scheduled release date. Gordy barely knew it even existed and had yet to hear a single note. He was preoccupied with the gathering storm around the Supremes.

Few would argue against the assertion that Florence Ballard had become increasingly unreliable and that her standards of professionalism had slipped. She was drinking heavily, missing group meetings, and had become pessimistic about her career, which seemed to be casting her in an unflattering light as a backing singer. The perfect harmony that had once united the Supremes had permanently soured. On two previous occasions, Ballard had been in material breach of her Motown contract and failed to turn up at a recording session and a press conference. Gordy had grown tired of negotiating with the three girls and Motown's senior management had arranged for a local vocalist, Marlene Barrow, a member of Motown's studio backing group the Andantes, to be on call and to cover for Ballard.

The three most recognisable and photogenic women in Detroit were entrenched in personal warfare. Until now Gordy had kept a quiet counsel about the in-fighting and had only talked about Ballard's behaviour to family and close allies. But in January 1967 he resolved to start the year afresh. He had made up his mind that Blondie had to go. It was a resolution he was determined to keep, but as events took their own direction it proved to be harder than he ever imagined. More than anything else he did in his remarkable career, it was the decision to sack Florence Ballard that was to shape Berry Gordy's reputation for ever.

Desperate Housewives. A group of Detroit housewives are taught hand-gun skills, as fear of crime escalates in the city.

FEBRUARY

Crime

Florence Ballard was half asleep and slumped in the back of a taxi heading slowly through the sleet to her home at 3767 Buena Vista. Motown had screwed up the limousine service, so rather than wait at the airport she'd travelled home by cab, tired and disillusioned. The journey from Metro Airport had taken twice as long as usual, and it was dark by the time she climbed the few steps to her home, carrying luggage and laden with presents. She hunted down a set of keys deep in the side pockets of her mink coat, which had a torn lining and was weighed down on one side with loose nickels and dimes. She had flown home from a one-night-only show in Pittsburgh, turning down a five-star hotel bed for the familiar comfort of her own home. Daily flights from one city to another had worn Ballard down, and although she had been reassured time and again that she could take a break, it never came to be.

She had reached a point where touring with the Supremes was akin to suffering. Her once distinctive auburn-blonde hair had lost its radiance, and her cherubic face had given way to lined tiredness. The one great love of her life – singing in front of an enthusiastic audience – had turned into demeaning drudgery. A colleague who had toured with her during the summer months of 1966 described hearing her through hotel walls sighing from the pit of her stomach, as if she was giving voice to an inner pain. By now the Supremes had spent four relentless years on the road, and each one of them was more or less worn down by demands. In her younger days, when the Supremes had first found fame in 1965, there was a sense of excitement about checking in at reception, taking an elevator to the most expensive suite, and ringing for room service, but the novelty had long since faded, and she had grown to loathe hotels. Newly laundered sheets no longer felt special or even comforting, and she longed for the dishevelled welcome of her family home. She once told her mother that she preferred to wrap herself in her coat than sleep in sheets.

Back home, she kicked off her shoes, rummaged through her bags, and arranged gift boxes along the wall like statues. Returning to her family was a therapy of sorts. They called it homesickness, and in Florence Ballard's case it had become exactly that – a deep emotional sickness that neither antidepressants nor drink could cure. She had been hospitalised twice and visited by numerous doctors brought to hotels by worried road crew. On more than one occasion, she'd fallen asleep in her dressing room and had to be woken to go onstage. Nor was she alone. Diana Ross had been hospitalised too, and Mary Wilson talked of near permanent exhaustion. Although Ballard was unaware of it, in early February Aretha Franklin had flown into Detroit from Memphis in a state of emotional breakdown and was in hiding. She had turned her back on her recording obligations and was holed up in the Franklins' family mansion near Hitsville. The two women had met each other intermittently since childhood, but they were not close and had not seen each other face to face for many months. Neither knew that they had both reached the lowest point of emotional exhaustion, victims of a weariness of the soul.

★

The deep snow had gone, but a rusting smog had settled low above the rooftops of the Wayne County morgue, which sat on the southeastern corner of Brush and Lafayette. Detroit was struggling to cope with a sudden surge in dead bodies, many of them murder victims, and by 1967 the city's faux Egyptian morgue had reached the advanced stages of organisational chaos. A body had gone missing, and to complicate an already embarrassing situation, the morgue's staff were struggling to account for its disappearance. The corpse of Michael Ovcarich, a seventy-eight-year-old Croatian bachelor, had vanished on its way from a local funeral home. Bizarrely, while the staff were trying to account for the missing corpse, another one, the body of an unknown and entirely different man, mysteriously turned up in its place.

Deputy Medical Examiner Dr Clara Raven launched an internal investigation into the affair but was unsure whether her department was dealing with a bureaucratic mix-up among the 'white tiles and crypts' or whether it was a case of bodysnatching, a crime that had not been widely known in Detroit since the nineteenth century. It soon transpired that the missing body was a result of human error. In the hurried activity that often surrounds death, an employee had confused the body of Michael Ovcarich with a recently deceased vagrant some thirty years younger. It was a farcical mistake, but the incident pointed to a wider malaise in the city of Detroit. Public services were stretched to breaking point, and escalating crime figures had put a strain on the city's resources. The morgue handled over 10,000 bodies a year, relying on ancient creaking metal filing cabinets and an austere system of white-tiled drawers into which bodies of every shape and size were placed. Dr Raven admitted that the missing body was an embarrassment but assured the local press that it was an anomaly. 'This has never happened before,' she said defensively. 'I can't understand how a body identified at the scene of death, brought here for storage, and then released to an undertaker, could not be the same.'

Raven's concerns for the missing body spoke to a wider concern: the city's urban pathology. There was growing public concern about the safety of downtown Detroit. The *Detroit News*, in association with its sister radio station, WWJ, had long been planning a $100,000 reward programme aimed at combatting crime and providing 'substantial assistance to the overburdened police'. It was a carefully calculated promotional campaign that occupied a thin blue line between civic goodwill and commercial self-interest. The campaign was to be known as the Secret Witness programme. In effect, citizens could contact the newspaper through a secret coupon system, divulge anonymous information about crimes, and win money. It touched the city's rawest nerves, playing on a growing fear of urban youth among the newspaper's predominantly older white readership.

Crime sells newspapers, but it also has a uniquely corrosive effect. Every day, the front pages of the *Detroit News* reported incidents of rape, robberies and violent crimes, which obviously had the greatest impact. At the launch of the campaign, the first appeal for witnesses was for information on the slaying of eighty-four-year-old Frances Keirnicka, whose body had been discovered on the back porch of her home at 4618 Rivard. It was a calculated choice. Both the crime and the victim established trends that would recur across 1967 as the police and their favoured newspaper reporters told a growingly familiar narrative: ageing and powerless citizens were vulnerable to youth crime even in the supposed sanctity of their homes.

Although the *Detroit News* sold mainly to a socially conservative white readership, it was careful to avoid blatant racial prejudice. Editorial fingers had been severely burned back in 1961 during an acrimonious mayoral election when incumbent mayor Louis Miriani was defeated by Cavanagh. Miriani had run an ugly campaign coordinated along racial lines and eventually lost out as urban communities turned against him. Aware of the potential pitfalls, the editorial team of the *Detroit News* was careful not to demonise the African-American community, and so the crimes highlighted at the launch of the Secret Witness programme were chosen from across the social index: small-town crime in Macomb County, white-collar crime in the suburbs, and inner-city crime in the ghettos. There were appeals for information on the murder of a white teenage runaway, Connie Crossland, the murder of a Hamburg drugstore worker, George Reck Sr, and the slaying of a Saginaw doctor, Archer A. Clayton, by two teenagers. In a macabre twist of fate, it transpired that the dead doctor had delivered both his killers at birth.

Gun crime was the most prominent concern, but the *Detroit News* had chosen a specific angle on that, too, an angle that at least in part protected the integrity of honest Detroit. Many of the guns used to commit crimes in 1967 could be traced to a network of small arms shops across state lines in Ohio, where more lenient gun laws were in place. Toledo was only seventy miles away along Interstate 75, and criminals routinely made the short drive to buy cheap handguns in defiance of Michigan law. Although Detroit had inherited the problems of gun crime, the local media were keen to deflect the blame elsewhere.

In a rush to appeal to the populace, the Secret Witness campaign adopted the language of network television shows such as the police procedural *Dragnet*. Suspects were given fictionalised names like the Trailer Bank Bandit or the Fresh-Faced Felon, lending their crimes a dramatic distinctiveness. One criminal who frequently showed up in the Secret Witness campaign stalked the areas around Motown's Hitsville studio and went by the name of Michigan Avenue Slim. Slim was a hold-up man. He was known to be a young African-American whose crimes were mostly committed on Detroit's near West Side along West Grand Boulevard, and his target area was a cluster of townhouses that hosted small businesses and the nearby homes of aspiring middle-income families. In the first few months of 1967, he conducted a spate of robberies, including a raid on a jewellery store owned by a sixty-two-year-old man named John Skuratiwicz. Most of Slim's victims were elderly white residents, first- or second-generation immigrants from Eastern Europe. It was a contentious theme that fascinated the news media. Commonly, stories would pit older Eastern European-born males from Czechoslovakia, Russia or Poland against poorly educated black teenagers, a faultline that was already dividing Detroit and marking out cultural differences between young and old, black and white, and particularly between older European immigrants and disaffected African-American youth. As tensions grew during 1967, this faultline was to become a chasm, creating resentments that were destined to blow up as the year became hotter and increasingly tense.

Florence Ballard was not a big reader. She rarely bought newspapers, preferring to flip though music and fashion magazines, but like her boss she periodically read the entertainment columns of the *Michigan Chronicle*, looking for a mention of her name or of the stars she had grown up with. If she was ever aware of the Secret Witness campaign, it was only at a vague distance, but she had her own buried and very private reasons to be interested in the focus of the *Detroit News*'s next major criminal. A suspect described as a male African-American had been stalking women in parking lots along Woodward Avenue, and after a series of violent rapes he had become known to the police and the media as the Parking-Lot Rapist.

The story resonated with Ballard, who back in 1960 had been raped in a parking lot on Woodward Avenue, when she was only seventeen years old. She had gone with her brother to a segregated Negro-only night at the Graystone Ballroom on the corner of Woodward and Canfield to see DJ Frantic Ernie Durham. The ballroom was packed with black teenagers from the nearby projects, and as the night unfolded Ballard became separated from her brother. She agreed to take a lift home from a local high-school basketball star named Reggie Harding; they had already met on the local dance-hall circuit and knew each other casually. Harding drove the car a few blocks north on Woodward and veered into an empty parking lot, where he pulled a knife, held it to Ballard's throat, and raped her. Although she was an outgoing teenager who was already an aspiring R&B singer on the fringes of Detroit's music scene, Ballard was still a virgin. She never returned to the Graystone and avoided driving past the intersection where she had been attacked. Although he was entirely unaware of the story and knew nothing of Ballard's rape, Gordy eventually used Motown cash to buy the Graystone Ballroom for $130,000 and brought the old dancehall's segregationist policies to an end.

By February 1967 Harding was on the road to ruining his own life. Ballard chose not to report the crime, argued with her brothers that they should not take revenge, and changed the subject if Harding's name cropped up in conversation. Many of her friends and most of the singers at Motown knew nothing about the rape; Ballard only ever confided her feelings to a tight group of women: her mother, her sisters, the other girls in the Supremes, and Gladys Horton, a vocalist with the Marvelettes. For a brief period in the early sixties, Ballard had been a substitute singer for the Marvelettes when her Motown colleague Wanda Young was pregnant. Ballard had roomed with Horton and struck up a lifelong friendship. Horton was an orphan who had been taken into care before being fostered out to a family in Inkster, Michigan, and in the intimacy of faceless motel rooms far from home, the two singers often talked about the traumas in their past. 'Florence was a loner,' Horton said. 'She really liked her privacy, but sometimes she just needed to confide in someone. We got back to the motel after the show, and it all came out.'

At the time of the rape, Harding was a school friend of Florence's brother Billy at Eastern High, and for a time he was considerably more famous than his victim. He was a well-known character around the corners of Mack Avenue and East Grand Boulevard where he led a local street gang. Fired up by power, youthful ego and his towering height, Harding cut an intimidating figure, and many contemporaries admitted they lived in fear of him. He was a giant of a boy who entered the record books as the first seven-footer to play in the Detroit Public School League, and when he joined the Detroit Pistons as a fourth-round draft pick during the 1964 season, he became the first player to go straight from high school to the NBA. However, it was not long before he was in trouble with the NBA, racking up fines, suspensions and final warnings. When Reggie Harding raped Florence Ballard he was still in high school, but his success as a basketball player had brought him early wealth as a well-paid member of Goose Tatum's Harlem Roadkings, a competitor franchise of the Harlem Globetrotters. Harding was paid in cash at the end of Roadkings exhibition matches across the Midwest and went on wild spending sprees. His gangly frame often appeared comical, but almost everything else about

Harding was brutal, unlikeable and out of control. Many teenagers, including Florence and her brother, found his fame and fast cash superficially attractive, but many more simply avoided him, sensing a dangerous side to his personality. Nothing was quite right in Harding's life. Despite his gigantic frame, he lived in a shrunken wooden-frame home on the East Side, on a street that looked like something from rural Mississippi rather than a bustling city.

Describing the aftermath of the rape many years later, Florence's sister Maxine wrote in her brave and candid book, *The True Story of Florence Ballard*, that 'There was a lot of confusion in the middle of all the loud voices. I was told to stay in the room and I did just that, but I made sure I could hear everything. I wanted to crawl into a big hole when I heard Flo tell Momma that Bill's friend took her someplace and then he raped her. My family was in uproar over this, and they vowed to find him and have him locked up.' But, ultimately, the Ballard family made a decision that was not uncommon at the time. Deeply suspicious of the Detroit police and intimidated by Harding's reputation, they did not report the incident and closed the lid on it as best they could. For Florence Ballard it left memories that were impossible to close down and were never really resolved. 'I sat on the porch and cried and cried,' she said many years later. 'I had some pretty blue days.'

According to Mary Wilson, the rape 'ate away at Flo's insides' and never seemed to let her settle. She had frequent nightmares and slept restlessly. 'Despite her self-assured attitude,' Wilson wrote in *Dreamgirl*, 'she was an innocent. From this day on, I'd see Flo's basic personality undergo a metamorphosis, from being reticent and shy with a sassy front to being skeptical, cynical, and afraid of everyone and everything.' Florence Ballard knew she would never be slim like Diana Ross or as attractive to men as the magnetic Mary Wilson, but she could sing, and in a musical world that still valued suffering, she had more to sing about than any of them. People often described her singing privately to herself, on the road, in airports, and in empty hotel lobbies. She seemed to be mouthing her own personal lyrics. Slowly but surely, the vagaries of fame, the shifting power politics within Motown and the aftermath of sexual assault were eroding her self-confidence: she was becoming invisible.

Tellingly, when the Supremes were touring, Ballard used the telephone more than any of the others, often talking for hours at a time to her mother and sisters back in Detroit. She would save up spare coins for payphones in the pockets of her expensive fur coats. Mary Wilson watched the phone calls increase, as if they were some kind of lifeline, but she came to believe they were not helping. 'Her family's love for Flo would become a guarded fortress, with Flo sequestered inside and everyone outside considered a stranger, an enemy. From this day on, Flo would turn to them, not us, and their advice would color her every move . . . She would talk with them for hours and tell them all her problems.' Sadly, her family could not offer much constructive advice, nor give Ballard sorely needed perspective. They believed she should express herself and not let them 'push her around'.

Rape had cast Florence Ballard as a victim, and her family, unclear about what they could really do to help, reinforced that role. Her sister once wrote, 'While looking back at that night and thinking about the pain of trying to put this horrible ordeal behind her, no one could imagine this would be the first of many "rapes" that Flo would endure. These betrayals continued to eat at her like a vicious spreading evil trying to surround her and forcing her to fight to hold on to her very existence.' Wilson has described Ballard's long sighs and depressive silences: 'Some people took Flo's silence as a mark of her maturity; in fact she was often quiet because she feared being ridiculed. Her family still held on to those country ways and made no pretense of being more sophisticated than they were.'

By February 1967 deep feelings of persecution had entered Ballard's embattled soul. She imagined that the Motown Record Corporation was against her, that the music industry was conspiratorial, and that the only place she could find unconditional love was with her family back home in Detroit.

The Ballard family was a blues family. Ballard's father, Jesse Lambert Ballard, had migrated north from Rosetta, Mississippi, in 1929 as the Depression began to bite. A Jazz Age visitor to the city captured the sense of yearning that Detroit held for rural Southerners like Jesse Ballard: 'Detroit is El Dorado. It is staccato American. It is shockingly dynamic.' The Ballards, like thousands of other dirt-poor families, were attracted to the promise of a better life. From the age of twenty-one, Jesse Ballard worked at General Motors in the most punishing areas of auto manufacturing, labouring in the intense and unforgiving heat of the foundries. Although migrant black workers from the South were a minority in the workforce, they were heavily concentrated in low-status jobs. The majority worked in Ford's giant River Rouge plant, while others were heavily concentrated at Buick No. 70 in Flint and in foundries in Pontiac and Saginaw. Jesse Ballard was an amateur blues singer who played box guitar and, like many who played alongside him, he was fatally attracted to cheap liquor. Among his contemporaries on the Detroit blues scene were Doc Ross, who worked with him at General Motors, Bobo Jenkins, who worked a lifetime at the nearby Chrysler plant, and 'Washboard Willie' Hensley, who raucously strummed a washboard with thimbles and calloused fingers. But the most memorable of Jesse Ballard's social network was the legendary John Lee Hooker, who worked at a steel foundry that supplied the plant where Ballard worked. Foundry work was often described as the 'slave inferno' – back-breaking, relentless and burning hot – and Ballard frequently came back to his crowded home with scorched skin and facial burns. Over the years he had fathered a noisy family of thirteen (Florence was the eighth child). According to her sister Maxine, her father would drink himself into oblivion on the weekend. 'Although he was hardworking,' she wrote, 'he was also an alcoholic. My father's drinking worried me a lot as a child.' Without much evidence to back it up, one of Diana Ross's biographers claimed that Jesse Ballard was 'a hobo who slept in graveyards and picked the blues guitar', but in a more candid admission of her childhood, Maxine Ballard claimed she once saw her drunken father wiping his own shit with a five-dollar bill.

Unlike Berry Gordy's family, who were middle-class blacks who owned a chain of small businesses, the Ballards were frequently forced to turn to neighbours or to the church to provide them with food. They lived in a series of ramshackle overcrowded homes across the city: first in a condemned building; then a shelter for the poor on East McDougall, where they slept five to a bed; then a housing project on Ethel and Eight Mile Road; and ultimately in the Brewster Projects, where the fledgling story of the Supremes was born. The Brewster Housing Projects was a housing complex built for Detroit's 'working poor'. The Ballard family moved there sometime in the mid fifties with a reputation as a musical family; a cousin, Hank Ballard, was known at the time for his sexual soul song 'Work With Me Annie', a raw classic of the Detroit R&B scene, and later became famous for 'The Twist', the novelty song that was latterly covered by Philadelphia poultry worker Chubby Checker, who kick-started the Twist craze.

Mary Wilson first set eyes on Florence Ballard when they auditioned as soloists at a local talent show and was struck by her apparent self-confidence. 'I would see her walking around the neighborhood and think that she was such a pretty girl, with her fair skin, auburn hair, long legs, and curvaceous figure.' Remembering her in the days before the sexual assault, Mary claimed she was a very different person. 'In those days a large bust-line was considered a prerequisite of female beauty and, compared to the rest of us, Flo looked like a movie star. Even without make-up Flo's face was perfect; her big brown eyes perfectly balanced with her full sensuous lips and Valentine-pointed chin. Because her hair was relatively light, everyone called her "Blondie".' Berry Gordy was initially attracted to her and flirted with her incessantly and openly, deferring to her as the group's natural leader. As a teenager Ballard seemed worldlier than the more delicate Diane Ross, who at the time was studying fashion at Cass Tech and nervous about the quality of her voice. There was no flashpoint or incendiary moment that shifted the balance of their relationship – it was gradual and probably inevitable.

Maxine Ballard described her sister as 'smart and aggressive', but after years of effort and thwarted ambitions to be a solo singer, Ballard had begun to miss important engagements. She was frequently late for interviews, and in contrast to the expectations of Motown's talent-management system, had become surly and impolite. Ballard blamed the pressures of touring, but Gordy saw it differently. He worried that her increasingly erratic and provocative behaviour was undermining Motown's professional standards and that she ran the risk of humiliating the Supremes in a very public way. Flo had taken to hiding small liquor bottles in her luggage and in the pockets of her white mink coat. According to Mary Wilson, she was definitely not an alcoholic, but like others in her family she was vulnerable to drink. Her grandmother had been an alcoholic, so too was her father, who died of cancer in 1959, and her brother Calvin died in his early thirties of liver problems. She was easily intoxicated and could appear drunk even after sipping a single beer. Flo argued that drinking before a show calmed her nerves and that the other girls did it, too, and Mary Wilson has always partially backed her claims. 'Diane and I could drink without suffering any ill-effects, but Flo's tolerance for alcohol was almost nil.'

Ballard dropped out of high school in her mid teens, hiding her failures from an older brother, Cornell, who had assumed the role of surrogate guardian after their father's death. She grew up quickly – possibly too quickly – and her formidable voice disguised her immaturity. Rather than attend school, Flo spent much of her free time hanging about on the worn grass outside Motown's Hitsville studio. Describing her teenage self many years later, she admitted that she was equally enthralled by singing and by men. 'I'm the one that used to chase those fine-ass niggers around in the projects,' she said. 'Just so I could see them singing and standing on the street corners looking good as hell.' Her sister described the same sense of teen spirit: 'We used to fly through the projects like we owned them.' Ballard's pursuit of 'fine-ass niggers' brought her into contact with a local harmony group called the Primes, managed by local hustler Milton Jenkins, a flamboyant character who eventually married Flo's older sister, Maxine. Jenkins cut an impressive sight. The girls claimed they first saw him emerging from a red Cadillac, dressed in a sharp coat and wearing a sling on one arm, the result of a road accident several weeks before. Jenkins was a self-styled human peacock and wore clothes that could captivate a woman at fifty yards, compared to the ghetto teenagers who swarmed around him – and he had cash. Jenkins 'rented rooms' near Fourteenth Street and, like his infamous contemporary, music producer Diamond Jim Riley, he worked in the shadow territory between music and prostitution.

Jenkins was originally from Birmingham, Alabama, and had travelled north to Detroit with three southern-born singers, Kell Osborne, Paul Williams and Eddie Kendricks, who formed the nucleus of the Primes and who in the years to come would morph into the Temptations. The gregarious Jenkins hatched the idea of a sister group called the Primettes, blithely unaware that in that passing thought he had laid the foundations of the greatest girl group ever. Flo Ballard was fifteen; her neighbourhood friend Mary was only fourteen; they had recently met a third girl, Diane Ross, who was also fourteen; and a fourth girl was another teenager from the Brewster Projects, Betty McGlown, the oldest at seventeen. McGlown subsequently left to get married and was replaced by Barbara Martin, but she too moved on, leaving the Primettes as a perfect trio. As the groups took shape, Jenkins's fortunes changed dramatically. His broken arm, which he had paraded as if it were a fashion statement, became gangrenous, and he died from related infections without reaping any of the rewards of originating two of the greatest groups in the history of soul music – the Temptations and the Supremes.

Motown were initially sceptical about the Primettes. They appeared raw and untutored, and were nowhere near the shortlist of local hopefuls that Berry Gordy was recruiting for his growing empire. At first Motown used the Primettes' age as an excuse and told them to come back when they had graduated from high school, dismissing them as inexperienced, directionless and offering nothing that differentiated them from the hundreds of other girl groups in the crowded streets of Detroit soul. Compared with Motown's most successful girl group, the Marvelettes, who had already delivered hits, the Primettes still dressed in bobby sox and schoolgirl cardigans, and looked naïve, dated and perilously close to doo-wop.

In the Primettes' early days, Ballard was the lead singer and had a passionate gospel-tinged blues style that stood out even in the most competitive company. Marvin Gaye described her as 'a hell of a singer, probably the strongest of the . . . girls'. Seemingly cursed with a thin nasal pop voice, Diane Ross stood behind her onstage singing background harmonies, privately in awe of her teenage friend. Ross often conceded that Flo's voice was something special. 'She was absolutely regal, and the strength in her voice matched her carriage. She was capable of such high volume that with the proper training maybe she could have sung opera if she had had the money or the knowledge to pursue that kind of career.'

A local mail man and sometime Motown songwriter named Freddie Gorman had a delivery route that took him through the Brewster Projects. He was tentatively making his way as a songwriter but had yet to build enough resources or reputation to leave his full-time job. Gorman was a peripheral character at Motown but had contributed lyrical inspiration to the Marvelettes' hit 'Please Mr. Postman', and he co-wrote the catchy 1960 song 'I Want A Guy' for the Supremes. After pressure from several Motown staff members who lived in the Brewster Projects, Gordy gave in and assigned Smokey Robinson to record the Primettes. He made one non-negotiable stipulation: their name had to change. In a rushed meeting at his office, he gave the lead singer an hour to come up with something more original. He handed Ballard a list of potential names, which included suggestions such as the Darleens, the Sweet Ps, and the Jewelettes. But she chose a name of her own making: the Supremes. Carolynn Gill, a vocalist with rival group the Velvelettes, witnessed the exchanges and has remained adamant that the Supremes were Ballard's group. 'Florence was the original lead singer,' she once said. 'When the group came to Motown, it was Flo's group; she had formed it and named it.'

By 1967 the Supremes had been with Motown for six years. The girls were minors when they signed their first employment contract, and as a courtesy Motown had invited their mothers in to oversee the paperwork and countersign the contracts. There was no legal counsel present, nor was one requested by the families. Ballard did not even know what legal counsel was, nor did she particularly care. The contract was the summit of her aspirations, and to sign with Motown was a ghetto dream come true. The label offered demanding contracts but nothing unusual for the time. The girls would be given a small wage, and company costs were to be deducted from their royalties. This simple and widely practised 'net value' clause was to become a festering sore across the years as the group's income and expenditure soared. Much has been written and said about the contracts that Motown's young artists signed, but paradoxically it was the Supremes who were in breach of contract. They had already made a written commitment to Milton Jenkins, who by now was married to Maxine Ballard. Jenkins lacked the will to sue his own sister-in-law or to pursue her new employers at Motown, so he simply let it go. The Supremes were by no means an instant success, either. Motown subsidised them for four fruitless years, shouldering the financial burden of non-recoupable rehearsal time, barren studio sessions and failed releases. On the purest measure of profit and loss, Gordy cash flowed to the Supremes for years, sometimes against his better judgement. By 1962 Ballard, already disillusioned and sensing that her career as a member of the fledgling group had stalled, accepted a role as a stand-in singer with Motown's more successful girl group, the Marvelettes. For six months the Supremes ceased to exist, and it was only when Ballard returned to Detroit in September 1962 that they reformed and tried again to shake off the stigma of being the 'No Hit' Supremes.

Like many aspiring Detroit acts, the Supremes were sent out to tour on the now notorious Motortown Revues, an intensive boot camp on wheels, including seventeen one-night stands in a row. The relentless regime of touring took the Supremes on the so-called Chitlin' Circuit of small towns, city ghettos and flea-ridden venues. They lived on a tour bus, slept in their day clothes, and struck up fleeting friendships. Ballard had a short love affair with Otis Williams of the Temptations, only one of many Motown love affairs that complicated an already emotionally charged creative community. Although the Revues have long been mythologised, in fact they were punishing trips that took busloads of young Detroiters to some of the most squalid areas of urban America and to confrontation with the deepest prejudices of the segregated South. Ballard witnessed conditions that were unbelievably bad. 'Roaches, broken-down facilities, bad plumbing, face bowls and stuff,' she once said. 'Some of them didn't even have bathtubs . . . like a flophouse. But you're black – you've got to stay there.'

The spring of 1964 marked a watershed moment. The Supremes were seen as also-rans in the frenetic glamour of Detroit and, still hiding the emotional trauma of rape from all but her closest friends, Ballard thought of giving up music entirely until Motown's ace production team, Holland-Dozier-Holland, approached the group with a jaunty pop-soul song called 'Where Did Our Love Go'. It was initially conceived of as a beat ballad and was intended for the Marvelettes, but inexplicably they turned it down, and only by default or desperation did it end up with the Supremes. They had reservations, but having plummeted to the bottom of the Motown pecking order, they had precious few options. Ballard agreed that Ross's reedy voice was more suited to the track than her more forceful R&B style. It proved to be a fateful mistake: she'd inadvertently conceded the role of lead singer to Ross.

The Supremes had recently been turned down by Dick Clark's *Caravan of Stars*, a live version of the TV series *American Bandstand*, but sensing a potential hit, Gordy begged Clark to reconsider. By sheer coincidence another group dropped out, and with no contract and no absolute guarantee that they would appear on the television show, the Supremes hurriedly joined the live tour. It was while they were on the road as stand-ins that 'Where Did Our Love Go' unpredictably rocketed to the top of the charts. By the time they flew home from California to Detroit Metro Airport, their lives had changed for ever, and the balance of their friendship had shifted.

It was clear from the outset that the Supremes had competing personalities, but further complicating the tense chemistry of the group, there were also different versions of Florence Ballard. Marvin Gaye described her as 'a beautiful person – loving and warm'; to her biographer, Peter Benjaminson, she was the 'spunky funny one'; and to her fellow Supreme Mary Wilson, she was simply 'misunderstood'. Although the Motown publicity machine had taught her the basics of etiquette, Ballard had never graduated from high school and came across as a bundle of contradictions: streetwise yet shy, moody yet opinionated, uneducated yet glamorous. Perhaps the most revealing description of her character came from a former boyfriend, Roger Pearson, the son of a trust-fund millionaire. Pearson was a white college student from Connecticut who had met Ballard in January 1966 at the El San Juan Hotel in Puerto Rico, where the wealthy student was celebrating his twentieth birthday. He detected a fundamental tension. 'Flo was caught between poverty and opulence,' he said tellingly. 'She was only two years out of the projects and into a whole new reality of opulence when she became a star.'

Tension between wealth and poverty was common to many at Motown, but for Ballard it was extreme. Her family had always struggled financially, and in a painfully honest account of their childhood her sister Maxine admitted that the family had furnished their home from Famous Furniture, the Detroit store that extended credit to ghetto families, and that when the teenage sisters menstruated, they stuffed torn rags into their pants, unable to afford sanitary towels. In stark contrast to her hand-to-mouth upbringing, Ballard's life as a Supreme exposed her to untold wealth. Touring brought them into contact with Las Vegas high-rollers and old European wealth. On a tour of the United Kingdom in 1965, Gordy befriended an English aristocrat named Alexander Charles Robert Vane-Tempest-Stewart, the ninth Marquis of Londonderry, a black-music obsessive who once sang in a short-lived aristo-jazz band called the Eton Five. Briefly besotted by the Supremes, he invited them to stay at his stately home at Wynyard Park in County Durham (they were appearing locally at Newcastle City Hall and the Stockton ABC in the northeast of England). The girls described being in awe of his 'hundred-room mansion, dining amid antique china and crystal'. The servants' quarters were grander than the home Ballard had grown up in, and Diana Ross described the gardens as being big enough to accommodate the entire Brewster

Housing Projects. The marquis took Flo for a walk through his manicured gardens to see the family burial grounds, including the resting place of one of the most famous racehorses of the eighteenth century, Hambletonian.

Although she was always quick to adopt the surface veneer of glamour, Ballard was deeply uncomfortable in the company of wealth and struggled to make perfect sense of her adult life. She was never fully immersed in stardom and found success exhausting. 'We had charge accounts at Saks, Hudson's and places like that,' she once said disbelievingly. 'Whatever we charged, the bill didn't come to us; it went to Motown . . . It was fantastic to be able to go out and buy everything we wanted and put it on and look like a million dollars.' By the time she was twenty-four years old, Ballard had visited Tokyo, Paris and London; she had performed onstage at Harlem's Apollo, the Copacabana and all the major Las Vegas casinos. She was outwardly comfortable in furs, but nagging doubts about her past and the loneliness of travelling made her uncomfortable within herself. Witnesses described Ballard standing apart as if she were watching herself, never quite sure if her career was real or imaginary. Whatever image she projected outwardly, she had become one of the most uncertain stars in Detroit's glittering galaxy and, according to *Detroit Free Press* journalist Peter Benjaminson, she was harbouring the first fateful signs of a grudge: 'Right or wrong, she believed that her founding and early domination of the group, along with her talent, should have made her the Supremes' permanent leader and that she should have the enduring right to sing lead on at least some songs. When leadership was denied her, she sometimes became sullen and angry.'

As Ballard's self-doubt deepened, her belligerence increased. She often confronted Gordy, demanding respect and wanting to be acknowledged as the group's original leader. Then, just as inexplicably, she would retreat into herself, often refusing to talk to him for days on end. Her face had always been round and had the lively quality of someone who, according to Mary Wilson, had a 'great laugh . . . a hearty laugh'. But it was a face of many masks: black eyeliner was drawn heavily around her eyes and then flicked into sharp triumphant scars, and long teardrop earrings hung from her ears. More significantly, behind the ebony foundation and thick mascara, her eyes had the puffy despair of a woman who had cried too much.

Gordy had come to personalise her behaviour and imagined that he was the sole object of her rage. 'Flo was Flo and everyone loved her,' he wrote. 'She was a unique character whose wit, sarcasm and deadpan comments kept us laughing. At times she was outgoing, fun-loving and even challenging. At other times [she was] withdrawn and depressed.' The depression worsened with alcohol and the next anonymous hotel lobby. For those who knew nothing of her background, she could at times seem rude, detached and unprofessional, and then just as suddenly light up a room. She was quick to notice hierarchies within the group and felt that Ross was accorded favours, or that she and Mary were disciplined more often than Ross. She frequently talked about being on trial, as if she were being watched by the Motown Record Corporation. It was not all paranoia. Gordy was, of course, closer to Ross and was prone to taking sides.

Discipline had begun to worry Gordy. Onstage, on tour and in the company of journalists, all Motown artists were expected to conduct themselves with decorum and were trained to do so. The label had even founded its own training academy and 'charm school', overseen by the imperious Maxine Powell, whose Detroit-based Finishing and Modeling School had been a magnet for aspirational young black girls since the Second World War. Ballard seemed to be deliberately bending the rules, as if she were testing Gordy. He had seen with his own eyes the sporadic drunkenness and lapses in professionalism. She'd once responded to a throwaway insult by soaking him with drink in a hotel bar and, according to Diana Ross biographer J. Randy Tarborelli, she had overstepped the mark when she threatened to expose Gordy's business practices to the press. It is a claim that has never been independently verified, nor is it entirely clear what Ballard meant by the threat; she had no great knowledge of the corporation's accounts or tax returns, but at the very moment she needed to reassure Gordy of her loyalty and win his approval, Ballard alienated him still further.

The most likely explanation is that Ballard had become so disenchanted with the exhausting workload that she voiced her disrespect more loudly than others. For most Motown acts, touring was a necessary evil – at its most intense from Memorial Day to Labor Day, May to September. The punishing schedules and promotional demands often scattered neighbourhood friends to different parts of the world. Relationships became increasingly remote, secret love affairs were common, and the tangled grapevine of gossip was exacerbated by distance.

Being on the road had lost its early sense of adventure, and acts who were associated with each other in the minds of the record-buying public only met as they passed each other in the terminal of Metro Airport. It was here that Ballard periodically saw the man who raped her rushing for a plane. By 1967 Harding's basketball career was going everywhere and nowhere. The Detroit Pistons were in transition, having racked up record defeats and failed to make the play-offs. For a brief spell, Harding sat in the same locker room as point guard Dave Bing, who in later life became mayor of Detroit, and the NBA's youngest ever player-coach, Dave DeBusschere. But Harding pushed everyone to the edge of tolerance. He was a psychotic misfit entirely unsuited to the discipline of professional sport. He was educationally subnormal, routinely carried a knife, and was known to conceal a handgun in his duffel bag. His notoriety helped neither his career nor his local standing, and incoming Pistons coach Donnie Butcher quickly offloaded him.

At the very moment that Harding's career was stuttering, a group of investors pooled their resources to buy a basketball franchise in the fledgling American Basketball Association and founded the Indiana Pacers. They wanted to recruit players with NBA experience, and Harding fitted the bill. At the time there was even a supposition that the new franchise would remove Harding from the temptations of Detroit street life and save his once-promising career. It was a generous but utterly forlorn hope. Harding had been a criminal since elementary school, and throughout his teenage years the Detroit police had questioned him about a string of petty crimes and sexual assaults. The towering height that made him so adept at basketball had also cast him as a fully grown adult misfit by the age of ten. Although there is no direct or reliable evidence to suggest that Reggie Harding was Detroit's parking-lot rapist, he unquestionably matched the profile. At eighteen years old, Harding had been arrested for having carnal knowledge of an underage teenager and was charged with statutory rape. Only his potential as a rising basketball star helped him secure an acquittal. He had been abusing heroin since his mid teens and later in life spent two years incarcerated in southern Michigan's Jackson State Prison. Upon his release he said, 'Sure I was on the needle. But now I understand about drugs – you take drugs and you don't even know your identity.' It was a short-lived redemption. Harding was repeatedly apprehended for robbing liquor stores in Detroit and died, not yet thirty, in 1972, in a shootout a few blocks from the parking lot where he'd assaulted Ballard. A car pulled up, someone inside called his name, words were exchanged and the unknown assailant fired a gun, killing him instantly.

In February 1967, the Supremes were in residency at a Detroit supper club called the Roostertail, situated on the crest of Lake St Clair by the banks of the Detroit River. Motown had a joint venture with the management there and used the club to showcase new acts. All three members of the Supremes had been stricken by a winter virus and were suffering from recurring head colds, blocked sinuses and stomach complaints. They were allowed to stay locally in their own homes but were visited daily by a company doctor. Marlene Barrow of the Andantes had been contracted to be on stand-by throughout the residency and had been warned that there was a likelihood she would be called to replace Ballard. Fearing that all of the Supremes might be too ill to perform, Motown suggested to the Roostertail management that it would be expedient to pencil in a replacement group, so arrangements were made to secure the services of New York girl group, the Toys. This might not have been mere expedience. Behind the backs of both the Supremes and the management of the Roostertail, Motown staff members were accepting two network television bookings in

Hollywood and New York, and the Toys were a cover for a quick cancellation.

As it transpired, all three girls made it to the opening night at the Roostertail and it was a huge success. Senior Motown executives took photographs of the Supremes and their backing band partying backstage with co-star Bobby Darin. Ballard was missing. She did the show but then ducked out of the after-show drinks and returned home rather than mingle with Gordy and his guests. Mary Wilson described her behaviour as a 'metamorphosis' – 'I could see her suffering, and her eyes reflected a gamut of emotions – fright, embarrassment, distrust,' she wrote. Gordy had not told Ballard that her position in the group was at risk, and he avoided doing so for several months. But he had already discussed the possibility of a compromise deal with Motown's legal team, a new contract that would allow Ballard to work on some solo projects but cut her ties with the group. It was wishful thinking. Despite her many anxieties, Ballard was still defiantly proud of being one of the Supremes and frequently introduced herself to strangers as the leader of the group. Frustratingly for those around her, Ballard's pride was often communicated through the uninhibited voice of alcohol, and when reconciliation looked possible, another unexpected incident drove Gordy and Ballard further apart.

Gordy wanted to sideline Ballard but had no master plan to sack her. Only his sisters and his closest confidants at Motown knew how entrenched his feelings had become, and fatefully for his reputation, he began to 'improvise' solutions. Smokey Robinson and Gordy's brother-in-law Harvey Fuqua were among the small clique who knew of his plans to promote Diana Ross to lead singer and isolate Ballard. Robinson thought it was a great opportunity for some of the fringe Motown singers, but Gordy and Fuqua were lukewarm about promoting from within. They felt that hiring an outsider would be a grander gesture. Some have subsequently claimed that Gordy kept a secret dossier of potential replacements, but if he did, he kept it stored in his head. His sister Esther was keen to recruit Barbara Randolph, a local cabaret singer and the daughter of the actress Lillian Randolph, best known for the role of

Annie in *It's a Wonderful Life*. Randolph had great versatility as a performer and had shared the stage with the Supremes at a residency in San Juan, Puerto Rico. She knew their repertoire well. Sensing an opportunity, Gordy tentatively dropped her name into a conversation with Diana Ross. But according to Motown mythology, the air turned ice cold, and Randolph's name was struck off the list. 'Berry said there were problems and dissensions in the group and that I would be replacing Flo,' Barbara Randolph admitted many years later. 'But he said the final decision was Diana's [and] I wasn't sure I wanted to get involved.' In any case, Randolph's actress mother was hatching alternative plans. She had secured her daughter a supporting role in *Guess Who's Coming to Dinner*, the race-relations movie starring Sydney Poitier which was destined to become one of the landmark films of the year.

Marlene Barrow of the Andantes was another contender. She had been used as a substitute singer before and answered the call several more times as tension within the Supremes mounted. She knew all of their songs and, according to producer Lamont Dozier, she had featured on several recordings where her role was to 'fatten' out the group's sometimes thin sound, but Barrow had a settled family life in Detroit and was unwilling to make any long-term commitment to travelling. 'I didn't have any dreams of going further,' she claimed in the Andantes' story, *Motown from the Background* by journalist Vicki Wright. 'It was just filling in.' She was on permanent stand-by throughout the Roostertail residency and had driven to other shows in the Midwest when there was a risk that one of the girls would not make it onstage. She had even been a stand-by to history at the Civic Arena in Pennsylvania when the Supremes broke the venue's one-night performance record, a record previously set by the Beatles. Despite anxieties back in Detroit, Ballard showed up for the Pennsylvania show, but was not called upon to perform. According to reviews, another Motown group, the Spinners, opened the show and warmed up the crowd with a virtuoso medley of sixties soul hits in which they impersonated the manic dance routine of the Contours, the elegant shuffling of the Temptations, and the endearing contortions of Little Stevie Wonder.

On 7 February Berry Gordy rose with the light. Without bothering to shave or eat breakfast, he set off from his home for Motown's newly acquired Golden World Studios at 3246 West Davison, his driver Tommy Chapman at the wheel. As they drove in bumper-to-bumper traffic along the freeway, Gordy took care to avoid discussing Motown business and stuck to general conversations about the traffic, or the forthcoming Ali and Terrell fight. He no longer trusted Chapman. Gordy had been suspicious of the chauffeur for many months now and felt his driver listened too intently to backseat conversations, habitually glancing in the rear-view mirror, his long nose and sharp features periodically breaking into a smile. Chapman was a well-established chauffeur on the R&B circuit who had broken into the recording industry as a driver for Etta James in the early day of her heroin addiction, and it was through James that he had met Harvey Fuqua and secured work with the Gordy family. By 1967 he was in love with Florence Ballard. The first spark of friendship had ignited when Chapman drove Ballard home from a late-night recording session, and it had been rekindled when they travelled together as part of the Motown entourage when the Supremes toured Japan in 1966. It was on board the Northwest Orient flight to Tokyo that they really got to know each other. Gordy had watched their love affair deepen but had no reasonable grounds to sack Chapman, nor had he any solid proof that the chauffeur was doing anything to undermine Motown. Nonetheless, he had much to be private about. He was keeping secrets on several fronts: his home life was in flux again, and he was having simultaneous affairs.

The Golden World Studios were about the best that Detroit had to offer. Members of the Detroit Symphony Orchestra were counted among the freelancers, and some of the city's best musicians worked together under the collective pseudonym of the San Remo Golden Strings. The studios had been subsumed into the Motown Empire, the deal had been brokered in the fall of 1966, and the *Michigan Chronicle* reported: 'The purchase price is in six figures and includes real estate, recording studios, and the company's catalog of master discs and tapes.' In addition, Motown had purchased the copyright catalogue of rival publishing company Myto Music and the recording contracts of two of the city's most formidable male singers, Edwin Starr and J. J. Barnes. Gordy thought it was a great deal and liked to talk about it as a triumph. It eliminated competition and took one of Motown's rival indies out of the way, but with success stretching Hitsville to breaking point, the real motivation was to increase studio capacity.

Gordy planned to record two songs there with a white singer named Chris Clark – first, the self-penned 'I Want To Go Back There Again', and a second, 'I Love You', co-written by Marvin Gaye and his wife, Gordy's sister Anna. Clark was from Santa Cruz, California, and was stylistically similar to the British R&B singer Dusty Springfield. Her peroxide-blonde hair was arranged in a fashionable beehive style, and her heavily accentuated black eyeliner gave her the de rigueur look of a British Mod. She was a strikingly attractive woman and was immediately drawn to Gordy. Like Gordy's lover Diana Ross, she was drawn not so much by his money or power but his charismatic determination to pursue success. Gordy was a fastidious producer and spent most of the day strengthening the lead vocals on 'I Want To Go Back There Again', a song that he cherished more than most. 'It didn't get too big, but it meant a lot to me,' he later wrote in his autobiography. Clark was not the greatest singer he could have turned to, but she had a smouldering jazz soul voice that was both contemporary and cosmopolitan. Gordy saw her as a sophisticated woman and often turned to her for advice.

Gordy and Clark had embarked on a furtive interracial relationship that remained secret for several years. 'Chris and I became close,' he admitted years later. 'Very close. I loved her companionship and found her a different kind of security, a mental security.' There was undoubtedly a bond. 'Some people didn't know what to make of Chris's razor-sharp but extremely subtle wit or her rapid-fire jumps from one subject to the next.' Gordy liked to repeat a joke about mixed relationships he once heard the comic Godfrey Cambridge tell: 'If God had meant us to be kept separate, he wouldn't have standardized the parts.'

Society had yet to adjust to mixed-race relationships, and only a month or two after Gordy began sleeping with Chris Clark, his friend and collaborator Jackie Wilson was arrested with a white girl in a South Carolina motel and charged with immoral conduct. Detroit was only barely tolerant of interracial relationships and was not ready for a mixed-race version of the Supremes. 'I learned a lot from my experience with her about how the world looks at mixed couples,' Gordy said much later in his life. 'Color was never an issue between us, but we knew it was for many others, both black and white.'

According to Supremes biographer Mark Ribowsky, Gordy was careful to smuggle Clark into what was an already complicated private life. 'He was already cheating with Chris Clark, the white Motown singer who happened to be a gorgeous and sexy blonde,' he wrote luridly. 'Not willing to wait until he was back in Detroit to fool around with her, he would sometimes fly Clark to where he was on the road and have roadies smuggle her into his room – which, with a sense of danger and betrayal that must have been perversely exciting, was always right next to Diana's room.' Certainly Ross was kept in the dark about the intensity of Gordy's relationship with the creatively intimidating Clark.

Gordy's motives for keeping this relationship hidden were not just to do with the mores of mid sixties Detroit; he was prone to secrecy and had lived a life of sexual intrigue since he was a teenager. Gordy had a lengthy list of former one-night stands, show girls and secret dalliances. According to one former girlfriend, 'he kept the faith in a faithless kind of way', and loved women indiscriminately. Gordy had an alert mind and a good memory – and he needed one. He was married and divorced three times and fathered eight children. (His publishing company, Jobete – the financial powerhouse of Motown – was taken from the first letters of the names of his three oldest children, Joy, Berry and Terry.) His first wife, Thelma Coleman, still lived locally. His second wife, Raynoma Gordy, was two months pregnant and due to return to Motown after a period of estrangement during which she had run an ill-fated rival company, Shrine Records of Washington DC.

A third lover, Margaret Norton, also lived in Detroit. No marriage certificate has ever come to light, but Gordy may also have married her sometime in 1964. What was not in doubt was that they had a son together, Gordy's fifth child. It was this relationship more than any other that exacerbated an already rancorous war with his former wife Raynoma and a vindictive dispute between the two women festered for several years, conducted mostly by vicious telephone insults and embarrassing street fights. But Gordy did not stop there. Despite the emotional chaos surrounding him, he was in love with Diana Ross, and yet by December 1966 he was sexually involved with Clark.

The Chris Clark sessions at Golden World coincided with a reef knot in Gordy's increasingly tangled personal life. Even by Gordy's promiscuous standards, having an affair with Clark was a difficult trick to pull off. To add another layer of complexity, lawyers acting on behalf of Raynoma were trying to challenge the validity of their divorce, which Gordy had hurriedly secured under Mexican law. Yet things were about to get worse. The eventual B-side of Clark's Motown debut on the VIP subsidiary was a song simply called 'I Love You'. It was co-written by Gordy's sister Anna and Marvin Gaye, who visited the studio to sit in on sessions; Gaye contributed as a studio producer and Anna observed from the sides. Golden World crackled with infidelity. Gaye was easily distracted, too, and was already fighting with Anna over their marital problems.

Later that week Gordy, Gaye and their gambling buddies from Motown went to the Olympia – home of the ice hockey team the Detroit Red Wings and known locally as the Old Red Barn – to watch a satellite telecast of Muhammad Ali's title fight against Chicago's Ernie Terrell, live from the Houston Astrodome. More than 30,000 fans had crammed into the venue, shattering the record for an indoor fight, and thousands more gathered to watch the fight on the giant screen in Detroit. Both fighters were showmen who flirted with the fringes of the music business. Ali had recorded a version of the old Ben E. King standard 'Stand By Me', and Terrell was already part of the burgeoning Chicago soul scene, where he performed with his band, Ernie Terrell and the Heavyweights.

Ali had only recently converted to Islam, and his new name had become a matter of honour. In a pre-match publicity event, the fighters had hammed it up for the cameras, but in an unscripted moment of verbal sparring, Ernie Terrell inadvertently called his opponent what Ali referred to as his 'slave name', Cassius Clay. It was a slip of the tongue with no serious intent to offend, but in Ali's eyes it demeaned both him and his faith. Ali retaliated by branding Terrell an Uncle Tom. A week of name-calling had set the scene for a fight that ranks as one of the greatest ever. Ali teased and taunted Terrell, and in the fifteenth and final round, as he pummelled the beaten Terrell into the bloodstained canvas, he chanted, 'What's my name? What's my name?' It was a scene that took on the nasty edge of torture as Terrell drifted into unconsciousness.

Gordy and his entourage streamed out of the Olympia in stunned silence. Tex Maule, a reporter for *Sports Illustrated,* described the Shakespearean brutality of it all: 'Terrell is a pleasant, soft-spoken and gentle man,' he wrote, 'and he would make an admirable champion. He is, you might say, a prince among fighters. Unfortunately, he is fighting the king. Good night, sweet prince.' The day after the fight, the *Michigan Daily* claimed that 'Cassius Clay had turned butcher and gave Big Ernie Terrell a savage bloody beating.' Such was the power that Ali exerted over Terrell that many suspected some bewitching plot. A professor of psychiatry, Dr H. Peter Tarnesby, told *Jet* magazine it was entirely probable that Ali had hypnotised Terrell as he stared at him eye to eye, but *Newsweek* had a more grounded and timely analogy, describing the defeated Terrell as being 'wounded in combat'.

After the fight, Gordy and Gaye returned to Golden World to conclude the Chris Clark sessions. Gordy was due at Motown's offices the next day for a meeting with his legal executive, Ralph Seltzer, and other senior managers, including Motown's business affairs executive Harold Noveck and his accountant brother, Sidney Noveck. All three men wore sober suits, reported only to Gordy, and were deeply unpopular with the company's creative producers. Some of this was nothing more than the familiar tension between business affairs and creatives but something deeper was at work.

Money was flooding into Motown, but so too were bills, and the corporation had to control costs. Gordy had been slow to dump unprofitable acts, the payroll was out of control, and a civil war of sorts was looming. Sylvia Moy, a Motown staff writer, nailed Seltzer's reputation: 'Ralph was a brilliant company man, a Motown man, a Berry man. Everything he did was for Motown and Berry.' Seltzer represented the contractual interests of the company, and for that reason alone he found himself on the opposite side of the negotiating table from the talent. It is a familiar faultline in creative companies, but misunderstandings were driving a wedge into the company. One artist has since described Seltzer as a 'son of a bitch'; others claim he was 'abusive and foul-mouthed'. Ty Hunter, vocalist with the much admired Detroit super group the Voicemasters, which boasted Lamont Dozier, David Ruffin and Freddie Gorman among its members, blamed Seltzer for the eventual erosion of Motown's family spirit. 'Once Berry brought in Ralph Seltzer, the family atmosphere was finally destroyed,' he reportedly said.

On Friday, 10 February, Motown's innovative Jewish publicist, Allan 'Al' Abrams, wrote an internal memo to Ralph Seltzer proposing a contentious publicity scheme involving President Johnson. Abrams was an ambitious press officer, a masterful attention-seeker and a political networker. The memo requested permission to set up an unofficial 'Motown for Johnson Committee' to raise funds for the president and to act as a front to promote the Supremes in powerful celebrity circles. He had already negotiated for the Supremes to make a personal appearance at a presidential fundraiser in the summer and to attend a photo op with Vice-President Hubert Humphrey in Washington DC. In one of his more eccentric diversions, Abrams had once told journalists that Motown was on the brink of signing the president's twenty-three-year-old daughter, Lynda Johnson, as a solo singer. It was Abrams who had sealed a deal to print images of the Supremes on supermarket bread, and he secured their appearance on a War on Poverty telecast back in June 1965, in aid of President Johnson's Great Society initiatives. Abrams was a quixotic character best suited to freelance employment; behind Motown's back he promoted the singer Della Reese, and he had once worked for Andy Warhol to publicise Detroit's first 'mod wedding', in which the high priest of pop art gave a local Detroit couple away and hired the Velvet Underground as the wedding band. Abrams had known Ballard for several years, and since the autumn of 1966 he had been 'fire-fighting' press enquiries about her health, flatly denying rumours that there was trouble at the heart of the world's favourite girl group. Although he was well liked by old-school Motown artists, Abrams alienated senior management by undermining their authority, driving ahead with projects that had no sign-off. He later claimed that he had been sacked by Motown on Pearl Harbor Day, 7 December 1966, when Seltzer and Michael Roshkind hit him with the unkind parting shot, 'Consider yourself bombed.' But internal Motown records show he was still working with the company well into 1967 while negotiating with southern rival Stax Records in Memphis to join their ranks. Sensing deep discontent at the heart of the Supremes, Abrams had also spoken off the record to Ballard about being her personal publicist, and, alive to Aretha Franklin's growing success, he had met with her husband-manager, Ted White, to discuss promoting Franklin's career too. Abrams used his local contacts in the Democratic Party to propose that Detroit should honour the singer by declaring an annual Aretha Day to celebrate the achievements of a woman on the cusp of being hailed the Queen of Soul.

Aretha Franklin was huddled in a dressing gown and slumped on a deep sofa at her home at 7415 LaSalle Boulevard. Even though the room was darkened by heavy curtains, she still squinted through half-closed eyes. She hated the limelight and had come to hate daylight too. For ten depressive days in February, she was hidden away at home, tearful, listless and on the verge of abandoning her career as a singer. Doctors had diagnosed depression; one imagined her reluctance to face light to be a sign of meningitis; others simply described her condition as exhaustion. Whatever the real story, the pace of everyday life had driven Aretha Franklin deeper into herself, and she had not crossed the front door of her family home for nearly a week.

The Franklin family mansion sat like a tabernacle on the corner of Lamothe Street and LaSalle, the Reverend C. L. Franklin and his daughters, Erma, Carolyn and Aretha, having long been stars on the Christian gospel circuit and periodically crossed over to pop music. Erma Franklin had briefly worked with Berry Gordy in her younger days, but, possessively guarded by their father, none of the city's famous family ever signed with Motown. Music had shaped the great soul families of Detroit in subtly different ways. Ballard's family was a blues family, while the Franklins were pure gospel. Their travelling caravan had been a fixture on the lucrative gospel circuit for over two decades. With a pedigree as a child genius stretching back to infancy, Aretha had moved across the years from pure spiritual to elegant soul, signing with Columbia Records in New York. Despite being a seasoned live performer since her childhood she had yet to make a consistent impact on the record charts. Her career at Columbia was not a conspicuous success, and a string of promising solo albums had fallen off the radar. By mutual consent she left Columbia and, in what proved to be a historic move, went to Atlantic Records.

The Franklins also had secrets. Reverend Franklin dressed in flashy suits, sported ostentatious jewellery, and arranged his hair in the fashionable ghetto styles of the day, often shocking the staid members of his congregation by preaching the gospel in a 'conk' hairstyle more readily associated with Detroit's pimps and gangsters. According to his biographer, Nick Salvatore, Franklin sported 'alligator-skin shoes, diamond stickpins, flashy rings, [and] watches, and ministerial crosses complemented his colorful neckties. While he occasionally bought clothes on the road, his regular haberdasher was a downtown Detroit firm, Kosins.' By 1967 Franklin was a high-profile figure in the civil rights movement and a successful gospel artist in his own right. His thunderous voice had been recorded by Chicago's Chess Records and sold in R&B stores across ghetto America.

If anywhere could be described as the church of Motown, it was the Reverend Franklin's New Bethel Baptist Church. In 1965, when Smokey Robinson's friend and co-writer Warren 'Pete' Moore of the Miracles married Bonita Tyson at New Bethel, the marriage was witnessed by almost the entire Motown staff. Mary Wilson of the Supremes was one of the congregation's most enthusiastic singers and had grown up as a childhood friend of Carolyn Franklyn, whom she first met when they were in fifth grade. The two young singers were bussed together to Algers Elementary School, in what was then a predominantly white Detroit neighbourhood, as part of the city's policy of racial integration. Mary Wilson once described Reverend Franklin as a 'sexual' preacher. 'Women loved him,' she said. 'He was a ladies' man! My mother adored him.' Franklin preached fire and brimstone but lived his life like a pop star. His wife had divorced him, leaving him a single father tending a family of four, but his charisma meant that the preacher was rarely if ever alone. A string of housekeepers, many recruited from the Bethel congregation, helped out, and Franklin had unofficial wives, including a long-standing love affair with the brilliant gospel singer Clara Ward, who in turn became Aretha Franklin's surrogate mother. Whatever the Scriptures told him, the Reverend Clarence L. Franklin had no great theological problems reconciling the restraints of the Old Testament with his adventurous sex life.

Aretha Franklin and Florence Ballard must rank among soul music's most troubled personalities, and both felt the need periodically to retreat into the security of their families. By February 1967 Ballard had buckled with the demands of constant travelling, and Franklin had escaped from a tempestuous recording session in Muscle Shoals, Alabama, when her first session for Atlantic Records went catastrophically off the rails. She was working with the quixotic Jerry Wexler, a Bronx window-cleaner turned R&B maestro. Wexler was a creative emperor at Franklin's new recording company, Atlantic Records – once described as 'the West Point of rhythm and blues' – and had hired Rick Hall's Fame Studios to capture the grittier southern sound that was emerging from the independent studios of Alabama and Memphis. Fame studios played host to some of the great leathery voices of the southern soul scene – Arthur Alexander, Clarence Carter, Don Covay, Jimmy Hughes,

Irma Thomas and Wilson Pickett – and had pioneered a sound that Wexler believed would resonate with Aretha. It was a decision that was misguided and inspired in equal measure.

Unlike Detroit, where the R&B recording scene was predominantly black, Muscle Shoals had a very different ethnic composition. Aretha was one of the very few black faces in the studio when a drunken fight broke out between her irascible husband, Ted White, and rogue trumpeter Ken Laxton, a talented but combustible studio musician. (Wexler described Laxton as 'real obnoxious trash', and others have since dismissed him as a redneck with a horn.) When the fight escalated, the session was brought to an abrupt end, and Aretha stormed out and returned alone to her room at the Downtowner Motel, followed by her drunken husband and Wexler. In his book *A Life in American Music*, Wexler has described what happened next as 'Walpurgisnacht, a Wagnerian shitstorm'. After a night of raised voices, banging doors and then gunfire, Franklin and White ended their relationship, at least temporarily, and returned to Detroit. It was neither their first dispute nor their last. The R&B producer Clyde Otis claimed that Ted 'beat her down so unmercifully . . . This is a woman who is so insecure.' The disarmingly honest Etta James described a common bond among Florence Ballard, Aretha Franklin and herself. 'There was always an unspoken understanding between us. Over the years we'd be drawn to men – the wrong men, crafty, grafty men – who weren't in love with us but in love with who we were. We were used. We allowed ourselves to be used. We were attracted to cats who pretended to be protective but saw us as property, cats who didn't think twice about messing up [our] life.' It was a bond that remained unspoken. 'But we never had that discussion,' she said. 'We just put the feelings in our music.' One of Franklin's most precocious releases when she was a teenager at Columbia Records in 1962 was the rocking R&B song 'Rough Lover', in which she shocked the gospel circuit by demanding rough love, a cruel man, a 'mean sweet daddy who the devil wouldn't cross'.

Franklin's relationship with her husband could lurch from happiness to hostility within minutes, and perhaps inevitably White has been portrayed as a selfish villain and Franklin as a brilliant tortured genius. But the truth was more complex. In 1968 Ted White was forced to defend himself after *Time* magazine portrayed him as a violent wife-beater and represented Franklin as a depressive who 'sleeps till afternoon, then mopes in front of the television set, chain-smoking Kool cigarettes and snacking compulsively'. White claimed he was victorious in his defence and successfully sued *Time*, but no payment was made and the magazine never published an apology. It is more likely that the complaint simply ran out of steam before it came to court.

On her arrival home from Muscle Shoals, Aretha had taken a taxi from Metro to her father's home in floods of tears. Rather than spend time reconciling with White, she stayed indoors, ignoring calls, avoiding recording obligations, and hiding from her husband. She talked to her father about her self-doubt and considered the prospect of returning home to Detroit permanently, rejoining the Franklin family gospel caravan. Aretha was intensely close to her father, so close that their relationship provoked the malicious and unfounded rumour that he was the father of the child she bore in 1955 when she was only thirteen, and of her second son, born two years later when she was only fifteen. Rather than confront the gossip Franklin chose not to dignify it with a response. Out of a mixture of privacy and cussedness, she refused to name the father of her first child, restricting the release of the birth certificate and only ever saying that the matter was 'very, very personal, and nothing I care to discuss'.

For almost two weeks, Franklin ventured out only once, and that was behind the protection of dark glasses to a private booth at a celebrated local Polynesian restaurant called the Chin Tiki on Detroit's Cass Avenue. A local businessman named Marvin Chin had defied Detroit's cold weather and built a bizarre fantasy restaurant featuring Hawaiian dancers and Polynesian fire-eaters. Upstairs, a cascading waterfall and fake rock walls swept around a surf-shaped bar. On the lower floor, a waterfall and bamboo bridge led to quiet thatched booths where couples could hide from the world. Ballard and her sisters ate there regularly, hiding from Motown, and it was no great surprise that Franklin was also attracted to its obscure corners. Surrounded by clamour since childhood, Franklin was uncomfortable in noisy groups, hated nightclubs and often recoiled from meeting strangers, preferring quiet corners or eating at home. The more that fame required her to take centre stage, the more she curled up into self-comforting agoraphobia.

Franklin knew Ballard only by reputation. They moved in different Detroit circles but their lives seemed to have simultaneously unravelled. Both women suffered from depression and, in their own distinct ways, mild paranoia. In a famously accurate description, Wexler christened Franklin 'Our Lady of Mysterious Sorrows'. In his book he said, 'Her eyes are incredible, luminous eyes covering inexplicable pain. Her depressions could be as deep as the dark sea. I don't pretend to know the sources of her anguish, but anguish surrounds Aretha as surely as the glory of her musical aura.' The black community leader Jesse Jackson also hinted at her impenetrable divinity, introducing Franklin to the stage as 'our sister beloved, the one who wears a coat of many colors'.

A young Linda McCartney, then an aspiring photographer, sensed her anguish. Linda had met her husband, Paul McCartney of the Beatles, at a photo shoot for *Sgt. Pepper's Lonely Hearts Club Band* and had gained access to other major musicians, including Franklin. 'We met at the Hilton Hotel in Los Angeles and she was in tears,' McCartney later recalled. 'She was sort of drinking vodka, and she was just a mess, so depressed. I took pictures of her . . . and the sadness was amazing.' The impetuous R&B singer Etta James also witnessed her depressive moods: 'Like me, Aretha was having heartaches too big to hide in some white-bread song. Her man was doing her wrong and making her crazy. The power of her pain comes right at you when you listen to her early Atlantic records.' Motown singer Gladys Knight, a young contemporary dating back to the days when they sang gospel as children, saw an icier personality and described in her memoirs a woman who had a protective shell that was at times far from pleasant. When they met on the road or in hotel lobbies, 'there [was] always a distinct chill in the air,' she once said. 'Sometimes it goes in the deep freeze and she simply ignores me.'

Paradoxically, the songs that Aretha Franklin recorded in the fractious atmosphere of Muscle Shoals were blessed with something special. The aching brilliance of the session gave Jerry Wexler renewed hope that all was not wasted, and the song 'I Never Loved A Man' was destined to become an all-time soul classic. After days of recuperation in Detroit, Franklin was encouraged to call Wexler, who was so ecstatic with what he had heard from the recent sessions that he had already hatched a plan to release 'I Never Loved A Man' as a single. With no obvious B-side, he convinced Franklin that he could recreate the Muscle Shoals sound this time in New York. They agreed by phone that she would head for midtown Manhattan, well away from the racial tinderbox of the Deep South, and, for reassurance, her sisters Erma and Carolyn and a long-time family friend, the gospel singer Cissy Houston, would be hired as backing singers.

Franklin packed her bags, left Detroit and flew to New York, where she recorded the torch song 'Respect', which she had sung live onstage but never recorded. At the time, 'Respect' was more immediately associated with Stax singer Otis Redding, and locally in Michigan with a recording by Ann Arbor garage band the Rationals, who had spent six weeks on the WKNR/Keener charts with their version in 1966. But Aretha Franklin's rendition trumped them all. She completely refashioned the song, imagining it not as a domestic love song but as an anthem of women's self-assertion and civil rights. When Otis Redding heard Franklin's version for the first time, he acknowledged its pure brilliance, simply saying, 'That woman has stolen my song.'

After the drama of self-imposed exile faded, 'I Never Loved A Man', with the song 'Do Right Woman' on the B-side, was hurriedly released and became Aretha Franklin's first million-selling single, spending seven weeks at the pinnacle of the R&B charts. Valentine's Day in 1967 was to become an epic moment in the history of Atlantic Records. Wexler brought producer Arif Mardin into Manhattan for an intense day of creativity. Together they cut 'Don't Let Me Lose This Dream' and 'Baby, Baby, Baby', a song co-written by Franklin and her sister Carolyn. The remaining songs were mainly cover versions from the Franklin family household favourites, including Ray Charles's 'Drown In My Own Tears' and Sam Cooke's 'A Change Is Gonna Come'. By the same day Franklin had temporarily reconciled with Ted White, and their ill-fated love affair was back on. Her reconfiguration of 'Respect' and her recording of 'A Change Is Gonna Come' propelled her to the front line of soul music's resistance movement. It was the apotheosis of her family's long association with the civil rights movement and their closeness to Martin Luther King's SCLC. Through the power of her voice, Aretha had risen up through the aristocracy of soul music and taken her place at the forefront of the march to freedom.

On 16 February Motown's sales force was on full alert. Box loads of a new song, 'Bernadette', by the Four Tops, were ready to roll at distribution points across America. Gordy had high hopes for the song, although lead singer Levi Stubbs was anxious about it being too cloyingly romantic. Others felt its clever use of a girl's name would guarantee enough first-week sales to take it high in the charts. When producer Phil Spector heard it played on the radio, he supposedly described it as 'a black man singing Bob Dylan'. Although the quote was to enter pop history, no one has ever successfully traced it back to Spector and it seems to have first appeared in a press release written by the imaginative Al Abrams, a man whose promotional stunts were never limited by the truth. 'Bernadette' was destined to become yet another pop-soul classic. Although it had none of the political undercarriage of Aretha's songs, what it lacked it meaning was made up for in youthful energy.

As Detroit soul music dominated charts around the world, the city's darker underbelly was exposing itself. A spate of crimes targeting storekeepers escalated throughout February. On 18 February a corner-store grocer named Abraham Swad fired three shots as he chased bandits out of his shop on Charlevoix. A few days later, a Polish grocer, Edward Polomski, was confronted by a gunman in his store on East Warren; he drew his own handgun and shot the intruder in self-defence. The following day, William

Zachman, the owner of the Log Cabin Grocery, critically wounded a young intruder caught breaking into the store. Both Zachman and Polomski had taken lessons at a gun clinic for grocers, a controversial scheme that had been set up by the civic authorities to teach shopkeepers how to arm and defend themselves. There were seven shootings in little more than a month. The attackers were described by the press as 'teenage Negroes', and in most cases the grocers were older Eastern European men intent on defending their property. It was a social stand-off that was to grow in intensity as the snows of 1967 finally receded.

Crime was growing but the perception was worse, and the events that unfolded at the Tocco Family Grocery at 700 Joseph Campau proved both tragic and unprecedented. Two young men entered the shop with what appeared to be a girlfriend dressed in the soul fashion of the day: a jet-black wig in the Motown style, a belted suede coat and large cascading gold earrings. All three went to different parts of the shop, an action known by most storekeepers to be a familiar prequel to robbery. One of the men focused on the office at the rear, where seventy-three-year-old owner Peter Tocco – distantly related to an infamous Detroit Mafia family – was guarding the safe. His daughter became suspicious of the new customers and reached for her father's handgun. She had never fired a gun before but began to shoot wildly at the suspects, hitting one of the men in the throat and blasting the woman in her head and chest. The robbers were rushed to the hospital and the woman, Helene Smith, was pronounced dead on arrival. As they transported her body to the morgue, it transpired that she was not a woman at all but a fourteen-year-old truant from the city's Northeastern High School who lived in the Brewster Projects. Stripped of her wig and make-up, she was a disarmingly beautiful young girl. It turned out that she had become so fascinated by the city's nightlife that she had faked her age to gain entry to the 20 Grand. Fatally, she had pretended through much of her short life to be twenty-one and by tragic chance she had met the male robbers only four hours before. A mixture of naïveté and adventure had led Smith to her untimely death.

Helene Smith's death divided opinion. Some saw her as a victim, others as just another teenager scaring the life out of the city. Grocers and shopkeepers across Detroit were demanding that Mayor Cavanagh institute measures that could protect their businesses. The Associated Food Dealers of Greater Detroit, which included Pops Gordy among its members, published statistics that showed a 134.7 per cent rise in robberies of grocery stores between 1965 and 1966, and as February drew to a close they were hatching plans to picket a major crime conference in the city. To generate publicity for their cause, the storekeepers eventually picketed the conference, dressed in grocers' aprons, and handed out leaflets offering small-arms training. The marksmanship courses on offer were sanctioned by the National Rifle Association at a gun club located beneath a billiard parlour at 4752 Chene but it was a reaction founded on emotion, not logic. In a few short months, grocers had killed seven 'bandits'. The deaths served only to exaggerate a faultline that pitted store owners and urban youth as mortal enemies.

On 19 February Detroit's escalating crime rates made national news. The publication of a report by the Crime Commission, chaired by Attorney General Nicholas Katzenbach, described Detroit as a city vulnerable to a crime epidemic. The commission claimed that the US justice system was still in the 'horse and buggy stage' and needed fundamental reform. Forty-three per cent of respondents said they stayed off the streets, thirty-five per cent said they no longer spoke to strangers, and twenty-one per cent said they only used a car at night and would not contemplate walking the streets. Most troubling for Detroit was that a sizeable twenty per cent of all US residents claimed they were contemplating leaving cities for the suburbs. Ironically, one of the commission's leading conclusions was that people were more troubled by the 'fear of crime' than by crime itself, ignoring the fact that the newspaper's own high-profile Secret Witness campaign was a daily contributing factor.

The *Detroit News*'s Secret Witness campaign increased sales, won the endorsement of the police, and heaped pressure on Mayor Cavanagh's administration to increase funding for the police. The *News* was the shopkeepers' paper and instinctively took the side of the small-business community against what it perceived as lawless youth. At the height of the shopkeeper killings, one of Detroit's most reprehensible characters, Mary V. Beck, the first woman elected to the Detroit City Council, wrote an inflammatory open letter to the mayor. She claimed that 'no woman or child appears to be safe either on the streets, or in their homes, or in any business place'. Beck had a taste for political opportunism and was never afraid to upset the delicate balance of race relations. Cavanagh was quick to retaliate, dismissing her letter as crude demagoguery and sensing that it was inspired by grandstanding and bigotry. Beck had Ukrainian parentage and spoke passionately on behalf of those nations seeking to break from Russia's Soviet grip, so however distasteful her attitude towards young black teenagers became, she had the emotional support of many thousands of Eastern European immigrants. Some saw her as a breath of fresh air and a voice for the underrepresented, but many more felt her diatribes came with the sharp taint of racism.

Embattled police commissioner Ray Girardin was losing the battle to bring order to a police force that was in the advanced stages of organisational disarray. Four thousand five hundred officers were struggling to police one and a half million citizens, and as Girardin sifted through statistics on his desk at police headquarters at 1300 Beaubien, the signs indicated that homicide rates would spiral in 1967. In the previous year, there had been 232 homicides, more than in any year since Prohibition and a substantial 13.7 per cent rise over the reported figures for 1965. Girardin was a story in his own right, the kind of figure who could have fallen from the pages of an Elmore Leonard novel. Bizarrely for a police commissioner, he had once been a true-crime reporter and was still known for his hard-boiled newspaper features, written as if from the front line of crime-ridden Detroit. He was a forceful presence in the city and once described Detroit in a local magazine with all the drama of film noir nihilism: 'A disturbing sickness has infected many cities, including Detroit,' he said. 'It may be the malaise of an unsettled world.'

Change was not a word that the Detroit police had ever embraced.

Although 35 per cent of the city was black, there were only 217 black officers in a force of 4,709. Despite frequent publicity campaigns and a community-awareness scheme involving 320 different social groups across the city, the police department remained stubbornly white. Attitudes among young African-American teenagers were particularly frosty, and Commissioner Girardin had hired a prominent black preacher, Reverend Hubert G. Locke, to try to build better relationships between the police and black communities. Recruitment of black officers remained bureaucratically slow, and the city's highest-crime area, the Tenth Precinct at Livernois Station, was proving virtually impossible to police.

By 1967 small enclaves of the city were lost to crime. The notorious strips along Fourteenth Street and Twelfth Street were populated by brothels, unlicensed soul clubs and late-night drinking dens known locally as 'blind pigs'. Another trouble spot was the once-desirable Highland Park neighbourhood, which had been a village in its own right before Chrysler's Brush-Maxwell plant had encroached on the area and the village became subsumed by a manufacturing ghetto. According to a local government report, Highland Park had become a place of 'obsolescence, poverty, and social disorganization' where most of the buildings were over fifty years old, sub-standard, in dire need of repair, and inhabited by low-income families earning less than $3,000 a year. Fifteen per cent of adults were unemployed. Smokey Robinson and Jackie Wilson had both lived there as teenagers and had seen their old neighbourhood caught up in a spiral of industrial neglect, poverty and crime.

Police had targeted yet another troubled area, a warren of inner-city streets on the far East Side at Kercheval, where the city's young Black Power radicals had set up base near the premises of the Afro-American Youth Movement. The intersection of Kercheval and McCellan Street was described at the time as 'America at the crossroads'. The Supremes' most recent single, 'Love Is Here And Now You're Gone', was still high on the charts when a police tactical patrol squad from the city's central division approached two men acting suspiciously. One of them reportedly resisted arrest and grappled with Patrolman James Pierzinski. In the ensuing fight, the officer was wounded in the face and taken to Detroit General Hospital – or at least that was the version of events that the Detroit police's information department fed to the local press. But it was not quite what it seemed. The suspect was a confident and combustible character called General Gordon Baker, whose unusual given name made him stand out among Detroit's small cadre of revolutionary street radicals. Baker was a founding member of Detroit's Black Power group Uhuru (Swahili for 'freedom') and earlier in the decade had travelled to Cuba as part of a controversial delegation of Detroit Marxists to visit Fidel Castro.

Baker had been in the audience at Stokely Carmichael's incendiary speech the previous month, and had been posting flyers in Kercheval, seeking volunteers to join a teenage militia known as the Black Guards. Baker and his associates were already in dispute with the Black Panther Party nationally and on the verge of forming the more industrial Detroit League of Revolutionary Black Workers, a rival Black Power group focused on workplace activism. Despite the military associations of his given name, General Baker was opposed to the American presence in Vietnam, and because of his revolutionary politics he was deemed unsuitable for military service. Baker and two other prominent street militants, Glanton Dowdell and Rufus Griffin, had been arrested the previous summer on charges of harbouring concealed weapons. The arrests had been part of a summer of insurrection known as the Kercheval Incident, when the police narrowly managed to suppress a full-scale riot as members of the Afro-American Youth Association armed themselves with a .45 pistol, two M-1 rifles and 120 rounds of ammunition. Dowdell was destined to become yet another colourful character in the story of 1967. Feared by the mainstream and feted by the intelligentsia, he was a convict-turned-artist whose radical artwork, a painting of a black Madonna and child, became one of the most strident statements of black self-determination of the era.

Baker and his cohorts had been arrested as the result of an FBI tip after they had illegally wiretapped an East Side apartment block. Police and FBI surveillance was already commonplace and destined to grow in both scale and subterfuge throughout the year. Like John Sinclair and the mysterious Steering Committee, the young black militants were already on a secret list of local Detroit radicals whom the police were tracking. By the end of 1967, Baker became the most infamous black worker in Detroit when he founded DRUM, the Detroit Revolutionary Union Movement, a cadre of radical workers employed at Chrysler's Hamtramck assembly plant, known colloquially as Dodge Main.

The Detroit police department and its affiliates within the Michigan state police had a long-standing reputation as one of America's most secretive and repressive forces. The departmental files on young activists like Baker, Dowdell and Griffin were thicker than winter fog, and there was an unofficial directive to harass them wherever they went. Confronted by the restlessness they faced on the streets, the police were compromised. They lacked the support systems to police a city of so many competing communities and made the basic mistake of employing an unsophisticated force, fatefully using their notorious Big Four vehicles or 'Tac Squads' to patrol sensitive areas of the city. Each unit was made up of *four* officers whose presence was meant to snuff out trouble and reassure citizens. The consequences were obvious. The Big Fours came to be seen as mobile intimidation units, particularly by young people, and became the target of resentment, abuse and anti-police violence.

Seen from on high, the map of the city had not only been redrawn by the new freeways creating a concrete grid of avenues and access roads, but on closer examination Detroit was in fact a set of people and subcultures who cohabited but never really met. There was the hippie Steering Committee, the young rock gods of the Grande Ballroom, the disgruntled officers of the Detroit police, and a legion of car-assembly workers drawn from the tense communities of Polish and African-Americans. There were disenchanted young men who moved from unemployment to Vietnam, the radical soldiers of Black Power, the independent producers who saw soul music as their Klondike, and the caravan of older gospel Christians who had seen their homes destroyed to make way for freeways.

In the last week of February 1967, Motown's studios hit a logjam. Every waking hour was taken up with recording, and many sessions were overrunning. Producers Barrett Strong and Norman Whitfield were working on early tests of Marvin Gaye on 'I Heard It Through The Grapevine', a song that Berry Gordy was lukewarm about and had already rejected on three separate occasions. Even when it became a global hit, Gordy never really warmed to it, but a version of the song recorded by Gladys Knight and the Pips would end the year as one of the company's top-selling releases, and Gaye's follow-up version was destined to become a legacy song for decades to come. Motown had a contracted agreement to provide a roster of artists for a concert at Sesquigras '67, a series of events to celebrate the University of Michigan's 150th anniversary. The show was to be held at Hill Auditorium in Ann Arbor at the end of February. Six Motown acts were contracted: Smokey Robinson and the Miracles, Martha and the Vandellas, Jimmy Ruffin, Tammi Terrell, the Spinners and Motown-supporting act Choker Campbell and His Orchestra. A retinue of managers, electricians and costume assistants packed the equipment into a small convoy of cars and trucks and set off for Ann Arbor. Robinson's triumphant caravan of stars proved to be a huge hit with students, and a front-page review in the university newspaper simply said, 'Smokey Burns at Hill'. It proved to be a historic month for the campus concert hall. Exactly ten days earlier, the guru of psychedelia, Dr Timothy Leary, had sat cross-legged on the same stage, advocating the public use of LSD. 'We forget that we were meant to live in a Garden of Eden,' he proclaimed. 'Turn on, tune in, and drop out.' Leary outraged the local Michigan police by urging students to drop acid tabs into their parents' coffee. 'Each of you go home tonight and turn on Mom and Dad. Don't use words, just do it.'

For the increasingly exhausted and irritable members of the Supremes, their relentless schedule continued. Motown had been commissioned to provide the title track for a forthcoming

Hollywood feature film, *The Happening*, and the Holland-Dozier-Holland production team cranked into action. Having already watched a rough cut of the film in Hollywood, they tried to lay down the basis of the song in L.A. Frustrated that they could not get the sound or musicianship they wanted, the production team returned home to Detroit accompanied by the movie's composer, Frank De Vol, who had already racked up Oscar nominations for the scores of *Pillow Talk* and *Cat Ballou*. The Supremes were instructed to make their way to Hitsville. Ballard was driven reluctantly from her home on Buena Vista by her chauffeur-boyfriend, Tommy Chapman. Gordy had tried to discourage the relationship and had encouraged Ross to talk to Ballard about the hierarchy of fame – she was a star and Chapman was not. Others agreed with this view. Always a Motown and Gordy loyalist, Smokey saw Ballard's relationship with Chapman as a turning point. 'Little by little he convinced Flo that Berry was out to get her. He messed with her mind. I think he pushed her off track, persuading her that there was more money to be made outside Motown,' Robinson claimed. 'Florence also suffered from envy. She deluded herself by believing that she deserved the same recognition as Diana. She really believed she was as great a talent.' Whatever skewed advice Ballard was hearing from Chapman, he was still a source of comfort to her. 'It's frightening to go all the way to the top and someone says to you that you have to be a star, that you can't mingle with certain people,' Ballard once said. 'People to me has always meant people, and I've always felt that if I don't have people, then I don't have anything.'

At first Mary Wilson welcomed Ballard's new boyfriend. She knew him; they had travelled extensively together, and Chapman at least appeared to offer an alternative to Ballard's reliance on her family. 'Knowing how difficult it was for Flo to be intimate with a man, I was happy that she had Tommy,' Wilson claimed in *Dreamgirl*. 'Whenever Tommy was around, she stopped obsessing about Berry and Diane, whom she'd come to regard as a single entity. As Diane moved further to the front, Flo became not only defiant but bitter.' But even members of Ballard's own family were sceptical; her cousin Ray Gibson later said, 'It didn't *feel* like real love. To me it was like an addiction. I think they were both addicted to each other, for their own separate reasons. Florence needed to be loved and Tommy to find a pot of gold.'

By now the Supremes had signed a second and improved contract with Motown, giving them greater security and better deal points. They were now guaranteed a share of just below eight per cent of net sales but tellingly, this time around their income was tied to the wholesale price of a record, not its retail price. Statistics provided by Motown claimed that 'Where Did Our Love Go' sold 1,072,290 stock copies, leaving each of the Supremes with revenues of $7,237.96, and from that, income development and studio costs had to be deducted. It was a better deal than before, but far from a great one. Superficially it was much more money, the girls could earn increased wages, and their income rose from $50 a week each to $225 a week, but like many before and since, the Supremes' attention was diverted to wages and cash money rather than longer-term rights protection or revenue on future sales. Without questioning, or seeking recourse to lawyers, all three girls signed the new deal, one that has since been described as 'a contract so one-sided that it became the model for all future Motown contracts'. This level of naïveté was not uncommon. Motown's southern rival Stax signed a major national distribution deal with the New York-based Atlantic Records on the basis of a conversation, and Sid Nathan's King Records out of Cincinnati, the home of James Brown and Florence Ballard's cousin Hank Ballard, issued contracts that were, in the words of one industry insider, 'a legal gun to the head'. Singer Martha Reeves has admitted that she had signed contracts that were onerous, but knowingly conceded that Motown provided an escape from the Brewster Projects and the assembly lines. 'Motown had signed us all to ironclad contracts, and they turned us into international stars.'

Buried within those contracts was a clause that was to prove injurious in the years to come. Motown was to maintain ownership of the name 'The Supremes', irrespective of who sang under that banner. The girls could argue all they wanted about money, complain about early-morning flight times, and bitch about hotel rooms, but Berry Gordy was adamant that he owned Motown, he owned the Supremes' name, and he had the right to decide who would star in America's greatest girl group. The law, at least for now, seemed firmly on his side.

The Houses on Buena Vista. Enriched by their success, The Supremes bought houses near each other on Detroit's Buena Vista Street. Mary Wilson celebrates outside her new home at 4099 Buena Vista, which was soon to feature in the intrigue around Florence Ballard's departure.

MARCH

Home

On the evening of 1 March 1967, a herd of Elks congregated at a ranch-style home on Outer Drive, carrying handbags, silk purses and hopes of change. It was a gathering of Christian mothers of Detroit and a glimpse into a world that could not have been further removed from the flash exuberance of soul music. Berry Gordy and his girlfriend, Diana Ross, approached the doorway and stepped back in time to a much older Detroit. The Gordy family home was festooned with red and white carnations, bright crimson ribbons streamed through the hallway, and the place smelled of fresh coffee. A crowd of elderly black ladies stood around the home, chattering politely and defiantly about life. Bertha Gordy greeted her son effusively. Her hair was thatched grey and her heavy winged eyeglasses pointed up to heaven and to the Lord. Bertha Gordy carried herself with a dumpy decorum, but despite her age and conservative ways she still exerted a forceful influence on her son, fussing over him, scolding him, and smothering him with attention.

Bertha was hosting a coffee evening in her role as past Grand Exalted Ruler of the Lady Camille Temple of the Michigan Elks, a benevolent charity that was a throwback to a past era. The family home resembled a church service. Floral handbags, matching frocks and elegant hats turned the sitting room into a chorus of colour. Men were marginal figures, and although Jasper Hairston, the president of the Detroit Metropolitan Lodge, gave the formal welcome, he was in a tiny minority including Berry Gordy, Harvey Fuqua, and a few attentive husbands who mostly looked incongruous on the sidelines. Diana Ross's mother, Ernestine, was the co-hostess of the evening, representing Beulahland Temple #569, an Elk community that met on West Warren, near the Kronk Recreation Center. She hugged her famous daughter periodically, proud to be in her company.

This was a room of elderly women who valued status, took pride in their families, and cared deeply about emancipation. Most had raised their families in Detroit's post-war society, and they were in every respect the backbone of Motown. Bertha also ran the Friends Club, a philanthropic group that raised money for the Congress for Racial Equality (CORE), the NAACP, and the Freedom Fighters in Mississippi, who in the spring of 1967 were embroiled in a Supreme Court case to have a Ku Klux Klan member sentenced for murder in the infamous Mississippi Burning case. The money raised at the social evening would be used to help with legal costs.

Ernestine had worked periodically for Motown since 1961, acting as a chaperone and ensuring that the Supremes, who were then underage, were given protection on tour (she liked to tell people that her role was to 'keep the girls away from any Temptations', heavily accentuating the name of one of Motown's most boisterous groups). She had witnessed several disputes over the years and was deeply divided in her mind about Florence Ballard. She was sympathetic to the girl's unhappiness, and felt she had not had the best of upbringings, but a subtle generational shift was in play too. Ernestine came from a generation that was appalled by bad manners, unprofessionalism or laziness. It was a simple and at times unhelpful view, but she was of the belief that Ballard did not work hard enough and certainly not as hard as her daughter Diane.

Berry Gordy and Diana Ross were in love, but they felt a professional need to hide it from the world, so they had a habit of touching each other discreetly, surreptitiously. They were rarely seen kissing in public, preferred holding hands in private, and never allowed intimacy to become unprofessional. The critic Nelson George, in *Where Did Our Love Go*, described something deeper than love, almost an emotional need. 'Only a blind man or a fool could ignore the special care Berry put into her career and the worshipful, loving way she spoke of him. They were more than lovers; they were creations of each other. Diana would never have been the star she was without him. And Diana, by her very makeup – her pop voice, her ambition, and her willingness to be loyal and to learn, to be his sex symbol and his daughter – had made Berry's dream come true.'

The first couple of Motown were more accustomed to dining with celebrities and record-company moguls, and so a visit home to see their parents came with a mix of obligation and nostalgia. Strong tea was served in bone china cups decorated with red carnations and the ornamental milk jug was passed around the room from one gloved hand to another with genteel precision. A rumour had swept through Detroit neighbourhoods that milk was being deliberately poisoned, after a hoax call from a disenchanted farmer claimed that all fresh milk heading for the city had been laced with arsenic. Strikes and industrial disputes were rife throughout 1967, and in the days running up to the Elks' meeting, agricultural workers in Monroe County, on the periphery of Detroit, were enraged at low pricing and poor pay. A group of striking farm labourers had allegedly contaminated milk as the protest escalated. Bertha Gordy reassured her guests that the milk was from her husband's store and that it was safe to drink but she was less sure about the cakes. People laughed politely. Bakers Union Local 326 was also on strike, and 700 members were picketing the city's main bakery wholesalers, including Schaefer's, the bakery that had sublicensed image rights from Motown and built their reputation selling Supremes sliced bread. The March *Michigan Chronicle* was passed around the house like a precious album. A photo of the unmistakeable Berry 'Pops' Gordy Sr, posing at a Booker T. Washington business luncheon, dominated the front page.

Berry Gordy Jr spent most of the evening reminiscing with one of his mother's oldest friends, the Detroit beautician Carmen Murphy, owner of a franchise of beauty shops called the House of Beauty (HOB) aimed at African-American women. In the post-war period she had built one of the most successful businesses in the Midwest, offering hairstyling and manicure and pedicure services to teenagers and housewives. Diana Ross and Martha Reeves had grown up visiting the HOB salon and had learned basic make-up and grooming tips there. Many early R&B groups borrowed wigs and false eyelashes from the store in advance of local shows. Like the Gordys, Carmen Murphy had an unshakeable belief in black entrepreneurship. Her husband told *Ebony* magazine that his wife had applied assembly-line thinking to the beauty business. 'Leave my wife alone,' he told the magazine, 'and the House of Beauty would be as large as the Ford plant at River Rouge.'

Carmen Murphy had played a key role in the evolution of soul music too. She hosted a small recording studio in the basement of her beauty store on Mack Avenue, one of numerous primitive sound studios dotted across the city. For a while in the early fifties, she had been one of Berry Gordy's most influential mentors, periodically acting as an executive producer and releasing records on her own HOB label and distributing local records by pre-Motown artists like Herman Griffin and the Rayber Singers, including songs written and produced by Gordy himself. Although she made her fortune from beauty and style, Murphy stayed close to the church and also sold Christian gospel music via a distribution deal with Wand Records in New York. She became a self-taught business guru and a local celebrity in her own right, and she liked to tease Gordy that she had taught him all he knew. One lesson she frequently stressed was that Gordy was not in the recording business – he was in the *distribution* business. It didn't matter how great a song was; if it wasn't in the stores, it wouldn't sell. To underline the point, one of Murphy's contemporaries, the irrepressible Johnnie Mae Matthews, drove day and night across Detroit in a '57 Buick with boxes of records in the boot, hawking them to record shops and convenience stores, even selling them at street corners as if they were hamburgers. It was a distribution model common in Gordy's youth but one that Motown and its industrious sales force was already transforming.

Despite a mild anxiety about poisoned milk, there was a sense of warm achievement in the ranch house on Outer Drive, a neighbourhood where only ten years earlier no black family had ever owned property. Although they would never inherit significant wealth themselves, this was the parental generation that had allowed soul music to flourish and who through their quiet resistance and sometimes understated politics had changed the lives of their children for ever. Black Power could not have existed without their gentle persistence.

Carmen Murphy had always been generous with her advice but she had made one other small gesture that helped to shape Motown: she offered Gordy the marketing rights to a music label she no longer had much use for. The label was called Soul. In Murphy's mind it was a word that looked backward to the church and the old wooden pews of her own childhood. Sensing that the name might have long-term value, Gordy had a contract drawn up and paid Murphy the agreed peppercorn value of one US dollar.

Soul became a Motown subsidiary label on which Gladys Knight and the Pips, Jimmy Ruffin, Junior Walker and the All Stars, and lesser-known aspirants like Frances Nero ultimately appeared but, more importantly, it came to define a musical genre, symbolising everything that was transformational about black music – looking forwards to the charts and backwards at the Lord. James Brown had noisily called himself the Godfather of Soul, Aretha Franklin was known as the Queen of Soul, but it was a Detroit beautician with a white lace frock, a floral-print handbag, and coconut wax on the tips of her hair who had gifted the term 'soul' to her friend's son and thus to the world.

The next release on the Soul label was already at Motown's

Midwest pressing plants. It was Gladys Knight and the Pips' 'Take Me In Your Arms And Love Me', written by a triumvirate of in-house musicians, Barrett Strong and teenage friends Rodger Penzabene and Cornelius Grant. Although Gordy had built his Motown empire on an image of youthful exuberance and young love, what was less obvious was that a matriarchy of powerful older women had provided the offstage support structures. His mentor, Carmen Murphy, and his mother, Bertha, were informal advisers to the business, and his formidable sisters were ubiquitous at Motown – Loucye ran the Jobete publishing division until her untimely death through brain cancer in 1965, and her older sister Esther occupied senior management roles, eventually becoming Motown's CEO.

In an indirect way, this generation of stately African-American women acted as a safety net and a route out of the ghetto thinking that often trapped black music. None more so than the exquisite duchess, Maxine Powell, who ran Motown's charm school and whose job it was to teach the streetwise Motown singers interview techniques, table manners and social decorum. One member of the Temptations who was particularly resistant to charm training famously complained, 'I don't want to learn how to be white.'

By Elk tradition, eleven o'clock is the hour of recollection, when the hostess leads a moment of reflection for the dead. Bertha peered through her Coke-bottle glasses and recited the words, 'You have heard the tolling of eleven strokes. This is to remind you that the hour of eleven has a tender significance. It is the golden hour of recollection. Living or dead, we are never forgotten, never forsaken . . . The chimes of memory shall be pealing forth the friendly message. To our absent members.' The room replied, 'To our absent members,' and raised their china cups aloft.

The following day, 2 March, would be a landmark day. In a burst of creative vigour, the Supremes recorded three songs in a single day: 'Reflections', 'In And Out Of Love' and 'The Happening', which was the tenth successive number-one hit written by the Holland-

Dozier-Holland production team. The session also marked the end of the songwriting trio's relationship with Motown, and a bitter dispute with Gordy lay ahead.

Berry Gordy and Diana Ross had left the coffee evening early, apologising for their busy schedule. The Supremes were due to appear on a live ABC network tribute to Rodgers and Hart, featuring Bobby Darin, the Mamas and the Papas, and Count Basie and His Orchestra. At the time, Gordy was weighing the possibility of releasing a duet by Diana Ross and Bobby Darin that had already been prerecorded at ABC's old Monogram studio lot in Los Angeles by the show's musical director, Quincy Jones, but the plan came to nothing. As soon as the show was over, the Supremes flew on to Puerto Rico to take up residency at the Americana Hotel, San Juan, and despite her deepening anxieties about being away from Detroit, Ballard travelled with them. For the time being, stand-by Supreme Marlene Barrow returned to her day job as a studio singer with the Andantes.

A major new concert film, *T.A.M.I. Show* (the Teenage Awards Music International Show), was on general release. It starred the Supremes, Marvin Gaye, Chuck Berry and James Brown performing frantic dance routines and was provoking near riots at ghetto cinemas. *T.A.M.I. Show* was a co-feature aimed at attracting young audiences to the movies by pioneering a technological innovation called Electronovision, in which high-resolution videotape was transferred to film and then projected in movie theatres. Ironically, the success of the film in rundown inner-city cinemas and with the poorest audiences belied Motown's growing fascination with rich supper-club residencies. It was a tension that was never fully resolved, and in a flagship interview with *Newsweek* magazine Gordy was asked to account for the success of Motown artists. In an unguarded moment, he told them it was 'rats, roaches, struggle, talent, guts, love', a strange and convoluted expression improvised to suit the moment and playing to the crasser stereotypes in the press. It was a phrase that would come to haunt Gordy, repeated time and again by other journalists in subsequent articles, and one that he was obliged to apologise for, particularly to his own mother.

Gordy had grown up in a family that was immersed in the social sensitivities of the time and the phrase 'rats, roaches, struggle, talent, guts, love' was one that that his enterprising mother came to detest. She frowned in disapproval if it was ever mentioned in her presence, and often scolded her millionaire son in public as if he were a child. Her attitude was understandable. At face value, the phrase implied that Gordy had emerged from a rat-infested urban ghetto, which he most certainly had not. Bertha's home had never been infested, ghetto attitudes were discouraged, and the messages drummed into her children were about achievement, thrift and hard work. Although Berry was a fully grown man with his own global business empire, Bertha was adamant that the phrase about rats and roaches must never be uttered again. Gordy's throwaway remark was clearly a generalisation about living conditions for substantial numbers of black people in Detroit, but it was not his own personal experience.

Coincidentally, at a time when housing in Detroit was in flux, a lesser-known soul singer named Leah Dawson conducted a high-profile campaign against the Motor City's slumlords. Dawson was a gifted gospel singer in her mid twenties who had given birth to four daughters in six years. Her recording experience was limited, confined mostly to session singing and a couple of low-key releases on one of the myriad local independent labels, Magic City Records, whose roster included other hopefuls like Thelma Lindsay, Bonnie Brisker and Cynthia and the Imaginations. Dawson had a close working relationship with Motown saxophonist Walter 'Choker' Campbell and had released a song in partnership with him called 'My Mechanical Man'. It brought her tantalisingly close to Motown, where Choker Campbell and His Orchestra were one of a preferred group of back-up musicians used to support Marvin Gaye and Stevie Wonder when they performed at the city's Fox Theater or on regional tours in the Midwest.

Dawson aspired to sign with Motown and had sent them several demo tapes, but they never made the cut and for all she knew they might have lain unloved in the piles of hopeful tapes sent in by fans and musicians alike. Dawson's recording career was restricted to a dance record on Magic City and a dated but powerful blues song 'A Good Man (Is All I Want)' released on Johnnie Mae Matthews' Big Hit Records and sold from the trunk of her car. By 1967 Leah Dawson's distinctive look – an urban afro coupled with elegant ball gowns – made her one of the most eye-catching singers on the local club circuit but her career had failed to ignite and her income was precarious. Dawson's statuesque beauty masked a challenging home life; her living conditions were poor, and the slum conditions risked the health of her children. Rather than fade into the background of ghetto life, Dawson decided to launch a unique protest on behalf of better housing, and for several weeks she mobilised her neighbours to picket against slumlords, targeting specifically her apartment owner, an absent white landlady named Carol Mason.

Dawson lived at 2906 Whitney in a dilapidated apartment eight blocks from Motown's West Grand Boulevard address, and while picketing the building, she sometimes did impromptu soul sets with a makeshift microphone and amplifier. Her protest defied normal expectations about poverty and ghetto life as Dawson did not live in an inner-city tower block or in the tangled social cement of the Brewster Projects. She lived on a tree-lined side street in a neighbourhood that was superficially pleasant, but the suffocating overgrowth and decaying trees nearby had created a prairie ghetto. Dawson's was an overcrowded home with no lighting, shabby sleeping arrangements, and cramped conditions; her gas had been disconnected; and there was rat-infested squalor at the back. The singer was fearful that one of her children would be attacked as they slept. This was the world that Gordy had inadvertently described when he told *Newsweek* of an upbringing of 'rats, roaches, struggle, talent, guts, love'.

Housing in Detroit was a crucial subplot to Motown's growth as a company. By March 1967 Detroit's long odyssey of home ownership was brought into stark relief by Motown's success. Gordy was negotiating with real-estate agents to buy a palatial three-storey mansion at 918 West Boston Boulevard in the city's Boston-Edison neighbourhood, which had once been home to Detroit's entre-preneurial barons, such as auto magnate Henry Ford and S. S. Kresge, whose retail stores were a precursor to Kmart. It was a faux Renaissance mansion that had been built in 1927 but was now refurbished as the most ostentatious home in the city, boasting a two-lane bowling alley, its own snooker room and an Olympic-size swimming pool.

Motown Mansion had not been Gordy's first choice. In the latter months of 1966, he had pursued several other statement properties in Detroit, including a home in the whites-only enclave of Sherwood Forest, a small neighbourhood of winding roads on the northern edges of the Palmer Park, known for its distinctive homes and understated racism. The wealthy residents of Sherwood Forest had organised to protect the vicinity, and in the early sixties they had successfully halted the spread of factories along Seven Mile Road and blocked plans for a new city airport nearby. More questionably, they had also curtailed the spread of black families northward into the area. Sherwood Forest employed one of the first private security patrols in the United States and applied 'restrictive covenants' that discouraged existing home-owners from selling their houses to African-Americans. The no-Negroes clause in local covenants was illegal and breached Detroit's open-housing policy, but custom and practice had proved more powerful than the law, and Sherwood Forest's discrimination by stealth prevented even Gordy from finding a home.

The Gordy family had played its own small role in the fight to desegregate Detroit. Bertha's local insurance agency gave African-American families financial security, which protected family and friends from having to borrow capital in the often racist loan market. It was this modest kitchen-table trust fund that initially invested in Motown and transformed soul music, but by March 1967 Gordy and the successful Motown acts no longer needed loan capital or family help; they could pay for homes with hard cash or employ Motown lawyers to help them take on rental leases. Suddenly and without precedent, cash money came into the hands of the top tier of soul musicians, giving them a unique buying power. The Gordy family, the Four Tops, the Supremes, Stevie Wonder and the Temptations all bought or leased properties in Detroit neighbourhoods from which their parents had been racially excluded. When Stevie Wonder began to rack up hits, Motown arranged for his family to move to a new home at 18074 Greenlawn, where only two black families had ever lived.

Big hits bought bigger houses. When 'Baby, I Need Your Loving', an early hit for the Four Tops, entered the pop charts in the summer of 1964, singer Abdul 'Duke' Fakir sought an advance on royalties and bought property. 'I went to Berry for the advance, because my mama was working as a domestic,' he recounted years later, 'and I said, "I need an advance really bad." Berry said, "What do you need? What for?" I said, "I want to buy my mom a house – she needs it bad." He said, "How much do you think you need?" I said, "Oh, about ten thousand dollars." He said, "Well, here's fifteen thousand dollars." That was the happiest weekend of my life. Bought my mom that house, bought me a Cadillac – powder blue and white.' It was an investment that had a deeper back story. At the time, the Fakir family was crowded into a small rented apartment on Alger Street. Fakir's mother was a young Negro migrant from the Deep South, but his father was one of a few hundred immigrants from West Bengal who'd travelled to Detroit from India. He'd found work as a crane operator and had no hope of a mortgage loan.

Detroit was blighted by a discriminatory system of home lending known as 'red-lining', which in effect denied financial services to neighbourhoods based on race, ethnicity or economic status. Red-lining was the apartheid system of the financial services sector, which offered access to mortgages and investment capital to white families but not always to others. Finance companies had literally drawn a series of red lines across the map of Detroit, delineating those areas where loans could be granted and those where restrictions would apply. The contours of the map crudely followed racial lines and underscored a racially restrictive logic: white neighbourhoods were seen as low-risk, black or racially mixed areas were deemed high-risk, and some areas where high concentrations of blacks lived in substandard homes were deemed not worth the risk at all. The eminent social historian scientist Thomas J. Sugrue, in his towering book *The Origins of the Urban Crisis*, excoriated those hidden practices for turning Detroit from being 'a magnet of opportunity to a reservation for the poor'.

In areas where white residents were anxious that incoming black families might drag down property values, unscrupulous agents fed those anxieties. By deliberately cultivating prejudice, agents could secure property at 'panic' prices. Some sent bogus sales information about incoming families, and others paid young black teenagers to circulate real-estate agent information in areas vulnerable to change. A frequent tactic was to offer attractive inducements to young black families to move into an all-white block, thereby 'busting' an area's ethnic composition, and so the term 'blockbusting' was born.

Guy Nunn, a union leader with the United Automobile Workers (UAW), described the process of blockbusting in an emotional outburst on local radio, in what turned out to be a prescient perspective on modern Detroit: 'The real estate board pursues – and enforces – a policy which will in time spread to the ghetto, block by block, until it becomes the entire heart of the city. You can watch it happening day by day. As a Negro family moves a block away from the ghetto's former boundary, real estate agents go to work on the fears of the white residents in that block. The prospect of a double sale is created: a new home to the panicked white seller, an old one to another Negro. Block by block, it works.' Blockbusting was one of the lesser-known ironies of the Motown success story. The Supremes and the Four Tops were frequently lauded on radio and television for their 'blockbuster hits', yet outside the city most people were unaware of the term's very specific racial meaning. However, the cash that came with success allowed the young black musicians of Detroit at last to buck the system.

Wealth still clung to Detroit's old industrial heart. In early March the Supremes were hired to sing at a private party at the Grosse Pointe Country Club to celebrate the twenty-first birthday of

Judith Fisher, the debutante daughter of the family who owned the Fisher Body automobile company. Grosse Pointe was one of Detroit's richest neighbourhoods, much of it generated by the automobile industry. The Fishers, who had made their dynastic fortune in automobile manufacturing and consequently held a majority of stock in General Motors, were among the city's most affluent families.

It was unusual for the Supremes to accept a show with such a small invited audience and with no prospect of television coverage, but an undisclosed fee negotiated between Motown and the Fisher family secured their services. Mary Wilson later hinted that it was among the most lucrative amounts the Supremes ever received for a single performance, but for reasons now lost in time, Florence Ballard withdrew from the private show. Some said she had the flu, others blamed exhaustion, and more mischievous explanations said she was 'incapable' of appearing. Whatever the real reason, Motown had a safeguard in place: Marlene Barrow of the Andantes. Meanwhile, a senior Motown aide named Larry Maxwell was busily assisting Gordy with a shortlist of more permanent replacements. Maxwell had joined Motown after his own independent soul label, Maxx Records, had crashed into bankruptcy, and he brought a network of connections with him that included Gladys Knight and the Pips. He had already made a tentative phone call to Camden, New Jersey, to the family home of Cindy Birdsong, a member of the Philly-based group Patti LaBelle and the Bluebelles, inviting her to Detroit to meet Gordy.

Marlene Barrow was by now accustomed to stepping in on short notice, sometimes as a studio stand-in for Ballard. 'Holland-Dozier-Holland took me aside quietly and asked me to come into the studio and sing, so I did,' she recalled. 'That is me and Mary [Wilson] on "You Can't Hurry Love". There are a few others on which I sing,' she told writer Vicki Wright. In truth, Barrow's stand-in performances were of no great significance in themselves. Motown was accustomed to trying out different singers on different songs. Innovation and improvisation were common, and backing singers often stepped in to add ballast to a recording session. But providing backing vocals was one thing; replacing one of the Supremes onstage was something quite different. 'It was Harvey Fuqua who approached me and asked me to fill in for Florence,' Barrow claimed, although the agreement between her and Motown was kept secret. Barrow was taken out of her normal studio roster and given intensive training to polish her stage presence. Though she had many of the vocal characteristics of the Supremes down to a tee, she was unfamiliar with the stage routines. Unknown to Ballard, who was easily wounded by Motown's scheming, Barrow rehearsed dance moves with Mary Wilson at Wilson's red-brick duplex home on Buena Vista, which had been converted to accommodate a basement dance studio and was often used as a rehearsal space. Motown choreographer Cholly Atkins and his wife lived beneath Wilson on the ground floor of the house, and Atkins routinely used the studio to choreograph routines and train Motown artists.

It was down in the basement of Wilson's house that Barrow learned the now iconic hand signs that supported the onstage performance of the Supremes' classic love song 'Stop In The Name Of Love'. 'The next thing I knew, I was working night and day at Mary's house trying to learn the Supremes' stage act,' Barrow recalled many years later. 'I was also given a budget to go to Saks Fifth Avenue to buy expensive clothes because I ordinarily didn't dress like they dressed.' These secret rehearsals were a necessary short-term solution, but they implicated both Barrow and Wilson in intrigue that was not of their making. Although they moved in the same circles, Barrow simply avoided Ballard and the whispered gossip, but Wilson felt more deeply involved and faced a moral dilemma that haunted her for years to come. Her loyalties were stretched in every direction: as a friend, an employee and a professional singer. It was not an easy or pleasant role to play and, without initiating any of the secret plans, she was caught in no man's land and about to be trapped in the cross-fire of an increasingly vindictive dispute.

Harvey Fuqua and Larry Maxwell made arrangements for Cindy Birdsong to visit Detroit. She was hidden away in a local hotel in a cloak-and-dagger operation, and Barrow, who has kept quiet ever since, simply claimed, 'I didn't see Florence during this time, and it was kept very quiet that Cindy was in Detroit.' Negotiations were slow. It was not clear whether Ballard would bounce back from her depressive illnesses and rebuild her relationship with Gordy, or whether she would turn her back on fame. Nothing seemed simple. Birdsong was contracted to a rival group, and securing her services was not going to be easy. Gordy still clung to the belief that Detroit was rich in female talent and remained lukewarm about Birdsong. Another potential candidate he favoured was Pat Lewis, a graduate of Central High School and member of the popular Detroit group the Adorables, who had a local hit called 'Warning' on Solid Hit Bound Records, a song that Gordy felt had escaped his clutches. According to Motown myth, he also mooted the radical idea that his secret lover, Chris Clark, could join the Supremes, transforming them into a multiracial group, but that was an idea fraught with risk at the time. Gordy could not be certain that mainstream America would embrace such a group, and, more personally, it would mean taking the reckless gamble of combining two of his lovers into the same group.

Several Motown stars were on tour, and for a brief period in March the pressure on recording time eased. Stevie Wonder, Tammi Terrell, Jimmy Ruffin and Gladys Knight and the Pips had all travelled to Ithaca, New York, to make guest appearances at Negro Heritage Week at Cornell University, an annual event celebrating African-American history and desegregation. Diana Ross, Mary Wilson and substitute singer Marlene Barrow were allocated a hurriedly assembled back-up band from Hitsville, and their equipment was transported by truck to the Grosse Pointe Country Club to prepare for Judith Fisher's debutante party.

Although she was in a position to seize one of the most high-profile jobs in the history of soul music, Marlene Barrow stoically let the offer pass, believing that the demands would be irreconcilable with her home life. She had no great desire to replace Ballard permanently and so told Motown management that she wanted to remain a studio singer and working mother, subsequently admitting to feeling uneasy about Motown's plotting and sticking firmly to her decision not to join the group.

The Supremes travelled to Grosse Pointe by limousine, taking a route that was a stark reminder of the race divide in the city. They drove east along Kercheval, where Black Power posters punctuated the storefronts, until the ghettos gave way to suburbia and a very different America. For decades the only blacks to be seen in Grosse Pointe were Negro servants, who were still discouraged from using front entrances. It was the city's most affluent area and a doggedly white neighbourhood. At the time of the party, the grounds of the palatial Grosse Pointe Country Club were being renovated, a brand-new Robert Trent Jones Golf Course had just been completed, and a tree-planting programme to replace diseased Dutch elms was underway. The Motown limousine was directed to park outside the Great Hall in the ancient heart of a country club with no black members. But by 1967 Grosse Pointe had developed a nagging social conscience. Nearby in a local church, a small group of interfaith residents and dedicated integrationists were planning to break the local colour bar. They had printed more than 50,000 leaflets to distribute locally. 'We who live in Grosse Pointe believe that any family should be free to choose its place of residence. We welcome neighbors on a personal basis, without regard to race, color, or creed,' it read. Among their ranks was Dr Douglas Sargent, a paediatrician at Wayne County Child Guidance Clinic who argued that racial integration was important to child development. He told the local press that a narrow white-only experience created an experience of 'such homogeneity that [children's] marshmallow-like characters are shocked when they are eventually exposed to the real world'.

Motown had contracted the Supremes to participate in two films in March 1967, a Hollywood comedy called *The Happening* and a public-service film promoting youth opportunities. They could not have been more different. The Hollywood film was a comedy romp in which a group of young hipsters kidnap a jaded Mafia crook played by Anthony Quinn; the other was a fundraising vehicle for a prominent Detroit charity, the United Foundation's Torch Drive, and was scheduled to be filmed in and around the public housing projects where the girls had grown up.

On 9 March Motown released Brenda Holloway's 'Just Look What You've Done' on the Tamla label, written and produced by Frank Wilson. The flip side, 'Starting The Hurt All Over Again', was a Motown debut for another new and soon-to-be influential writing team, Nick Ashford and Valerie Simpson. Significantly, neither was from Detroit. Ashford and Simpson had relocated from Harlem to be closer to the Motown hit factory; Wilson and Holloway were from Motown's nascent West Coast operation, later to become known as MoWest. Holloway had been raised in the by now notorious Watts ghetto of Los Angeles, which had flared up in a week of rebellious rioting in 1965. When she first visited Detroit, her arrival triggered days of gossip at Hitsville. Holloway was universally thought to be the most stunning woman signed to Motown. Her beauty and figure-hugging gold lamé dresses touched jealous nerves with rival singers, and from her earliest days at Motown she had to deflect Gordy's advances. According to her version of events, Holloway gave him an ultimatum: 'Either I sing or I'm your mistress, but it's one or the other.' Within days she was in the studios and had moved in with Gordy's parents, who had also provided a marital room in their cavernous home to Harvey Fuqua and their daughter Gwen.

For several years Brenda Holloway promised to be another superstar and came to personify Motown's growing interest in West Coast opportunities as the creative traffic between Hollywood and Detroit gathered steam. Motown had hired a West Coast representative, an ex-actor named Shelly Berger whose job was to secure more network television shows and higher-profile L.A. bookings. Berger struck a deal to showcase Motown acts with a self-professed crooked cop named Elmer Valentine, who once told *Vanity Fair* magazine that an elementary school teacher predicted he would be sent to the electric chair someday. Valentine had turned an old bank building in Hollywood into the coolest music venue in the world. The Whisky a Go Go was colour blind, attracting Bob Dylan, the Beatles, Jimi Hendrix, Van Morrison, and Frank Zappa, and in a hectic spurt of shows Marvin Gaye and Tammi Terrell, Smokey Robinson and the Miracles, and Gladys Knight and the Pips all performed there. Within only a few months of his arrival at Motown, Berger secured shows for lesser Motown acts at other L.A. nightspots, including PJs, Ciro's, and the Trip, a hippie hangout next to the towering Playboy Club on the Strip. His ebullience made him seem arrogant, but he had contacts in Hollywood that went way beyond the insular R&B circuit. Berger's influence was crucial to Motown's diversification and Gordy – who was not naturally inclined to modesty himself – sneakily admired Berger's shameless name-dropping, though once commented on Berger's more audacious plans, 'Either he's on drugs or he's an idiot.' It was clear he was not the latter.

Berger secured a commission with Columbia Pictures for the Supremes to perform the title track for the upcoming comedy-heist movie, *The Happening*. Brian Holland and Lamont Dozier worked on the song for two months, aiming to hit a non-negotiable release date of mid March. The initial recordings began in Hollywood, but Holland and Dozier were disappointed with the quality of session musicians and so returned to Detroit to work with the erratic but brilliant Funk Brothers, who could conjure sound effects using ingenious props like chains and spoons, and even an innovative echo chamber, which was no more than a hole cut in the studio ceiling. The title track of *The Happening* had a vague countercultural feel, the title itself hinting at avant garde art happenings and hippie protest, but Motown's indelible imprint was there too: the up-tempo beat, the charismatic hook lines and the engagingly popular choruses. It was a song that did not need a movie, let alone a low-budget schlock movie, to hang onto.

The Happening was released on 20 March backed with the effusive 'All I Know About You', a song of such shameless joy it was closer to Eurovision pop than soul. The release was a milestone of sorts. Although none of the central players knew it at the time, it was the last record marketed under the Supremes' name and the last to feature the dream-girl triumvirate of Diana Ross, Mary

Wilson and Florence Ballard. The next release, 'Reflections', would be credited under the name 'Diana Ross and the Supremes', affirming Ross's status as the group's lead vocalist and paving the way for her ascent to solo success.

Upon signing new and improved second contracts, Motown had advised the Supremes to buy their first homes and invest some of their earnings in property. They had hired road manager Don Foster's girlfriend to act as a decoy purchaser and pose as a cash buyer with inherited wealth. She met with various real estate agents over several days, focusing her attention on an area of the city that had long been predominantly white but was becoming popular with wealthy and aspiring African-Americans. Deals were quickly concluded, and all three singers bought homes within a two-mile stretch of West Buena Vista Street, off Dexter Avenue. Wilson bought 4099 West Buena Vista and promptly asked to have mirrors installed on the bedroom ceiling. She was discouraged by Esther Gordy, who feared it might be misunderstood by the press and damage the group's carefully calculated image of romantic love, not kinky sex. Ross bought 3762 Buena Vista but spent most of her time on the road or in hotel suites. Ballard bought the property at 3767 Buena Vista, diagonal to Ross, and both conceded later in life that having homes in such close proximity exaggerated the tension that was growing between them.

Diana Ross was always more ambitious than the other Supremes. In the spring of 1967, she took a day off from her singing engagements in L.A. and travelled to the set of the 'feminist Western' movie *The Ballad of Josie* at Universal's studio lot to meet film star Doris Day. Ross was already immersed in the outward trappings of stardom and had distanced herself from the Detroit R&B scene of her youth. She planned to pursue a career in Hollywood as a screen actress, but in a more metaphorical sense Ross had become the screen itself, and for years people projected images onto her, not all of which were true or fair. She was described variously as self-centred, vain, jealous, bitchy, manipulative, egotistical and then, triumphantly, a diva. It was her foresight and ambition that propelled her forward and so irritated others.

Mary Wilson described her as having 'a low tolerance of criticism'. Ross was aware of the impression she created, and even her own family considered her spoiled and demanding as a child. 'Just because I have my standards they think I'm a bitch,' she once snapped at colleagues who fell below her obsessive levels of professionalism. Ross resented the Motown group the Contours, whose flash and aggressive behaviour she felt was beneath contempt, and she refused to share a stage with them. Peter Benjaminson, a writer for the *Free Press*, reported that she 'fought bitterly with other female vocalists over such items as hairspray, the borrowing of a pair of shoes and the use of the mirror in the bus's one bathroom. [She] clearly believed that she was always right and that anyone who clashed with her was always wrong.' Later in her career, Motown creative assistant Suzanne De Passe once described seeing Ross in the elevator of Essex House on Central Park in New York: 'The elevator stopped and the doors opened, and there, in a Pucci dress, holding her Maltese puppy, with a Sassoon wig and shoes covered in the same material as the Pucci dress, was the breathtaking Diana Ross – more glamorous than any human thing I'd ever seen in my life.'

As Smokey Robinson witnessed from the very earliest days, her taste was fortified by a tireless determination. 'Diana Ross was the most hardworking, most diligent student at Artist Development [referring to Motown's talent academy],' he said. 'Everybody else would be gone and she would still be there. Diana Ross wanted to be . . . Diana Ross.' Most of those who rushed to criticise her saw only shimmering surfaces and snobbery, but her signature phrase, 'I have my standards,' carried many deeper meanings. 'Standards' was a commodity that was measured daily in her childhood home and was a core value of her family as they'd navigated the pressures of post-war Detroit, first reaching and then leaving the Brewster Projects. Her mother, Ernestine, and her strict father, Fred Ross, had a strained marriage, but they shared an unshakeable belief that their children would not simply survive but strive for a better life and command respect. Reflecting back to the projects, Ballard's sister Maxine remembered a moment in the Ross household that provided a unique insight into the different home lives of the Supremes: 'Diane's mother always had such a nice table setting . . . I needed someone like Mrs Ross. I felt she knew everything and was willing to share.' To understand Diana Ross and why she eventually usurped Ballard's role as leader of the Supremes, there are clues in her mother's fussy table settings and the brooding quasi-military presence of her father. Although they both lived in the Brewster Projects and sang the same teenage ballads, Ballard and Ross came from strikingly different families: one was wayward and raucous, the other obsessive and focused. Fred Ross described the projects not as a ghetto waiting to happen but as an aspirational place: 'If you got in, you were one of the lucky ones,' he once said. 'At that time, a stigma hadn't been attached to the projects. The front yards had nice lawns, the housing was decent and there were courtyards . . . It wasn't so terrible, believe me.'

Fred Ross was born on Independence Day, 1920, in West Virginia and grew into an imposing character with grey-goose hair and a neatly trimmed moustache. Unlike the rural poverty and segregated racism that many migrants to Detroit had experienced, Ross had grown up as the son of a professor at West Virginia State College. He saw education as a currency even more powerful than the dollar, and by 1937 he had moved to Detroit, graduated from the city's selective high school, Cass Tech, and found gainful employment. Like Gordy, Ross was briefly successful as a local boxer, but neither sport nor music could divert him from the path of self-improvement, and with punishing determination he enrolled at Wayne State College, studying an early-day MBA in business administration. Ross had a motto that he repeated almost daily: 'Life is too short to be poor.' His wife, Ernestine, had standards too. She was the daughter of a Baptist minister in Bessemer, Alabama, and remained close to the church throughout her life. A neighbour described her as 'the consummate mother, always at home sewing and cooking, [and she] kept her daughters fastidiously clean'. Mary Wilson saw them as role models: 'Unlike many other families then,' she wrote, 'the Rosses didn't cling to the old idea that the family came before the individual. Instead they emphasized the importance of each child's personal achievements, and education was considered crucial. Diane always had a streak of daring and independence.'

It was Ernestine Ross who encouraged her daughter's singing career, helped sew stage costumes, hosted group meetings, and pushed her daughter forward. Diana later claimed that if it had not been for her mother's support, she would not have become a professional singer. For many years Diana Ross was an also-ran, easily drowned out by the siren emotions of the many gospel-raised singers she grew up with. She seemed embarrassed by her thin frame and nasal voice, and stood back from the front line. She accepted that there was a hierarchy. Florence Ballard and Aretha Franklin could conjure sounds from their mouths that Diana Ross could only dream of; Mary Wilson could imitate great voices from jazz to soul to opera, and earthy R&B singers like Mable John and her brother Little Willie John had throats like sandpaper and could dig a song out of the gravel. But Diana's mother persisted, pushing her forward, and Ross somehow turned her slenderness and reedy vocals into a virtue, fashioning a singing style that marked her as one of the greatest cross-over acts in the history of black American music. Gil Askey, musical director of the Supremes, put it succinctly: 'Diana Ross had an ideal commercial voice. When she had to, she could go out and get the butter.'

Mary Wilson spent a lifetime trying to fathom Diana Ross. 'Even at a young age, I could see that Diane was trying to build up her own self-confidence,' she once wrote. 'Her haughtiness was just a front; deep down, she believed she wasn't as pretty as the other girls. She craved attention, and in her attempts to get it, she could seem almost ruthless.' By the mid sixties Ross had found the near-perfect defence. Accustomed to having her vocal skill questioned, she retaliated in her own inimitable way, questioning whether she was really a singer at all. 'I'm not really a songwriter,' she said gnomically, 'I'm an interpreter. So in a sense I am an actress first and foremost. I act out the songs, and I lead with my heart.' By 1967 there was no question that Diana Ross had beaten her teenage insecurity. Manhattan novelist Rona Jaffe, who wrote several books on fame and femininity, described Ross as if she were an amalgam of very different women: 'She is a delicately-boned, gentle, intelligent, trembling electric wire of a girl – part guts, part geisha, all radar. It's what makes her a star. Chic, witty, high-fashion tastes in clothes, with a style of her own. The curviest skinny girl I've ever seen.'

One of the few decisions that Diana Ross made with her father's full blessing was to enrol at his alma mater, Cass Tech High School, where she aspired to join the school's selective sorority, the Hexagons. Cass offered a curriculum of fashion and design, which suited Ross's teenage fascination with clothes, make-up and the fashion industry. Attending Cass Tech set her apart in the eyes of her teenage contemporaries. Most youngsters from the Brewster Projects went to the rough-and-ready Northeastern High School, which in 1967 was in a predominantly Polish neighbourhood. Ross chose not to. The origins of her apparent imperiousness or aloofness from the rest of Motown began from the age of sixteen, when she was often assumed to be less rooted in the simmering ghetto mindset of the projects. She even managed to secure a temporary job at Hudson's on Woodward, which had Detroit's most exclusive women's clothing department and had set up training clinics to train black sales girls in diligence and people skills.

Ross's reputation as a difficult and demanding person had its origins in a report published in the *Chicago Tribune*. The Supremes had flown into the city two hours late for a concert at the Arie Crown Theater on McCormick Place, and a reporter at the airport heard Ross complaining about the delay and asking for an explanation from the ground crew. She was parodied in the magazine with her 'giant celebrity glasses', and much was made of her fox fur-trimmed coat. This image of a flamboyant drama queen stuck, but what the image did not account for was a more rounded truth: the coat was being paid for in instalments from her wages at Motown and was something of a personal milestone. For the first time in her life, she was able to afford a coat bought from the store that had employed her as a teenager.

★

Detroit society was essentially working-class and blue-collar, but it was also one rich in nuance and class division. In their early years as the Primettes, Ballard, Ross, Wilson and their friend Betty McGlown often performed on the local labour-union circuit in the cavernous workers' halls that sat astride the automobile plants. Wilson remembered nervously playing a concert with local singer Freda Payne for an audience of what she describes to this day as 'elites'. Pronounced 'ee-lights', it is a distinctive Motor City expression used by Wilson to describe foremen, black office workers and those employees whose status had been elevated by senior union membership or the small privileges that the car plants bestowed. It was for many a small, almost imperceptible step up the social ladder, and according to Wilson, the elite life baffled her: 'Perhaps they were better educated, or their skin was lighter, or they had managed to banish any Southern accent or language from their speech. Those blacks frowned on other blacks.'

What was clear from the mid fifties onward was that Ross's family had joined the growing ranks of the 'ee-lights': comfortable, morally rooted, but not yet rich. Ross faced trying times as a child. She was never close to her father and never would be, and so to compensate she clung emotionally to her mother, seeking her approval, confiding in her, and vying for her attention. Ernestine Ross's support was always close at hand, her protective antennae always alert to her daughter's best interests. Her marriage had been under strain for many years, and the couple eventually separated and then divorced. It was no great surprise that Diana sided with her mother. For her entire adult life, few could remember a time when mother and daughter were at odds, and when it did happen, it was memorable for both. In 1950, when Diana was only six, Ernestine fell seriously ill with tuberculosis and was hospitalised in a sanatorium. Diana was dispatched to her grandparents for almost a year to allow her mother to recuperate. The Deep South was a wake-up call. 'You could just feel the bigotry in the air,' she remembered in her adult years. 'You could slice it with a knife like stinking cheese.'

Many years later, at the height of her fame with the Supremes, she described those feelings in a magazine interview and unintentionally mentioned being separated when her mother was ill with tuberculosis. For the conservative and socially upstanding Ernestine, this was as close as her daughter ever came to personal betrayal. They argued heatedly over many weeks. Ross had intended no hurt; it was nothing more than a piece of colour in an endless round of interviews, but for her mother, who had never done an interview in her life, it was devastating to read about her private life in such stark detail. Even into the sixties, a stigma still attached itself to consumptive tuberculosis, which for many of the older generation was seen as a disease of poverty. Ernestine found her illness demeaning and painful to talk about, having spent a lifetime trying to better her life and never to be seen as either poor or needy; to be portrayed as such by her own daughter hurt her deeply.

There was a dignity about the older black women around Motown that consistently put social respectability before the hype of the music industry. Ross came to understand it later in her career and habitually corrected journalists who lazily described her success as a story of rags to riches. 'We were never raggedy,' she would say, out of respect to her mother. Wilson was equally scathing about the easy stereotypes of the ghetto. 'The truth is that Berry never signed anyone to Motown who needed to be "remade",' she once said. 'The uncouth, boisterous and slovenly couldn't get a foot in the door anyway. Almost everyone who came to Motown wanted to move up in the world . . . We were all trying to get ahead, and it's always bothered me that some people have assumed that by accepting what some consider "white" values, we sold out. It's just not true.'

Funk overlord James Brown had styled himself as the hardest-working man in showbiz, but even Brown's nightly itinerary of live shows fell far short of the workload that burdened the Supremes between 1965 and 1967. It was a punishing and ultimately divisive schedule that would have exhausted even the most robust individual. Wilson frequently fought swollen glands and migraines to make it onstage; Ballard was diagnosed with pneumonia and had persistent head colds; and Ross was flown home after she collapsed onstage in Boston and was hospitalised in the Henry Ford Hospital near Hitsville. Her weight had plummeted to ninety pounds. 'Sometimes the stress got so bad I couldn't eat,' Ross said. 'I just couldn't swallow anything. I'd put food in my mouth, but my jaws would clamp together and I couldn't chew. It got so that I couldn't even tolerate the smell of food. It was too pungent for me. Perhaps it was a form of anorexia. I was becoming skin and bones.'

History has blamed Berry Gordy for driving the Supremes to the point of collapse, but it was success that was the real taskmaster. Eddie Holland saw it close up: 'We didn't write songs; we wrote hits. But I'll say this: making a hit is a collaborative process. And by that time the Supremes were hardly ever there. They were always out on the road, doing this club, that TV show, this hotel. The only time they saw Detroit was when they flew over it. We'd have to grab them for a few hours at a time every two, three months. And they'd be tired and didn't really want to come.' Diana Ross fought through the demanding schedule as if it were bipolar disorder. She claims, 'The highs were high, but the tension that accompanied them and the work that was required to maintain our performance in quality during the recording and extensive touring was overwhelming and debilitating.'

In the spring of 1966, Wilson claimed to notice a change in her two friends. Diana Ross was chastising the Motown road staff and bickering about small details. Ballard's drinking had tipped from social excess to habitual need. 'I began to notice that Flo's drinking was becoming a habit,' Wilson said. 'She never drank before a show, but after we finished our set, we would change and go out and partake of the local nightlife or attend private parties. This was when Flo drank. A normal person leading a normal life could have slept it off and carried on. But we were not leading normal lives. After a show we might fly to another city to finish recording or prepare for our next engagement or television appearance . . . Many nights we were lucky to get two hours' sleep before facing the public again.'

On 20 March 1967, coinciding with the world premiere of the movie *The Happening* at the Adams Theater in downtown Detroit,

Motown released the film's title track. The movie posters made heady claims, calling it 'the most fantastic three-million-dollar caper that ever happened. A mobster, a chick and three young guys pull of the wildest hold-up of them all.' The tag line was 'It's crazy, it's cool, and it's supreme'. Unfortunately, it wasn't. By far the most memorable aspects of the movie were the title track and the debut of Faye Dunaway, who, later in the year, was nominated for an Oscar for her role in *Bonnie and Clyde*. *The Happening* had mostly been shot in Dunaway's native Florida, but no suitable premiere could be negotiated there or in Hollywood, so the producers hitched their film to the Motown bandwagon and reluctantly accepted their third choice, Detroit, a city unfamiliar with opening nights. Dunaway tried hard to promote the film, but it was to no great avail. *Time* magazine slaughtered it, turning its guns on executive producer Sam Speigel, who had previously made landmark films like *Lawrence of Arabia* and *Bridge Over the River Kwai*. It 'bears all the earmarks of the amateur effort,' *Time* wrote condescendingly. '*The Happening* is a homemade bomb. Next time Speigel should reapply for foreign aid.'

It became clear to most critics that *The Happening* had one redeeming feature: a title track sung by three women who neither appeared in the movie nor had seen a single frame of the film prior to its release. The choice of a Detroit theatre for the premiere confirmed *The Happening*'s low self-esteem: the Adams Theater was one of a rare breed of cinemas known as 'alley jumpers', in which the entrance and the auditorium were housed in separate buildings in order to make the entrance appear grand while saving on real estate costs by having the audience walk to a theatre located in cheaper property via a rear alley. In the case of the Adams Theater, the entrance and lobby were housed in the Fine Arts Building overlooking Grand Circus Park, but a tunnel carried moviegoers a block away to a faceless building.

Having never thought of the film as appealing to black audiences, the promotion team reversed gear and desperately tried to whip up enthusiasm via Detroit local radio. On the day of the premiere, several live radio shows camped out at the Adams Theater. From

10.30 a.m. to 1.30 p.m. DJ and community broadcaster Martha Jean 'the Queen' Steinberg broadcast live from the lobby on WJLB; from 3 p.m. to 5 p.m. WXYZ's Pat Murphy occupied the grand entrance; at 7.45 p.m. Jay Butler's *Teen Club* on WHCB took over; and later in the evening, the movie was promoted live on Bob Keen's *Happening on Keener* (WKNR). In the days immediately before and after the premiere, promo staff distributed handbills along Twelfth Street, a ghetto artery that had its own unique connection to the city's thriving independent soul scene. Fourteen blocks north of Motown's complex of office studios on West Grand Boulevard, Twelfth Street, at its intersection with Clairmount, was a hive of small clubs, including the Chit Chat, where members of the Funk Brothers regularly moonlighted. The intersection had become infamous as an area frequented by 'prostitutes, pushers and pilferers', but for a week it also became the last desperate haunt of movie promoters more accustomed to Sunset Boulevard.

Twelfth Street was stark proof of the social demography of Detroit. The *Michigan Chronicle* described the area's restless immorality. 'By daylight a congested narrow avenue with no depth from curb stone to storefront, Twelfth Street by night is a mixture of gaudiness and furtive shadows,' wrote a staff writer, using the language of pulp fiction. 'Cars cruise the street, slowing at the dark corners, their occupants seeking a rendezvous.' Hidden behind the film noir imagery were some truly alarming statistics. The local neighbourhood had 145,000 people jammed into six square miles, and in every social survey it led the city's crime statistics in rape, armed robbery and auto theft, and accounted for one quarter of all the burglaries in the city. It was housing that set the area apart. Rows of crowded and dilapidated buildings had become an eyesore. In 1940 no black families lived in the neighbourhood at all: it was 98.7 per cent white. By 1950, 37.2 per cent of local residents were non-white, and by 1960 the proportion of blacks to whites had virtually reversed. Only 3.8 per cent were now white. The area around Twelfth Street had witnessed complete transformation in twenty years as white residents fled the area to new buildings, better neighbourhoods or the encroaching suburbs. In a contemporary survey by the University of Michigan's Psychology Department, the area was described as a community of high stress where an overwhelming majority of the residents were disenchanted with their living conditions. Of those interviewed, 93 per cent said they wanted to move out; 73 per cent felt that the streets were not safe; 91 per cent believed that a person was likely to be robbed or beaten at night; 57 per cent were worried about fires; and most tellingly of all, 78 per cent believed police did not respond promptly when they were summoned for help. It was a blighted area about to take centre stage.

Easter Sunday, 1967, was Diana Ross's twenty-third birthday, and she spent the day with Berry Gordy. Temperatures were comfortably into the sixties, and the city's most wealthy families congregated on the 'spongy lawns' of St Paul's on Lake Shore. The sun shone down on a strange kind of civic apartheid. Detroit prayed to God but mostly apart. Few congregations were racially mixed. European immigrants still flocked to the churches of their cultural past, to the branched candlesticks of Russian orthodoxy or to the domed Greek cathedral. African-Americans had historically seen their churches as a refuge from racism and a place of self-improvement, and black ministers often acted as employment agents for the Ford car plants, providing recruitment information and references for their parishioners. To secure employment, many unemployed workers were dependent on the church for letters of recommendation. Set against this lurked a deeper religious intransigence; some Catholic churches secretly maintained parish covenants that prevented black families from living in their parish. Elsewhere politics were hatching beneath the altars of prayer.

The Reverend Albert B. Cleage Jr's Central United Church of Christ had laid plans to unveil a painting of a black Madonna, a radical piece of iconography portraying the Virgin Mary as a feisty black woman. The Franklins and Cleage had fallen out over the role religion should play in forcing social change, The Franklins favouring a form of Christian gradualism that followed the non-violent creed of Martin Luther King, while Cleage espoused a more radical Black Power agenda. Both saw the church as a moral compass, but their disagreements were exacerbated by egotism. Each in his own way imagined himself as the de facto leader of the black community. Cleage had commissioned prison artist and Black Power soldier Glanton Dowdell to create the painting. Dowdell had served more than ten years in Jackson State Penitentiary. He had come to the attention of Michigan's art establishment after painting a sombre composition called *South East Corner of My Cell*. For his black Madonna, he reputedly walked around Kercheval until he spotted a young mother named Rose Waldon, who became the model for his ethnic vision of the Virgin Mary. Waldon was painted cradling the black baby Jesus in her arms on an eighteen-foot canvas which arched above the altar of Cleage's church. The unveiling caused a storm of debate, challenging congregations to reconsider the origins of the nativity and the history of Christianity itself. In a dramatic coincidence, Dowdell was due in court the following day, where he stood side by side with Black Power militant General Baker; both men had been charged with carrying guns and ammunition on Kercheval and Pennsylvania. For Glanton Dowdell, court appearances were nothing new. He was a fifth-grade dropout who had been put in a home for the mentally retarded at the age of thirteen and dismissed as 'a lunatic' with severe learning difficulties. He had been incarcerated most of his life, and on his release he had become caught up in local gang culture where, for several years, he was a hold-up man who committed armed robberies in illegal soul clubs. Dowdell had been radicalised in prison, and rather than keep the money for himself he redistributed the stolen cash to fund political activism and social welfare programmes. What was truly remarkable and did not come to light until 1967 was that Dowdell was not retarded; on the contrary, he was an artist of daring creativity – a true savant.

Marlene Barrow had come to realise that cooperating with Motown had made her strangely vulnerable. Her recent appearances as a surrogate Supreme had wrenched her from the invisibility of the Snake Pit studio into a limelight where she risked being compromised in what was an increasingly unpleasant dispute. It was with mixed feelings that she took a call from Motown's offices asking her to fly immediately to New Orleans to replace Florence Ballard yet again. Nobody would tell Barrow what had happened on the road to necessitate such a long and urgent flight, but it was clearly not good news. The Supremes were midway though a sweeping tour of the southern states that took in Miami, Memphis and New Orleans. Their Los Angeles-based media agent, Shelly Berger, had travelled with them to the Florida residencies at the Deauville Hotel and the Eden Roc on Miami Beach. Berger later claimed that Florence Ballard was drunk all the time; most other accounts said she was only drinking sporadically. The shows in Miami were tense yet relatively uneventful, but it proved to be the calm before the storm. Ballard's drinking increased and became more flagrant. The Supremes did a one-night student show at Middle State University's campus in Murfreesboro, Tennessee, and then journeyed to Atlanta and on to Memphis. The flights were short, but Florence disobeyed advice from the backstage staff and smuggled drink on board, and by the time Motown's entourage touched down in Memphis, she was visibly drunk. On arrival at the prestigious Peabody Hotel, Ballard was incapable of filling in her check-in details. Diana Ross phoned Gordy from the lobby and described the scene to him while Mary Wilson tried to cover things up and arranged for Ballard to be helped to her room. It was an ignominious arrival in soul music's second city, the home of Stax Records, Motown's great southern rival. The Memphis show began late but with no great drama, and reviews the next day were universally positive. But there was a laxness that would have enraged Gordy. Ballard had showered and sobered up enough to play her part, but on her return to the hotel she was unable to sleep and sank into depression. She drank heavily through the night and missed the prearranged breakfast rendezvous. Concerned about her safety, Ross and Wilson got the keys to her room, opened the door, and found her slumped on the bed, fully clothed and half asleep. Tissues were scattered around the room, empty bottles filled the waste basket, and hotel records showed that Ballard had run up a huge phone bill with numerous calls back to Detroit.

Motown's road managers, Don Foster and Joe Schaffner, were dispatched to Ballard's room. They quickly organised her luggage and raced to the airport in time to catch the flight to New Orleans. According to close witnesses, Ballard sat in silence throughout the journey. Paradoxically, Schaffner had once dated Ballard when they were younger, but their relationship had petered out and he had gone on to marry one of the Marvelettes, Katherine Anderson. Schaffner later remembered taking a call from Gordy when they arrived in New Orleans and described the incident in all its painful detail: 'Berry told me very calmly to put Florence on the next plane back to Detroit. He wasn't angry, he was just disgusted. I put her coat on her, grabbed her suitcases, and drove her back to the airport. Before we left, she went up to Diana and just smiled in her face, as if to say, "You ain't got me, lady, I was leaving anyway." It was the most heartbreaking sight. On the way to the airport she just cried and cried. She was so miserable, so unhappy.'

Musical director and trumpeter Gil Askey witnessed it all, but he was soon to leave Detroit and migrate to Australia. He has since described a nervous anxiety taking hold of the tour, and when the decision arrived from Detroit that the Supremes would perform as a duet, he watched an emotional meltdown at the heart of the group. According to one of Askey's friends, he went into the lead dressing room to find Ross slumped in a chair like a weeping child, 'just skin and bones sticking out of a dress – no human form'. That evening, excuses were made to the New Orleans crowd, and the Supremes appeared as a duet. Ross claimed it was touch and go: 'Mary and I were frantic. We ended up having to go on without her. We abandoned the regular choreography, and, after grabbing the hand mics, we walked around the stage and sang, just the two of us.' The two remaining girls managed to get through the show, but the perfect symmetry of the three Supremes was shattered. Marlene Barrow had been called at her home and was already at Metro Airport, ready to fly south to stand in for Ballard in the last few remaining shows of the southern tour, but for one night only the Supremes had been forced to sing as a duet, and that would never be allowed to happen again.

With hindsight, no single person had perspective on the civil war at the heart of the Supremes. Berry Gordy was increasingly angry at being disobeyed but was unaware that Ballard had been raped as a teenager and so dismissed her deepening depression as surly drunkenness. Her family was unaware that her unhappiness had tipped into sullen unprofessionalism, and most Motown employees were unaware of the scheme to recruit Cindy Birdsong. Wilson talked vaguely about Gordy's plans in her memoirs and said he attended 'a meeting with some upper-level people at Motown, Diane, and me', claiming that Birdsong was the meeting's unanimous choice, 'largely because she and Flo had a similar look'. Although the meeting was unanimous, the outcome was not. Birdsong had provided Motown with copies of her existing contract, and lawyers were fussing over clauses that prevented her from securing an immediate release from her duties. She also communicated concerns that any thought of leaving the Bluebelles by mutual consent would be obstructed by her fellow singer Nona Hendrix, cousin of rock god Jimi Hendrix and one of soul music's early feminist voices. Hendrix was a strident force within the Bluebelles and had no great love for the Supremes, and the secrecy was not helping either. 'I never knew for sure if Flo knew about Cindy,' Wilson reflected. 'If she did, she wouldn't have let on, I'm sure. I still prayed Flo would straighten up, but as the days passed, the possibility of that happening seemed less and less likely.'

Disputes among Motown's girl groups had reached a critical stage. The Marvelettes were in and out of Motown's Golden World Studios throughout March, recording a Smokey Robinson song called 'The Day You Take One (You Have To Take The Others)', which was to become the B-side of 'When You're Young And In Love', and laying down vocals for their next big song, 'My Baby Must Be A Magician'. It was an intensely emotional session; two founding members had already become casualties, Juanita Cowart had retired after what Motown described as 'a nervous breakdown' but which turned out to be diagnosed as manic depression, and another singer, Georgeanna Tillman, left the group when she was diagnosed with sickle-cell anaemia. The group's problem had parallels with the warring Supremes. Singers Gladys Horton and Wanda Rogers each believed they should be credited and recognised as the lead singer and were caught in an acrimonious and self-defeating dispute that made recording sessions difficult. The bitterness curdled over years and eventually damaged the group irreparably. Horton met and married Joe Tex's trumpeter, Sammy Coleman, while on tour but the relationship only lasted a year, and their child was born with cerebral palsy. Horton drifted from front-line entertainment and her career at Motown was over too.

Gordy, for his part, had run out of patience with his warring girl groups, and Florence Ballard in particular. 'It seemed the harsher the warning, the more flagrant Flo's behavior became,' he once wrote, convinced that her actions were designed to undermine his authority. He called a meeting of those who had witnessed the scenes in Memphis and New Orleans. Shelly Berger was there. 'Mr Gordy was sold on the idea that Florence had to go,' he recalled, 'and I have to tell you I was against it. I was against changes in acts because from my experience, any time an established act had been changed, the act had fallen apart.' Gordy listened to their various accounts and then spoke alone with Ross and Wilson. It is not clear if this private meeting ended with any consensus, and it has been shrouded in mystery and half-remembered gossip ever since. But Gordy took from the atmosphere of the meeting a tacit permission to dismiss Ballard and believed the other Supremes were in agreement. As March ended, Gordy had concluded the purchase of his mansion on Boston Boulevard but had yet to move in, and an extensive schedule of interior decorating was underway. The mansion had become a landmark purchase in the history of home ownership in Detroit, but it was soon to take on a very different meaning when it became the disputed backdrop for Gordy's eventual showdown with Ballard. Friendships that had been forged in the decaying Brewster Projects were about to crumble like rubble.

Love-In. A Detroit hippie dances at the city's infamous 'Love-In'
at Belle Isle Park, where the 'Holy Barbarians of Rock' MC5 performed
on a makeshift stage on a grass bank.

APRIL

Love

Love came but not alone. As the battle for the soul of the Supremes reached its crisis point, Detroit was rocked by a senseless killing that cut to the emotional core of the city's distrusted police department. George Overman Jr personified good citizenship; he was a well-behaved teenager who played trombone with the Finney High School band, but his promising young life ended in an anonymous service elevator at Cobo Hall, where he was stabbed by unknown assailants. The young man had been unpacking band equipment from a car parked outside a side entrance. Dressed in a bottle-green band uniform, a perfectly pressed shirt and a thin black bow tie, he was accosted by two youths demanding money. When he refused to hand over his cash, Overman was stabbed in the chest just below his neck. The attackers escaped with only two dollars, and within a few hours of the stabbing police had gathered enough witnesses to believe that the suspects were two young African-American truants who had been hanging around Cobo Hall over the previous few days.

On the day of the stabbing, Cobo Hall was busy. A UAW convention occupied most of the building, and a banquet for the Detroit Board of Education was scheduled for the evening. With blood gushing from his neck, George Overman Jr staggered into an elevator and was found dying by a ventilation engineer working nearby. Overman's death marked a new nadir for Detroit, feeding fears that crime was out of control and raising concern that the flagship Cobo Hall – supposedly a thrusting symbol of modern business – had become a magnet for criminals and wayward teens. The homicide had been the seventh violent attack within a matter of months and was a setback for race relations across the city. Mayor Cavanagh was forced onto the defensive, and pressure mounted on Inspector Arthur Schwaller, head of the homicide bureau, to make swift arrests. It was publicity the city could do without and was not helpful to internal relations within an increasingly beleaguered police force, either. The dead boy was the son of a prominent local policeman, George Overman Sr, director of the Detroit City Police Band, like his father before him. The Overmans were from a police dynasty, and like many serving officers the death of a son killed so cheaply cut to the quick among a police community who felt unsupported by their political masters.

April was a turbulent month. Fierce emotional winds swept through the city, and the word love was on everyone's lips. It had become a touchstone for the new counterculture and the rise of a youth movement that wanted to bring an increasingly unpopular foreign war to an end. The Supremes were in Miami performing at the Eden Roc alongside comedian Sonny Sands. Extra chaperones had been provided for the trip, and Gordy instructed the road crew to notify him if there was any recurrence of drinking on the road. The first few days of the month were eventful for Motown: 'There's A Ghost In My House', a surging novelty record by R. Dean Taylor, was released; the Four Tops opened a triumphant UK tour at the Royal Albert Hall, and 'Bernadette' entered the UK top twenty; local pop group Mitch Ryder and the Detroit Wheels were back home in Detroit performing at the Chatter on Gratiot; and the 'holy barbarians' of guitar rock, the MC5, were in near permanent residency at the Grande Ballroom, this time billed under yet another new tag line – 'the original avant rock'. John Sinclair was by now officially managing the group, and Detroit's much anticipated 'love-in' was only four weeks away. Ominously, it was to be held at the bandstand on Belle Isle, the site of the city's infamous 1943 race riots.

Back at Hitsville, Gordy and his sister Esther had concluded a contractual argument with a local Detroit charity called the United Foundation to employ the Supremes to front a fundraising documentary. The girls were to be filmed outside their old homes at the Brewster-Douglass Projects as part of an annual charity campaign known as Torch Drive. The trustees were drawn from Detroit's high society, and among their ranks were executives from the automobile industry, city bankers, and Michigan entrepreneurs. Motown agreed that the public-service film could use the group's current hit, 'The Happening', as a promotional soundtrack. The 16mm film had a tight budget of $1,000, and all the filming was to be completed in a day.

The girls travelled to the rendezvous separately, Ross in a jacquard-weave suit, Wilson in a crocheted cape, and Ballard draped in her trademark fur stole. They linked arms together and strolled through the Brewster Projects as if they were bosom buddies. Kids poured onto the streets to watch, and local residents looked down from their tower blocks. No one could have guessed the simmering resentment hidden behind their promotional smiles. But trouble was not long in coming. The script required all three girls to speak a line about their love of Detroit, but on the day Gordy intervened and changed the narration, insisting that all the lines be delivered by Ross. It was a small but heavy-handed change, improvised on the spot to save filming time, and although it was driven by pragmatism rather than anything sinister, Ballard saw it as a demotion and further evidence that the Supremes were becoming Diana Ross's group. A squabble erupted on location, witnessed by hundreds of local residents and leaving Wilson in the unenviable position of silent witness. According to subsequent reports, clearly embellished with time, Ballard refused to play the role of onlooker. 'I ain't playin' second fiddle to Miss Ross,' she said sarcastically. 'Especially here in the projects where we used to be equals.' It was common for Ballard to appeal to Wilson to intervene, but the increasingly compromised Wilson tried to remain neutral, caught between two opposing and at times implacable forces. It would be the last time they would ever appear in their childhood neighbourhood together.

Early that evening one of Motown's senior receptionists, Janie Bradford, called the girls individually and invited them to a meeting at Gordy's home. She was guarded about the purpose of the meeting, but it was a harbinger of more bad news and clearly not a social event. Wilson complained to Bradford at the time about feeling trapped between the unhappy Ballard and the ambitious Ross, and told Bradford that she felt she was becoming squeezed into an unpleasant and unfair role. 'Looking back, I shouldn't have been surprised to see that, as our career grew, so did feelings of competitiveness, jealousy, and distrust,' she wrote in *Dreamgirl*. 'It upset me once in a while, but I became an expert at stifling my feelings if I thought expressing them would endanger the group.'

Although she spent much of her time mediating between warring friends, Mary Wilson had her own unique story to tell. Wilson had been born in the small town of Greenville, Mississippi, known locally as 'the heart and soul of the Delta', and moved to Detroit as an infant. Born into an unstable family, her birth father, Sam Wilson, worked the riverboats on the Mississippi and was an inveterate gambler who believed in one of life's most flawed concepts – easy money – and so wasted his adult life pursuing wealth via blackjack and roulette. 'It was obvious that he loved the fast life,' Wilson wrote in her autobiography, admitting that her grandparents resented her father's fecklessness. 'Although he had a trade, he couldn't hold a job and had long been a drifter, and worst of all, he was a compulsive gambler. To proud and religious people like my mother's kin, Sam Wilson was just plain weak. My mother was always the quietest and most reserved of siblings, but when it came to Sam, nothing they said could change her mind. She loved him.'

Wilson's natural mother, Johnnie Mae, struggled to raise her children, and when she 'was frightened down to her last few dollars and still without a job', she reluctantly agreed that Mary be adopted by her aunt and uncle, Ivory and John Pippin. They had invested a $7,100 GI loan into a small newly built house in Dearborn, Michigan, and planned a more prosperous future in the Mecca of the north, Detroit. Thoughtlessly, Wilson's aunt told the young child that she was not her natural mother and that her real mother, Johnnie Mae Wilson, now single and shot of her feckless husband, was travelling north to take her away. Tearful and confused, Mary went with her real mother, and they moved into a smaller house in southwest Detroit, then again to an apartment in the Brewster Projects in 1956. In this brief spell, Mary had experienced the comforts of living with her aunt in Dearborn and the poverty of being taken to various rundown apartments with her real mother. 'Many people would have considered a move to the projects to be a step down,' Wilson said. 'But for me, having already stepped down from a middle-class neighbourhood to various apartments in the inner city, this was a step back up.'

Passed from one family to another, becoming the subject of a custody dispute between her adoptive mother and her real family, and before that the subject of emotionally disruptive fights between her mother and father, Mary had grown up feeling as if she was born to be in the middle of trouble. And so it proved at Motown. She was frequently caught not only in the midst of arguments within the Supremes but in disagreements with other groups too. The Supremes and Martha and the Vandellas loathed each other; it was partly due to unhealthy competition but more perniciously because of the strong women that fronted the two groups. Martha Reeves and Diana Ross did not get along, and neither was the type to acquiesce. 'I would get caught in the middle,' Wilson said subsequently, 'and although we both liked all the Vandellas – Martha, Rosalind Ashford and Annette Sterling – our relationship with Martha was strained by her feuds with Diane. Flo and I would admit privately who was right, and it wasn't always Diane. But she was in our group, and solidarity was crucial, right or wrong.'

Tribalism between the two groups became exaggerated by professional jealousy as the Supremes surpassed Martha and the Vandellas in popularity. From 1965 onward they began to dominate the charts and became a greater priority for Motown. Ross's close relationship with Gordy did not help either, and any advantage gained by the Supremes was seen by Martha Reeves as a by-product of Gordy's preferential treatment.

It was inevitable that Mary would be caught in the cross-fire. By far the most successful with men, she compartmentalised her life. She was more gregarious than Ross and more streetwise than Ballard, and by 1967 she had managed to build up a formidable list of conquests, including a long-time love affair with Abdul 'Duke' Fakir of the Four Tops and a 'holiday romance' with the English film director David Puttnam, who in 1967 was a successful advertising executive. Later in the year, in Las Vegas, she fell in love with the Welsh pop singer Tom Jones, by then a married man.

April was the month that LSD arrived in earnest. It came with surreal and spectacular consequences. LSD – lysergic acid diethylamide – was nearly twenty-five years old when it was absorbed into the kinaesthetic body of American counterculture. Invented by the Swiss chemist Albert Hofmann back in 1943 as a profitable over-the-counter cure for migraines, there were high hopes that it would join Valium and Dexedrine in the pharmacy of everyday life. But while experimenting with lysergic acid, Hofmann began to hallucinate, and imagined it as a drug with a role to play in mental health care. 'It was obvious that a substance with such fantastic effects on mental perception . . . would arouse interest outside medical science,' he once wrote, and he was right.

By 1967 there had been three congressional hearings about the increase in non-medicinal uses of LSD, and despite the limited circulation of the drug, it added to anxieties about hippie counter-culture and the so-called 'dropout' generation. Illegal LSD was manufactured in makeshift garage laboratories, with supplies mostly concentrated in and around university towns. Michigan police reported several DIY manufacturing hubs in Ann Arbor, home of the University of Michigan, which by the mid sixties was a hive of liberalism and hosted the first 'teach-ins' against the war in Vietnam. LSD had aroused interest in two different communities, and they converged on Detroit in April 1967. Hippies and peaceniks from across the Midwest were planning to attend the city's first 'love-in' on Belle Isle, while the cream of America's psycho-analytical community were due to arrive for their annual convention at Cobo Hall, part of which was still cordoned off as a murder scene.

In the aftermath of the murder of George Overman Jr, Detroit's leaders became concerned that conventions might be cancelled and reservations shifted to other conference cities. The American Psychoanalytic Association had booked the Statler Hilton, and the American Psychiatric Association (APA) had reserved the main convention facilities at Cobo Hall. Both reported receiving anxious enquiries from delegates, and a few late cancellations, but the Motor City did its best to project a business-as-usual attitude. A key item on the agenda of the forthcoming APA convention was fashionable and timely: the psychiatric effects of LSD.

Ann Arbor was the gateway to the LSD abuse in Detroit, and, predictably, it was John Sinclair who negotiated the first shipments. Sinclair frequently paid homage to the power of LSD in his jazz columns, and while his polemical writing style was often prone to evangelical overstatement, he was in every sense a visionary. In one column he argued that acid had the capacity to transform youth culture and make garage-rock bands like MC5 forces for social change. 'LSD was the catalyst which transformed rock and roll from music of simple rebellion to a *revolutionary* music,' he wrote in his book *Guitar Army*. 'The music was what gave us our energy and our drive, but it took the magic sacramental acid to give us the ideology which could direct that energy. Marijuana, which had come to us directly from black people and black musicians, in particular, had given us a start in this direction, but LSD opened the road into the future as wide as the sky and we were soaring.'

Although lysergic acid fascinated academia, it was the politically charged youth who were destined to become the public face of LSD, which meant in turn that the popular press would ensure it became a substance tainted by fear and exaggeration. The *Detroit Free Press* refused to run an ad promoting a new low-budget drug-exploitation movie *The Weird World of LSD*, which knowingly positioned itself as exploring 'the reefer madness of the '60s'. It was one of a spate of fast-turnaround films that sought to exploit public curiosity about hallucinogenic drugs. Nor was moral outrage uncommon. Detroit's hippie community had become politicised by civil rights, the Vietnam War and the corrosion of the city's industrial base, and it had access to a network of underground venues and magazines. LSD intensified this sense of resistance. Hippies might have been a joke elsewhere, but not in Detroit. Concerned about the political threat they posed, the FBI embarked on a three-year campaign of surveillance, declaring a cadre of Detroit hippies as 'potentially the largest and most dangerous revolutionary organisations in the United States'.

LSD was by no means unique to Warren Forest's revolutionary guitar army. Motown's Martha Reeves was hospitalised in the early days of LSD when, according to her version of events, someone dropped an acid tab in a glass of champagne she was drinking in a Detroit nightclub. In her autobiography she attributed her emotional breakdown to the drug, and at least partially blamed it for a hiatus from what was already another troubled and unhappy Motown group. Reeves believed that the experience had triggered a psychotic crisis and feelings of anxiety and entrapment, which Professor Walter N. Pahnke explained neurologically when he spoke to delegates at the APA convention at the Statler Hilton downtown. He described the negative effects of LSD as 'very intense, negative, dysphoric, and hellish by those who have been through it'. It was through the professor's academic research that the concept of the 'bad trip' entered the language of the mainstream.

Although Reeves confessed to abusing drugs many years later, the full creative impact of LSD did not affect Motown until much later in the dying days of 1967, when the term 'psychedelic soul' came into more common usage. Gordy was deeply resistant to the new development but came up against a determined advocate in producer Norman Whitfield, who was already pushing the boundaries of Detroit soul and had positioned himself as a restless innovator ambitious to win Gordy's approval and seize any opportunity to climb the Motown ladder.

By April 1967 John Sinclair and the Steering Committee had assumed yet another new identity. They were now a full-blown creative cooperative called Trans-Love Energies, which managed counterculture events across Michigan and published a network of small incendiary magazines such as the *Warren-Forest Sun* and the polemical *Guerrilla*, bearing the masthead 'A Newspaper of Cultural Revolution'. They were sold via radical bookshops by an army of high-school hippies and to the increasingly ecstatic audiences that flocked to the Grande Ballroom.

In the early days of April, Sinclair was mentoring a group of Detroit high-school radicals to help them edit and distribute their own underground newspapers using primitive printing presses at the Trans-Love Energies headquarters at the Detroit Artists Workshop at 4857 John Lodge. Among the most successful at the time were: *Kultur*, the unofficial newspaper of Grosse Pointe High School; *Yellow*, published by students from Diana Ross's school, Cass Tech; *Elevator*, published by students from Mumford High School, where musician Cornelius Grant and lyricist Rodger Penzabene had been classmates; and *Rank*, published by Thurston High School in Redford Township. There was clearly an orchestration of content. All four underground titles promoted a conference against the draft, a smoke-in event promoting illegal dope in Grand Circus Park, and the biggest event on the counterculture calendar, the forthcoming love-in scheduled to take place on Belle Isle on the last weekend of April and featuring the MC5. The student papers attracted the concerned attention of high-school boards across Michigan, and when the *Detroit News* reported that this new style of high-school newspaper was an unwelcome phenomenon containing 'vulgarities' and articles that were 'pro-marijuana and pro-free love', several schools informed the police and asked them to investigate.

It was amid this already heady mixture of drugs and disenfranchised youth that Detroit found a new antihero, Lawrence

Robert 'Pun' Plamondon, a charismatic young hippie who, like his hero Jimi Hendrix, relished his bastardised Native American roots and played up the image of being Michigan's ultimate voodoo child. Pun Plamondon was born in Traverse City, the illegitimate son of a 'half-breed Ottawa Indian and a long-distance operator'. He took pleasure in promoting an image of otherworldliness, but in fact he had been adopted into a respectable middle-class home by foster parents. Plamondon had been a restless and difficult teenager and ran away from home aged sixteen to retrace the steps of Jack Kerouac and hitchhike around the United States. He finally reached the West Coast, where he worked with migrant Hispanic farmers in Los Angeles, and a few years later Plamondon's winding travels brought him back full circle to Michigan and to the headquarters of Trans-Love Energies, where John Sinclair's holy barbarians greeted him like a long-lost prodigal son.

Plamondon arrived in Detroit in mid April 1967, when Sinclair was sharing his plans for the 'love-in' with a sceptical Detroit police. Sinclair was out on bail for drug offences and, in the eyes of the police, the most dangerous hippie in the city, but inexplicably he managed to convince the authorities that the event would be trouble-free, well-managed and good press at a bad time for Detroit. A moustachioed Italian-American police inspector named Anthony Bertoni was assigned to the role of liaison officer. He was a career cop who was credited with initiating Detroit's Tactical Mobile Unit (TMU), a brutal city-wide patrol force that frequently recruited ex-Marines into its ranks. Police officers nicknamed them *Bertoni's Commandos*, yet somehow Sinclair convinced the dubious cop that Trans-Love Energies could provide its own private security firm. With typical hyperbole, Sinclair boasted that it would be the world's first hippie police force, and he dubbed them 'the Psychedelic Rangers'. It might well have been that Bertoni was seduced by another so-called 'special force', but promises of peace and love proved to be fruitless. By agreeing to Sinclair's requests for a love-in, the Detroit police were about to make a catastrophic misjudgement that would not only taint their reputation but also deepen public concern about inner-city safety.

The police were blissfully unaware that Plamondon, a man who was destined a few years later to join the FBI's Most Wanted list, had arrived in the city ready to add even more anti-authoritarian zeal to a growing and combustible counterculture.

Youth culture was fragmenting into a mosaic of different tribes. Industrial Detroit had long been a biker town where decaying working-class neighbourhoods and the encroaching suburbs had spawned numerous gangs, among them the Justice Riders, the Road Agents, the Scorpions, and, on the East Side, one of America's most notorious biker gangs, the Outlaws, sworn enemies of the Hells Angels, and who used the slogan 'ADIOS' (Angels Die In Outlaw States). The Outlaws were established on Route 66 in Matilda's Bar in McCook, Illinois, southwest of Chicago. Membership was limited to those who owned American-made motorcycles and who swore allegiance to their logo, a skull and crossed pistons. By 1967 the gang had expanded rapidly across the United States, but their heartland remained in white-only neighbourhoods in the Midwest. Outlaw youth seemed out of control, and the publication of new statistics on sexual infection and venereal disease seemed to support an impression of promiscuity and lawlessness. According to figures from the US Public Health Service, Detroit had the fastest-rising rates of syphilis in the United States, with 900 current cases of infection, the highest since the invention of penicillin. Infection rates for gonorrhea were predictably higher among teenagers and running at double the rate of older adults. Dr Benjamin Schwimmer, head of the Detroit Health Department's Social Hygiene Clinic, argued manfully that the city's commitment to fighting sexual diseases had led to more effective clinical diagnosis and that this explained the rise, but it was only a whisper of sanity among yet more lurid headlines.

In mid April, as the weekend drew to a cold conclusion, a series of twisters ripped through the Midwest, killing fifty-one people and wrecking rural communities from Detroit to Chicago. A Chrysler spokesman reported that the twisters had wrecked the Plymouth-Dodge assembly plant in Belvidere, Detroit, 'opening it up like a can of tuna'. Tornadoes devastated the southern edges of the town of Owosso, Michigan, a farming community that sat incongruously between the giant motor plants of Detroit and Flint. A tornado tore through East Main Street where Motown's pressing plant, the American Record Pressing Company, was located, halting production of Marvin Gaye and Tammi Terrell's 'Ain't No Mountain High Enough', scheduled for release on Tamla the following weekend. Detroit was on the outer circle of the damage, narrowly avoiding the worst of the carnage, but there were fears of civil unrest, and the National Guard was mobilised to clear fallen trees and dangerous rubble.

The storms paralleled the growing turbulence at Motown. By the spring of 1967, four different factions were testing the management's patience at Hitsville. Discontent within the Supremes loomed largest, but the Funk Brothers were also complaining about being cut out of production credits and losing out to producers. There was some merit in their arguments. Many of the semi-improvised backing tracks that underpinned numerous Motown songs owed their inventive style to Earl Van Dyke and his band of studio brothers, but they rarely benefited from royalties. A third disgruntled faction was a clutch of less successful acts who felt sidelined, and since the end of 1966 some of them had held regular meetings at the home of producer Clarence Paul. A labour union of sorts emerged from those social gatherings, and they grumbled more loudly and lobbied for improved access to recording facilities. But when it came to profitability and the bottom line, it was a fourth pocket of discontent that was to prove most threatening to Motown. Holland-Dozier-Holland, the label's most successful writing team, had become resentful about the level of royalty payments and disillusioned that they had not been offered Motown stock and given a stake in the business. The previous twelve months had heightened their resentment. Along with John Lennon and Paul McCartney of the Beatles, Holland-Dozier-Holland was the most successful songwriting team in the world, and they felt undervalued. It was not a simple case of exploitation either. The music value chain was far from simple. Producers often resented the attention that the singers attracted; singers came to understand that the real money was in compositional credits, not in performing; and the management knew that records were not always hits, and that many recordings had to be cross-subsidised. At the end of that production chain were the Funk Brothers, making historic music for next to no reward.

The storms had subsided by the time Gordy flew to New York City in mid April to receive a national business award from the Interracial Council for Business Opportunity at the Biltmore Hotel in Manhattan. The award was presented to him by the bespectacled Rodman C. Rockefeller, the eldest son of former vice-president Nelson Rockefeller and trustee of the Rockefeller family fortunes. In his citation Rockefeller said, 'Mr Gordy has accomplished more than creating a leading recording and entertainment company. Besides fashioning a new dimension in American music with the Motown Sound, he has demonstrated the opportunities existing in business today and has inspired other young people to plan business careers.' It was a citation that meant a lot to Gordy – the commitment to self-improvement still rushed through him like adrenaline. He had been hardwired since childhood to seek success and often quoted the creed of his father's hero, Booker T. Washington, that the surest way for blacks to gain equality was to demonstrate 'industry, thrift, intelligence, and property', or, as Martin Luther King was fond of saying, 'taking their own steps on the staircase'.

By mid April, Martin Luther King was criss-crossing America, delivering a series of fiery and controversial speeches on civil rights and the escalating war in Vietnam. 'A nation that continues year after year to spend more money on military defense than on programs of social uplift is approaching spiritual doom,' he argued, having taken the risky decision to cross the Rubicon and oppose the war. It was at a landmark speech to a congregation at the Riverside Church in New York that King made his most public attack on American involvement in Vietnam. It came in advance of a month of anti-war protests across America, and a contingent from Detroit's Committee to End the War hired ten train coaches to carry them to New York for the rally there. King spoke eloquently and at times openly of Detroit and how it was losing out in the financial battle between social spending and the cost of the war abroad. 'Perhaps the more tragic recognition of reality took place when it became clear to me that the war was doing far more than devastating the hopes of the poor at home. It was sending their sons and their brothers and their husbands to fight and to die in extraordinarily high proportions relative to the rest of the population . . . So we have been repeatedly faced with the cruel irony of watching Negro and white boys on TV screens as they kill and die together for a nation that has been unable to seat them together in the same schools. So we watch them in brutal solidarity burning the huts of a poor village, but we realize that they would never live on the same block in Detroit. I could not be silent in the face of such cruel manipulation of the poor.'

Berry Gordy and his family instinctively understood King's importance to the black community, and back in 1963, upon the cajoling of his sister Esther, Gordy agreed that Motown would record King's speeches and release them on a commemorative album. At a podium in Cobo Hall, King recited his most famous speech in its original form: 'I have a dream this afternoon that one day right here in Detroit, Negroes will be able to buy a house or rent a house anywhere that their money will carry them, and they will be able to get a job . . . Yes, I have a dream this afternoon that one day in this land the words of Amos will become real and justice will roll down like waters, and righteousness like a mighty stream.'

Although he remained stridently committed to non-violence as a means of bringing about change, King predicted that violence was on the horizon. In the spring of 1967, he warned that at least ten cities 'could explode in racial violence this summer'. The prediction proved to be prescient and irrefutable; minor disturbances broke out in Louisville, Cleveland, Chicago, San Francisco, Nashville and Houston. Then in June, Boston and Tampa witnessed serious disorder, followed by historic riots in Newark, New Jersey, which led to twenty-five deaths and over 1,300 arrests. Despite a deeply fractured community spirit, many in Detroit were still convinced that no serious disturbances would occur in the Model City. Ironically, when public disorder did erupt, it came not in the turbulent ghettos but through the spectacular antics of the city's new left counterculture.

The death of George Overman Jr hung like a pall of smoke over the city. Within a day of the murder, the mayor's most persistent opponent, local demagogue and councilwoman Mary Beck, demanded his instant resignation and opened campaign headquarters in a vacant ice-cream store in northwest Detroit to mobilise support for having Mayor Cavanagh recalled. Detroiters were confused about what they thought. Some saw Cobo Hall as an asset to the city's business tourism, while others saw an urban jungle of walkways, entrances and loading bays that attracted urban criminals. Plans to make Cobo safer with tighter security and increased police patrols were too little, too late. And to confound the city's problems, a string of major concerts and conventions was imminent. Cobo was already advertising tickets for a Frank Sinatra concert in May, an exhibition fight featuring Muhammad Ali and a local Detroit heavyweight, Alvin 'Blue' Lewis, and most anxiously of all, James Brown and His Famous Flames were due to appear downtown in June. Brown was a combustible character who not only attracted noisy audiences of young black men but also had tentacles that reached into the darkest parts of the criminal ghetto, and many felt that heavy police activity in the streets would promote anxiety rather than quell it. Eleven teams of homicide detectives questioned thirty-five youths at addresses across the city, many woken in dawn raids, and some of whom were taken into custody in a showy act of desperation. The pressure on the police to make arrests came from the public, the press and from the mayor's office, where the increasingly stressed Jerome Cavanagh seemed no longer blessed with the good luck that had marked his inaugural years.

The Motown machine cranked on. After the delay in pressing due to the April storms, 'Ain't No Mountain High Enough' was finally available in stores on the Tamla label. Two days later the Funk Brothers improvised the backing tracks for 'I Wish It Would Rain', a song initially assigned to the singer Jimmy Ruffin but then reassigned to the Temptations. Then, over two successive studio days, the studio musicians laid down tracks for two subsequent releases by the Supremes, 'In And Out Of Love' and 'Forever Came Today'.

On Sunday afternoon, 23 April, Berry Gordy hosted a private meeting at his home that proved to be one of the most infamous moments in the history of soul music and a landmark in the disintegration of Detroit's most famous female group. It lasted less than an hour, but it determined the future of the Supremes and disfigured Gordy's reputation for ever. It was such a contentious meeting that it is impossible to separate fact from fiction, but most published versions of the events cast Berry Gordy in a dreadful light and portray Diana Ross and Mary Wilson as his accomplices in an act of personal treachery.

Strangely for a meeting of such significance, nobody is certain where it actually took place. Gordy has refused to talk about it, Ross has avoided the subject throughout her life, and Ballard's recollections were almost certainly clouded by deep personal disillusion. Only Wilson has reported on the meeting at any length, and long after it took place. The Supremes were back in Detroit recording at Hitsville and were scheduled to fly to Los Angeles later that month for a charity concert but they had not spoken or seen each other face to face for at least a week, and their last public appearance had been in Miami earlier in the month. The relative silence of the key witnesses has allowed other commentators to fill the vacuum with grand fictions. Almost all have chosen to locate the meeting in Gordy's grandiose new mansion on Boston Boulevard. But, according to Wilson, the meeting actually took place in Gordy's old home on Outer Drive, which he was about to give to his sister Anna and Marvin Gaye, and their newly adopted baby. The location matters in one significant respect – by placing the meeting in the grandiose Motown house, the setting has been used to 'psychologise' Gordy, conferring on him a cruel arrogance and dominance.

The mansion was audacious and epic in scale. It featured a traditional London pub, bedrooms painted in gold leaf, French chandeliers dangling from corniced ceilings, and a painting of Gordy dressed as Napoleon Bonaparte, which his sisters had commissioned as a family joke. But despite being tongue-in-cheek, in the minds of those who disliked Gordy, it was taken to be a symbol of full-blown megalomania. Numerous reports of the April meeting have been committed to print, and almost all of them mention the Napoleon painting – adding entirely fictional detail. Wilson has since described how she was late, probably arriving at the Outer Drive house around three o'clock on what was a chilly and blustery Sunday afternoon. Gordy was not working from a fixed script or clear plan. He improvised his way through the meeting, and for some inexplicable reason did not dismiss Ballard – nor, crucially, did she resign. There were no Motown lawyers present, no one to record the events, and no paperwork. Ballard, for her part, was defensive but not blind to her faults; she admitted she had been drinking on the road and suffered from bouts of loneliness and depression, and she admitted to taking time off, mostly by agreement but on other days without Motown's consent. Ballard was also aware that Marlene Barrow had stood in for her on several occasions, but the mention of understudies swung the meeting in a new direction, and Gordy improvised about big shows on Broadway and in Las Vegas hotels, where understudies were standard practice. He implied the system could be introduced for the Supremes, and soon after, Diana Ross referred to the idea of understudies on a network television programme when she praised the Broadway system, describing newcomer Cindy Birdsong as an 'understudy' – although, in a clumsy act of bravado, she claimed that she herself was irreplaceable. Throughout the meeting, Wilson said, Gordy was careful never to enrage Ballard: 'There were no insults or accusations; he knew better than to provoke Flo. She had a violent temper. It was clear that she just wanted to get it over with.' Maxine Ballard confirmed this: 'Flo told me that it was getting to the point where they couldn't be in the same room together without an argument or a fight. I knew if Flo got angry, someone was going to get an ass-kicking.' Ballard always admitted to having a fearsome temper, but although she had many fights with Gordy over the years, this was not one of them. As the meeting lurched from one scenario to another, she remembered Gordy saying, 'Florence, you're a millionaire. You're just twenty-four years old and you can retire any time you want.' Ballard interpreted this not as an option but as a coded rejection: 'I got the feeling I wasn't wanted.'

Cindy Birdsong arrived at the house around four and waited by the entrance. Gordy was by now improvising other outcomes, including Ballard taking an extended break from the group. 'Suddenly everything got tense,' Wilson claimed. 'I realized that Diana and Berry had come to this meeting not knowing what I was going to say or whose side I would take. For a second I thought to myself, "Why doesn't Flo speak up?"' But according to Wilson, 'Flo said nothing . . . Then I realized that Flo was waiting for me to rescue her, waiting for me to tell Diana and Berry how they mistreated Flo, and how wrong they were . . . While Flo no doubt would have appreciated me defending [her], she refused to defend herself. She wanted out more than anything else, and she knew that I knew it.'

Even her most ardent and committed supporters have struggled to explain Ballard's silence and so the meeting turned to what the other girls thought. Mary Wilson claimed in her memoirs: 'As I stared at Mrs. Ballard, I drew upon every ounce of courage I had. I loved Diana and I loved Flo equally, more than anything else in the world. But my two best friends had each taken a different course, and this is where it led . . . It hurt me, but I said, "Mrs. Ballard, Flo doesn't want to be in the group anymore. Yes, I want her in the group, but what can I do? She no longer wants us."' It was a short exchange that Florence Ballard took to heart. She was unambiguous in her condemnation of Mary Wilson, telling family members that she had been 'stabbed in the back'. Incredibly, she turned her anger not on Gordy or Ross but on the girl in the middle, later claiming that 'Mary alone was holding all the cards in her hand. She held all the power. Everybody in the room was just waiting to see which way she swam, and it ended up three to one.' That might have been how it was interpreted, but it was not how it felt. Wilson has always described feeling trapped, and painfully recalled that 'in those nine seconds I saw nine years of work and love and happiness fade away . . . With one look at Flo, I knew that dreams don't die, people just stop dreaming.' It was those words that inspired the Broadway show *Dreamgirls*, in 1981, and a subsequent feature film, a fiction that took the betrayal to new levels of mythology.

From the earliest snowbound days of 1967, Berry Gordy had resolved to replace Florence Ballard, but he did not set out to humiliate her or expel her from Motown. Despite Motown's global success, most of the artists who had left the company had either withered away or left of their own volition. Few, if any, had been sacked. In the early sixties, a small group of old-style R&B singers including Singing Sammy Ward, Hattie Littles and Gordy's old friend Mable John had left when Motown began to pursue commercial pop, and in every case their contracts simply expired. Ward continued to record locally, Hattie Littles spent time in jail after killing her abusive husband, and Mable John signed to Motown rival Stax. Berry Gordy's actions were a masterclass in managerial confusion. The meeting ended in confused silence rather than in fury. Wilson saw resignation on Ballard's part: 'Flo's response was frighteningly cold and distant. She was detached, yet seemed satisfied with the outcome. Flo and her mother left, with Mrs. Ballard in tears. I stood at the window and watched them get into Flo's Cadillac and drive away.'

No one was quite clear what had been agreed, if anything. Gordy had supposedly hinted at a solo contract as a sweetener, and Ballard certainly pursued the prospect in the following months. Wilson was even more confused: 'maybe she would be back; maybe she would not'. Securing Cindy Birdsong's release from her existing contract with the Bluebelles was proving tougher than anyone had imagined, and for a few ambiguous months in the spring of 1967, Birdsong was unsure whether she was a member of the Supremes, a short-term stand-in, or neither. It was not clear whether Birdsong was being groomed as Ballard's replacement or to occupy the role that Marlene Barrow of the Andantes had turned down. It is quite possible that when she arrived in Detroit, it was only as an understudy, but the messy realities of spring 1967 were not as powerful a story as the megalomaniac with a Napoleon complex, and so it became the preferred view of almost every subsequent history of Motown that Gordy had invited Ballard to his home as a final act of humiliation, for no other reason than to demonstrate his power. That impression stuck to Gordy throughout his long career but is almost certainly an exaggeration.

As the dramatic yet inconclusive Motown meeting drew to a close, homicide inspector Albert Schwaller led a Detroit police unit into a downtown home at 450 East Elizabeth, just north of Grand Circus Park. A search of the premises produced a brown-handled pocketknife believed to be the murder weapon in the killing of George Overman Jr. Detectives had been working on various leads and had quizzed several teenagers who were known to hang around the convention centre. Among the prime suspects were Larry Porter, one of thirteen children who lived in abject poverty in a rundown frame home at 3746 Crane near Mack Avenue, and a fifteen-year-old giant of a boy named Freddie Lane, who at six foot two towered above his fellow suspect. They were not at the same school, lived in very different parts of the city, and neither of the families had ever met. Their common bond was truancy and hanging around the periphery of Cobo Hall.

Although there was little doubt that Porter and Lane were the perpetrators, there was significant doubt about Lane's capacity to stand trial. For nearly two years, his father, Nathaniel Lane, had battled the Detroit school system to have his son declared mentally ill. At the time of the murder, Freddie had the mental age of a six-year-old and was enrolled in special-education classes at Garfield Elementary, he had been in trouble with the law repeatedly, and was known by other children to be easily led. Freddie Lane was not in a fit state to be interrogated as an adult, but mindful of their own exposed reputation, the Detroit police briefed local journalists that the boy had been chaperoned and that Judge James H. Lincoln of the juvenile court was present during a four-hour interrogation. The suspects were held without bond at the Wayne County Youth Home on East Forest. As Florence Ballard arrived home depressed from her hour-long meeting with Gordy, a message was radioed to all police patrol cars: 'Teletype 5509 fatal stabbing at Cobo Hall is canceled. Suspects in custody.'

Gordy hurriedly dressed to attend a black-tie function that night. He was a top-table guest at the annual hundred-dollar-a-plate dinner in aid of the Fight for Freedom Fund, an NAACP fundraiser that attracted the elite of Michigan's African-American community. Marvin Gaye was the headline act, supported by the Jimmy Wilkins Band, a local substitute for Earl Van Dyke's Funk Brothers. It had been a tense day for Gordy. Fidgeting and chewing at his tongue, he sat uneasily in the company of the mayor, the police commissioner, and the president of the UAW, Walter Reuther. A few yards away, holding court at the Gordy family table, was Pops Gordy, who flirted with Motown staff and shared cocktails with his daughters, entirely unaware that the showdown with the Supremes had even taken place. The speeches were long, self-serving and unduly formal, and none of the speakers broke with polite convention to mention the teenage trombonist who had died there only a few days before.

The next day the Supremes drove separately and wearily to the Motown studios. Meanwhile, the suspects in the murder of George Overman Jr were in custody, and the prosecutor's office was preparing to argue that, irrespective of his mental age, Freddie Lane should be tried as an adult. Harmony was in short supply. None of the musicians in the studio had been told about the events of the previous few days. All three girls attended the session and went through the motions but avoided each other, sitting apart in grim silence. It was unclear what the future would hold. Cindy Birdsong was still in the city, rehearsing dance routines and stage moves with the choreographer Cholly Atkins in the basement of Wilson's house on Buena Vista, thus compounding Flo's feelings of betrayal.

Office staff were making travel plans to fly the Supremes from Detroit to Los Angeles to perform at the Hollywood Bowl in a benefit concert for the United Negro College Fund. The day would have been consigned to insignificance had it not been for the travel arrangements: Esther Gordy told office staff not to reserve tickets in Florence Ballard's name and that Cindy Birdsong would travel in her place.

Towards the end of April 1967, and for one night only, the two great strands of mid sixties Detroit music met on the same stage when Motown group the Elgins were implausibly supported onstage by the holy barbarians of Motor City rock, the MC5. It was an unlikely encounter. The Elgins had only a couple of minor hits to their name, including the evergreen 'Heaven Must Have Sent You', and lead singer Saundra Edwards was heavily pregnant and unable to travel long distances. Restricted to local engagements only, Motown had hired the Elgins out to a student function at Wayne State University. The organisers had also independently booked MC5, whose rehearsal rooms were nearby at the Detroit Artists Workshop. It was the only time that a Motown act and Detroit's guitar-noise merchants played together on the same stage. The men of the headline act dressed in suits and bow ties, and the pregnant Edwards was resplendent in a stretchy nylon cocktail dress. They carefully managed their stage routines to protect her, and yet their support group, who had recently acquired $3,000 state-of-the-art Vox amplifiers powerful enough to shatter the eardrums of the respectful or the uninitiated, raged through the hall.

In the rooms above MC5's rehearsal space, a special edition of the alternative newspaper the *Warren-Forest Sun* was hurriedly being printed. It reported last-minute nerves about Detroit's forthcoming love-in. The police had given permission for the event, but hemmed in by recent teen murders, they were backtracking on promises and clumsily threw oil on already simmering fires. They launched another drug raid that focused on the perimeter of Wayne State University, the offices of Trans-Love Energies, MC5's rehearsal space and the homes of prominent anti-war radicals.

On the last Friday of April, a gig featuring the acid-rock band Seventh Seal was scheduled for the Wayne State campus, but it was disrupted when the university's security police refused entry to outsiders. Enfant terrible John Sinclair immediately moved the show to the Artists Workshop, but the relocated concert was further disrupted after bogus claims of a shooting within the building. When the police came to investigate the shooting, it was not the homicide squad that responded but Sinclair's nemesis, the Detroit police narcotics division. Yet again the underground community known collectively as the Steering Committee made the front pages of the Detroit press. Spooked by the negative publicity, commercial sponsors of the Belle Isle love-in grew nervous; on the eve of the event, Coca-Cola withdrew its offer of free drinks, and Hertz backed out of donating two rental trucks that were supposed to be used as makeshift stages. When MC5 eventually got up to play, the 'stage' was nonexistent. Instead they assembled their deafening speakers on grassy banks and improvised a performance area on the hillocks of a public park.

On Saturday, 29 April, the eve of the Detroit love-in, the Supremes were backstage at the giant Hollywood Bowl. Motown had hired a big band with a fifteen-piece string orchestra comprising some of the best musicians on the West Coast. Band leader Ben Barrett and L.A.'s premier saxophonist, Preston Love, were among their number. It was an unusually cold night in California, and the musicians complained of being exposed to the night air, but their discomfort was nothing compared to the chill among the Supremes. The new line-up was Diana Ross, Mary Wilson and Cindy Birdsong. Ballard was at home in Detroit and had vowed to sever all relationships with her former pals. The concert was a fundraiser for the United Negro College Fund (UNCF), an educational charity founded in 1943 by the great educator Frederick D. Patterson. By 1967 the UNCF had taken on a special status in the R&B scene and was a preeminent charity for celebrities, musicians and Democrats. In 1959, before his presidency, Senator John F. Kennedy had donated the proceeds from his Pulitzer Prize-winning book, *Profiles in Courage*, to the fund. The Gordys were major donors; so too was the soul crooner Lou Rawls, and Muhammad Ali became the fund's biggest single donor when he gifted $10,000 from the proceeds of his title fight with Ernie Terrell.

Motown had agreed to donate a scholarship to UCLA to be known as the Motown Scholarship for Musical Excellence. To maximise publicity, they agreed that the Supremes would headline at the fundraiser. When the idea was first hatched, it made perfect sense. Nobody could have predicted the emotional meltdown within the group, nor that it would mark Cindy Birdsong's debut performance as a member of the Supremes. Neither Motown nor the UNCF announced the winner of the 1967 UCLA scholarship, although one of the recipients of 'general educational support' was Lionel Richie, a teenage student at the Tuskegee Institute who had formed a campus group called the Commodores. The group signed with Motown soon after their graduation.

The Supremes shared the stage with Johnny Rivers, Buffalo Springfield, the Seeds, the 5th Dimension and fellow Motown singer Brenda Holloway, whom Diana Ross had previously blocked as a stand-in Supreme. Cindy Birdsong's debut concert was sponsored by AM radio station 93 KHJ in Los Angeles and came at the height of what was known as the Boss Radio era, a new and eccentric free-form style of broadcasting pioneered by DJ 'the Real Don Steele', who broadcast three hours a day to what he called 'the magnificent megalopolis of Boss Angeles', using the deliberately eccentric and obtuse catchphrase 'Tina Delgado is alive, *alive!*' KHJ festooned the stage at the Hollywood Bowl with Boss Radio paraphernalia, and Steele shamelessly plugged the show for days on end, blissfully unaware of the wrangling behind the scenes. No one was ever told that Ballard was missing or that Birdsong was her stand-in. The Supremes simply arrived, performed and left.

The night before the show, choreographer Cholly Atkins made a point of telling Diana Ross not to draw attention to either Ballard or Birdsong. The silence was inevitably misinterpreted back in Detroit as further evidence of conspiracy. Few people in the auditorium had a close-up view of the acts, so another well-worn myth emerged that Birdsong had been chosen as Ballard's replacement because she was a body double with the same basic shape as Ballard and so Motown in an act of cruel stinginess would not need to purchase new costumes. Neither assertion is borne out by fact. The Supremes sang a curtailed set and chose their own clothes for the outdoor arena. Diana Ross wore a lightweight coat, Mary Wilson wore a striped polo shirt and miniskirt, and Cindy Birdsong wore her own A-line dress. There were no wigs, no Supremes costumes, and no significant attempt to deceive. Many reviewers simply didn't bother to ask. The *New Pittsburgh Courier*, a major African-American paper that regularly promoted Motown shows, reviewed the concert assuming it was business as usual and published a stock shot of the three girls featuring Florence Ballard.

At the end of the concert, the Supremes were driven to a Hollywood fundraising party high in Beverly Hills, where Shirley MacLaine, Natalie Wood, Robert Wagner and father–daughter team Henry and Jane Fonda politely applauded their entrance. Jane Fonda was by now a committed opponent of the war in Vietnam and worked the room, talking at length to the Supremes. Again, no one mentioned the new line-up, nor was it raised. The next morning a shop on Rodeo Drive opened early to allow the Supremes to shop privately, and by mid morning they were at Los Angeles airport going their separate ways. Wilson and Ross flew back to Detroit, and Birdsong returned to Philadelphia to face the simmering rage of her own group, the Bluebelles, who had yet to agree to her departure.

Thousands streamed across McArthur Bridge. A few hopeful families were headed for the botanical gardens at Whitcomb Conservatory, but the majority were young people drawn by curiosity to the Detroit love-in. The band shell on Belle Isle was unexpectedly cordoned off that day, and despite promises made to the organisers, it had been rendered out of bounds. Temporary staging was unavailable, and up to twenty local rock bands improvised solutions all day. MC5, Billy C and the Shells, and Seventh Seal pirated power where possible and set up banks of speakers in raised clearings around the park. Crowds flocked around the bands in huddles, and hundreds climbed trees throughout the park to get a better vantage point. For the first three hours, hippie security force the Psychedelic Rangers, under the command of an untrained student named Bryan Collins, managed to contain the boisterous but largely peaceful crowd. Unfortunately for the city's battered reputation, a few sporadic incidents before dusk led to chaos. Members of the Outlaws, some wearing chains and Nazi memorabilia, sprayed beer on the crowd and chanted '*Zeig Heil*' at the hippies. The Outlaws drove their bikes threateningly at a crowd of acid-rock fans, scattering them. Police moved in to arrest the culprits, and bottles flew in the direction of the trouble. Within minutes a small-scale riot had erupted, and Detroit's riot-trained Tactical Mobile Unit was brought in to disperse the crowd. Lawlessness spread backwards towards the bridge, and the crowd – whether peaceful or angry, sober or drunk – was forced onto Jefferson Avenue, where cars were overturned, windows smashed, and property vandalised. It took the police two hours to contain the disturbances, and journalists who had come to the love-in, to file soft lifestyle features on the hippie phenomenon, suddenly had front-page news. 'Riot at Love-In; Ten Jailed' screamed the headline in the *Detroit News*. The blame was placed exclusively on the Outlaws, and although there were now strained relationships between the police and John Sinclair's 'holy barbarians', they both held to the same line: the hippies had come in peace, but the event had been hijacked by dark forces and motorcycle gangs.

An editorial in the *Detroit Free Press* thundered against the love-in: 'It was not the love which got out of hand on Belle Isle Sunday. It was the hate. The outcasts of a decent society, the organized motorcycle gangs like the Outlaws, revel in harm and destruction . . . The love-in was invaded by the greasy-haired, filthily dressed hoodlums who would probably come unglued in a bathtub. Instead of soda pop, pretzels and garlands of dandelions, they brought beer, wine, motorcycles and an itch for a rumble.' Yet again there were calls for Mayor Cavanagh to get tough on crime. Letters to the papers encouraged the police to be less lenient on the city's youth and their belligerent subcultures and for the hippies to join the real world. 'The truth,' the editorial said, 'is that this is the real world – a world of cars and industry and an economic system, a world of good people and a few bad ones, and the hippies are going to have to live in it.' Most commentators dismissed the love-in as part of a wider malaise of a society that had no respect for authority. Anticipating that the love-in would be a major success, another attention-seeking event for the following day was announced. Advertised as a 'smoke-in', it was a demonstration in support of the legalisation of marijuana to be held at Grand Circus Park in downtown Detroit. After the fiasco on Belle Isle, they hurriedly cancelled the event at the eleventh hour but news of the cancellation did not travel widely enough and gangs of hippies surrounded by nearly 200 spectators congregated to protest against Michigan's drug laws by smoking 'mellow yellow', a briefly fashionable 'drug' made from banana peels. Biochemists had helped the craze gain credence by publishing reports that scrapings from the inside of banana peels contained serotonin and norepinephrine, chemicals that were related to the hallucinogens in LSD. The name mellow yellow riffed on the colour of the peels and the mellow feelings the drug was supposed to induce. Like the Trans-Love Energies commune, the name had been borrowed from a hit record by the Scottish acid-folk singer Donovan.

As April 1967 drew to a close, the transient interest in smoking bananas reached its brief height. Michigan already had draconian laws forbidding marijuana use, laws that Sinclair himself had fallen afoul of, but as yet there was nothing on the books to ban bananas. Although hardened legislators were briefly distracted by the new craze, a comment in the New York counterculture magazine *The Village Voice* clarified the predicament facing law enforcement: 'What legislator would dare affix his name to the Banana Control Act of 1968?' No one did. And so the theatrical countercultural warriors of downtown Detroit smoked bananas until the month of May.

Detroit, I Do Mind Dying. An assembly worker at Chrysler's Automobile Plant,
Dodge Main, in Hamtramck, Michigan.

MAY

Strike

A peculiar illness dogged Detroit. The symptoms were similar to a heavy cold or influenza, victims felt listless and were unable to work, and doctors across the city were bewildered by the cause of this mystery virus. Detroit police officers had begun to call in sick in record numbers, having made the unofficial decision to use the symptoms of flu as a proxy for striking. Officers were contractually banned from withdrawing their labour but had stumbled on a unique form of protest: reporting unfit for duty. The virus became known locally as 'the blue flu', and while it mostly infected police officers and firemen, the contagion had also spread to one of the city's most famous singers, Florence Ballard of the Supremes.

Buffeted by criticism and struggling to cope with a rising crime rate, the Detroit police habitually looked inward, suspicious of outsiders, cynical about social change, and convinced that they had lost the battle for public respect. Recruitment posters described them as 'the beating heart of the city' but they were widely disliked and disrespected in numerous communities. Relationships between the police and city hall were at their lowest ebb too. Mayor Cavanagh rejected pay demands, and although the police were well paid compared to most manufacturing workers, lower-paid officers felt that their workplace was more geared to political expedience than to the victims of crime, and they persistently complained about feeling exposed when relatively small incidents across the city sparked out of hand. This was specifically true in the African-American communities, where a sense of social justice and civil rights had been ignited and where a generation of young and increasingly militant black lawyers encouraged teenagers to be more aware of their basic rights and to challenge the legality of street arrests.

Detroit's police force was ill equipped to fight an unwinnable war in the inner city, where crime, drug abuse and political restlessness were powerfully stacked against them. Most officers were white and often born into the job as the sons of police families, institutionally set in their ways and instinctively suspicious of social change. They had become embroiled in an intractable war with the eccentric hippies of Warren-Forest and Motown's generation of young African-American youths, and with no right to strike, the police often felt persecuted and disaffected. Many saw the blue flu as their only option.

In May 1967 the talk of strikes across the city increased, and the intricate supply chain that fed the automobile manufacturing plants was uniquely vulnerable to disruption. The Big Three car giants – Ford, General Motors and Chrysler – looked forward nervously to their annual salary negotiations in the fall. The manufacturers needed unbroken production schedules as 1968 model cars were made available to dealers, and the unions knew there was no more than a forty-one-day supply of cars. With a strike fund of $67 million, the UAW could close down the car plants for as many as ten successive weeks. The underlying health of the automotive industry was more vulnerable than the Detroit public fully grasped. Auto production was at its lowest level in six years, down 32.3 per cent from the previous year, mostly due to labour troubles, lagging sales and the paralysing effects of the winter storms. The cold weather was no longer an issue, so the source of the greatest unpredictability was 'wildcat' disputes, in which plants took their own local action irrespective of the UAW. A bitter dispute at the Fisher Body plant in Mansfield, Ohio, exposed the fragility of Detroit's manufacturing economy. Since the twenties, division of labour and the famous 'Fordist' manufacturing principles had given Detroit a reputation for industrial efficiency, but the supply chain of car parts and components was now disaggregated in plants across the Midwest, and the manufacturing chain had weak links. The wildcat at Mansfield showed that a break in one part of the chain could undermine the whole operation. Over twenty General Motors plants dependent on parts from the striking plant risked grinding to a halt, leaving 80,000 workers facing short-time work.

Motown was not exempt from Detroit's disputational culture. Since the departure of Mickey Stevenson in January, Gordy had been approached by numerous employees looking for higher wages, new deals or more advantageous positions. The approaches varied in tenacity. Some were content to joke and jostle with Gordy about their lot in life, others brooded malignantly in the background, and some were so persistent in their demands that it became their modus operandi. The Funk Brothers had appointed keyboardist Earl Van Dyke as their go-between. The balding well-built Van Dyke would approach Gordy and his Motown executives on a monthly basis about disenchantment in the studio. Van Dyke was widely respected by the less well-paid musicians at Motown and had engineered the corporation's first wildcat strike on April Fool's Day 1965, when Motown musicians refused to take the stage at the Odeon in Glasgow, on the Scottish leg of an ill-fated UK tour. Faced with the disastrous consequences of cancelling the show, Gordy capitulated and bundles of cash were drawn from a local bank and the strike abandoned. Although the flurry of threats quickly subsided, it bequeathed Earl Van Dyke with a formidable reputation among freelance musicians as someone who could bargain with Gordy and win.

At least in a superficial way, production at Motown had some similarities with automobile assembly plants. The African-American academic Suzanne E. Smith has used the term 'automotive' to describe Motown's marketing, citing as a representational highpoint a video in which a CBS television crew filmed Martha and the Vandellas singing 'Nowhere To Run' on the assembly lines at Ford's River Rouge plant. By 1965 Motown was commonly described as a hit machine, and journalistic comparisons with the Detroit car plants were routine. But the assembly line of soul had many underlying differences. Producers enjoyed significant creative freedom, and recording sessions shifted effortlessly from slow beat ballads to rousing gospel-inspired soul, from newly composed material to cover versions. Perhaps a more accurate industrial metaphor for Motown would be to describe the component parts of a song. The Funk Brothers often improvised powerful backing tracks that were used and re-used by different producers and engineers. The Andantes provided choral support and the vocal undercarriage to assist lead singers, and a string of accomplished baritone saxophonists, including Andrew 'Mike' Terry, the purveyor of the legendary 'bari tracks', delivered rasping support to many Motor City hits. All of these component parts came together to create music that is now instantly recognisable, but at the time it was assembled on the basis of who was available, how much studio time was allocated, and who had priority in the jealous hierarchies at Hitsville.

Motown songs often sounded similar, and some used the same backing tracks, but they were never identical, and so the profound difference that set them apart from the assembly lines of Ford and Chrysler was individual creativity. The singers, producers and musicians of Motown wanted to hear themselves in the music, and each song had its own distinctiveness and musical idiosyncrasies. Given this well-oiled and often ego-fuelled division of labour at Motown, it was inevitable that a strike would break out there too. When it came, it was a labour dispute that would change Motown for ever and strike a near-fatal blow to the very heart of the so-called hit machine. Holland, Dozier and Holland, the corporation's greatest producers, were on the verge of withdrawing their cooperation and refusing to write any more songs. It was a dispute that had yet to reach its final crisis point, but it was only a matter of time.

Towards the end of May, the Supremes had been contracted to perform at a series of universities in the Midwest. The shows were all in striking distance of Detroit, and although the semi-detached Florence Ballard had agreed to appear, Motown doubted her commitment, so Marlene Barrow of the Andantes was placed on stand-by. A more daunting task loomed: the Supremes were scheduled to return to the world-famous Copacabana club in New York City, where they now had a residency. The nightclub had been a crucial launching pad for them, but it carried painful memories, and successive appearances at the Copa between 1965 and 1967 had corroded the very soul of the group.

Everything about the Copacabana screamed glamour – the Brazilian decor, the celebrity clientele, the Manhattan ambience and the show-tune costumes. All came together to create a place of champagne and sorcery. According to showbiz legend, this was where a group of young and immature ghetto girls from Detroit were magically transformed into stars; it's a powerful myth but one that hides the tracks of a hundred tears. During a series of exhausting and tetchy rehearsals for their 1965 show, differences between Ballard and Gordy first erupted, and by their return residency in 1966 tensions between the two had become an open wound. The prospect of returning to a place of bad blood for a third time in the spring of 1967 was not something that anyone at Motown relished.

The Copacabana proved to be a place of severe emotional breakdown. The higher the social stakes, the more intensely controlling Berry Gordy became, and the bigger the risk of failure, the more the Motown machine ground the Supremes like a pressing plant. For three years the girls had been to hell and back on the road, and far from being a landmark in their glittering career, the Copacabana had become their metaphoric Vietnam, a place they feared rather than enjoyed. Since the fifties the Copacabana had been a well-known Mafia-controlled club, indirectly owned by Mob boss Francesco Castiglia, aka Frank Costello, and managed by his right-hand man, Jules Podell, who ran the club on a day-to-day basis. In the fifties Podell had operated a no-blacks policy, and while the ban on black artists and customers had fallen away with time, he remained cautious and unconvinced by the black music industry and sceptical that Detroit artists had the sophistication to cut it in Manhattan. Gordy described Podell as 'a cigar-smoking, gravel-voiced, no-nonsense wheeler-dealer whose reputation hinted at underworld ties'. They were pretty heavy hints too. Podell was a pugnacious Jewish businessman who ran the Copa on a mix of frenetic activity and chilling fear. He often screamed at imaginary staff, unleashing his frustrated and intolerant catchphrase 'I couldn't care less! Couldn't care less!' at walls, bar stools and people who were not even around to hear him.

Beneath the superficial glamour the club was grubby and lawless. It ignored fire regulations, flouted liquor laws and, by Gordy's own description, operated like 'a madhouse'. The whiff of Mafia connections gave the Copacabana a certain cachet with Manhattan's cool set, and when the Supremes first opened at the Copa the buzz that they attracted fuelled the fantastical rumour that Motown had Mob connections and that Gordy was in their pay.

Podell agreed to showcase two Motown acts a year, but only on the proviso that they were popular in the charts at the time and could bring an array of show tunes, current hits, and cover versions to the Copa stage. He was adamant to the point of obsession about one very specific contractual point: groups performing at the Copacabana were to appear with their original named members and not use stand-ins. This was to offset any perception that the Copa's well-heeled audience was being short-changed, or that sub-standard acts could show up and dupe the paying public. It was not a wholly unreasonable stipulation. Sending 'decoy' groups out on the road was common in independent soul music in the sixties, and by 1967 the long and dishonourable history of meeting multiple engagements with different line-ups of the same group was common practice.

An agreement signed with the Copacabana in the early days of 1965 required Motown to deliver the Supremes in their most famous manifestation – Mary Wilson, Florence Ballard and, as she was legally known, Diane Ross. The prospect of replacing Ballard with either a stand-in from the Andantes or with Cindy Birdsong was legally a non-starter, and so Motown was forced into another uneasy truce. Rather than default on its Copacabana contract, Gordy was forced to shift ground and send his sister to reason with Ballard at her home. She was coaxed back into the line-up and accepted the 1967 Copacabana residency and another key residency at the Flamingo club in Las Vegas in the summer. Far from following a cunning master plan, it now seemed that Gordy was making it up as he went along and that the new era of the Supremes had tipped into farce. Billboards along East 60th Street in Manhattan's theatre district were already promoting the return of the Supremes for a string of late-night supper-club shows between 11 and 24 May. Ballard was on the billboards, and to turn up without her was a material breach of contract that put payment schedules at risk. Podell had already hinted that he always punished acts that tried to pull a fast one.

Berry Gordy traditionally cleared the decks when the Copacabana residency came around and took executive control. He was a perfectionist whose relentless focus on detail sometimes bordered on autistic, and when major shows came around he insisted on rehearsing key moments over and over again, beating spontaneity out of performances. Gordy was a tough taskmaster, but he reserved his most severe criticism for his lover. Those who thought he was biased in favour of Diana Ross were also forced to acknowledge the intense pressure he heaped on her. Critic Nelson George described a fierce approach to rehearsal: 'Berry was brutal about little mistakes,' he wrote. 'Diana bore the brunt of his criticism, for it was she whom Berry had made the group's focal point. Diana was to carry the show, and when she didn't do it with the verve Berry desired, his temper would flare and she'd end up crying under his demanding gaze . . . It was carrot and stick with Berry and Diana, love and discipline, as he pumped and deflated her ego at his whim.' Gordy had expectations of Ross that he never demanded of the other two Supremes, and if he was a tyrant and bully – and many say he was – then the greatest victim was the woman he loved, not the woman he had come to distrust – Florence Ballard.

Under pressure to win over the mainstream, Gordy resorted to a preferred formula, stripping away Detroit's more urban and abrasive R&B sound and replacing it with glitzier show tunes, extravagant costumes and comedy routines. He insisted that current Broadway standards be included in the set, and it was agreed that one of the numbers would be 'People (Who Need People)', from the successful Barbra Streisand musical *Funny Girl*. It was a late decision. *Funny Girl* was on an extended run at the Broadway Theater near the Copa in midtown Manhattan and at the time was vying with *Hello, Dolly!* as musical of the year. It was agreed that 'People' suited Ballard's voice, with a second option that all three girls might share shifting lead vocals. 'As the recording date for the live album drew near,' Wilson recalled, 'we had to finalize our repertoire . . . Things came to a head when it was announced that Flo would no longer be doing her solo number, "People" from *Funny Girl* . . . We all suspected that Berry had taken the song from Flo, but Flo was thoroughly convinced of it and she was crushed.' According to Nelson George, Gordy had previously intervened when the song was being rehearsed. Ballard was four bars into the song when he supposedly shouted from the auditorium, 'Let Diana do it.' It was a wound that never healed. From that moment on, Wilson said, 'Flo regarded what was the highlight of her career as a disaster.' Although the song remained in the repertoire, it did not feature on the Supremes' subsequent live album, and while it fell out of fashion as a pop song and disappeared from their act, it hung around unpleasantly in the background, like an unresolved insult.

Gordy was a nervous wreck throughout the first Copacabana residency. Each night he sat close to the stage, taking notes and quietly mouthing the rehearsed introductions. 'If you don't know us, on the end is Florence Ballard. She's the quiet one. In the middle is Mary Wilson. And she's the sexy one. My name is Diana Ross.

I'm the intelligent one.' They sang the show song 'Somewhere', from the musical *West Side Story*, and towards the end Ballard was allowed to improvise some teasing comedy about money. It was a piece of harmless shtick that owed more to Broadway actress Pearl Bailey than to Detroit R&B, but it always got a polite laugh from the audience, and nerves settled again. Ballard was reduced to harmonising in the background as Diana Ross, a less naturally gifted singer, sang the lead vocals of 'People'. Gordy clumsily invited Cindy Birdsong to sit with him in the audience and watch the performance. Unnerved by her rival's presence, Ballard retreated deeper into herself and refused to travel in the group's limousine, preferring to be driven to and from the hotel in Tommy Chapman's Lincoln Continental.

In May the *New Pittsburgh Courier* ran an uncorroborated piece claiming that Ballard was on the point of leaving. Under the rhetorical headline 'Are the Supremes Ready to Break Up?', the story claimed to have been filed from New York and might have been from a rogue source who had witnessed the backstage events at the Copacabana. The story described a 'smoldering feud' and claimed that Ballard intended to leave the group after a series of scuffles with Diana Ross. Although the media were still two or three months behind the facts, Motown was losing control of the story. Al Abrams, who was personally close to Ballard and who by May was acting as a freelance publicist for Motown's Memphis-based rival Stax, had been leaking stories to the press to paint Ballard in a positive light and demonise Motown's management. He regularly told journalists that backstage tensions often flared because of Gordy's love affair with Ross. The rumours gathered pace throughout May and even began to appear in the normally loyal *Michigan Chronicle*. While the paper liked to trumpet its editorial independence, it was nervous about the advertising income it got from Motown, and to be sure that Gordy stayed faithful to the paper he had delivered as a boy, the *Chronicle*'s managing editor, Al Dunmore, took direct control of reporting favourably on Motown.

Around 15 May, Wilson and Ballard flew back to Detroit on a

short break and stayed at their respective homes overnight. Although Ballard later claimed that she felt betrayed by Wilson, a report in the *Michigan Chronicle* described them sitting together in the 20 Grand amid a celebrity audience invited to see Memphis double act Sam and Dave, whose short tour of the Midwest was being promoted by Al Abrams. The show had a tense symmetry. The Georgia-born act was famed for wildly energetic stage shows and tumultuous personalities. They earned the nickname Double Dynamite but from the mid sixties onward did not speak to each other offstage, and as their partnership worsened they travelled separately to shows, had separate dressing rooms, and rarely made eye contact onstage. Ballard and Wilson had not reached that level of distrust, but their friendship was profoundly damaged and their smiles on that night seemed contrived. Ed Perle, Motown's public relations director, was insistent that the night out was all about friendship and closed the book on any press suggestions that the Supremes were at war.

Towards the end of May, the Supremes embarked on another round of television engagements, mostly filmed by day and targeted at New York TV studios within striking distance of the Copacabana, where they sang nightly. They appeared as mystery guests on *What's My Line?*, recorded at the CBS Manhattan studios, and on 21 May they performed on *The Ed Sullivan Show* live from the Expo 67 Theater in Montreal, wearing flapper costumes and singing a medley of show tunes from *Thoroughly Modern Millie*, *Second Hand Rose*, and *Mame*. On 22 May, after a return flight from a show in Canada, Ballard made her last television performance as a member of the Supremes on NBC's *Tonight Show* with Johnny Carson, recorded at the NBC studios in Rockefeller Center. The Supremes performed 'The Happening' and two songs from the Copa residency, 'The Lady Is A Tramp' and 'Blue Moon'. It was a significant moment. Johnny Carson asked them outright on national television if it were true that they were breaking up. Diana Ross, by now always the nominated spokesperson, fielded the question: 'If all the rumors were true, we'd have six children and would've all been married six times.' It was a cute answer but untruthful. All three girls had sensed that this would be Florence's last network television appearance as a Supreme and that the clock was ticking on her relevance to Motown. Another bit of onstage detail spoke volumes: without any prior warning, Ross had decided to change her wig for the show, jettisoning the group's traditional waved wigs in favour of a short British Mod cut. Even in appearance the girls looked divided.

Johnny Carson's persistence took the Supremes by surprise. Thrown off by his questioning, Ross ended by admitting that Barbara Randolph and Marlene Barrow had already performed as stand-in Supremes. She finished with a response that has been held against her ever since. 'The show must go on,' she said, 'except for me. They can't stand in for me.' It was a crass response said nervously to cover her tracks, but it came across as arrogant, self-centred and humourless. Perhaps more than any other remark she ever made, it drove a stake into the heart of the group. Wilson said nothing but looked visibly surprised, and Ballard had given up caring.

Urban life became hotter and more volatile as the spring turned to summer. There was widespread political anxiety about unemployment in the inner cities and 900,000 young Americans were expected to drop out of formal education. President Johnson asked Congress for up to $20 million 'so that our country will not suffer this terrible loss in its human resources', but he was candid about another motivation: to head off the threat of riots in forthcoming summer months. The federal government launched a national stay-in-school campaign, and among a whole battery of Great Society task forces was the Youth Opportunity Task Force, a cross-country push to stimulate 10,000 new jobs daily. To ensure the job creation push touched all industrial sectors and gained traction in the inner-city ghettos, civil servant managers and Democratic Party activists approached independent soul labels across the United States to gain their buy-in. Motown still cared and made polite noises, but unlike Stax Records in Memphis and Ramsey Lewis's Ramsel Records in Chicago, the company was distracted by success and allowed its rivals to fill the vacuum. Stax ran a high-profile album campaign – 'Stay in School: Don't Be a Dropout' – featuring Otis Redding and William Bell, and jazz-soul pianist Ramsey Lewis – whose chart-topping instrumental 'Wade In The Water' had given him status in his hometown – pulled strings with the editor of the *Chicago Defender*. They partnered with Stay Cool Summer, a project that took music into the inner city and addressed widespread fears that Chicago's South Side was a powder keg and that social unrest was inevitable.

In a brief flurry of political campaigning and high-society networking, Stax shamed Motown. The vice-president and the secretary of labor, Willard Wirtz, endorsed Stax's project and attached Democratic campaign workers to promote the album by distributing 10,000 promotional copies to major record stores. According to government statistics, over 5,000 radio stations, 700 television stations and the influential Voice of America network all received a campaign kit, providing the rawer and less sophisticated Stax sound with an unprecedented promotional vehicle and a reputation for good corporate citizenship. The *Stay In School* album consisted of songs and public service announcements by Otis Redding, Eddie Floyd, William Bell, and Sam and Dave. One track featured a group discussion with Sam and Dave, Booker T. Jones, and the Detroit singer-songwriter Mack Rice, who had relocated to Memphis to pursue his career. It took the form of an unscripted bull session in which the Stax performers shared their reasons why ghetto teenagers should not give up on education. On the back of the album was an open letter from Vice-President Humphrey, which read:

> First, I want to commend the Stax/Volt family of recording artists for their special interest in trying to help yourself.
>
> These artists know the value of a good education and what it will do for you.
>
> By singing their songs and talking to you on this album, they are trying to give encouragement and direction to those young people who are struggling against hardship and difficulty. They are trying to make sure that you understand, fully, the difference an education will make in your life.

These artists know that the high school dropout is headed for disappointment and frustration when he tries to get for a job. He'll meet disappointment when he tries to get a good-paying job, and then face frustration when the job he finally gets does not last too long. Machines are taking over more and more of the unskilled jobs that the uneducated used to get.

Today's good jobs are going to young people who are educated, who have "brain power" and skills. The name of the game is this: *Those who learn more, earn more.* That high school diploma could mean the difference between a real future and a mere existence.

As you listen to what the talented Stax/Volt artists sing and say, make up your minds to complete your education. Remember, THOSE WHO LEARN MORE . . . EARN MORE! My young friends, that's where the action is!!!

Sincerely,

Hubert H. Humphrey

Stax seemed to have swamped Motown in the spring of 1967, reaching deeper into inner-city ghettos and securing more respect nationally. On 13 May newspapers carried lifestyle features on Otis Redding and Carla Thomas, promoting another simultaneous release, the *King & Queen* album, which featured hit singles 'Tramp' and 'Knock On Wood' and carried liner notes attributed to Republican senator Howard H. Baker of Tennessee, a former ambassador to Japan known in Washington circles as 'the great conciliator'. Stax launched the album at Washington DC's legendary jazz club the Bohemian Cavern, where Carla Thomas presented a gold record of *King & Queen* to Senator Baker and thanked him for his high-profile endorsement of Memphis and the Stax cause. Many of the connections with the political elite had been forged by Al Abrams, now closer to Stax and the embittered group of artists that felt undermined by Motown, among them his friend Florence.

Compared with Stax's federally funded national campaign, Motown's efforts were local and small beer. General Motors in Detroit had signed on to the government's job creation scheme and struck a deal with Motown that a song by the Temptations, 'Don't Look Back', could be used as a local campaign song. Gordy was not instinctively drawn to campaign songs, believing that great pop was about love and affection and rarely about politics. His instinctive conservatism, which he had proudly inherited from his father, not only edged him away from being overtly political but also made him nervous about the growing creative power of the counterculture. He discouraged several efforts to draw Motown artists into the impending Summer of Love, and in late May 1967 his sister Esther, four foot ten and notoriously bossy, was by then the de facto chief operating officer of the company. She had been approached by the organisers of the Monterey Jazz Festival, who invited Motown artists to play at the open-air concert in California. Monterey was already a West Coast institution and predated the rise of counterculture by a decade. In 1958 Billie Holiday and Louis Armstrong headlined at the festival, and each successive year became an international showcase for jazz and blues musicians, but by 1967 Monterey was diversifying into rock and featuring some of the stand-out bands of sixties counterculture, including The Who, Jimi Hendrix, and the Mamas and the Papas. Motown's Smokey Robinson and members of the Beatles had joined a hastily convened international committee, but arrangements were chaotic and communication abysmal. The Kinks were invited but could not get a travel visa and Donovan was refused entry due to drug charges. Despite Smokey Robinson's pleas, no major Detroit artists agreed to play at Monterey. It was not entirely due to stubbornness either. The organisers had left decisions until painfully late, and most of the names they wanted were already contracted to other major shows.

Gordy had no great desire to compromise. He was not a fan of the hippie cult, a reluctance partly informed by the disturbances at the Detroit love-in, but more instinctively he had a hunch that hippie festivals were destined to be either troublesome or fraught with bad publicity. Time was to prove him wrong. Monterey went on to become a significant success and a landmark showcase for new music. With the clock ticking and only two weeks remaining until the festival, Monterey producer Lou Adler gave up on Motown and turned his attentions to Stax, immediately securing the services of Otis Redding, who was so eager to appear he cancelled an operation on polyps on his throat. Monterey was the making of Redding, and his mesmerising performance, driven by the southern fatback sound of back-up band Booker T. and the MGs, propelled him to international stardom. Onstage at the Monterey County fairgrounds, Redding simply said, 'So this is the love crowd?' before cranking into a set that ranks among the greatest in the history of R&B.

Back at 1300 Beaubien, the police department was in internal melt-down: morale was low, and widespread absenteeism was endangering law and order. Detroit's 4,000 officers had to police a city of 139 square miles, and community concern about police brutality did not help. There was intense anger about the so-called Big Four police cruisers, which according to contemporary news reports had 'a Gestapo-like image' in the eyes of the black community. There had been fifty-seven homicides already in the first six months of 1967, but a clear message was being missed in tangled police data: the black citizens of Detroit were more likely to be the victims of crime than their white counterparts. Mayor Cavanagh launched a high-profile recruitment drive within the black community, arguing that 'the roots of crime overlap the roots of poverty'. The mayor was right, but it was a subtle sociological point easily drowned out by the noisy clamour for tougher policing. Beleaguered by the simmering resentment they faced in the street, many older police officers drawn from the city's Polish, Ukrainian and Eastern European communities began to stay home from work. Officer James Radke made headlines when he defied a senior officer and refused to accept an assignment in the city's notorious Livernois Precinct, a 6.5-square-mile area north of Motown's West Grand Boulevard, because he was required to drive a police car alone in a ghetto neighbourhood.

James Brown's much feared concert at the Cobo Hall was packed to the rafters, and a heavy police presence circled the downtown area. Typically, Brown had arrived in Detroit with a bang. Only a few days earlier, an attempt had been made on his life when a gunman broke into the singer's motel room at the Ramada Inn near Chicago's O'Hare Airport. The would-be assassin was arrested, and Brown arrived in Detroit under a cloud, with rumours circulating that the incident had been provoked by the Godfather of Soul's two great weaknesses: money and sex. Although he was an egotistical and morally questionable character, Brown was at the height of his ability to influence the mood of the ghetto. He had been a leading figurehead in soul music's Stay in School campaign and the previous summer had released 'Don't Be A Dropout'. He was a tireless performer addicted to attention and dependent on raucous applause; a showman first and social pioneer a very poor second. 'I visited schools and talked to kids,' he said. 'I told them to stay in school, listen to their teachers, and stay close to their books. They were there to take care of business. I told them about my own background, and I think that made it more vivid. If I hadn't been blessed with musical ability . . . I'd still be a janitor.'

A small number of police officers had threatened to boycott the James Brown concert. In part their actions were a mark of respect for Officer George Overman Sr, whose son had been stabbed to death at the venue. Those who followed through on their threat called in sick, claiming to be too ill to work. By mid 1967 the number of police officers stricken by blue flu had risen to 847 and was running at a rate of about twenty per cent of the force. The Detroit Police Officers Association (DPOA) announced that 300 officers had been stricken by the blue flu one day, 500 officers the next day, and 1,000 the next – a strike by proxy. The police department got tough and ferried police vehicles to take the 'sick' to medical examinations, and they issued an order that officers declaring themselves ill must report for medical examination at their precinct station. Commissioner Girardin suspended 186 officers; the DPOA retaliated by filing a suit against the city for harassing police officers. The straight-talking Girardin said characteristically, 'That was a bastard thing to go through. I was practically helpless. I couldn't force them to work.' Girardin made good on his threats. As the blue flu escalated, he asked for the state police to be on call and for the National Guard to be on emergency stand-by.

As the police used indirect means to strike, the car plants in Detroit were more militant. In May of 1967, the Big Three car companies were increasingly nervous about the annual set-piece negotiating with Walter Reuther's UAW. Faced with a record 7,500 union grievances and 200,000 skilled workers wanting a raise of at least thirteen per cent, there was scant room for agreement. Management was reluctant to admit that the manufacture of 1968 models was at an all-time low. Ford vice-president Lee Iacocca predicted a nine-million-car year but admitted that a strike would blow that prediction 'sky high'.

The UAW had its own problems too. It had become overly fixated with annual set-piece negotiations and was increasingly out of touch with the white heat of the furnaces or the assembly plant floors. The union leadership was nearing retirement age, while more than forty per cent of the membership they represented was only thirty years old. Senior union officials were not always aware of the day-to-day resentments of racism in the workplace, where poisonous chemicals, deafening noise and punishing schedules could trigger fist fights and walkouts. Into all this came 'speed up', the system that was designed to increase productivity by either speeding up the assembly line or forcing manual staff to work relentlessly to keep up. More than any other issue – even pay rates and working hours – it was 'speed up' or the conduct of a bullying foreman, who was often drawn from the ranks of the city's Eastern European immigrants, that divided workplace Detroit and provoked the greatest number of wildcat strikes.

The local blues singer Joe Lee Carter never found great fame in music. He was a friend of Florence Ballard's father, but both were dwarfed in the Detroit blues scene by their contemporary, John Lee Hooker. Carter's music was too raw and 'old-fashioned' to attract the attention of Motown, and his era had come and gone when urban renewal tore down the old Hastings Street slums and

Detroit's freeways were built. Carter recorded under the name Joe L. and released a frantic blues song, '(I'm Not Gonna Be) Worried', on the Clissac label, long forgotten until the B-side, 'Please Mr. Foreman', touched a raw nerve locally and was brought to the attention of the UAW by a local indie-soul producer and long-time Gordy rival, Mike Hanks. The song attracted some popularity within the union movement and was subsequently used by the League of Revolutionary Black Workers in a film protesting against poor working conditions. It told its story of an auto worker ground down by the noise and exhausted by 'speed up'. Fearing for his safety as the heavy-metal noise of the assembly line gathers pace, the worker pleads to the foreman for mercy. The song contains a short, poignant lyric that has since passed into the social history of Detroit – 'I don't mind working but I do mind dying' – and as the pace of strikes in the late sixties gathered, the otherwise obscure blues song became a wildcat rallying cry. The slogan 'Detroit: I Do Mind Dying' became one of the enduring statements of the era.

A new generation of young black workers were organising, often beyond the reach and reference points of traditional labour unions, and strikes erupted in almost every industry. A movement called DRUM (Dodge Revolutionary Union Movement) began mobilising in Chrysler's Hamtramck assembly plant – colloquially known as Dodge Main – a plant that reflected the faultlines alienating Detroit's black majority from the police. Over seventy per cent of the workforce at Dodge Main was black, while the lower-managerial positions and the contentious foreman roles were almost entirely dominated by older Polish-American workers whose behaviour stubbornly inhibited the local union, UAW Local 3, from resolving problems around plant safety. In the absence of support from mainstream unionism, it was inevitable that Detroit's wildcat warriors would take their own action.

Towards the end of May, the Detroit press announced that Ali would fight in Detroit. An exhibition bout was to be held at Cobo Hall, and although there would be no title at stake, the fight was scheduled at a truly important moment in the young boxer's life. Ali had threatened to refuse the draft, and the Detroit fight was scheduled to take place only days before his army induction deadline in Houston, Texas. In another bizarre twist, the man Ali would fight was a local heavyweight with his own story to tell. He was a career criminal incarcerated in Jackson State Penitentiary. The authorities had agreed that he could be released under secure escort to fight Ali. A mood of restlessness and tense expectation was beginning to grip the Motor City, and although the weather remained mild, the prospect of a long and hot summer was all but inevitable. A self-confident young black man known simply as 'the Greatest' was coming to Detroit.

The Greatest in the Motor City. Muhammad Ali training at Brewster Recreation Center prior to his exhibition bout against local Detroit heavyweight Alvin 'Blue' Lewis. The fight took place a few days before Ali was stripped of his titles for resisting the war in Vietnam.

JUNE

War

Muhammad Ali arrived like a messenger from God. He had agreed to fight a two-hander against Orville 'Baby Boy' Qualls, a six-foot-six heavyweight out of Omaha, Nebraska, and Alvin 'Blue' Lewis, the most talked-about Detroit heavyweight since Joe Louis. The exhibition fight was scheduled for 15 June at the Cobo Hall, and as Ali trained with local sparring partners his lawyers were engaged in a bigger fight with the US military, which aimed to conscript the champ to fight in Vietnam.

Brewster Recreation Center was spartan and the heat unbearable. The thermostat was kept as high as hell to crank up the heat; condensation drizzled from the rusting ceiling pipes and dripped down on the speed bags and the urine-coloured canvas. Master trainer Luther Burgess barked out orders as fighters lurched from side to side. Some went there to avoid school, others to dodge the army recruitment teams, and others because they couldn't stomach working night shifts at the River Rouge plant. It was a place to avoid work and Vietnam.

In the first week of June, the Supremes were out of town, halfway through a two-week residency at the Shoreham in Washington DC, a luxury hotel in the city's embassy district near Rock Creek Park. The Shoreham was an up-market and well-connected venue that had played host to presidents and inaugural balls, a far cry from the Howard Theater in the 14th Street ghetto area – once dubbed 'the largest colored theater in the world' – the place where the Supremes had performed only three years earlier. The girls sang by night and networked by day, heading north of the beltway to visit the Walter Reed Army Hospital, where they entertained GIs and were photographed with bedridden soldiers and amputees recently returned from Vietnam. They doubled back later the same day for another photo op, this time with Vice-President Hubert Humphrey. Gordy went with them to hand over a donation to fund a swimming pool at Frederick Douglass Houses, a local government housing project in DC.

On 11 June 1967, the Supremes performed their final show in Washington and flew back to Detroit for a fleeting visit and to lay down vocals for a forthcoming release, 'In And Out Of Love'. There is no record that they ever made it to the studios, and if they did it was a brief visit to ensure the vocal tracks were laid to tape; Holland-Dozier-Holland used the Andantes to do vocal overdubs, a pragmatic decision, but with Ballard still hanging on to her probationary role, the session fuelled fanciful theories that Motown was trying to airbrush her from Motown history.

Boxing was in Detroit's blood, and Muhammad Ali's arrival could not have been more timely. Ali was due to fly to Houston a few days later to attend court for refusing the draft, and much of his time was taken up with legal meetings, briefing sessions with the Nation of Islam, and discussions with his management team, who were busily juggling several lucrative offers for Ali to defend his title for what would be the third time that year.

Wherever Ali went, he brought chaotic theater with him. His downtown suite at the Sheraton Chrysler Hotel was pandemonium. The phone rang incessantly; corridors were crowded with journalists, hangers-on and spiritual advisers; and camera crews assembled outside, hoping to capture the excitement of his visit. Ali's conversion to Islam had outraged the boxing establishment and put him on a collision course with authority. Unknown to Ali and his confidants within the Nation of Islam, local FBI field officers were assigned to follow him throughout his stay. They occupied nearby rooms in the Sheraton Chrysler and watched Ali clandestinely from a distance. It was not their first intrusion into the world of Islam. The FBI in Washington DC now had voluminous files on the Nation of Islam dating back to 1942, when Elijah Muhammad and his son Emmanuel Kareem were charged with sedition for failing to register for the draft during the Second World War.

Ali was eulogised in the street and castigated in the press. His FBI files described him as 'the great mouth' and often cast him as a now familiar ghetto stereotype – the arrogant young black man who would not conform. The noise and fuss surrounding his arrival raised the temperature in an already volatile city. There was concern that Ali could become a target for protests or even assassination, so the Nation of Islam kept the hotel suite downtown to host press briefings but took occupancy of a 'safe house' in northwest Detroit, moving into a detached villa at the intersection of West Buena Vista and Petosky Avenue, a short walk from Mary Wilson's home and adjacent to the home of the irrepressible Diamond Jim Riley, the would-be boxing promoter, self-publicist and local record producer. Diamond Jim knew Ali of old, and they were frequently seen around town together, Riley acting as a flashy host, insinuating his way into Ali's entourage and imposing himself on the boxer. When Diamond Jim escorted Ali into the 20 Grand, the MC, Ziggy Johnson, stopped the music and paid homage to the champ. Even the jaded house musicians knew they were in the company of greatness and broke out into spontaneous applause.

June 1967 was supposed to be a turning point in the Vietnam War, but it proved to be the contrary. President Johnson had once predicted that this was the month the war would end, but it was an ill-judged hunch founded on false hope. American forces in Vietnam had reached 385,000 in number, and an additional 60,000 sailors were stationed offshore. More than 6,000 Americans had been killed in the previous year alone, and on a daily basis throughout 1967 the Michigan press reported ever more casualties. June had hardly begun when a group of Detroit Marines fighting with the Fourth Infantry Division was attacked on a reconnaissance mission in the Central Highlands of Vietnam. Melvin Leroy Shields, Joseph Calhoun, Paul Domke and Emmanuel Fenech all lost their lives in the dense jungles of Pleiku Province. New recruits were being drafted daily at army recruitment centres across Detroit, some of them strategically positioned outside the car plants, targeting the underpaid, the bored and the disillusioned.

Ali had travelled to Detroit with his girlfriend, Belinda X. Boyd, a seventeen-year-old devout Muslim girl he had met at the University of Islam and whom he would marry two months later. Dressed in a pure white jilbaab, she cut an impressive figure. Teenagers swarmed around Ali as he ate in a Muslim restaurant near the Linwood mosque. Others sparred with him on the corner of LaSalle, imitating his trademark jive talk. Few young people had money to spend on tickets for the exhibition bout, and some young blacks had been discouraged from going to the area around Cobo Hall after recent violence. Policing was high-profile, and the mayor had instructed the city to install security cameras to deter crime.

For the Nation of Islam, the most important part of Muhammad Ali's rushed itinerary was not so much the fight itself but a photo session at Temple No. 1, the most venerable of Detroit's Muslim temples. Temple No. 1 could trace its origins back to the Great Depression and to the elusive W. D. Fard, the founder of the Nation of Islam. Although it had had various locations across the years, like C. L. Franklin's church, Temple No. 1 had relocated from Detroit's old Black Bottom ghetto and was now situated on Linwood Boulevard. Malcolm X had been a regular speaker there, and now the most famous Muslim in the United States – a boxer, celebrity and visionary – was about to grace it with his presence. Ali was an unlikely symbol of resistance to the war. His brushes with the military dated back to 1960, when as the teenage Cassius Clay he registered for the draft with Selective Service Local Board

47 in his native Louisville. Nearly four years later, a month before he fought Sonny Liston for the heavyweight championship of the world, Clay was ordered to attend a military aptitude test at an induction centre in Florida. He had not been specifically singled out. Like many young men of his generation, he was part of the military's general trawl of likely recruits, a victim of random bureaucracy rather than of racism or collusion. Despite the fast-talking style that had earned him the nickname the 'Louisville Lip', Cassius Clay had a low IQ and poor literacy skills. He failed the military test and was officially classified as 1-Y, unqualified for military service. 'I said I was the greatest, not the smartest,' Ali joked years later, but his failure to meet even the most basic levels of literacy hurt him deeply and led to years of ostentatious overcompensation. He frequently portrayed himself as a street-smart thinker and demeaned his boxing rivals as thick or slow-witted. He nicknamed Sonny Liston 'the Ugly Bear', and the counter-attacking style he used to snare over-zealous opponents became known as 'rope-a-dope'. One by one, talented boxers like Liston, Ernie Terrell and ultimately Smokin' Joe Frazier (whom Ali called 'the Gorilla') were mercilessly taunted for their stupidity or their political conformity.

Ali's poor educational accomplishment was significant in another key respect. Recruiting officers regularly toured Detroit's inner-city ghettos under what was known as Project 100,000, an initiative introduced by Secretary of Defense Robert McNamara to provide remedial education for potential recruits, particularly those that who been rejected for failing to meet the army's mental aptitude requirements. In Vietnam they were cruelly nicknamed 'the Moron Corps', and when they entered combat there was a clear racial dynamic. Forty-one per cent of those recruits were black, compared with only twelve per cent in the armed forces as a whole. It was a scheme with a built-in social bias and one that some Black Power radicals described as 'state-sponsored genocide'.

Although he failed his first aptitude test, Muhammad Ali was never shy about his ability in the ring. 'I am the astronaut of boxing. Joe Louis and Dempsey were just jet pilots,' he once boasted. It was a remark that divided opinion, especially in Detroit, where Joe Louis was as close as a human ever gets to being God. Ali's style and ghetto spontaneity made him popular in the projects, but that was in marked contrast to the cooler reactions of the cognoscenti. The fight authorities had yet to embrace the vociferous excitable young champ, and his conversion to Islam had shaken the conservative world of boxing to its core. Columnist Jimmy Cannon of the *New York Post*, a gifted writer who had once described boxing as 'the red-light district of sports', despised Ali. He described Rocky Marciano as 'a rose in a garbage dump' but could not find words to endorse Ali and considered him to be a coward and a draft dodger. Cannon saw Ali's draft evasion as symptomatic of the sixties and refused to call Ali by his Muslim name. In one diatribe he wrote off not just Ali but an entire generation: 'Clay is part of the Beatle movement,' he wrote scathingly. 'He fits in with the famous singers no one can hear and the punks riding motorcycles with iron crosses pinned to their leather jackets and Batman and the boys with their long dirty hair and the girls with the unwashed looks and the college kids dancing naked at secret proms held in apartments and the revolt of the students who get a check from Dad every first of the month and the painters who copy labels off soup cans and the surf bums who refuse to work and the whole pampered style-making of the bored young.'

As the sun burned down on Detroit's decaying trees, events were crowding in on Muhammad Ali. Secretary McNamara agreed to a reclassification of the criteria for military service, and as a result Ali was reclassified as 1-A – 'fit for military service' – and his previous failures were consigned to the past. He was instructed to report for induction in Louisville. Lawyers managed to delay the date and shift the venue to Houston to allow Ali to prepare for his fight with Zora Folley, but by the time the delayed date for his induction approached, Ali had become more critical of the draft and more outspoken about the integrity of the war itself.

Ali argued that he was a conscientious objector and not a coward, but he had run out of road, and the military set a final and non-negotiable date for his induction. On 28 June 1967, after his

Detroit fight, he was required to report to the armed forces examining and entrance station on San Jacinto Street in Houston to be inducted into the US military. The Houston centre processed 440 inductees a month, all bound for Vietnam. Outside on the sidewalk, a small posse of one hundred protesters gathered in support of Ali, one carrying the smartass placard 'Draft Beer, Not Ali'. Another young black demonstrator, risking immediate arrest, set fire to his draft card and held it aloft to the cheering crowd. Inside, names were duly called out in alphabetical order and, inevitably, the name Cassius Marcellus Clay was announced. Ali stood rigidly still, and when it became clear he would neither acknowledge the name nor step forward and accept the draft, a navy lieutenant escorted him to a room further down the hall and informed him that he had committed a felony by breaching the Universal Military Training and Service Act. Ali acknowledged the charge but again refused to acknowledge his name and was invited to agree a statement. Already infamous for saying 'I ain't got no quarrel with those Vietcong. Ain't no Vietcong ever call me a nigger', he agreed to a more restrained statement. It read: 'I refuse to be inducted into the armed forces of the United States because I claim to be exempt as a minister of the religion of Islam.'

Muhammad Ali's refusal to fight in Vietnam threw boxing into chaos. The New York State Athletic Commission, the British Boxing Board of Control and the European Boxing Union all agreed to strip Ali of his titles and that an elimination contest would be the best way to determine a new world champion. On the list of contenders were Ernie Terrell, Floyd Patterson, Philadelphia's Joe Frazier, Canada's George Chuvalo, and Germany's Karl Mildenberger. An outside possibility was Detroit's top heavyweight, Alvin 'Blue' Lewis.

Lewis had been raised in the now bulldozed Black Bottom ghetto and was the recent product of America's brutal prison life. He had done time in Jackson State for murder and armed robbery, but by 1967 he was a partially reformed character who had played a critical role in stemming a prison riot. The governor at Jackson

State had repaid Lewis by agreeing to early parole on the basis of his promise as a boxer, but early release in itself did not disguise Lewis's fearsome record for violence. He had committed over one hundred armed robberies and seriously injured a man who later died of his head injuries. Even in the context of Detroit's epidemic crime rates, the charges against Lewis were frightening. At the age of seventeen, he was jailed for twenty to thirty-five years, and on his arrival at Jackson State he joined two of his brothers who were already incarcerated. Although both of Lewis's brothers were hardened street criminals, Alvin Lewis was turning his life around. He was already on the sparring circuit of the elite heavyweights, and his rock-hard hands and orthodox style had taken him to the Detroit Golden Gloves championship.

On the morning of Thursday, 15 June, Alvin Lewis woke early. He did some light training in Palmer Park and shadowboxed in the gym. The hard work was over and it was now down to self-belief and luck. In a moment of supreme showmanship, Muhammad Ali called Lewis into the ring. His unmistakeable voice rang around the Cobo Hall, and his charismatic boastfulness rattled from the walls. It promised to be a fight of contrasts. Not since Ali fought Sonny Liston back in 1964 had the champ encountered such a lawless street fighter as Lewis. Ali was always a more technically sophisticated fighter and had risen through the tutored ranks of the US Olympic team, but Lewis was ghetto hard man and unlikely to be beaten down. Moreover, he was focused and Ali was distracted, his mind drifting to the draft, to Vietnam, and to a possible prison sentence. Both fighters wore headgear, but it was never likely to be a training session.

A firecracker erupted behind Ali's corner when his name was announced, and screeches of support backed Lewis noisily throughout. Bizarrely, Lewis had two quite separate sets of supporters within the arena – local street gangsters who had grown up with him in Detroit and, incredibly, two rows of Jackson State prison guards who had travelled to see their inmate take on the most famous boxer in the world. When Lewis was a teenager, his local street gang had used a shrill whistling sound as a gang signifier. It sounded a bit like a frightened crow, and when he entered the ring Detroit teenagers let out piercing cries in homage to their fighter. It was a blood-curdling noise that momentarily confused Ali and one that few outside the Brewster Projects would even have understood. Lewis fought hard, delivering a series of body punches, and while the judges narrowly favoured Ali, Lewis had forced his way into contention for the future.

The following day's papers were hostile to Ali's stance on Vietnam. Al Stark, a staff writer for the *Detroit News*, was unforgiving. He saw Vietnam in every shuffle, and although he had not been at the ringside, he vividly described the encounter: 'But it was enough for the crowd . . . to see the perfectly formed muscles in the young champion's back and legs uncoil so swiftly his opponent could only gape. Shrapnel does terrible things to young muscles, and no one likes it when a hand grenade or a mortar shell explodes. The pieces of metal are made white-hot by the explosion and they cut deeply into young bodies. Shrapnel gouges out chunks of flesh. It leaves scars on the head, where hair will never grow. It rips and kills.' Stark's report was the first of many that would taunt Ali, contrasting his protests on the home front with the harsh reality of war. The FBI continued to monitor Ali around the clock as he toured campuses and spoke out against the war. His movements were tracked and his phones tapped, and his hectic travel schedule involved a relay of FBI field officers. In Atlanta, agent R. R. Nichols, who was in charge of the local field station's wiretap unit, intercepted a series of phone calls between Ali and Martin Luther King in which they discussed the boxer's legal predicament, his conversion to Islam, and their shared opposition to the war. King recommended that Ali make contact with a close associate, the Chicago-based lawyer Chauncey Eskridge, who acted as legal counsel for King's Southern Christian Leadership Conference. (Fatefully, Eskridge would be with King on the balcony of the Lorraine Motel in Memphis on the day in April 1968 when King was assassinated.) Ali and Eskridge signed an agreement that took them on a long journey to the US court of appeals, where Ali's status as a conscientious objector was finally resolved.

The war was beginning to expose uncomfortable demographic truths on the home front. By 1965, when the war had yet to peak, African-Americans already accounted for at least twenty-three per cent of the enlisted soldiers who were killed in action. Only eight per cent of personnel who served within the borders of South Vietnam were classified as black, but over 12.1 per cent, or 5,711, of casualties were African-American. Although statistics can tell multiple stories, there was an increasingly settled perception that young African-American men were now disproportionate victims in Vietnam, and the anti-war movement cultivated the impression that young and often uneducated black youths were being used as 'cannon fodder'.

Concern spread throughout Motown, where many staff members had family in Vietnam. G. C. Cameron, destined to return and become the lead singer of the Spinners, was serving in the Marines, and Mary Wilson and Diana Ross both had brothers on active duty. Ross described her brother Earl Fred Ross Jr as a man racked by self-doubt: 'Many of his friends were dying of drug addiction either in Vietnam or when they came back, and he had lost faith in nearly everybody. It was sad to see what had happened to him. We used to send him letters and packages with little things we knew he missed, like mustard . . . He wrote us about how scared he was and how his friends kept dying over there. He was afraid of people he wasn't supposed to be afraid of – other Americans, especially some of the officers. He felt he couldn't trust them.'

James Franklin 'Frankie' Boyce, a band member with the soul harmony group the Parliaments, was another victim. The Parliaments were another set of local hopefuls led by the eccentric George Clinton and at the time were enjoying some small-time national success with their song 'I Wanna Testify' on the local Revilot label. Boyce signed up for military service on its release and within a little more than year he had died at the Battle of Dak To in a place *Time* magazine described as 'the jungled peaks and malarial valleys of the central highlands', where 'the triple canopy of jungle foliage shadows the ground in a perpetual, skyless twilight'. Frankie's guitar was sent home with his body, and among his personal effects were the lyrics to an unrecorded song, 'Soul Soldier'.

African-Americans bore a heavy burden of bereavement, and the deaths of three graduates from Detroit's Northwestern High School brought the story to Motown's doorstep. George Dorsey Jr had graduated from Northwestern two years earlier and was opposed to the war but believed it was a matter of duty and honour to fight in Vietnam, and so on his graduation he joined the First Squadron of the Eleventh Armored Cavalry. He was a point man for his patrol in Tay Ninh Province when he noticed an abandoned bicycle lying in dense brush. Suspecting a guerrilla ambush, he returned to warn a second patrol and was killed in cross-fire. Ironically, at the time of his death he had been receiving medication for eczema and a severe skin allergy to jungle vegetation and should have been on medical leave. Dorsey was awarded the Purple Heart for valour, and his body was shipped back to his adopted sister, a member of the Women's Army Corps. He had been a popular student at an inordinately special school. Northwestern was one of the biggest and best of Motown's many talent academies across the Detroit school system. Mary Wells was a prominent member of the Northwestern Choir when Dorsey first attended the school there; James Jamerson, one of Motown's pre-eminent session guitarists and a legendary member of the Funk Brothers, had studied at Northwestern in the late fifties; at least two of the Temptations, Otis Williams and Melvin Franklin, also attended Northwestern; and the affable and gigantic keyboard maestro Richard 'Popcorn' Wylie was also a graduate. Wylie had been a Motown employee in the company's early years but left after a dispute over money to pursue an independent career as a writer and composer, releasing a bizarre novelty hit, 'Rosemary What Happened', on Ollie McLaughlin's Karen Records out of Ann Arbor. It was an answer song to Roman Polanski's film *Rosemary's Baby* and dominated Detroit radio stations in 1968 when the Mia Farrow movie was showing in cinemas nationwide.

As the coffins returned, grief deepened and anger rose. A twenty-year-old named Jeff Currethers was shot by sniper fire and died on arrival at the Eighth Field Hospital in the coastal town of Nha Trang. Currethers had also attended Northwestern and been one of the throng of local kids who hung around the streets to watch Motown stars arriving to record. But it was the return of the dead body of a third Northwestern graduate that had the most impact on the city's independent soul music scene. David Riley had served an apprenticeship as a sound engineer at a local independent studio but was conscripted to Vietnam and killed in Quang Tri Province in the fading days of Operation Prairie, an incursion against the North Vietnamese Army just south of the demilitarised zone.

Riley was the son of Diamond Jim Riley. A long-time Motown competitor who had been releasing R&B music in the city since the late fifties, Diamond Jim was in many ways a hip-hop character before his time. He owned bars, a restaurant and the Diamond Recording Studios on Linwood, and was a crime-hardened businessman who had earned money as a pimp and a street extortionist. Few, if any, had seen him cry until he buried his son. Initially Diamond Jim refused to accept the news from Vietnam. The military had made mistakes before, so he wrote to local congressman John Conyers, hoping against hope that the information was incorrect and that the army had made a catastrophic blunder. It was false hope. An official telegram from General Wallace Greene, the commander of the Marine Corps, was hand-delivered to Riley's townhouse on West Buena Vista. Seeing the evidence with his own eyes, Diamond Jim wrecked his home in an uncontrollable rage, collapsed in inconsolable grief and spent the next few days, eyes rimmed with red, liaising with the Marines and planning a full military funeral. Although the incorrigible Riley was disliked by many, the local R&B scene stood as one, and the cream of Detroit music turned up at the funeral to pay their respects. Riley continued with his old swaggering ways, but a shaft of vulnerability had eroded his tough-guy credibility, and his threats no longer carried the same bravado. A few years later, Riley was shot to death in a nightclub dispute. His son had died a dead hero on a foreign field; Diamond Jim died on the floor of the Mozambique jazz club on Fenkell Street, the victim of his own ego and criminality.

Detroit's unique geography made it a terminus for those evading the draft. By the summer of 1967, newspapers carried stories of military personnel going AWOL. Some portrayed the absent servicemen as cowards; others saw their escape as a legitimate act of protest in the face of an unpopular war. Many young people hid out in Detroit, awaiting their chance to disappear across the Ambassador Bridge to Canada and beyond US jurisdiction. At least 50,000 crossed the bridge, and a further 100,000 escaped abroad. Detroit was a staging area with historic symmetry. It had been the last station of the Underground Railroad, the network of people and places that assisted black fugitives to escape from slavery.

It was 1970 before Motown broke ranks and recorded a Vietnam song that was unambiguously critical of the war. Producer Norman Whitfield recorded an album track with the Temptations simply called 'War'. It attracted the attention of progressive DJs across the country, but Motown shied away from releasing it as a single. Determined to give the song greater prominence, Norman Whitfield and Barrett Strong co-opted a relatively unknown local singer, Edwin Hatcher, better known by his stage name, Edwin Starr, whose declamatory and throaty voice reinvented the Vietnam soul song. The unambiguous hook – 'War. What is it good for? Absolutely nothing!' – made the song an instant and evergreen hit.

Edwin Starr's raw and emotional protest song came with the shock of the new, but nothing music could conjure up came close to the self-immolation protesters engaged in as they made the ultimate sacrifice to denounce the war. It was a statement that would be replicated across the world, from South East Asia to Detroit. In 1963 a group in Saigon celebrating the birthday of the Buddha was dispersed by police gunfire, and a woman and eight children were killed fleeing the scene. Enraged Buddhist leaders asked for volunteers to commit suicide as an act of defiance, and a sixty-six-year-old Buddhist monk named Thich Quang Du volunteered. He sat down in the middle of a busy Saigon road surrounded by nuns who then poured gasoline over his head and set him alight. 'As he burned,' an eyewitness said, 'he never moved a muscle, never uttered a sound, his outward composure in sharp contrast to the wailing people around him.' The following year another five Vietnamese monks had committed suicide in acts of self-immolation. And then, suddenly and dramatically, the trend moved to Detroit.

On 16 March 1965, an eighty-two-year-old German immigrant and peace activist by the name of Alice Herz set fire to herself in the Motor City, pouring cleaning fluid on herself and igniting her body. Passers-by tried to beat out the flames, and she was taken to the hospital in a critical condition. She told emergency workers, 'I did it to protest the arms race all over the world. I wanted to burn myself like the monks in Vietnam.' She died of her injuries ten days later. Herz's daughter Helga, who worked at Detroit's public library on Woodward, claimed that her mother's act 'wasn't mental derangement or a psychological compulsion' but 'an idea about the need to do something that would call attention to the gravity of the situation'. Prior to her death, Herz had confided to a friend in Detroit's extensive pacifist community that she was tired of conventional protest. She had marched peacefully, written letters to the press, and picketed politicians, but she felt driven to set fire to herself to make people understand the depth of her feelings. Others followed. Norman Morrison, a father of three and a devout Quaker, immolated himself outside the Pentagon after he had read an article about the destruction of a village by napalm. Morrison had brought his infant daughter with him to witness his suicide. A *Newsweek* report described his death as a 'macabre act of protest [that] almost included the sacrificial murder of his baby daughter'.

Thomas Davis was a child of Motown who had grown up on Detroit's East Side and was unemployed. When a letter arrived instructing him to report for the draft, Davis went AWOL. Like many escapees he had nowhere to run and no grand plan, so he drifted back to his old haunts. He became embroiled in a fight with his elder brother at the family home. Davis's brother tried to convince Thomas to surrender to the military authorities, but he refused, and as the fight escalated he grabbed an axe and tried to smash through the walls of the house. At the height of his rage, Davis lit a match and turned himself into a human torch, then ran at his brother and tried to embrace him in the flames. By the time the police arrived, the young escapee was dying on the sidewalk on Iroquois from third-degree burns. A thirty-nine-year-old mother followed suit. Inez Mathews left a suicide note for her husband, used a hose to douse herself in gasoline, and then set fire to herself in a parking lot at Grand River and Fenkell. She was rushed to Mount Carmel Mercy Hospital in a critical condition, and although she survived, it had not been her intention. Mathews had failed to cope when her husband was conscripted – and she was not alone.

Paradoxically, it was neither a battlefield death nor a dramatic suicide by burning that drove the real discriminatory cost of Vietnam home to the African-American community. It was the quiet storm of local churches, many of which congregated around the case of a local boy, Ronald Ward, a former football star at Eastern High School who had won a scholarship to Kentucky State before being drafted to fight in Vietnam. In June 1967, he jumped from a helicopter in a routine combat operation and injured his foot. He was given medical attention on his return to the Long Binh military installation, home to over 50,000 troops. Ward was convinced his ankle was broken and refused to return to combat. He argued with a senior officer, then returned to duty, but when the pain overcame him he disobeyed orders and took a troop helicopter back to base, effectively going AWOL. Ward was charged with cowardice and taken to the notorious Vietnam Installation Stockade, an army prison designed to house criminals and drug abusers. The stockade at Long Binh was nicknamed Camp LBJ, a contemptuous dig at President Johnson, and was run along segregated lines; black inmates stayed huddled together, separated from white prisoners, and the guards were faced with the unpleasant task of managing what was in effect a system of penal apartheid. Those like Ronnie Ward who kept their heads down served their sentence at Long Binh; those who rioted were taken back to the United States in handcuffs to the US Disciplinary Barracks at Fort Leavenworth, Kansas.

Ronnie Ward wrote a letter home that was published in the *Michigan Chronicle* and ignited indignation and disbelief back in Detroit. 'Poppa you just don't know what we being treated like here,' he said, describing conditions so primitive and racially divisive that they might have been from the chain-gang era of the Deep South. It was a moving letter from a son to his father, but it also exposed the inherent cruelties of the stockade. Racial tensions were worsened by overcrowding. The stockade had been built to hold 400 inmates, but by the time Ward was taken there, sometime in June 1967, the facilities housed nearly 700. Each prisoner had originally been allocated seventy square feet of living space, but by 1967 it had dwindled to around thirty-six square feet. Blacks represented ninety per cent of the inmates. Solitary confinement was in an area of the camp nicknamed Silver City, a row of converted shipping containers where temperatures often exceeded 110 degrees.

Ronnie Ward's father was no ordinary man. The Reverend Samuel Ward was one of Detroit's best-connected pastors, a friend of Aretha Franklin's father, and a cousin to his namesake, the former Motown vocalist 'Singing' Sammy Ward, one of the old-school R&B singers who had been purged by Motown in the early sixties. Ward belonged to the social elite of black achievers that the great civil rights leader W. E. B. Dubois had once described as 'the talented tenth', that vanguard of well-educated blacks whose mission was to challenge racism in all its forms. Ward Sr was a self-assured man who was undaunted by authority and spoke with an eloquent dignity. He rejected every explanation the army presented to him and threatened to take his son's case 'all the way to Washington' with the support of US congressman John Conyers Jr.

Independently Congressman Conyers had also been in touch with the parents of deceased Northwestern High School graduate George Dorsey, who had been forced to return to battle while incapacitated with an extreme skin condition. Conyers believed that black GIs were dying in combat at twice the rate of whites because of institutional bias in the armed forces. Dorsey's mother joined the gathering indignation and talked of rampant racism in Vietnam. 'We have received information that when Negro boys are considered to be "smart alecks" or "big mouths", sometimes they are sent out on a field mission as punishment,' she told the *Michigan Chronicle*. 'It's too late to save my son . . . [but] maybe it will save some other boy from getting killed just because he talks back to a white man.'

While Dorsey's family mourned his death, Ronnie Ward was holed up in the Silver City solitary confinement block, accused of desertion in the face of the enemy. Ward's congregation raised $600 to employ a local white attorney, Ernest Goodman, to fight his case. Goodman had a reputation for civil rights and had defended six leaders of the Michigan Communist Party charged with conspiring to teach and advocate the overthrow of the US government. He travelled to Vietnam, where he found himself up against the uncompromising heat of the military. Making the best of a bad situation, Goodman managed to fend off the most serious charge of desertion, but Ward was found guilty of disobeying a commanding officer and sentenced to two years' imprisonment.

In mid June the Supremes flew to the West Coast to honour a long-standing contract to perform a residency at the Cocoanut Grove in Los Angeles. Simultaneously, Motown had also agreed to a side contract with White House aides that on the final night there, the girls would be rushed through the late-night Los Angeles traffic to perform for the president, who was in town on a fundraising visit. A week before their presidential engagement, Diana Ross had laid down the lead vocals for the song 'Forever Came Today' at Motown's L.A. studios, and on the following day Mary Wilson and Florence Ballard drove to the studios to record background vocals. Ballard had taken to ignoring Ross if she caught sight of her in their hotel and Motown were forced to warn the singers about decorum in front of the president.

On Friday, 23 June, President Johnson was the guest of honour at a $500-a-plate President's Club dinner at the Century Plaza Hotel. Local radicals had anticipated the visit, and a coalition group of students and pacifists were mobilising 50,000 demonstrators, predicting 'the biggest antiwar demonstration in history'. Fearing for the president's safety, his aides abandoned the traditional police motorcade and put in place secret plans to land LBJ at the rear of the hotel via helicopter. Protesters gathered at the nearby Cheviot Hills Recreation Center to hear Muhammad Ali and Benjamin Spock give emotional speeches. As dusk fell, the demonstrators began the mile-long march to the president's hotel. Although they had secured a legal permit to demonstrate, a last-minute injunction from the Santa Monica Superior Court forbade the protesters from stopping at the hotel entrance. As the streets surrounding the Century Plaza became jammed, the sheer volume of marchers made that an impossible condition, and one of the largest security forces ever gathered in California laid siege on the crowd. More than a thousand police were present, and a brutal riot erupted. As the violence flared, Air Force One descended into Los Angeles International Airport at 7.30 p.m. On board were the president; his wife Lady Bird; nine leading congressmen; a small hand-picked group of presidential staff; and an even smaller press corps. Agent Thomas 'Lem' Johns of the Secret Service stayed close to Johnson throughout. He had been in Dealey Plaza in Dallas when President Kennedy was assassinated, and now had the special role of shielding the president.

LBJ was putting the final touches on an unpopular announcement; he had received recommendations from Secretary of Defense Robert McNamara and General William C. Westmoreland requesting further investment in troop numbers. By now the United States had 470,000 active service personnel in Vietnam, and the president was about to announce another 45,000. The extra troops threatened to take the fiscal budget soaring beyond $8.5 billion. Johnson faced the perfect storm: a deeply unpopular war, the prospect of increased taxation to fund its expansion, and a $29 billion budget deficit, the biggest since 1945. They were, according to the president, 'hard and inescapable facts'. The omens were not good. A three-page ad in the dinner's commemorative menu had been bought by opponents of the war. It made uncomfortable reading for LBJ: 'As of this date, we eight thousand Democrats of Southern California are disassociating ourselves from you because of your conduct in the war in Vietnam.'

At 10 p.m., comedian Jack Benny stood up to host the dinner, and at 10.30, less than twenty minutes after they had vacated the Cocoanut Grove, the Supremes took to the stage. Diana Ross thanked the president, and as she blew him a trademark kiss, protests raged outside. FBI agents and the Secret Service prepared for a hurried and ignominious presidential departure via the back stairs and a waiting helicopter. Johnson hurriedly asked for autographs for his daughter Lynda, and by 11.45 p.m. the president was back at Los Angeles International with his closest aides in the conference room of Air Force One. It had been a disastrous day.

The anti-war protest smouldered into the night as the Supremes returned to their suites high above the damage below, unclear about the war and what they had come to represent in the eyes of many black people. It seemed to some that they appeared to live in a bubble of fame, increasingly out of touch with the new militancy in the black community and the rising fury of their hometown. Many years afterward Mary Wilson defended her support for the president as a choice they made for positive political reasons. 'Though we had never met him,' she wrote, 'we were impressed by his social policies, especially in the area of civil rights, so we were happy to help him.' It was a post-facto rationalisation. The forces of liberal protest, including many of black America's civil rights activists, were outside the hotel protesting while the Supremes were inside, seemingly backing the war.

Muhammad Ali was never a great fan of the Supremes and rarely spoke kindly of Motown, but he said enough to friends to leave the impression that the Supremes had sided against him over Vietnam. Ali had no great relationship with Berry Gordy either, and although their paths crossed on the ebony achievement circuit, they were never close. With Chauncey Eskridge leading his defence, Ali finally won his battle with the US military, but only on a legal technicality. Case law determined that to qualify as a conscientious objector, three basic tenets had to be met: opposition to war, religious conviction, and a deep abiding sincerity. Taken together, Supreme Court judgements required Ali to meet all three. 'He must show that he is conscientiously opposed to war in any form. He must show that this opposition is based upon religious training and belief. And he must show this objection was sincere.' Paradoxically, it was the first tenet that caught the Nation of Islam and Muhammad in a bind. Ali was opposed to the Vietnam War, but according to the government's legal team, he was not opposed to war 'in any form'. His religion – and the teachings of the Koran – required him to wage war against unbelievers and to embrace the concept of holy war, and his appeal nearly collapsed on the interpretation of a single word: jihad. It was a term known only to a narrow constituency of people, a word whose time had yet to come.

Finally, after intense legal wrangling, a technicality came to Muhammad Ali's rescue; the law had not been specific enough about which of the three tenets they were finding against, and so they lost. It was a victory narrower than anything Ali had achieved in the ring, but however grimly won, it allowed Ali to return to professional boxing. Within a year of the judicial outcome, he was defending his world championship yet again, this time in Dublin's Croke Park, the home of the Gaelic Athletic Association. By another bizarre coincidence, his opponent then was Alvin 'Blue' Lewis, the Detroit prisoner whom he had last seen in the ring in June 1967.

On Friday, 23 June 1967, Detroit woke up to another racial crisis. A twenty-seven-year-old black army veteran named Danny Thomas was murdered near the city's Rouge Park while trying to protect his pregnant wife from a gang of white youths. Thomas was a Vietnam veteran who had returned to work at Ford after military service and was out walking with his wife in the parklands that skirted the principally white suburb of Warren. Over the course of an hour, the couple was tracked, insulted and harassed by a gang of Polish-American youths who had been holding a kegger in the park's incongruously named White House. The gang chanted 'niggers out' and threw stones and bottles at the couple. Frightened off by the gang, the couple tried to seek refuge in a locked picnic shelter but found they were trapped with no escape route. Guns were drawn. Danny Thomas was shot dead, and his pregnant wife miscarried on the spot. Police arrested gang leader Michael W. Palchlopek and an unnamed teenager for the murder, although his accomplices walked free when the traumatised wife could not identify them in a police line-up. The episode led many in the African-American community to distrust not only the fairness of law enforcement but the disrespect shown to returning black war veterans. Those two anxieties were to resurface with catastrophic consequences a month later as the heat of summer intensified.

June ended with blistering sun and volatile rhetoric. Detroit's second annual Black Arts Convention began on the last Thursday of the month and the keynote speaker was Daniel Watts, editor of the revolutionary magazine *Liberator*. Watts was a Columbia graduate and a suave architect with the Park Avenue firm Skidmore, Owings and Murrell; he was also a man who defied stereotypes. New York's *Village Voice* described him as a man who appeared to have 'a martini in one hand and a Molotov cocktail in the other'. Unlike his fellow guest speaker H. Rap Brown, the hardened civil rights activist, Watts was smooth, emollient and capable of mixing in any company. Brown by contrast was a proven firebrand. His address to the assembled delegates was characteristically emotional: 'Let white America know that the name of the game is tit for tat,' he hollered, a fist held symbolically in the air, 'an eye for an eye, a tooth for a tooth, and life for a life . . . Motown, if you don't come around, we are going to burn you down.'

Those rebellious words turned out to be the most prophetic words the city had ever heard.

On Guard. Armed officers of the Detroit Police and Michigan National Guard took to the streets in a vain attempt to quieten the rebellions of July 1967.

JULY

Riot

By midnight on Tuesday, 26 July, Detroit's skyline was scorched red with burning gas fumes. The writer John Hersey described it as 'a night of hallucinations', a moment when all the worst visions of urban crisis came frighteningly to life. They said it couldn't happen to Detroit, but it had. A ball of confusion swept through the Motor City, and the local music scene came face to face with forces it was powerless to contain. Sixties soul would continue its bittersweet journey for many years to come, but something happened in the brutal month of July that changed Detroit's image for ever and weakened its once majestic grip on music.

Four-year-old Tanya Blanding would normally have been in bed by midnight, but the relentless screech of sirens and the rasping flames were keeping her and her family awake. It was already several hours after curfew when a tank occupied by the Michigan National Guard took up position in front of the Blandings' second-floor apartment at 1756 West Euclid. The young family had obeyed the public service announcements; their curtains were drawn and the room was in semi-darkness. Only a very small flicker of light could be seen from the street below. It was a fatal flicker. Tanya Blanding's teenage uncle had lit a cigarette in the darkened room, and a National Guardsman below thought it was a gun discharging. Believing he was about to come under sniper fire, Sergeant Mortimer Leblanc fired the first shot, and his colleagues followed suit. Bullets tore through the window and ripped into the apartment walls. Tanya was killed instantly when the gunfire burst through her chest as she crawled up towards the window. Her twenty-one-year-old aunt, Valerie Hood, had her arm nearly severed at the shoulder as the room filled with screams. Tanya Blanding was the youngest and most tragic victim of a riot that had brought Detroit to its knees. In an unscripted instant, marred by mistake more than malice, a beleaguered white Guardsman from the Michigan suburbs had killed a black child from the ghetto. The Detroit police issued a statement shielded by the language of bureaucracy: 'The little girl's death was regrettable.'

The dramatic events had begun three nights earlier in the vacant premises of the Economy Printing Company, a bankrupt business in a rundown industrial building at 9125 Twelfth Street on the intersection with Clairmount. Undercover officers from the Detroit vice squad had attempted to enter the premises of what was known as a 'blind pig', the local colloquialism for an illicit drinking den or speakeasy. It was a term that dated back to Prohibition days, when the infamous Purple Gang controlled Detroit's illegal liquor trade. The derelict printing company offices were being used as a makeshift community centre run by the United Community for Civic Action, and the building that had once housed low-cost industrial printing presses had been transformed into an unlicensed blues and soul club, one of a network of drinking dens clustered near the Strip, a neon-drenched red-light district on Twelfth Street.

Law enforcement required that vice squad officers were not only to gain entry but also to provide evidence that illegal liquor was being sold on the premises, so most blind pigs in the vicinity were well fortified. At first the officers masqueraded as out-oftowners, claiming to be members of a Cincinnati basketball team, but the doorman rumbled their story and refused entry. Rather than argue, the vice officers discreetly moved on, returning hours later. It was in the dying hours of early morning, around 3.45, when officers Charles Henry and Joseph Brown returned to the illegal soul club and tried again. Both officers were black and had been on attachment as undercover vice officers for many months, so they were familiar with the rituals of the area. One officer befriended three women near the entrance and managed to gain entry by pretending to be part of a bigger group of revellers.

Soul music seeped through the brick walls: the Soul Twins' 'Quick Change Artist', Buddy Lamp's 'Save Your Love', and a big local hit, the Parliaments' 'I Wanna (Testify)'. The vice squad officers expected to find about twenty-five drinkers hidden away in the building, but they stumbled on a much bigger party, with a hundred or more people celebrating the return of two servicemen recently demobilised from Vietnam. Officer Charles Henry successfully bought a drink, and in doing so he had entrapped the club in an illegal act.

Usually those arrested in the neighbourhood would be secreted down a back alley and hustled into waiting paddy wagons away from the busy intersection, but the rear doors of the building had been bolted in violation of fire regulations, and the arresting officers were forced to improvise. Sergeant Arthur Howison of the Tenth Precinct's clean-up squad assumed control and, in what proved to be a fatal overreaction, tried to arrest seventy-three customers and the bartender. With no hidden way out, the drinkers had to be accompanied downstairs and out the front exit onto the noisy crossroads at Twelfth and Clairmount. According to the owner's son, 'some people refused to leave and were dragged out after the occurrence of a few fights'. In the ensuing chaos, the club's jukebox was smashed by the police in an attempt to silence the music, and one youth was handcuffed and beaten down the two flights of stairs leading to the street. It was by now the early hours of Sunday morning. Back-up was thin on the ground. Standard police paddy wagons could only hold fourteen people, so six or more were required to arrest the crowd. One got lost on the way, and others were slow to respond. But rather than disperse some of the revellers, Howison insisted that they stay in line. Knowing that their worst fate was a small fine, the throng raised their voices, mocked the police, and exchanged jokes with passers-by. A crowd of 200-odd soon gathered, and the atmosphere became increasingly intimidating. While a squad car slowly ferried the first group to the Livernois station, the crowd grew in confidence. 'Just as we were pulling away,' Sergeant Howison said, 'a bottle smashed a squad-car window.'

A rumour quickly spread that a man had been bayoneted by the police. It was untrue, but just one of many that were to disorientate the authorities in the dramatic days to come. Bricks were thrown and then a salvo of beer bottles. Some saw an opportunity to resist arrest and used the hail of missiles to escape the law.

By 4.40 a.m. the situation was out of control, and the remaining police officers were ordered out of the area in the hope that their absence would quell the crowd. It didn't work. A trashcan was smashed through a shop window, and within minutes a small but still containable riot erupted along Twelfth Street. At 5.20 the Tenth Precinct received its first complaint about burglar alarms as windows were smashed and televisions, bracelets, guns and groceries were looted from local shops. An eyewitness blamed the 'inhabitants of the night' – the pimps, the pushers and 'the Cadillac and silk suit crowd'. The police instinctively thought it was a 'pocket riot', easily contained and unlikely to spread, but that was wishful thinking; local teenagers from the crowded sidestreets were drawn to the intersection as rioting spread. By 5.30 police commissioner Ray Girardin had been woken by a call on his red emergency telephone telling him that a riot had begun. At first he thought the police were exaggerating the problem, but he later told the *Saturday Evening Post*, 'Our policemen have been instructed to meet force with force and also temper justice with mercy, but plainly there was the danger that many people would be killed, whether from fire or gunfire.' Girardin was right. The disturbances would last for four days and leave forty-three people dead, 1,189 injured, and the inner city of Detroit in ruins.

The timeline of what ultimately became known in African-American communities as the 1967 rebellions showed Detroit as a city struggling to cope with racial division, police brutality and endemic poverty, but all of those were subservient to a more lethal force – pure chance. Criminologists argued that the area had a deeply ingrained criminal underworld problem and a subculture of vice and prostitution; sociologists claimed that riots had been spreading since Harlem erupted in 1964, blown by the winds of social deprivation; racist commentators argued that Detroit had been an accident waiting to happen since the twenties, when racial segregation began to break down; still others blamed revolutionaries and said that the warnings were there the summer before, when a cadre of black nationalists from the Afro-American Youth Movement fought police on the corner of Kercheval and Pennsylvania in the so-called Kercheval Incident. But none of those theories fully explain what really happened on the last weekend of July 1967.

The first recorded injury was sustained by Lieutenant Raymond Good, who was struck by a rock and concussed. His last memory before being rushed to Henry Ford Hospital was of the flailing arms of a man wearing a shirt with distinctive green sleeves. By morning the name 'Greensleeves' had entered street vocabulary. Police reported that an African-American youth wearing a light jersey with green sleeves had been seen throwing missiles and goading the crowd. No one knew who he was or how he came to be at the corner of Twelfth and Clairmount, and, in a vacuum of real information, stories multiplied. Unreliable witnesses claimed to have seen him later that morning at the intersection of Twelfth and Hazelwood as looters laid siege on local shops, so the police released an all-points bulletin, and the hunt was on for a rioter known only as Greensleeves. He was variously thought to be an agent provocateur, a visiting agitator from out of town, or a Black Power radical schooled in the militancy of the local auto plants. Greensleeves was just another 'folk devil' in the long list of shadowy figures the police and local media were to pursue among the debris of Detroit.

By 7.10 a.m. smoking clouds billowed overhead as looting spread outwards from the Strip. The National Guard commander at Camp Grayling was notified, and in an attempt to disperse the growing crowds, a unit of armed police officers prepared an advancing V shape and swept through the mob, trying to clear the streets – the first of many futile efforts to regain control. By mid morning over 1,100 police officers – a quarter of the Detroit police force – had reported for duty. The composition told its own stark story. In a city that was one-third black, ninety-five per cent of the men were white.

Congressman John Conyers Jr lived a few blocks from the Strip and speedily organised an emergency residents' meeting at the Grace Episcopal Church on Virginia Park Street. Twenty local clergymen joined the meeting, but it too proved to be a futile congregation. The teenagers who composed most of the rioting mobs had ceased to care about mainstream 'Negro leadership', and when Conyers drove up Twelfth Street with a local minister turned police administrator, Dr Hubert Locke, and the deputy school superintendent, Arthur Johnson, it proved to be a huge setback for the community elders. They were shouted down by the crowds, dismissed as 'Uncle Toms', and when Conyers tried to remonstrate with the aid of a bullhorn, a bottle flew through the air and the community elders evaporated, fearing for their safety.

Mayor Cavanagh held an emergency press conference, naïvely claiming that the situation was under control, but by the time the assembled press left the conference looting had spread eastward to the John Lodge Freeway and west to Livernois. Cavanagh had once said that Detroit was different – 'you don't need to throw a brick to communicate with city hall' – and it was a quote his enemies would remember in the weeks to come. Fire crews who responded to alarms or urgent calls were pelted with stones, and at one point the fury of missiles was so threatening that firefighters abandoned their hoses in the streets and fled. Media coverage did not help, but nor was it wholly to blame. Over thirty-nine per cent of those involved in rioting first heard information from friends and neighbours, not from TV or radio. But that too was to change as the virus of anxiety spread and mutated. By mid afternoon the city's resources could no longer cope, and a request was made to bring in police reinforcements from towns across Michigan. Over 300 officers assembled at the Detroit Artillery Armory, the marshalling point for an initiative dubbed Operation Sundown, and an hour later several hundred National Guard troops who were in the area on training duty were also drafted in.

Police officers were instructed to protect Tiger Stadium, where 34,000 fans were attending a double-header between the Detroit Tigers and the New York Yankees, unaware that a major riot was erupting ten blocks away. Willie Horton, a Detroit sports legend who had grown up a few blocks from the blind pig, was urged to drive to the main riot area after the game dressed in his Tiger gear to try to quell the disturbances. He stood on a car in the middle of the crowd but his heroism backfired and the crowd seemed fortified by his appearance, chanting his name as if it were a mantra of rebellion. Ironically Horton had only recently been featured in a radio campaign called 'Detroit is Happening' to promote the city to visitors. The promo spots had been recorded at Hitsville, with Holland-Dozier-Holland producing, and featured the voices of Mary Wilson and Florence Ballard. Diana Ross had been unavailable.

The Fox Theater's interior was a riot of styles and colours. A network of lobbies framed by ornate columns led spectacularly to a proscenium arch playhouse where a matinee performance of a local soul show, the *Swingin' Time Review*, was in full voice. The MC, Robin Seymour, welcomed the headline act, Martha and the Vandellas. From the stage Reeves looked up and out to a theatre decorated with plaster bears and outlandish wildlife resting beneath cavernous ceilings styled like a rounded tent and supported by decorative spears. The show was being broadcast live on *The Big Eight* on Ontario's CLKW-TV, an entrepreneurial TV station based across the river in Canada. Among the assembled cast were a popular acrobatic soul-dancer, Lester Tipton, and a silky-voiced vocalist named J. J. Barnes who at the time was signed to the local Groovesville label. Reputedly Reeves had launched her set with a raucous version of the hit song 'Dancing In The Street' when the police directed a stagehand to stop her. Unaware of what was happening out in the streets, Reeves danced offstage sideways, where she was told that the theatre had to be evacuated. The matinee show traditionally attracted a young crowd, who police feared might spill onto the streets outside and become drawn into the spreading riot. Backstage in crowded dressing rooms were some of Detroit soul music's rising stars – the Parliaments, who at the time were signed to Revilot Records, Deon Jackson of Carla Records, and local teen sensations the Dramatics, whose novelty song 'Inky Dinky Wang Dang Doo' was tearing up the local pop charts. For the Dramatics the show would be the prequel to the most tragic and deadly weekend of their young lives.

Martha Reeves followed police orders. She later said in her biography, 'With microphone in hand I went to center stage and as calmly as possible announced that widespread rioting had broken out and Detroit was on fire . . . I will never forget the kind of responsibility I felt to announce something like that and not start a stampede of people running for their lives.' It was a moment that triggered a bizarre reaction. The song 'Dancing In The Street', an otherwise innocent piece of teenage pop, became inextricably linked to social unrest, and for months afterwards there was a potent although unverified rumour that black radio stations were discouraged by Washington from playing the song. Notoriety had already surrounded L.A. radio jock the Magnificent Montague, whose catchphrase 'Burn, baby, burn' had taken on a seditious meaning during the Watts riots of 1965, and for many in authority 'Dancing In The Street' had the same kind of sinister association. Some on the outer reaches of credibility even believed the song was a clarion call by black radicals plotting a summer of inner-city disturbances.

Within ten minutes of receiving police instructions, audiences hurried from the opulent auditorium and dispersed through the lobbies to the streets. Musicians and half-dressed support acts hurriedly vacated the stage area, leaving personal effects behind. The Dramatics and their entourage of teenage friends left by the main exit, following the audience onto Woodward Avenue, where they managed to catch a passing bus. As fate would have it, it was heading in the general direction of the rioting and would become the most fateful bus journey in the history of Detroit soul music – one that was to resonate through the city's court system for years to come. Ron Banks, the seventeen-year-old lead singer of the Dramatics, divided their modest performance fee among the members of the group and, in a moment of misfortune, they headed for a notorious hangout called the Algiers Motel, unwittingly heading towards an experience that one of the Dramatics described later as 'the worst day of our lives'. By the end of the weekend, three of their associates would be shot dead and two of the group beaten to a state of semi-consciousness and traumatised for life.

As the Dramatics travelled north on Woodward, the first death of the riots of 1967 was reported. A sixty-eight-year-old Armenian store owner by the name of Krikor Messerlian died defending his shoe repair shop at 7711 Linwood Avenue near Twelfth Street. A gang of African-American youths with southern accents had stopped at a nearby dry cleaner, threateningly close to Messerlian's shop. After a spate of incidents at his own store, Messerlian resented young black teenagers. And his volatile temper did not help control events. He ran out into the street with a twenty-inch ceremonial sabre and swung wildly at the gang, slashing a teenager's shoulder. The youths encircled him and Messerlian was clubbed to the ground with an axe handle and left with a fractured skull. An hour after that attack, twenty-year-old Darryl McCurtis from Birmingham, Alabama, who had been in Detroit less than six weeks, arrived at Henry Ford Hospital on West Grand, diagonally opposite Motown's Hitsville studios. McCurtis's behaviour aroused suspicions. Pathetically, he was still carrying the axe handle with which he had bludgeoned Messerlian to death, and he was arrested for first-degree murder.

★

By 5.25 the National Guard had arrived in the city, setting up a temporary base at Central High School. Home-owners, shopkeepers and small gangs of vigilantes had been quicker to react. Along key arteries in the city, citizens stood armed with hunting rifles and licensed guns, standing guard over shops and homes. A fear had taken hold that would not subside for many months. When fires spread along a row of well-maintained wooden homes on Pingree Street, the signal went out that family homes and personal property were at risk. Store owners tried to second-guess the mob. Many scrawled 'Soul Brother' or 'Black Owned' on storefronts, hoping that their businesses would be spared. Some got lucky, but most did not. Sixty-five per cent of Detroit's inner-city population was black, but only thirty-eight per cent of the businesses were owned by African-Americans, and of those the majority were single-store owners with an income of less than $8,000 a year. Whatever the rioters thought of the stores they were wrecking, they were largely the property of relatively disadvantaged people, and few were owned by the wealthy.

Sensing that the city was slipping out of control, Governor Romney authorised the National Guard to leave their base at Central High and take to the streets. Four thousand National Guard troops were patrolling inner-city Detroit, but it was too late to save one of soul music's most cherished institutions: Joe Von Battle's gospel and R&B store. The pioneering record store had opened in the old Hastings Street ghetto and relocated to Twelfth Street in the early sixties. At the age of fourteen, Aretha Franklin had recorded her first album for Von Battle's indie label, JVB. Gordy had shopped there as a kid and briefly ran a rival store when he set up his first failed business venture, the 3-D Record Mart. By 1967 Von Battle's store had been forced by changing tastes to diversify away from gospel to reflect the upsurge in R&B, and he even stocked Gordy's million-selling labels alongside a bewildering array of smaller independent labels like Groove City, Kool Kat and Magic City. When Von Battle arrived at his burned-out store, his daughter Marsha Mickens described him as looking distraught and powerless, as if 'his whole life's work had been destroyed'.

R&B records were carried through the streets in triumph or left to melt in the flames. 'I think that Joe Von Battle really died the day he returned to his shop,' his daughter said, 'to trudge through mounds of charred and melted records and fire-hose-soaked reel-to-reel tapes, unwound and slithering like water snakes; thousands of songs, sounds, and voices of an era, most never pressed onto records – gone forever.'

A sinister party atmosphere pervaded the neighbourhood, looting spread, stores were torched, and a string of up-market boutiques in a five-block stretch from Livernois to Seven Mile Road called the Avenue of Fashion was ransacked, with mannequins left strewn across the street like lifeless bodies. When looters were taken to Palmer Station under arrest, some were still wearing stolen cashmere coats and homburg hats.

At 7.45 Mayor Cavanagh announced that a curfew would be put in place. People were instructed to vacate the streets and stay indoors between the hours of nine at night and five in the morning. Police ordered the early closure of theatres, liquor stores and neighbourhood bars. Fearing that gasoline could find its way into the wrong hands, the fire chief ordered that all gas stations close down and sales of flammable liquids be curtailed. Two young looters named Willie Hunter and Prince Williams were next to die. They had migrated to Detroit from the southern states to work in the Ford auto plants and were last seen walking by Brown's Drug Store on Twelfth Street. Overcome by carbon monoxide poisoning, their charred bodies were discovered trapped in the basement of the store.

Darkness was supposed to bring respite, but only seven minutes into the curfew hour, police received the first confirmed report of sniper fire in the 1600 block of Seward. Thomas 'Beans' Bowles, the gangly Motown bandleader, claimed that fear of sniper fire spooked the Detroit police and forced them to overheat. 'They were like cowboys, quick-draw artists, and they practiced on black people,' he said. At the height of the riots, he remembered 'eating graham crackers and drinking milk' with his two young sons when a National Guard jeep pulled up to his apartment and shone a flashlight through the window. The innocent act of putting a cracker in his mouth had looked in the dark like the actions of a sniper.

Paranoia about rooftop snipers took hold, and across the next three fatal days it would lead to numerous misunderstandings. The first victim of sniper fire was Sheren George, a twenty-three-year-old white mother of two who worked as an exotic dancer at the Hollywood Ballroom. She was riding home in a car driven by her husband, going north on Woodward, when they saw a white man being beaten by a crowd of African-American youths. They slowed down to navigate a way around the trouble spot when a bullet struck the left rear door. Sheren George was hit below her left breast and died at Detroit General a few hours later. She was four months' pregnant at the time of her death, and her life had been a catalogue of tragedies: she had drifted into the sex industry while trying to raise two children, having failed to come to terms with the unsolved murder of her first husband.

Walter Grzanka had a drink problem. He sat on his back porch near Second and Charlotte Street, watching fires glow across the city skyline. Grzanka was the son of first-generation Polish immigrants, and had a police record for petty offences. After darkness fell some locals broke into a nearby store, looting groceries and liquor. A young black man was filling a cardboard container with goods and handing out alcohol, and Grzanka was drawn to the incident like a moth to light. Onlookers described a party atmosphere, but when the proprietor turned up the mood suddenly changed. Hamid Audish Yacoub was a thirty-year-old Arab-American and an aspiring local businessman who had only just bought the store, and suddenly saw his livelihood being ripped apart. His first sight was the half-drunk Grzanka leaving the store with more loot. Yacoub fired one direct shot and two more to scatter the looters. Grzanka fell to the ground with a chest wound and was pronounced dead on arrival at Detroit General. In his pocket was the pathetic haul from his night as a looter: seven cigars, four packs of tobacco and nine pairs of men's shoelaces.

★

Florence Ballard watched the riots on television, periodically getting up to look out her front windows as smoke circled above her home on West Buena Vista. Although the house was comparatively safe, fires had broken out on Dexter Avenue and at nearby intersections. Ballard's desire to pursue a solo career and break free from Motown and Diana Ross had grown in its intensity. She had mistakenly placed her affairs under the questionable management of her boyfriend, Tommy Chapman, a slow reader with no managerial experience and no legal training. Chapman had been told by a contact that Ballard's binding contract with Motown might work against a solo career, so he reached the conclusion that it would be best if Ballard severed her links with Motown. It was the first of many hurried and ill-advised decisions he would make on behalf of his girlfriend. Ballard was scheduled to meet Motown lawyers in the days to come.

Coincidentally the riots marked the release date of the love song 'Reflections', which the Supremes had recorded fractiously back in March. It was issued under the group's new moniker, Diana Ross and the Supremes. Feeling humiliated and demoted, Ballard refused to have a copy of the record in her home, and her resentment towards Gordy and Ross festered. Gwen Gordy, the family's youngest sister, who had argued with her husband, Harvey Fuqua, about how Ballard was being treated, tried to encourage Ballard to talk her way back into the group, even if that meant apologising to the Motown management. But it was never likely to happen. Although the riots were to play a role in devastating much of Detroit's soul music infrastructure, most of Motown's headline acts were out of town and far from the troubles. Stevie Wonder was onstage with Ray Charles and Dionne Warwick in Baltimore, and although his mother's home on Greenlawn Street was surrounded by fires, it survived. His chaperone and blind tutor, Ted Hull, who was employed by Motown in partnership with the Lansing Institute of the Blind, returned early from Baltimore to find that 'the scent and sight of black smoke filling the sky' had grown 'more and more menacing'. Tammi Terrell was living with her volatile boyfriend, David Ruffin of the Temptations, in a rented apartment on Dexter near the intersection with Clairmount. She described looking out fearfully on the burning city, too scared to leave her increasingly tense home. Hitsville stayed open throughout the riots. 'We continued business as usual,' Gordy said, 'but outside were constant reminders of the turbulence surrounding us: flames jumping, broken glass and debris from shattered windows and looted stores. Despite martial law, the rioters were still out there, running up and down the streets with stuff – toasters, sofas, stereos, TVs, everything they could carry.'

Late on the second day of rioting, Otis Williams of the Temptations drove across town and made an instinctive decision to break with routine. Normally he would have headed for the Chit Chat Club on Twelfth Street to have a nightcap or shoot pool. Back home he watched events on TV. 'Watching the news was like seeing a nightmare,' Williams wrote. 'The violence, looting, and burning got worse by the hour.' At one point the carnage became so great that he slept in the hallway of his apartment, too frightened to pass by windows and fearful of being burned to death: 'They were firing rounds all over the place and it didn't seem to stop.'

Maull's Bar at Joy and Yosemite had also been attacked. Resident group the Detroit Emeralds were on tour, and their replacement for the night was another group of local hopefuls, Dennis Edwards and the Firebirds, who were forced to shelter under tables inside the club. Edwards had auditioned at Motown in the preceding weeks, and within a matter of months he would be promoted out of the bar-room soul scene to become a lead singer of the Temptations when the reckless David Ruffin was fired.

Sirens blared like inner-city blues. By 11.02 a.m. on Sunday, 23 July 1967, the 82nd Airborne Division's Third Brigade was dispatched from Fort Bragg, North Carolina, heading for Detroit. Its last military action had been as part of Operation Power Pack, the defence of the Dominican Republic against Communist insurgents. On the brigade's arrival, the military planned that it would be supported by the 101st Airborne from Fort Campbell, Kentucky, fresh from a tour of duty in Vietnam. To ensure his back was adequately covered on the ground, the president dispatched special envoy Cyrus Vance, the assistant to Secretary of Defense Robert McNamara, but by the time Vance arrived in Detroit another death had been reported. This victim was Daniel Jennings, a thirty-six-year-old father of fourteen children. Jennings had dropped out of Pershing High School, where he had been a classmate of Mable John, one of Motown's first recording artists. He had recently lost his job as a wrecker at a salvage yard, and with a small gang of friends goading him on he broke into Stanley's Patent Medicine and Package Store, a corner store owned by Polish trader Stanley Meszezenski. Jennings broke the panes of glass in the front door, and as he climbed into the store a single shot rang out, hitting him in the chest. Jennings was pronounced dead on arrival at Detroit General, shot by the store's owner, who had been lying in wait.

The next four victims were also looters. One of them, Joseph Chandler, a Korean War veteran, was shot by police, trying to escape with armfuls of groceries at the Food Time Market on Second Avenue. His body was later discovered under a car, raising suspicions about the police version of events. The circumstances of Chandler's death were to assume a chilling significance in the months to come. He was shot by a Detroit police officer named David Senak, who was also implicated in the killing and torture of a group of black teenagers, some of them members of the soul group the Dramatics, in what became infamously known as the Algiers Motel killings. Chandler's death began as an impersonal reference number, Complaint DD 386913. He was pronounced dead on arrival at Henry Ford Hospital and his body was routinely dispatched to the Wayne County morgue, where the stressed and overworked medical examiner, Dr Clara Raven, performed an autopsy and recorded the cause of Chandler's death as 'a shotgun wound to the right buttock, penetrating liver and right lung with massive hemorrhage'.

Looting was by now epidemic and the root cause of many more deaths. The police were angered, exhausted and out of control, and as a consequence misunderstandings and human recklessness were conspiring to ratchet up the death toll. Few were as unlucky as Alfred Peachlum, a thirty-five-year-old African-American who died at four in the afternoon of 24 July. Peachlum was a welder at General Motors, a father of three, and an avid Tigers fan who had been at Tiger Stadium when the first news of rioting circulated. Either through curiosity or the thrill of crime, he passed an A&P supermarket at 3430 Joy Road where widespread looting was already underway, entered the store, and was caught inside when the police arrived. The patrolmen panicked when they saw a shiny object in his hand. Thinking it was a gun, they opened fire and Peachlum was struck in the chest. He staggered outside to the back alley, where he died. He had been holding a piece of beef wrapped in aluminum foil.

A gulf was opening up between police reports and eyewitness accounts. The death of another African-American victim, Charles Kemp, seemed to underline the theory that young black men were being targeted. He died on the afternoon of Monday, 24 July, in an incident involving police and a National Guard sergeant, and on the basis of his wounds alone it was closer to execution than justice. Kemp's death was a pathetic mixture of bad luck and poor judgement and began to raise the spectre of a police force in meltdown. Kemp had moved to the city from Alabama in the months before the riots and worked at a gas station in the city. The pay was modest but the job was secure, or so it seemed until the authorities decided to ration gas. The decision was a body blow to small gas stations, including Charles Kemp's employers, who laid him off. Unemployed by the riots, looting seemed a low-risk alternative to Kemp, who approached the Borgli Brothers Market on Mack Avenue. The police had already visited the store several times that day to scare off looters and were on their way to another incident when the unemployed Kemp was shot running from the premises with the grand haul of five packets of cigars.

Detroit General resembled a war zone and the police were stretched in every direction. But they had not entirely given up their long-standing feud with Trans-Love Energies and the countercultural community in the Warren Forest neighbourhood. MC5 guitarist Wayne Kramer was an unlikely riot victim. The band had been playing at the Grande Ballroom as a support act for the then unknown Tim Buckley when rioting broke out. Promoter Russ Gibb remembers that 'the ballroom was not air-conditioned; it was often the custom to cool off and party a bit on the breezy roof of the building after a particularly sweaty show or between acts. In the wee hours of Sunday, however, the staff and band noticed a particularly large glow in the sky from the direction of Twelfth Street and Clairmount . . . to the northeast. Unbeknownst to those present, this glow was in fact fires stoking the epicenter of the Detroit riots.' Buckley and his band remained in Detroit for two days, trapped in the gathering insurrection. They innocently drove to a barbecue in Kensington State Park, thirty miles west of Detroit, and returned to the Grande to rescue their equipment. Kramer drove directly to his apartment and claimed to have spent the night stoned watching Detroit burn through an amateur telescope protruding from the apartment window. As the night wore on, police mistook the telescope for a rifle and National Guard troops stormed the apartment. Kramer was arrested for aiding and abetting snipers. MC5 took an incendiary influence from the disturbances and went on to record one of their most declamatory and polemic songs, the blues-tinged 'The Motor City Is Burning', a John Lee Hooker blues classic, backed by guitarist Buddy Guy. Hooker had recorded the song in Chicago in the immediate aftermath of the riots. Its strident and uncompromising tone appealed to MC5, who included it in their set and eventually covered it on an album, fortified by the message: 'All the cities will burn, you are the people that will build up the ashes.'

At the stroke of midnight, President Johnson went live on television from Washington to announce that federal troops were being dispatched to Detroit. He was insistent that this was at the request of the state governor, George Romney. 'I am sure the American people will realize that I take this action with the greatest regret,' he said solemnly, 'and only because of the clear, unmistakable, and undisputed evidence that Governor Romney and the local officials have been unable to bring the situation under control.' He was not simply deflecting any possible blame but reasserting his defence that this was not a presidential attack on the black community. Seven times the president mentioned Romney's name, papering over the cracks of a horrendous dispute behind the scenes and leaving the American public in little doubt where the buck stopped. The 82nd Airborne was mobilised, and although the troops remained east of Woodward to inhibit the spread of rioting, word spread that Detroit was under martial law. The 'arsenal of democracy' had just got a lot tougher: M-16 rifles, M-79 grenade launchers and tear gas were now being deployed. At two o'clock on Tuesday morning, police officers were called to guard firemen at the corner of Vicksburg and Linwood, where there were reports of blazing stores and random sniping. Suspicion had hardened into prejudice: almost any young African-American male was seen as a threat. A car carrying three black teenagers was stopped by National Guardsmen, and in the confusion gunshots splintered through the windshield, hitting one of the boys. Shots were fired from the car, and unfortunately fireman Carl Smith became separated from his unit. He took cover behind a row of trashcans but was shot and fell forward into the intersection. Because of the intensity of gunfire, it took police forty minutes to reach the fatally injured fireman; he had been killed by a single bullet passing through his head. Smith's death was followed ominously by another death in the line of duty. This time it was a police officer from the Thirteenth Precinct, Jerome 'Jerry' Olshove. It was his death that would unleash a macabre set of events. Olshove was on temporary duty at Kiefer command, a special tactical response centre set up on the grounds of Herman Kiefer Hospital on Hamilton Avenue, when his scout car was dispatched to an A&P store at the corner of John R. and Holbrook. A local man, Albert Phillips, was staggering around the parking lot, his face partially disfigured by shotgun wounds. In the store were two looters, Danny Royster and Charles Latimer. According to police reports, the looters were told to line up against a wall. Latimer followed orders and was immediately handcuffed by Officer

Olshove. Royster resisted arrest and, according to the police report, he tried to grab another officer's gun, which discharged, killing Officer Olshove.

Although Olshove was reported dead at 3 a.m., most of his colleagues were not told until later that morning, when a new shift arrived for duty. The death was almost certainly accidental, but Royster and Latimer, who had been handcuffed throughout the incident, were charged with first-degree murder. Olshove's death was a tipping point and unlocked a torrent of rage within the police that resulted in acts of lawless revenge. Within forty-five minutes of the first police death, two more victims died. William Jones and Ronald Evans were shot by police while stealing beer from a corner store. They were reported in police logs as 'fleeing felons', although Evans had probably been executed, shot fourteen times by police guns. Over the next twenty-four hours, colleagues of the dead officer from the Thirteenth Precinct lost their emotional grip and a bitter pathology was in play, pitting white police officers against young black teenagers. Officer David Senak, one of Olshove's colleagues and a principal character in the events that were about to engulf the soul group the Dramatics, described a precinct in grief: 'We had guys there at roll call that were like brothers to him. [They] couldn't go on the streets for half an hour, forty-five minutes. They were crying like babies.' Olshove had been due to leave the police later that month to take a job at IBM. He left a widow and an infant child.

Federal paratroopers under the command of Colonel A. R. Bolling arrived at Southeastern High School, and at long last the ill-equipped and strategically naïve National Guard had substantial support. The 101st Airborne included battle-hardened Vietnam veterans, many of whom were black, but one of the great paradoxes was that at the very moment that help arrived, a Detroit police unit had been thrown into battered and emotional disorder. The greatest threat to the city's reputation was not looting and social unrest but the hardened grievances of a police force that was neither in control of the city nor of themselves. According to a

Time magazine report, 'Detroit's convulsion' continued: 'By Tuesday morning, Detroit was shrouded in acrid smoke, the Edsel Ford and John C. Lodge freeways were nearly deserted, and tens of thousands of office and factory workers stayed home. Downtown streets were almost empty, giving gangs of looters free passage. They smashed the windows of a Saks Fifth Avenue branch near the General Motors office building, making off with furs and dresses; grocery stores were wrecked and plundered throughout the city, and fresh food became scarce. Profiteering began as merchants overcharged for bread and milk.'

Martha Jean 'the Queen' Steinberg, the towering R&B radio personality, broadcast her radio show *Inspiration Time* live for forty-eight uninterrupted hours, preaching non-violence and pleading with residents to clear the streets. It was reassuring to those who listened to her popular show on FM powerhouse WJLB, but the Queen now spoke principally to an older generation. For young African-American men, she was just another figurehead talking into a microphone and was unable to convert her words into actions. Reports of sniper fire were receding, and by mid morning banks and government buildings were reopened, but many staff still stayed away. At midday Mayor Cavanagh allowed gasoline sales to resume but limited sales to five gallons per vehicle. A stubborn fear still had a grip on the city, and the Tigers postponed their evening game against the Baltimore Orioles, eventually relocating it to Maryland.

For a few brief hours on Tuesday, 25 July, the authorities thought optimistically that they were witnessing the calm after the storm, but yet again the hope was short-lived. At 3.25 a.m. two thirty-six-year-old African-American men, Arthur Johnson and Perry Williams, died inside a looted pawnshop at 1401 Holbrook. Police reports said a unit shot at looters and the men died as felons resisting arrest. Contradictory witness statements described two different police units. The first shot at the front windows of the looted shop, and a second entered the building when the firing died down. By then out of sight of witnesses on the street, the second group of officers claimed that Johnson and Williams attacked them with clubs, and so they shot the men in self-defence. The victims were poorly educated high-school drop-outs, and their version of events would remain unknown.

Detroit was sketching its own dark history. As another night of curfew fell, a thirty-eight-year-old African-American became the next victim of the riot, and this time the circumstances were poignant rather than conspiratorial. Jack Sydnor, drunk in his apartment block at 2753 Hazelwood, fired a pistol at nothing in particular, the shot was interpreted as sniper fire, and neighbours summoned the National Guard, who surrounded the building. A local patrolman, Roger Poike, broke down the door, and Sydnor shot at the police. The response was unforgiving. A barrage of bullets tore through the apartment, and the force drove Sydnor through the window. He fell three floors to the street below. Sydnor was described in police logs as a sniper, and technically that was true, but as the writer John Hersey said, 'He did not fit the picture of the dedicated, educated, intellectually sharpened, politically aware, suicidally inclined black revolutionary zealot of the sort those who feared a national plot had been describing.' Sydnor was a mumbling incoherent drunk, intoxicated until his tragic death.

Tuesday night was far from quiet. There were frequent reports of firebombing, and between midnight and three, as Tuesday turned to Wednesday, there were 800 reports of rooftop snipers, and seven more Detroiters were killed. Several witnesses voiced growing concern that police patrols were now killing indiscriminately. Resentment about the death of Officer Jerry Olshove and a fear of rooftop snipers had taken a hold of a small number of police units, and anxiety increased further with the death of a fifty-one-year-old white woman named Helen Hall, who was visiting Detroit on business and staying at the Harlan House motel, a few blocks from Motown's Hitsville studios. Hall worked for a car components company that specialised in tachometers. Her company had plans to acquire a local Detroit firm and had sent Hall on a reconnaissance visit to the targeted company. She was shot by a nervous Guardsman who had been called to investigate reports of a sniper attack. Seeing activity at a window, the Guardsman fired at the motel, killing Hall and narrowly missing her colleague. Unexpectedly, it was a member of the National Guard who was to become the next victim of the disturbances. Larry Post was a bachelor, a disciplinarian and a car fanatic who had risen to the role of sergeant. He was working at a checkpoint on Dexter when he saw a car occupied by three white males approaching. Post shouted at them to stop and fired a warning shot in the air. The car ignored the orders and accelerated away from the roadblock. More shots were fired, and after an exchange of gunfire across the intersection, Post was wounded in the stomach.

At 3.00 a.m. Governor Romney and Mayor Cavanagh called a joint press conference. 'On the basis of our collective judgment,' the governor said, 'Wednesday will be a better day. We are making progress.' The declaration was unconvincing. The next three to die were George Tolbert, Julius Lust and Albert Robinson – all their deaths tragically avoidable. Tolbert was a production worker at Pontiac who was passing a checkpoint on LaSalle when he was shot by a Guardsman. Julius Lust was one of only two white males shot to death, who had stolen car parts from a junkyard on the edges of the General Motors plant. Police were called by a security guard, and Lust was shot trying to escape. The police thought he was brandishing a gun, but when they reached his body they found him holding a mechanic's wrench. Three days into the disturbances, the price of life had cheapened, and too many deaths were the result of misunderstandings, poor judgement or callous reactions. A vengeful police force and a nervous National Guard were now part of the problem – not the solution.

In the few days immediately before the riots, the Supremes appeared at the Yale Bowl in Connecticut. Local reports of the concert described Diana Ross as standing stock-still onstage with her palm out in front of her in the freeze-frame pose that always introduced the global hit 'Stop In The Name Of Love'. Flashbulbs exploded around the stadium, and a crowd of over 50,000 rose from their seats in an impromptu standing ovation. From

Connecticut the group had briefly returned to Detroit then on to Las Vegas for their annual residency at the Flamingo Hotel. Cindy Birdsong, who was not yet sure she was a member of the group, had joined them only discreetly. To avoid any confrontations with Ballard, Motown had booked Birdsong at Caesars Palace, where she stayed separately throughout the residency. She was instructed to make her own way to the shows and watch from the auditorium night after night. It was a plan destined to fail. 'I had to go to watch the show,' Birdsong told the *Detroit Free Press*. 'And I felt I was making her uneasy.' Bad press was by now accumulating daily, but for reasons that cannot be logically explained, Motown insisted that Florence Ballard was happy in her role. Gordy had agreed with the Flamingo management that the hotel's luminous pink-and-white marquee would carry the new name 'Diana Ross and the Supremes'. On seeing the signage, Ballard went into a rage and confronted Gordy in front of Motown staff, accusing him of conspiracy and cruelty, saying it was further evidence of his 'dirty work'. Gordy retaliated: 'Florence, what did I ever do to make you hate me? I'm the guy who made you a star!' Those who witnessed the argument said it was one of the few times they thought Gordy felt hurt. One witness said he was fighting back tears, while others described it more as sighs of resignation, and that his lower lip, which he chewed nervously, was raw. This time Gordy had an option and he acted decisively. He instructed the road-management team to contact Birdsong at Caesars Palace and prepare her to replace Ballard for the rest of the July residency. *Jet* magazine got wind of the dispute and wrongly assumed it was a backstage fight between Flo and her replacement Birdsong, describing unseemly public hair-pulling and raised voices.

Disputes at Motown were now multiplying daily. Holland-Dozier-Holland slowed the pace of production to a stop, and as the riots flared they chose to stay away from the studios. Martha and the Vandellas were also in personal disarray. Reeves had unexpectedly married and then acrimoniously divorced within a year. Emotionally battered by a gruelling tour schedule, she was addicted to antidepressants, and she had already fallen out with

Diana Ross and fired her friend and fellow Vandella Betty Kelley after a tortuous disagreement at a concert at the Latin Casino in Cherry Hill, New Jersey.

The dispute with Ballard over the exterior signage was one in a string of small fights that raged backstage in Las Vegas. One in particular about Ballard's onstage demeanour brought her relationship with Motown to a final and bitter end. Tour manager Joe Schaffner, probably one of the most reliable witnesses to the break-up of the Supremes, once said: 'Florence's lack of enthusiasm onstage bugged the hell out of Diana. There was a song they used to do ['Somewhere'] that was very dramatic and would make Diana cry and go through all this drama. When she would look over her shoulder and see that Flo didn't have the same kind of emotion or presence, she would not accept that.' During a well-rehearsed piece of onstage shtick between the girls, Flo would imitate the comedienne Pearl Bailey, teasing Ross about her thinness. It was a routine that went down well with audiences, but it had crackling, bitchy and tense undercurrents onstage. The pay-off line was Flo's gag, 'Fat is where it's at', a line that always provoked a laugh. Ballard delivered the line with her stomach sticking out to exaggerate the comic delivery, but her staged exaggerations were over-acted and interpreted as insubordinate by Gordy. It was a mild rebellion at best, but Gordy charged backstage and unceremoniously sacked Ballard on the spot. She walked out on the entourage to celebrate her twenty-fourth birthday with Tommy Chapman.

Sometime towards the end of July 1967, as riots raged closer to her home, Ballard was home alone and drunk. Bitter about events in Las Vegas, she called the home of her ex, Roger Pearson, in Greenwich, Connecticut. Pearson's father, Samuel, was an executive of the Dreyfus investment company. Pearson was not at home but members of his family who took the call reported that Ballard was upset, slurring her words and accusing Motown of marginalising her. She told Samuel Pearson that Diana Ross and Berry Gordy planned to sack her and asked him for advice. It might have been that she felt Pearson Sr could match Gordy's wealth and influence.

Roger Pearson subsequently told *Vanity Fair*, 'Florence called my home and, in my absence, complained bitterly to my father that they were changing the name of the group to Diana Ross and the Supremes. My father said she sounded drunk.'

By sunrise on Thursday, 27 July, the worst of the rioting had subsided. Shimmering fumes shrouded Motown's studios. The looting was only sporadic, and sniper fire had died away. Federal troops withdrew from the streets back to command posts, and Michigan state police were withdrawn entirely from within the city boundaries. Mayor Cavanagh announced that the curfew was to be lifted, but yet again he was forced into a U-turn when Detroit became the focus of a new macabre problem: riot tourism. Teenagers and petty criminals from the suburbs were flocking to the city to watch or in some cases to participate in looting. There were hundreds of reports of cars with out-of-state plates, and police engaged in a gun battle with a carload of white Kentucky hoodlums.

Amid this chaos, Florence was driven by Tommy to the Northland Inn in Southfield. It was by now the afternoon of 27 July. She had agreed to a personal appointment with Michael Roshkind, a corporate vice-president at Motown, but stipulated that she would not attend a meeting at Motown's studios and wanted a neutral venue. Roshkind flew in from New York and took a room at the Northland; he later hinted that he expected a long and fractious confrontation with Ballard and her lawyers but it was not to be. Roshkind was a hard-nosed New Yorker prone to exaggeration and, unlike many of the Detroit-based artists, he saw Motown as a business and not as a 'family'. He had managed to secure a senior role at Motown with the help of a hyped resumé, claiming to have worked as a senior PR man for Adlai Stevenson and John F. Kennedy, a claim that has never been wholly verified. Later in his life, he admitted to false representation when he made entirely bogus claims of being a war hero. Despite these inconsistencies, there was no questioning his authority at Motown and the power he exerted the day he met with Ballard. As they sat uneasily in the Northland lobby, Roshkind, who was still unsure why Ballard was alone and unaccompanied by lawyers, handed over a sheaf of documents. Among them was a severance agreement drawn up by Motown. After a brief and stilted conversation, Ballard glanced down at the documents, only taking a cursory look at them. 'I read a little bit of it,' Ballard later claimed. 'It said you're not supposed to ever say that you were a Supreme, or had anything to do with the Supremes whatsoever. You can never call yourself an ex-Supreme.'

Eaten up by anger, confusion and plans to free herself to pursue a solo career, the twenty-four-year-old who had actually chosen the group's name shakily signed one of the most contentious documents in the long and litigious history of pop music. Roshkind had given her a non-negotiable agreement promising $2,500 per year for six years, a total of $15,000, thus bringing to an end her life as a Supreme. To soften the blow, Ballard was given a purple Cadillac Eldorado with cream leather interior. General Motors was marketing the car under the nickname 'the Rat Pack', an ironic reminder of the high life Ballard had left behind in Las Vegas. She cried, signed the paperwork and, embarrassed about what to do next, wiped away her tears and left.

The liquor ban imposed on the first day of the riots was lifted in Livingston and Washtenaw Counties and later in the day at Fourteen Mile Road. Lines of people ready to buy beer snaked alongside shops. By evening the bars were crowded, and by Saturday night, almost a week after the disturbances had been triggered, the curfew was finally relaxed.

Getting the assembly lines running normally was crucial. According to social historians Sauter and Hines, the civic authorities saw the car plants as a crucial bellwether: 'Personnel directors in the life industry of the Motor City – the auto plants – were busy on telephones coaxing their employees to return to the assembly lines. General Motors announced that all but two of their plants were operating with only 50 per cent of the workers.' Officially Mayor Cavanagh declared the riot over. After ninety-two intense hours of criminal damage, more than 7,200 people had been arrested, of whom the vast majority, 6,400, were black. Almost 3,000 were picked up on the second day of the riot, and by midnight on Monday 4,000 were incarcerated in makeshift jails, some confined in an underground garage without toilet facilities.

Over 1,000 National Guardsmen, their reputation under increased scrutiny, were sent home, and the men of the more effective 82nd Airborne withdrew from their base at Southeastern High School. Shopkeepers across the city took the tentative step of reopening for business, and a local form of inflation kicked in – milk, bread and basic foodstuffs had tripled in price. As the city began to return to some kind of normality, the riots claimed its final victim, an unarmed nineteen-year-old African-American male named Ernest Roquemore, who was shot outside his home at 3484 St Jean Street by an American paratrooper who had recently returned from service in Vietnam. An army unit was spearheading an operation on premises selling looted merchandise, and as Roquemore was pursued home from a local store, the paratrooper thought he was holding a chrome revolver and instantly shot him dead. It transpired yet again that it was not a gun but a tiny transistor radio, the simple everyday device that had taken Detroit's music to the world.

As the clean-up continued, police made one seemingly significant arrest, catching the mysterious Greensleeves who had been accused days before of provoking the first disturbances outside the blind pig on Twelfth and Clairmount. As the riots escalated so had his notoriety. He had variously been described by the press as an outside agitator, a Black Power fanatic connected to the Afro-American Youth Movement, and a Communist militant hardened by wildcat strikes in the car plants. None of it was true. A man matching the description of Greensleeves was arrested for fire-bombing the George V drugstore at 12200 Dexter at the corner of Richton Street. It transpired that he was a twenty-two-year-old local man named Michael Lewis, who lived three blocks away from the looted drugstore and was neither an outsider nor a Communist. Lewis was a criminal opportunist who was taken to Livernois Station, where the arresting officer recognised him from witness descriptions. Lewis was in every sense an archetypal rioter – young, black and disenchanted. He had worked briefly at Ford's River Rouge plant but felt more at home on the street, where he was an excitable but otherwise anonymous character. The events of July 1967 had given him an exaggerated status and spoke to a now virulent fear of young black men.

When Berry Gordy returned from Las Vegas a few days after the curfew he willed the staff of Motown to continue life as normal. Diana Ross and the Supremes were only home for a few brief and bewildered days before they travelled with the Four Tops to perform at the Forest Hills Club, a 14,000-seat venue in New York. *Jet*, the influential Chicago-based society magazine, simultaneously published a damaging two-page revelation of the in-fighting behind the scenes of black America's most famous group and rightly predicted that Florence Ballard would not be onstage at Forest Hills. In fact, she would never travel to a major Motown show again.

The Hitsville studio escaped largely unscathed, except for damage to a front window caused by a tank shell fired across West Grand Boulevard. But Detroit's wooden-porch image as the home of soul music had been damaged to the core, and the family image that had been so crucial to the Motown story was brutally displaced by darker visions of a charred city under martial law. Profound damage had been done to the reputation and creative energy of Detroit's soul scene. The Great Rebellion, as it was soon to be dubbed, had given voice to the voiceless, but it had also wounded Detroit to the core. The nightclubs, the bars and the independent studios that had been the foundations of Detroit's soul scene had been burned to the ground, ransacked, or destroyed – one way or another put out of commission. The generation that had shaped one of the greatest periods in the history of popular music had seen its city devastated. For the Supremes and others within Motown, the riots were to become a metaphor for ruined harmonies and wrecked friendships. In a broader sense, the disturbances were also a requiem for Detroit's great industrial achievements and its declining manufacturing base.

Mayor Jerome Cavanagh, who had risen to civic stature along with Motown, surveyed the worst-affected areas in the days after the disturbances and vowed to rebuild the Model City. But it was clear even then that he was surveying not only the destruction from the riots but the debris of his own crumbling political career. Cavanagh told one newspaper melodramatically, 'It looks like Berlin in 1945.'

Curfew. Store owners protect their property fearing another night of mass looting. Some put 'Soul Brother' signs in windows to signify a black-owned business. But as July becomes August, a fear of rooftop snipers takes hold, and three young teenagers are murdered by the Detroit Police under cover of darkness.

AUGUST

Ordeal

A grieving black woman sat on the porch of a darkened home at 4599 Oregon near the thundering noise of the Jeffries Freeway. She was rocking methodically back and forth, crying to herself, hiding her face and periodically shouting out into the street. Mrs Rebecca Pollard had been tested to the very edge of her tolerance. Her seventeen-year-old son, Robert, was serving three to ten years in the Michigan Reformatory prison in Ionia, having stolen seven dollars from a local newsboy. Another son, Chaney, was repairing bridges on Route 12 in Vietnam under intense small-arms fire, and her third son was dead. For two years she had lived in fear that there would be a knock at the door and that a message would come from Vietnam. But when the bad news came, it was much closer to home. Her nineteen-year-old son, Aubrey, had been killed in a nearby motel, shot by the Detroit police. Neighbours helped her to bed as she sobbed. She was uncontrollable, flinging her fists at those who tried to comfort her. Rebecca Pollard sensed that something very bad had happened to her son, and she was right.

Smoke hung over the city, the aftermath of the riot fires mingling with the fumes from the foundries and glassworks as Detroit returned to work. A stench of injustice also pervaded the city, and it lingered for years to come. On the first day of August, four teenage pallbearers wearing suits with black silk handkerchiefs carried the tiny white casket of Tanya Blanding, the little girl who had been shot by a National Guardsman. Her funeral service was held at the Shrine of the Black Madonna.

When the writer John Hersey arrived in Detroit, he had little idea how many people were grieving and no great sense of what he would write. In the last burning days of July, the fifty-three-year-old English professor from Yale University had been approached by President Johnson to join the National Advisory Commission on Civil Disorders and make recommendations to the White House. After listening to early radio bulletins about the riots, Hersey was unsettled by the president's approach, and increasingly reluctant to compromise his writing by joining a federal commission. He turned down the White House request. But gradually the idea of conducting his own kind of inquiry began to take shape, and he embarked on a book that would dig deep into the subculture of the riots: the people, the places, and the prejudices.

John Hersey was a gnomic scholar who had burrowed his way into the elite of academia. With his shuffling demeanour and hooked nose, he looked like a small-town librarian. He was the Master of Pierson College, a Pulitzer Prize winner for his novel *A Bell for Adano*, and a peripheral advocate of new journalism, the stylised reporting that allowed the writer's voice and even fictional invention to shape hard fact. Although the movement was more readily associated with larger-than-life characters such as Tom Wolfe, Truman Capote and Hunter S. Thompson, Hersey was a more discreet and modest exponent. He reported the experiences of ordinary people at Hiroshima in exhaustive detail, and through their fictionalised lives told deeper truths about tragedy than any number of newspaper reports. Hersey was inspired to do the same for Detroit. He began as he typically did, by mapping out his work week. Every Monday and Tuesday he would pack his bags and his yellow legal pad and leave the quiet lawns of Yale to travel to Detroit and immerse himself in the city's hidden backstreets.

In an intensive burst of research, Hersey interviewed hundreds of ordinary folk caught up in the broken machinery of history. A few days into his first trip, in the first week of August 1967, he began to obsess about an incident that had happened in the last days of July at the height of the riots. A unit of Detroit police officers working in tandem with a troop of National Guardsmen had ritually executed three black teenagers in a shabby soul-music hangout called the Algiers Motel. For Hersey, the incident was to become a microcosm of 1967. He wrote: 'The episode contained all the mythic themes of racial strife in the United States: the arm of the law taking the law into its own hands; interracial sex; the subtle poison of racist thinking by "decent" men who deny they are racists; the societal limbo into which, ever since slavery, so many young black men have been driven by our country; ambiguous justice in the courts; and the devastation in both black and white human lives that follows in the wake of violence as surely as ruinous and indiscriminate flood after torrents.'

The Algiers Motel was located on the west side of Woodward Avenue near Virginia Park. At the rear was a three-storey building with an annexe called the manor house, which housed around fifteen kitchenette units used mostly by local musicians, drug dealers and prostitutes. It offered third-rate glamour: basic room service, a chlorine-blue swimming pool, and diseased palm trees that drooped sadly over the half-lit pool. The Algiers was a place where local musicians hung out and touring bands shacked up, often living five or six to a room. It was an after-show hangout halfway between a soul club and a brothel. Capsules of cocaine could be bought openly in its warren of corridors, and young people gathered by the ice-cold pool, some strung out enough to dive in and swim. The Algiers was part of a chain of three locally run motels. The Alamo was further south on Woodward, near Tiger Stadium, and the Rio Gran on West Grand was a convenience motel often used by Motown to house visiting session musicians.

Late in July three teenage boys had died at the Algiers Motel. They were Carl Cooper, Aubrey Pollard and Fred Temple. The circumstances of their deaths were angrily disputed, but what was beyond dispute was the utter horror of the night. One of the dead boys had been shot in the face and his testicles blown apart by police bullets. Hersey described the event as having the hallmarks of a 'ballistic lynching'.

The Dramatics had checked into the Algiers to celebrate one of their real paydays. The group all lived locally and had family homes to go to, but they saw the Algiers as a rite of passage for indie soul musicians and went there to hang out and be seen. At the time the Dramatics were young dreamers who had yet to find success in the fiercely competitive soul scene. Among their ranks were the group's leader, Ron Banks, along with Larry 'Squirrel' Demps, Cleveland 'Larry' Reed, Rod Davis, and a temporary member, guitarist Mike Calhoun. Most of them had met each other at Pershing High School, where the Four Tops had formed in the fifties, and although they were still underage, they had vigorously pursued a Motown contract. It was not to be. After an unmemorable audition at Hitsville, they were crowded out by more established acts and gave up on Motown to sign to Super-Sonic Productions, one of a myriad of small soul studios dotted across Detroit, and eventually released songs on the Sport and Wingate labels.

By 1967 the Dramatics were on the cusp of happening. They had built up a faithful following among ghetto teenagers who were hardwired to love the group's infuriatingly eccentric dance single, 'Inky Dinky Wang Dang Doo'. The Dramatics could sing like a church choir, with a shifting register of subtle voices, and they had honed a frantic adrenaline-fuelled stage show, rushing onstage to leap, spin and backdrop. Their vocal style was elegantly led by Demps, who belied his acrobatic image by working by day as a Detroit city clerk. The Dramatics sounded like the Temptations, but outwardly they were more like another Motown group, the Contours, a frenetic bunch of showmen who were renowned across Detroit for their athletic stagecraft and uncompromising lifestyles. 'Inky Dinky Wang Dang Doo' might have given the

Dramatics their first taste of local success, but in truth it had trivialised their act and left them rooted in no man's land, unsure of their direction.

On the first day of the riots, the Dramatics had secured an opening slot at the *Swinging Time Review* at the Fox Theater, sharing the bill with J. J. Barnes, the Parliaments and headliners Martha and the Vandellas. Excited to be opening a prestige Motown show, the Dramatics spread the word among their high-school friends that they had secured backstage passes and needed a couple of assistants for the day. Second tenor Reed invited Fred Temple, a friend who was well known to the group, to be his 'personal valet'. Temple was a high-school dropout who had a no-hope job at Dodge Main, where he worked alongside Banks, who in turn was so anxious that he would never make money from music that he had gone from school straight to the auto plants. When Reed distributed backstage passes at the Fox Theater's stage door, he reminded Temple to tell anyone who stopped him that he was the Dramatics' valet. It was a naïve gesture that would indirectly lead to Temple's tragic and gruesome death.

John Hersey's initial trip to Detroit coincided with near panic in police circles. The usually secretive police department had suspended an officer suspected of murder. Patrolman Robert Paille, thirty-one, was accused of the shooting of Fred Temple on the premises of the Algiers Motel in circumstances that were at best vague. The unusually quiet officer had spent a night in jail and was released on $5,000 bond – tellingly, a lower bond value than had been set for curfew violators during the riots. Temple's older brother, Eddie, only got wind of the full injustice of his brother's killing on the day of the funeral, when two battered and emotionally exhausted members of the Dramatics, Larry Reed and Rod Davis, turned up at the White House Funeral Home to pay respect to their dead friend. The two singers gave Eddie a rushed and garbled version of what had happened, overlapping and contradicting each other as they spoke, but what became clear was that both Reed and Davis were recovering from the darkest night of their lives. Reed was heavily bandaged, his head having been cracked open by a police gun, and the stitches closing his wounds had turned septic. Davis had been severely concussed and, according to those who knew him, spoke incoherently of what they had seen. No one seemed to have a grasp of the whole story, and the singers could only remember fragments of what had unfolded. Eddie Temple was not naïve either. He listened sceptically at first, aware that his brother and his friends in the Dramatics were by no means angels.

The story of the Algiers Motel killings is a novel in its own right, with so many subplots and twists that the truth may never be revealed. What is clear is that the central character was the motel itself. Extant reports describe the Algiers as a notorious 'haven for pimps, prostitutes, drug pushers and addicts, gamblers, number operators and other criminal elements'. It was permanently under police surveillance, and vice officers were perilously close to its trade in drugs and prostitution. When they arrived at the Algiers after their matinee show at the Fox Theater, the Dramatics entered by the front gates, passing a garish neon palm tree. The riots were only in their infancy. The Algiers receptionist was unsure she could find them a room because the motel was full to overflowing with an array of transient guests including sex trade workers, travelling soul musicians from Chicago, and after-show revellers from the 20 Grand nightclub nearby. No rooms were empty in the main motel, so the Dramatics and their guests were given rooms in the manor house. At some stage in their brief stay, the group members split up. Some stayed to party, while others, including lead singer Banks, defied the curfew and picked their way home through the burning streets. Those who stayed had secured enough food for two days. Singer Roderick Davis had made a trip to the Lucky Strike market on the corner of Woodward and Euclid to buy a supply of TV dinners, some rolls, apple turnovers, milk and pop. In a nearby room, two small-time prostitutes from Columbus, Ohio – Julie Hysell and Karen Malloy – were selling casual sex to residents. They had also befriended a restless young criminal from Detroit's North Clarendon Street named Carl Cooper.

Unknown to the Dramatics, Cooper had a string of recent convictions for petty crimes and had hidden in his room a starting pistol, which he had brought to the motel to show off. Cooper had been fooling around with the gun several hours before, sometimes pretending to be hotel security or an undercover cop. Shortly after midnight, which was by then the second night of rioting, Carl Cooper discharged the pistol as a practical joke. Coincidentally there had been reports of rooftop snipers in the vicinity of the motel, and two patrol units of the Detroit police and a National Guard unit were dispatched to the locale. Fearing they might be vulnerable to sniper attack from the roofs above the manor house annexe, they made their entrance through the rear of the building. Within a few chaotic minutes, the police charged at the Algiers Motel, barking out orders and screaming at the residents to freeze, and lie down. In the chaos that followed, Carl Cooper and Fred Temple were shot dead, and the remaining residents of the annexe were rounded up and badly beaten and humiliated.

The events that followed remain the subject of long-standing dispute but resulted in the death of a third youth, Aubrey Pollard. John Hersey became so intrigued with the competing versions of Pollard's death that he dedicated almost a year of his life to analysing what took place in what was less than thirty minutes of real time. Hersey sifted through the claims, counterclaims and conflicting testimonies. His standard approach was meticulous note taking, close analysis and acute observation of character. Like a master tailor, he tried to stitch together the remnants of what had happened and establish who was to blame. As an advocate of the new journalism, he was never convinced by linear logic. For him, great writing was not a simple line; it was a mosaic of broken fragments.

Hersey's book *The Algiers Motel Incident* was in every respect a product of modernist literature: words functioned like shrapnel and thoughts were chaotic; much of it was scattered and unintelligible, like the riotous events it sought to describe. But still doubt persisted. Neither the FBI nor even the scrupulously observant Hersey was ever able to fully assemble the true story, and so it remains unresolved. The families grieved separately because none of them really knew each other, so assembling the full story proved difficult even for them. On the day that Fred Temple was buried, the bodies of the two other victims, Carl Cooper and Aubrey Pollard, lay at separate funeral homes – Swanson Funeral Home and the J. T. Wilson Funeral Home, respectively.

'The police didn't notify us,' Mrs Pollard told a reporter at the funeral. 'That's a hurting thing.' All three families had heard fragments of the story, but no one knew the whole truth. Aubrey Pollard's father took his camera to the motel and, incredibly, was allowed into the building among the evidence. 'So I started from the top floor and worked to the bottom,' he told Hersey. 'That's when I went to finding the deer shots. That's what they killed Aubrey with, deer shots. They used double-barreled [guns]. I found a .300 high-speed Savage, and deer shots, and shotgun shells. I worked with the detectives. They were very nice to me.' The Savage he spoke of was a .300 rimless rifle cartridge. Mr Pollard's visit to the motel exposed three things: that the investigation was already chaotic; that evidence had been contaminated; and that the Detroit homicide detectives on site were more disposed to a local man who had wandered in from the street with his camera than to protecting the uniformed officers who had killed Aubrey Pollard. It spoke of chaos and internecine police wars. An internal inquiry had been launched, and the Detroit police press office came under hourly pressure to report its findings.

With the riots still not entirely quelled, a small team of community activists working alongside the Detroit branch of the NAACP had set up a safe haven at the offices of Congressman John Conyers Jr. Anyone with information about the riots who was too frightened to go to the police could approach them. Conyers' congressional district offices were situated in the Retail Store Employees Union Hall at 2550 West Grand, a few short blocks from Hitsville studios. When Eddie Temple arrived at Union Hall to record his brother's death, there was already a long queue. He had to wait patiently for over an hour to give his garbled second-hand version of his brother's death at the Algiers Motel. Temple recounted the scattered bits of information he had gleaned from the two injured members of the Dramatics and that his father had gathered from the crime scene. By sheer chance, it proved to be a remarkable brush with history: one of the women recording the story and committing it to handwritten testimony was the famous civil rights activist Rosa Parks, who had triggered the Alabama bus boycotts back in 1954. Parks had subsequently moved to Detroit and was a secretary in Conyers's office, where the riot victims were gathering to report criminal damage. It was with no great desire to be in the limelight that Eddie Temple – in part encouraged by Parks – told his version of the story and took on the mantle of spokesperson for the victims' families.

The press was pursuing the killings like bloodhounds. A *Daily News* reporter named Joseph Strickland had managed to track down a first-hand witness to the deaths, a paratrooper named Robert Greene who had been with prostitutes in the Algiers on the night concerned. Strickland tracked down Greene, who had recently been discharged from Vietnam, to his native Kentucky. To ensure he remained within the law, the journalist was accompanied by Charles Schlachter of the Detroit homicide bureau and an assistant prosecutor who took official witness statements. It was as a result of the interview with the Vietnam vet that the homicide bureau announced what many already suspected – that the 'Negro youths were executed in cold blood', and that Greene himself had only narrowly escaped death by 'pleading that he had just reenlisted in the army' and was due to return to Vietnam.

Greene's testimony was a tipping point. Others came forward, and the dam of reticence was slowly breached. Independent post-mortem examinations were funded by local newspapers eager to have an original angle on a breaking story. The post-mortems revealed that all three youths were killed at close range with twelve-gauge shotguns. Each new revelation heaped more pressure on the police. The *Detroit Free Press*, which was building a reputation for hard-hitting coverage of the riots, wrote a single condemnatory sentence: 'Officials now fear that the three Negroes were deliberately executed.'

Detroit was trying to return to normal, but that was no longer possible. Fires could be extinguished more quickly than the stink of injustice, and the unexplained murders of Aubrey Pollard, Carl Cooper and Fred Temple were to linger for many years to come. The first person to face trial in the Algiers Motel case was neither a police officer nor white. Melvin Dismukes was a low-paid black security guard with a closely trimmed beard and darting eyes who had been patrolling private property near the motel and had called the police when he suspected trouble. Hersey described him as 'a phlegmatic, big-bodied, twenty-six-year-old Negro private guard in the employ of an outfit called State Private Patrol'. Dismukes lived near Henry Ford Hospital in a small wooden-frame home at 2741 West Grand opposite Motown. He was from Birmingham, Alabama, the grandson of the pioneering Negro baseball star Dizzy Dismukes, and was a devout Christian. On the first full night of the riots, he had been encouraged to work overtime to protect the premises of the Lucky Strike supermarket a block north of the Algiers, where he had seen Rod Davis of the Dramatics buying TV dinners to take back to the motel. Dismukes had apparently developed a grudge against the criminal elements who hung around the motel and had frequently used his role as a security guard to register complaints about its wayward nightlife. He had been there to meet the arriving Guardsmen and police officers on the night of the killings and so formed part of the first group who stormed the motel's annexe around one in the morning. In the ensuing charge, he struck a friend of the three dead men, James Sortor, and so was charged with felonious assault. Carl Cooper's stepfather, Omar Gill, attended the court and told journalists that the testimony had helped him make more sense of his stepson's death and that he now believed he had been shot in this initial raiding party. Cooper had been playing a game of dice with others on the third floor and in the chaos had run downstairs, straight into a hail of bullets. The other families were markedly less sure. Several witnesses told investigating officers that the Detroit police had taken some of the boys into separate motel rooms and, out of sight of witnesses, gunshots were heard.

★

With the Algiers Motel incident now the subject of an internal investigation, Diana Ross and the Supremes, under their new official name, performed at the Allentown Agricultural Fair in Pennsylvania. After an overnight stay, they flew north to New York to a residency at the St Moritz Hotel. Cindy Birdsong was now contracted to Motown as a full-time replacement for Florence Ballard, but press speculation remained intense, and Motown insiders speaking to journalists off the record talked about a catastrophic breakdown in relationships among the original members of the group. *Jet* carried a waspish feature by Chester Higgins Jr – then a freelance journalist from Alabama but later to become a towering African-American photographer – which began with a teasing question: 'Did those sweet little girls, the fabulous singing Supremes, really stage a hair-pulling, knock-down-drag-out fight over a change of billing that would place their mercurial lead singer Diana Ross at the top?' . . . 'Show business circles were buzzing with the rumor that these nice little girls who grew up together in the seamy public projects of Detroit and blossomed to superstardom, where each now earns in excess of $750,000 yearly, went at it hammer and tongs during an engagement at Las Vegas's plush Flamingo, and when the smoke cleared, Diana Ross had won.'

Motown loathed articles of this kind. Even when events tipped out of control, Motown clung fiercely to its family image. Gordy was staying at the Central Plaza Hotel in Los Angeles when he was confronted with the story and quickly tried to deflect it by telling journalists that the Supremes had broken attendance records at their last six engagements, including the Copacabana, DC's Shoreham Hotel, the Ambassador in Los Angeles, and then the Flamingo. According to Gordy, new pinnacles of success had been reached and it was time to move on. But his surface calm hid an uncharacteristic rage. Ballard was not quite ready to move on either. She was back in Detroit, living permanently with her mother, Lurlee Ballard, and her boyfriend, Tommy Chapman, on West Buena Vista. Chapman had assumed the role of manager and was blundering around trying to secure a solo recording deal, with no great master plan and no apparent progress. Tentatively at first,

Ballard's family and disillusioned friends on the fringes of Motown questioned both the value and legality of the severance deal she had signed at the Northland Inn. Al Abrams, who was now a freelance publicity agent for Stax, had salvaged a decent friendship with Ballard and offered advice and his services as an agent. He was one of several people who counselled her to think again about the severance deal and to consider fighting Motown in court. It was an idea that gnawed away at Ballard throughout August, and the first seeds of a bitter legal battle with Gordy were sown.

Motown was by now a nervous place. Backstage at Allentown, Mary Wilson received a telegram from the Temptations, who were on a West Coast tour. Couched in the staccato language of the telegram, it sounded unintentionally threatening: 'Mary, stick by Florence. It may happen to you. Think about it – the Tempts.' To complicate an already confusing situation, the *Detroit Free Press* ran a story claiming that Ballard was only leaving the Supremes for a period of one month and that she would return. The information had come from Ross and Wilson, who had been interviewed a few days earlier. It is not clear among claim and counterclaim whether they were putting out peace signs or simply spinning a version of events led by Motown. More likely the two women were not wholly on top of events and had not been properly briefed by Motown management prior to the interview. Rather than simply denying the story, Motown seemed to endorse it, leading the industry to believe Motown had offered Ballard a new contract that guaranteed one week off every six weeks to allow her to overcome recurring illnesses.

On Friday, 7 August, after a fractious disagreement inside police headquarters at 1300 Beaubien, the Detroit police finally conceded. Three serving police officers were to be the subject of an internal investigation. The announcement was triggered by a damning internal report by the city's homicide bureau. It was a red-hot fourteen-page document that savaged the National Guard and their own colleagues, and went as far as to describe the events at the Algiers Motel as 'cold-blooded murder'. The report drove an irreparable wedge through the law enforcement community. Some accepted that it was a necessary response to the due process of law and order, while others saw a craven betrayal that threw colleagues to the wolves. The report was sufficiently detailed and cogent about the events at the motel for Prosecutor William Cahalan to authorise homicide warrants against Patrolman Ronald August, twenty-eight, for the slaying of Aubrey Pollard, and Patrolman Robert Paille, thirty-one, for the killing of Fred Temple. Both were charged with first-degree murder and held without bond. A third officer, Patrolman David Senak, challenged the terms of the internal investigation, and no charges against him were brought forward.

Another irony awaited Detroit. With two police officers charged with the murder of black teenagers, two local youths, Charles Latimer and Danny Royster, appeared in court accused of the murder of police officer Jerome Olshove, who had died at a supermarket on Holbrook when his colleague's gun was discharged as they wrestled with looters. The trial underlined the chasm of distrust that had grown up between black teenagers and the police. Police and the Motown generation of inner-city teenagers existed in different worlds and observed different codes of honour – it was 1300 Beaubien versus the 20 Grand.

Throughout the various proceedings of the Algiers Motel murder trials, which dragged on for many years after August 1967, the local soul club known as the 20 Grand became a silent witness. It was the most famous venue for young African-Americans across the city. The Dramatics had performed there several times, the three teenagers murdered at the Algiers Motel were all regulars, and Motown's galaxy of stars had all earned their spurs singing in the club's Driftwood Lounge. Marvin Gaye and Anna Gordy held their wedding reception there; Frantic Ernie Durham broadcast a weekly show from the club; and Smokey Robinson had dated his wife at its crowded tables. The 20 Grand was a nightclub, a cocktail lounge and a bowling alley all in one venue and was owned by two R&B club veterans, Bill Kabbush and Marty Eisner. The adjacent premises were owned by Motown's long-standing indie rival Ed Wingate, the former owner of Golden World Records and the proprietor of the overflow studios Gordy had acquired in 1966. The club had taken its name from a famous racehorse that had won the Kentucky Derby back in the Depression years and had subsequently lent its name to a brand of cigarettes popular in the post-war ghettos of urban America.

The 20 Grand was located at 5020 Fourteenth Street and Warren. It was always a legal club, but not everything about it was strictly law-abiding. One of the Algiers Motel murder victims, Aubrey Pollard, who had been a welder at River Rouge plant but subsequently fired for missing work, hung out there. Another victim, Carl Cooper, was described at the trials as a petty criminal and an urban dandy who 'dressed with a fierce and iridescent bravado'. On the day of his murder, Cooper made a 'natty sight; he was wearing brown loafers and brown socks, orange trousers, a brown sports coat over a white dress shirt, and a white straw hat'.

The police despised the peacock youths who frequented the 20 Grand and saw them as lawless and immoral. Each of the three officers at the centre of the Algiers Motel killings had made arrests at the 20 Grand and grown to resent the city's soul clubs. All three were junior officers and described being disorientated and fatigued from working twenty hours a day during the riots, but each had his unique pathology too. Patrolman Ronald August was a clarinetist in the police band under bandleader George Overman, whose son had been murdered at Cobo Hall earlier in the year. August had participated in the blue flu strikes of 1967, which he told Hersey had been a 'very bitter subject' and proved that senior officers were out of touch with the ordinary cop on patrol. He was a cautious man, almost melancholic, and seemed intimidated by brasher and more self-confident colleagues. Patrolman Robert Paille described feeling alienated in his own city and harboured resentment about young black men who failed to cooperate during the riots and goaded police officers as fires raged across the city. He told Hersey, 'Basically, I believe they are more immoral than corresponding white people.'

David Senak, the third officer, was the most resentful. He had worked with the city's vice squad patrolling the nightclubs and brothels on the Fourteenth Street strip and had witnessed prostitution, illegal gambling and sexual crimes close-up. He attributed the malaise in Detroit to a hard core of criminal black men who lived off immoral earnings and who were frequently to be found at the 20 Grand or the Algiers Motel. Senak's vice-squad job had made him paranoid about interracial sex, and he held racist attitudes towards young blacks. Paradoxically, Senak had been a student at Detroit's Cass Tech, where his time as a student had overlapped with a host of Motown talent, including Ivy Jo Hunter, arranger Paul Riser, producer Dale Warren and baritone saxophonist Andrew 'Mike' Terry. Senak graduated in the class of 1963 with Diana Ross, though neither knew each other well. Senak had studied architectural drawing and Ross fashion studies, but in a twist of fate, when Senak was initially charged with murder, he was sent home under internal investigation and remembered sitting in his living room watching Diana Ross and the Supremes on *American Bandstand* singing their 1967 hit 'Reflections'.

Motown's infrastructure survived the riots. Office staff returned to work as soon as the all-clear was sounded and began to prepare for the corporation's first national sales convention. A hectic timetable of recording and touring continued, and producers were expected to catch up on lost ground. In the first two weeks of August 1967, seventeen-year-old Stevie Wonder recorded a new album and a series of classics for the Christmas market, including Schubert's 'Ave Maria'. For most of his formative years at Motown, Wonder's creative development had been delegated to former gospel singer turned producer Clarence Paul in what was an odd relationship – not quite father and son, but not without its paternalism. Stevie Wonder was blind, ebullient and irritatingly prone to practical jokes, while Clarence Paul, a coalminer's son from a musical family in Bluefield, West Virginia, preferred a chilled-out and sedentary pace cushioned by marijuana. He had shortened his name from Pauling to Paul to distinguish him from his more famous brother, Lowman Pauling of the doo-wop group the 5 Royales, and earlier in his career had penned the dance-craze hit 'Hitch Hike' for

Marvin Gaye. Clarence Paul never managed to convert his early promise into sustained success, however, and as the sixties ignited for soul music, he had come to consider himself a victim of Motown's unspoken hierarchies.

Berry Gordy had stuck rigidly to a system that favoured piling resources behind the big sellers and letting the rest fight for attention. The Supremes were at the very top; below them were the Four Tops, the Temptations, Marvin Gaye and Smokey Robinson; and below them was a generation of talent that would have graced any rival city, including Stevie Wonder, Gladys Knight and Edwin Starr. The pecking order had worked well over the years, and those who couldn't make an impact either moved on or hung around waiting for unpredictable scraps of opportunity. Clarence Paul's stock was in decline, but he persisted on the fringes, hustling for studio time, tolerating Stevie Wonder, and dealing with thwarted ambition. Wonder was not an easy child. He had been born blind, the son of a feckless street hustler and a mother who was forced to work as a street prostitute. More than anyone he immersed himself in the noisy and increasingly superficial family atmosphere at Motown.

As Paul's career drifted, he took to throwing house parties where minor Motown acts and local backing singers frequently met to hang out. What began as irregular social events gradually evolved into something closer to a local union meeting. Disenchantment was aired, terms and conditions compared, and Motown's royalty payment system openly discussed. Gordy was aware of the grievances that were flaring up among the musicians, but he mistakenly shrugged them off as meetings of the miserable. He had yet to fully grasp that some of Motown's hardest-working talent, like Gladys Knight, the Originals and the Monitors, were also going along to the meetings, and that producers like Ivy Jo Hunter, who had co-written the now controversial riot song 'Dancing In The Street', were regulars.

With the full horror of the Algiers Motel incident outraging black Detroit, Diana Ross and the Supremes were now markedly out of touch with day-to-day events in their home city. In mid

August they embarked on an innovative set of shows at the old Steel Pier in Atlantic City, appearing in four short promotional shows a day, singing only their greatest hits. The show had the veneer of gospel, with Wilson and Birdsong wearing full-length white gowns and supporting the vocals with frantic tambourines. Audiences of 5,000 or more were packed in every hour. There were no seats, and the event frequently came close to getting out of hand; on some days the girls had to be rescued from the stage by security guards. Towards the end of the run, the Supremes returned to their hotel rooms to discover that they had been robbed and their rooms ransacked. Nine thousand dollars in furs and jewels, a wig worth $1,500 and a diamond necklace worth a further $4,000 were taken from Ross's room. Motown immediately moved the group to a new hotel and refunded the value of the stolen property, but an article in that month's *Jet* magazine, ostensibly a review of the Atlantic City concerts, also updated the story of Ballard, who had just been released from Henry Ford Hospital, where she had been treated for another illness, this time an intestinal virus. 'Meanwhile Florence, the former Supreme, sat in her comfortable northwest side Detroit home,' *Jet* reported. 'At twenty-four, Miss Ballard admits to being a wealthy woman without a financial care in the world. "Berry Gordy invested our money and he did it well," she said. Last year, she and the other Supremes – lead singer Diana Ross and Mary Wilson – earned more than $750,000 each. Much of their money is invested in blue-chip stocks, bonds, insurance, real estate, etc.' The robbery in Atlantic City brought wealth to the forefront at Motown, incensing those who were on low pay and infuriating those who felt that their talent was being overlooked, and the gulf in earnings inevitably alienated the Supremes from their now deposed founding member Florence Ballard even more.

A few days earlier, on 14 August 1967, Judge Robert E. DeMascio began the pre-trial examination in the *People of the State of Michigan v. Ronald August and Robert Paille*. The very fact that serving police officers had come to trial infuriated some of their colleagues, and fifty-five policemen jammed the Recorder's Court to protest. 'They are in the court to give moral support to these two police officers in the belief that they are innocent,' said Charles Withers, a representative of the Detroit Police Officers Association. 'As more and more get off duty, they will come to the courtroom too.' It was an intimidating experience for the small group of family members who turned up hoping that justice would be done. The two accused had spent time in the county jail after being arrested at their place of work – 1300 Beaubien, police headquarters.

Patrolman Robert Paille described the events as humiliating: 'It was the most awkward night of my life. During that time there, I tell you, it was really something. We were confined to an area there, isolated, and – we were both together – and jeez, it was, you know, it was almost unbreatheable in that place.' According to news reports, the other officer, Patrolman Ronald August, who was accused of the murder of Aubrey Pollard, 'appeared deeply depressed and on the verge of tears'. He was to become a compelling character throughout the proceedings, responsible for murder and yet, according to contemporaneous reports, the most passive and seemingly caring of the officers. It appeared as if he had been swept up by a police culture that was resentful, self-protective and conspiratorial. Senak said that he had seen neither of his colleagues fire a weapon and had not fired one himself. This contradicted remarks they had made internally to investigating officers, but due to court procedure Paille's 'oral confession', which was neither written down nor signed, was ruled inadmissible. The judge's summary described the charges against Ronald August as actions 'totally unlike defendant August', which was probably true but ran counter to all the material evidence. Pollard's father, Aubrey Pollard Sr, testified and so too did Fred Temple's brother Eddie, but the trial was cut short and the families were forced to accept the first of many delays and obfuscations.

John Hersey took the opportunity to make contact with Pollard Sr and interviewed him in depth about his son. According to Hersey, Aubrey's father sat 'square-shouldered and stiff with defiance on the edge of a sofa . . . He toyed with a knuckle of pork on a plate on a coffee table before him.' Now separated from his distraught wife, he ate his 'lonely supper' and described a son who had yet to find his way in life, a boy who was easily led and had been a good painter as a child. Hersey recorded his thoughts meticulously, right up to the point when the father described his son's death on the floor of a cheap motel. 'He never knew what hardness was. He had to crawl through a bucket of blood. The poor little fellow, he didn't know what life was really all about. Aubrey was a beautiful kid, but he was a baby, that's all, just a baby.' Pollard had died in apartment 3A of the motel's annexe, the room the Dramatics had hired for eleven dollars a night from the proceeds of their show at the Fox Theater. Witnesses described him writhing in his own blood in the last moments of life.

The Algiers Motel case had everything: disputed stories, deep-vested interests and an unparalleled sequence of events leading to macabre and ritualistic killings. The rituals became known as 'the death game', a term first coined by John Hersey as a way of describing the psychotic behaviour of the officers and the degradation their victims endured. By the time the game began, Carl Cooper and Fred Temple were already dead, killed by police or National Guard fire when the building was initially stormed. Both were slain at the rear of the annexe, where, among others, Paille, August and Dismukes had been the first contingent to enter the building.

Charging into the annexe and up the stairs, the police entered the Dramatics' room. It too was ransacked. 'They looked in closets, in the drawers, under the covers,' singer Rod Davis said. 'One of them put a gun to my head and shouted, "Get up."' Police screamed out through the motel corridors, demanding that all residents line up on the ground-floor lobby. Some did; others understandably tried to hide. Two other youths, James Sortor and his friend Lee Forsythe, hid in a linen cupboard. Larry Reed had been on the phone with his girlfriend, Glenda Tucker, a singer with a local soul group called the Fabulettes, who had recently recorded the song 'Mr. Policeman', in which Tucker and her fellow Fabulettes yearned for the love of a Detroit police officer. Still on the phone, Tucker heard noises in the background and was concerned she might have heard a shot. But then she was disconnected. Worried that Reed might have been caught up in trouble, she called the motel again, trying to be reconnected, but this time the motel receptionist claimed that no calls could be put through to the annexe due to an incident.

Eventually groups of people were rounded up and forced to line up along the lobby wall. They included the two remaining members of the Dramatics, Larry Reed and Rod Davis, along with prostitutes Julie Hysell and Karen Malloy, Vietnam veteran Robert Lee Green and a crowd of young soul revellers who earlier that night had been at the 20 Grand. Among those revellers were Aubrey Pollard, Michael Clark, Lee Forsythe and James Sortor. In all, there were nine people lined along the east wall of the annexe. Their arms were raised and they faced the wall, some without shoes, some in shorts, and some half asleep.

The Detroit police still believed there were snipers in the motel and demanded to seize guns that simply didn't exist. It was at this stage that Officer David Senak – nicknamed 'Snake' – took charge. Police behaviour had already been heavy-handed, but now it took on a sadistic character. According to his witness testimony, Rod Davis of the Dramatics reported that one officer screamed, 'We're going to kill all you black niggers off one at a time!' Davis was then beaten around the head seven or eight times. Police fired questions at him, and when he tried to answer they beat him again. They smashed his fingers with the butt of a gun, then forced him to lie down spread-eagled on the lobby floor and fired shots into the floor close to his body to frighten him.

The police interrogated those lined by the wall one by one. According to social historian Sidney Fine, 'the questioning was accompanied by further beatings and then in some instances by the firing of shots in the interrogation room, designed to convince those still in the line that their comrades had been executed for not revealing where the gun or guns were and that they would all be killed if they did not talk.' Clark and Davis of the Dramatics were taken into separate rooms, shots were fired into furniture or into the ceiling, and the two youths were forced to pretend they were dead. Davis was told to play dead and 'not budge an inch' so the rest of the line would believe the death game was for real. Senak now threatened to kill everyone in the line, barking at the men for being with naked white women and humiliating the two girls, calling them 'whores' and 'nigger lovers'.

Reed and Davis of the Dramatics were then told to say their last prayer before they died. Reed started to recite the Lord's Prayer at the top of his voice, and Davis joined in as if it was a gruesome rehearsal. They recited 'Now I Lay Me Down To Sleep', and as more blows rained down on them, Davis began to half sing the Twenty-Third Psalm, which the two youths had learned word for word as members of the Pershing High School Gospel Choir. They sang 'The Lord is my shepherd, I'll not want', and when they reached the line 'Even though I walk through the valley of the shadow of death', another member of the line screamed out 'Oh, Lord, please let me get out of this alive.' The Michigan National Guard and a few state police officers who had arrived at the scene retreated from the building, uneasy with the grotesque scenes they were witnessing. 'Detroit police are in charge in there,' one officer said, forcing his men off the premises. Patrolman David Senak was indeed in charge of events, but he was not in control of his own heightened and racist emotions. Three Detroit police officers remained. They continued to beat people in the line, thrashing their hands with gun butts, kicking their legs apart, and threatening to shoot the men in their testicles. Sensing that Ronald August was not participating in the attacks with the same gusto, Senak goaded him into taking the next suspect and interrogating him. August chose Aubrey Pollard at random. Pollard was forced to leave the line and accompany the reluctant officer to a nearby room. August, described in the court as 'refined', 'shy', and at times 'reluctant', found himself in apartment A3, faced with a petrified Pollard, who at the time wrongly thought the two other men had been executed and that he faced a similar fate.

For a few short dark moments, witnessed by no one, the Algiers Motel became a tableau of misunderstanding. In the room was a police bandsman who had worked exhausting shifts and had recently attended the funeral of a colleague's son who had been killed by a criminal black teenager, and a black teenager with no criminal record who happened to be in a place with a long record of criminal notoriety. Since he had given up his job as a welder at Ford, Pollard had been unemployed, was short of cash, and had no reason to trust the police. His father described him as 'smart in some ways', saying that 'he wanted to go a long ways. He loved to paint. He was a good artist. Everybody's dumb in some way. He was young.' It was a mess of unspoken fear and deep prejudice: a frightened police officer and a wayward but entirely innocent teenager scared out of his wits. Officer August was later adamant that he had kept assuring Pollard that he was not going to kill him, saying, 'Why would I kill you? I have never killed anyone in my life.' But no one heard that, and no one was close enough to bear witness. Pollard knew others had been shot, and he had seen the beatings close-up. Although he himself had not been as badly injured as his friends, he had every reason to believe his life was in danger. He lunged forward in self-defence – whether he was trying to escape or attempting to restrain the police officer is unclear – but his sudden reaction panicked August, and in the confusion the teenager was shot dead. He was the third young man to die inside the motel that night.

Back in the lobby, the remaining officers continued to beat, insult and pistol-whip the detained youths, some now so violently battered that blood spattered onto the faded wallpaper. In his court testimony National Guardsman Thomas filled in further detail: 'I told the police it was strictly their business and left the building.' Ronald August left the building soon after, too, and by his own admission leaned against the annexe wall and tried to vomit, sick about what he had seen and done. The patrolman slept restlessly, and on the morning after the killings the Detroit homicide bureau instructed all officers from the Thirteenth Precinct who had been at the motel to report to 1300 Beaubien. August met up with the others, and a consensus built among the group to deny conspiracy or brutality and to report the events in as matter-of-fact a way as possible.

Ronald August's handwritten report was economical with the truth. He did not mention the beatings, the game of death, the racist bullying, or the moment when he found himself alone in a room with Aubrey Pollard and shot him dead. But it was not all omission. August had embroidered one important part of the narrative: he exaggerated, along with his colleagues, the role of sniper fire, creating the illusion in the minds of his superiors and subsequently the court that the patrol had been under constant fire from rooftops around the motel. Soon after he had submitted his written report, August asked to speak in private to a senior officer, Lieutenant Gerald Hallmark, and made a more truthful confession. Sometime after, August was said to have told another officer that he'd confessed because 'he couldn't live with it'. A third officer described him as having 'a kind of sentimental atmosphere', a poetic way of saying that Ronald August was guilt-ridden and a threat to more belligerent colleagues.

John Hersey interviewed August after the pre-trial hearings 'in the spotless alcove of his house' and described him in his forensically accurate style as 'slender, dark and straight; with a gentle voice; with the slightly enlarged jaw muscles of a man who clenches his teeth; devoted husband of Genevieve'. Hersey painted a picture of an unremarkable man, devoted rather than brutal, anxious rather than arrogant. It was a picture that in every respect captured the banality of evil. This was not a man who had relished violence but one who had shot a young teenager at the height of an orgiastic police raid and was now facing a crisis of doubt.

The second day of the preliminary examinations heard Detective James Cowie say, 'A police officer is in a very peculiar position when there are criminal implications involved in a report that he may have to make to superior officers.' In effect, the accused's legal teams were now able to challenge whether the individual officers had been informed of their constitutional rights prior to filing their own reports, or when they were giving witness statements to senior officers. Put simply, had the police acted properly when interviewing the police?

The accused officers could potentially escape punishment by citing their Miranda rights. Had they been told of their right to remain silent? This was ironic to the point of incredulity; the Detroit police had been among the most vocal opponents of the Miranda warning, believing it was a constitutional right that benefited only criminals. In *Miranda v. Arizona*, a landmark case in 1963, Ernesto Miranda had been accused of kidnapping and raping a mentally challenged eighteen-year-old woman. When brought in for questioning, he confessed to the crime but was not told that he did not have to speak or that he could have a lawyer present. At his trial Miranda's legal team tried to get the confession thrown out. The motion was initially denied, but by 1966 the case had worked its way up to the Supreme Court, where a ruling established that statements made to the police could not be used as evidence, since Miranda had not been advised of his rights. Police across the United States resented the ruling because it made the bureaucracy of their job more onerous. Yet now, in the most public and dramatic of circumstances, the three accused Detroit officers were about to use the very ruling that the police took umbrage at.

The Algiers Motel hearings were a prequel to lengthy and unsatisfactory legal wrangles. Patrolman Robert Paille was released when Judge DeMascio pronounced that there was insufficient evidence and material witnesses to sustain a successful prosecution. The troubled Ronald August was charged with murder and faced further trial, while his partner, Officer David Senak, already identified as a ringleader by the media, had yet to face charges. Exhausted by the tension in the crowded court, Aubrey Pollard's mother finally broke down, yelling at the departing officers, 'Why did they do that to him? Why did they have to tear off his face? I know they did it.' She was helped from the court, sobbing uncontrollably. The last time she had seen her son was at the city's J. T. Wilson Funeral Home, with a plastic mask and reconstructed face staring up at her, so fragile she was not allowed to touch it or kiss it for a final time.

★

On Sunday, 20 August, the Supremes were in Montreal performing at Expo 67. It was a commercial haven protected from the social disturbances of inner-city America. Back home in Detroit, local soul-music promoter Don Davis drove down Woodward in suffocating heat. He owned a string of small independent labels and was staging an all-day Emancipation Dance at Detroit's Arcadia roller rink. He had struggled to get a licence for the event. The local authorities were scared of any major gathering of young African-American teenagers, and the show was to feature many of the city's emergent soul acts, including Groovesville recording artist Steve Mancha, the Fabulous Peps and a local group called the Holidays. By far the most newsworthy act on the extensive Arcadia roster was the Dramatics; it was to be the group's first public engagement since the riots. Ron Banks had managed to convince injured members Rod Davis and Larry Reed to perform, although both were still recovering from the beatings at the Algiers Motel and had been unable to rehearse. Davis's head was wrapped in bandages, and he had agreed to remove them and use heavy make-up to conceal his wounds.

As Davis negotiated the show with serious head injuries, black nationalist preacher Albert Cleage assembled a group of prominent Detroit radicals from the Citywide Citizens Action Committee to respond to the Algiers case. Enraged by the lack of justice for the families, they laid plans for a people's court to try the officers in absentia. Cleage and his acolytes told the press that the people's tribunal would be held at Detroit's Dexter Theater and would retry the police officers before a people's jury. A young Pontiac-based civil rights lawyer, Milton Henry, who had formerly set up the Malcolm X Society with his brother Richard Henry in their native Philadelphia, was elected to prosecute on behalf of the families. The tribunal split public opinion. Some saw a system of shadow justice; others a grotesque circus that was never intended to be fair. Fearing a backlash from the authorities, the Dexter Theater withdrew the booking, and at the eleventh hour the tribunal had to be hurriedly switched to Cleage's Shrine of the Black Madonna.

Coincidentally, Florence Ballard had driven by the church

earlier that day in her distinctive plum-coloured Cadillac Eldorado, heading downtown. Chauffeur Tommy was with her, but Ballard insisted on driving – the streamlined Eldorado, with its majestic back fins, a reassurance that her career was still on track. She was heading for a meeting with legal firm Okrent, Baun and Vulpe. At the time the thriving legal practice was led by the company's senior partner, Harry Okrent, an avuncular man whose office was decorated with all the trappings: a Rolodex, framed graduation certificates, family photos and a Tigers paperweight perched on piles of Michigan law papers. Okrent introduced Ballard and Chapman to his partner Leonard Baun, whom he liked to describe as 'the big friendly puppy dog' of the firm. Baun shook hands vigorously with his visitors and ushered them into an inner office. Within forty-five minutes, Florence Ballard had signed a new contract which was to prove every bit as contentious as her contracts with Motown and the ill-advised settlement she had signed at the Northland Inn. Baun presented her with a standard one-page Authority to Represent form. Neither unusual nor complex, it outlined that Florence Ballard agreed to be represented by Okrent, Baun and Vulpe in her claim for damages against 'Motown Record Corporation, Berry Gordy Jr., Enterprises Inc.' and 'Berry Gordy Jr' individually. The document was in effect a no-win/no-fee agreement that secured for the law firm twenty per cent of any amounts recovered from any settlement or litigation. The fee would only become payable in the event of a successful outcome and then immediately. Using the lawyer's own pen, Ballard signed. Her signature was much like an autograph: clear, fluid and with a flourish. What neither Ballard nor Okrent knew was that the lawyer who had taken her instructions had the beginnings of a brain tumour and was to prove a wholly unsuited figure to lead a legal fight with the resourceful lawyers of Motown.

By the end of August, the police had compiled a damning dossier on the Algiers Motel. They had always insisted it was a magnet for petty crime; in the previous six months, there had been fifty-seven arrests, of which sixteen were for robbery, sixteen were for violation of narcotics law, and the remainder for petty offences. There was no mention of either the arrested officers or of the executions of Carl Cooper, Aubrey Pollard and Fred Temple. Nonetheless Prosecutor William Cahalan filed suit in the Wayne County Circuit Court on the basis that between 24 April and 6 September 'sixteen persons had been arrested in [the Algiers's] rooms on narcotics charges'. The motel's days as a gathering place for Detroit's soul musicians were numbered.

Over five thousand people had gathered at the Dexter Theater to hear H. Rap Brown at a rally for the victims' families. In his high-octane voice, he engaged in his greatest skill: masterful polemic and unchecked rabble-rousing. 'If they are found guilty, the brothers should carry out an execution!' he roared, alienating himself further from the Detroit police. The tribunal divided the city. Some dismissed it as gimmicky, a 'mock trial by cop-haters', but others saw it as righteous retribution for a justice system that had failed to convict the police. Superficially, it was the events at the Algiers Motel that were on trial; more accurately, it was 1300 Beaubien and police corruption. Flyers were distributed to the crowds. 'Watch accurate justice administered by citizens of the community.' 'Witness the unbiased legal action of skilled black attorneys.' Milton R. Henry, subsequently a co-founder of the ultra-militant Republic of New Africa (RNA), served as one of the two prosecutors; Solomon A. Plapkin, a white attorney, and another Central Church member, Russell L. Brown Jr, were the defence counsel. The stenographer was Carolyn Cheeks Kilpatrick, mother of a future Detroit mayor, Kwame Kilpatrick, and among the jury members summoned to pass judgement were the novelist John Oliver Killens of the Harlem Writers Guild and the veteran activist Rosa Parks.

Eddie Temple, the brother of the dead teenager Fred Temple, was called as a witness. He recounted the feelings he had the day he saw his brother's corpse. 'I was there as a witness,' he said a short while later, 'actually as the person who identified my brother at the morgue. It had a tremendous value in that it exposed to a large number of people what had happened there, what these people had had to go through, the beatings, the fear.'

Detroit had become a specimen. For months it was analysed like a laboratory slide. The riots provoked a rash of very different surveys, each trying to make sense of the mayhem. One survey reported that seventy-nine per cent of citizens on the East Side wanted capital punishment for snipers caught during civil disturbances. Philip Meyer, a national correspondent for Knight Newspapers, which owned the *Detroit Free Press*, had just returned to the city after a sabbatical at Harvard and commissioned a survey known as 'The People beyond Twelfth Street'. He trained thirty black interviewers to go into riot-torn neighbourhoods to conduct the survey, and he established that the main grievances were overcrowded living conditions and police brutality. Another survey published in the *Michigan Chronicle* announced a subtle but seismic shift in the language of the city. Growing numbers of young African-Americans had stopped using the word 'riot' and were increasingly describing the events of late July as a 'rebellion'. It was more than mere semantics. A new sense of social awareness had settled on the city, and the term 'rebellion' implied something deeper and more purposeful: a sense of social action, retaliation and resistance.

The Algiers Motel case had come to symbolise the horror that had engulfed the city the previous month. The damage done to Detroit's reputation and social geography clouded some of the underlying detail. Although Motown had survived largely unscathed, the infrastructure of the city's independent soul-music scene was fatally damaged: studios burned to the ground, instruments destroyed, and shops ransacked. It was in many respects the end of the musical gold rush that had made Detroit the most creative black-music city ever. But that was nothing compared to the images of chaos and murder now etched in the minds of two young musicians who had witnessed darkness at the heart of the city.

It was 1.35 a.m. on a hot, sticky night. The Algiers Motel annexe was under police control. Glenda Tucker of the Fabulettes kept dialling reception, fearful that her boyfriend was dead. The National Guardsmen had retreated to the streets outside. Finally, after three killings, an hour of brutal beatings, and ritual humiliation at the hands of the three police officers, the young captives were sent in opposite directions. The two half-naked prostitutes were led back to the main motel. Others were forced back into their rooms, and those with no right to be in the motel were scattered through various exits. The last two members of the Dramatics to leave the Algiers Motel were forced out at gunpoint through the rear porch to Euclid and Woodward, to tense streets still governed by a curfew.

A few hours before, the two singers had been in their underwear, relaxing on motel beds; now they were on the streets, still not fully clothed. Hersey described their departure in remarkable detail: 'Roderick [Davis] started out in stockinged feet, and he was sharply surprised when, passing Room A2 on his way to the back door, he came on the body of Carl Cooper prone in a stain of blood in the carpet; he had not seen the body earlier, as most of the others had, and he had not believed even after all the shooting he had heard that uniformed men were actually killing people. He had to step over the body, for it blocked the room between one of the beds and the dresser.'

Outside, Davis desperately looked around, trying to find his fellow singer Larry Reed. Seeing the former captives emerge from the back of the motel, the National Guard troops cocked their rifles and forced them to lie face down on a plot of grass. One by one they were allowed up, instructed to put their hands on their heads, and then sent into the night under strict instructions to keep their hands in the air and not under any circumstances to look back. Eventually the two young singers were far enough way to run. Reed was a block ahead of Davis, but they both kept running until they felt safe enough to glance back. They couldn't see their school friend and part-time valet, Fred Temple, and assumed he must still be somewhere in the motel. In fact, he was lying in a pool of his own blood on the floor of apartment 3A next to Aubrey Pollard.

Rod Davis and Larry Reed's dark journey had not yet ended. Hersey wrote: 'Having walked forty-two blocks in stockinged feet, Roderick and Larry made their way across open lots and were about to cross some railroad tracks, near Dequindre, and a train came, and the lights of the locomotive shone on them, and they waited. After the train had passed they crossed the tracks, and some police and guardsmen stopped them. "Why are you all bloody?" The boys tried to tell them. "It's a good thing," the men said, "the light from the train was on you, because we were about to shoot.'" Briefly mistaken for looters, the two men were now by the Grand Trunk Railroad and in the custody of the National Guard, who handed them over to the Hamtramck police. They were now hopelessly lost in a bleak industrial area by the Detroit River. Finally, after another round of questioning, they were driven home, their feet grazed, their heads cut and bleeding, and their trademark pompadour haircuts ragged and untidy. Neither wanted to go to the hospital and, according to police, had a childlike desperation to get home. They talked guardedly in the police car, both still of the mistaken belief that Fred Temple had escaped and was out on the streets making his way home too. In fact, his body had been taken to the city morgue by the wagon patrol that Ronald August had summoned and was already tagged dead on arrival.

According to Fred's brother Eddie, who also knew the Dramatics from his time at Pershing High School, most of the survivors 'held up well', and he stayed in touch with them for a while. Roderick Davis was by all accounts the worst affected. He suffered from blinding headaches, drifted away from music, and was no longer enthusiastic about his greatest passion in life – singing. Towards the end of August, Eddie met Davis downtown. 'I just ran across him in . . . a department store,' he said. 'He wasn't looking well, and I talked to him, and he told me that his head had been bothering him tremendously, where he had been shot in the head. I tried to get him to see a doctor about this. Financially I don't think he had the money.'

A few weeks later, Davis's mother was interviewed by John Hersey. 'There is a difference in him,' she said. 'I took him to a neurologist but he wouldn't go on with the treatment. The doctor wanted him to have a head X-ray but he said he didn't want to do it unless there was something really bad, and if something was really bad he didn't want to know.' She described how he had become edgy and paranoid and that he often claimed his mother and sister were talking about him. They were, but only in the way concerned people do. On his second enforced visit to the neurologist, Davis was given an encephalogram, which revealed slowness on the left side of the brain where the worst of his wounds were raw, dark pink, and still healing. The neurologist was in no doubt that Davis's cognitive functions had been impaired irretrievably.

Roderick Davis and Larry Reed were still alive. But of all the survivors of the Algiers Motel incident, they had suffered the worst beatings and the deepest personal trauma. Soul music felt less relevant now, and within a matter of months both had drifted away from the Dramatics to be replaced by two more Detroit hopefuls, Willie Ford and William 'Wee-Gee' Howard. Roderick Davis stubbornly refused to seek help and would not consent to any further neurological scans, telling his mother repeatedly that he did not want to know how unwell he had become. His soul career was over, and within a few years he simply disappeared, drifting quietly into the dark anonymity of the city. He was the unheralded fourth victim of the Algiers Motel killings and one of Detroit soul music's greatest casualties.

Wiretapped. Martin Luther King makes a phone call from his hotel room.
Throughout 1967 he was under FBI surveillance, and his room
at Detroit's Ponchartrain Hotel was wiretapped.

SEPTEMBER

Surveillance

It was in the late summer of 1967 that Florence Ballard first mentioned hearing clicks on her phone line. Remarkably, she was not alone, and not even in a minority. A survey conducted by a supermarket magazine claimed that up to sixty per cent of adults across the United States believed their phone was bugged, and in Detroit seventy-five per cent of major corporations regularly swept their premises for bugs. The Michigan Bell Telephone Company, which serviced most private phone lines across the city, claimed that the most common customer concern after billing and directory enquiries was about bugging. The nervousness Florence Ballard felt echoed a wider anxiety of the time. She lived in a city increasingly fixated on surveillance, and in the aftermath of the summer rebellions Detroit made national headlines as the city most readily associated with electronic eavesdropping.

Many citizens were familiar with the dark arts of surveillance from magazine features on how to spot wiretapping, how to unscrew the mouthpiece of a phone, how to listen for clicks and echoes on the line, or how to detect telltale wires in Bell telephone junction boxes. It was a popular obsession, even for those who had nothing much to hide, and like most modern anxieties the concern was rife at Motown. Artists often joked that the boss was listening in or that the lawyers knew their every move. It was nothing more than an urban myth of the time, but for Ballard paranoia was no longer a joke. She felt intimidated by Motown and the praetorian guard of white lawyers Gordy had built around himself.

September was barely two days old when a highly confidential communiqué on surveillance techniques was distributed by hand to two Detroit-based FBI officers, Thomas P. Druken and John E. King. It had been handed to them by their special agent in charge, known only by the bureau's coded acronym, Detroit SAC. It had been despatched in secret in the last week of August from FBI headquarters in Washington, where it had been personally authorised by the director of the FBI, J. Edgar Hoover.

Neither King nor Druken were new to surveillance. Over the previous eighteen months, they had been part of undercover operations tracking Muhammad Ali during his short stay to fight Alvin 'Blue' Lewis and pursuing Martin Luther King when he preached locally. By the mid sixties the charismatic black leader had become a figure of obsession for the FBI. Hoover had instructed agents to probe into the lives of his political allies, the finances of his church, and, most scandalously, into the minister's adventurous sex life. Hoover was of the view that King was not only a threat to the established order but a hypocritical philanderer whose gospel exhortations disguised a string of sexual liaisons with married women. At a poisonous press conference in November 1964, Hoover had lashed out at King's criticism of the FBI by describing the civil rights leader as 'the most notorious liar in the country'.

The FBI field office in King's home town of Atlanta, Georgia, held voluminous files on King's activities filed under the codename 'Zorro'. The FBI were aware of several simultaneous threats to assassinate King with bounties offered by a right-wing cartel in St Louis and a $100,000 bounty offered by Samuel Bowers, the leader of the White Knights of the Ku Klux Klan. But by the summer of 1967 the bureau was less interested in the radical right. The communiqué in King and Druken's possession urged FBI field offices to widen their existing programmes of covert action and focus on urban black activists. It recommended intensifying the surveillance of Martin Luther King and launching a new campaign of mis-information against Black Power leaders such as Stokely Carmichael and H. Rap Brown. It was an instruction that implicitly targeted a cadre of Detroit-based radicals, many of them labour activists in the city's revolutionary black workers movement, later to become known as the Detroit Revolutionary Union Movement (DRUM). This highly controversial policy of covert action was to be known by the acronym COINTELPRO – the Counterintelligence Program.

August 25, 1967
[From] Director, FBI

PERSONAL ATTENTION TO ALL OFFICES

COUNTERINTELLIGENCE PROGRAM BLACK NATIONALIST – HATE GROUPS INTERNAL SECURITY

Offices receiving copies of this letter are instructed to immediately establish a control file captioned as above, and to assign responsibility for following and coordinating this new counterintelligence program to an experienced and imaginative Special Agent well versed in investigations relating to Black Nationalist, hate-type organizations…

The purpose of this new counterintelligence endeavor is to expose, disrupt, misdirect, discredit, or OTHERWISE NEUTRALIZE the activities of Black Nationalist hate-type organizations and groupings, their leadership, spokesmen, membership, and supporters, and to counter their propensity for violence and civil disorder.…The pernicious background of such groups, their duplicity, and devious maneuvers must be exposed to public scrutiny where such publicity will have a neutralizing effect. Efforts of the various groups to consolidate their forces or to recruit new or youthful adherents must be frustrated.

No opportunity should be missed to exploit through counter-intelligence techniques the organizational and personal conflicts of the leaderships of the groups and where possible an effort should be made to capitalize upon existing conflicts between competing Black Nationalist organizations. When an opportunity is apparent to disrupt or neutralize Black Nationalist, hate-type organizations through the cooperation of established local news media contacts or through such contact with sources available to the Seat of Government, in every instance careful attention must be given to the proposal to insure the targeted group is disrupted and not merely publicized. Consideration should be given to techniques to preclude violence-prone or rabble-rouser leaders of hate groups from spreading their philosophy publicly or through various mass communication media.

Many individuals currently active in Black Nationalist organizations have backgrounds of immorality, subversive activity, and criminal records. Through your investigation of key agitators, you should endeavor to establish their unsavory backgrounds. Be alert to determine evidence of misappropriation of funds or other types of personal misconduct on the part of militant nationalist leaders so any practical or warranted counter-intelligence may be instituted.

Intensified attention under this program should be afforded to the activities of such groups as the Student Nonviolent Coordinating Committee, the Southern Christian Leadership Conference, Revolutionary Action Movement, the Deacons for Defense and Justice, Congress of Racial Equality, and the Nation of Islam. Particular emphasis should be given to extremists who direct the activities and policies of revolutionary or militant groups such as Stokely Carmichael, H. "Rap" Brown, Elijah Muhammad, and Maxwell Stanford...

You are also cautioned that the nature of this new endeavor is such that under no circumstances should the existence of the program be made known outside the Bureau and appropriate within-office security should be afforded to sensitive operations and techniques considered under the program. No counter-intelligence action under this program may be initiated by the field without prior Bureau authorization. You are urged to take an enthusiastic and imaginative approach to this new counterintelligence endeavor and the Bureau will be pleased to entertain any suggestions or techniques you may recommend.

By the mid sixties the FBI were experts in black ops, deploying a range of dubious techniques to destabilise political groups – agents provocateur, anonymous hate mail, burglary, forgery, defamation and extortion. One popular technique of the time was 'snitch jacketing', in which an FBI agent would set up a legitimate activist to make him seem like a police informer, thus undermining trust within radical groups and fostering internal dissent. Harry C. McPherson Jr, a White House special counsel and LBJ's speechwriter, claimed that the aftermath of the summer of inner-city riots had created the perfect conditions for the FBI's expansion. The words 'law and order', he wrote, were simply the new 'code words for racism'.

Hoover described the summer disturbances as the 'catalytic effect of extremists', and throughout August and September 1967 the FBI flooded the White House with intelligence reports on Black Power activists to the extent that the president's staff felt bombarded by the obsessive volumes of evidence, some of it fanciful and questionable. According to historian Kenneth O'Reilly, the intelligence was 'short on facts and long on rhetoric', but a golden opportunity had arisen, and Hoover seized the chance to delve into the lives of black activists with hypocritical zeal. He once described Martin Luther King as 'a tomcat with obsessive degenerate sexual urges' and 'an instrument in the hands of subversive forces seeking to undermine our nation'.

Sometime back in 1965, FBI special agents Druken and King had set up a shadowy team to track King when he travelled to the Detroit area. They also had responsibility for keeping tabs on hippie leader John Sinclair and the MC5. Working in tandem with the Chicago field office, they tailed King throughout the Midwest, pursuing his local contacts vigorously and maintaining a daily log of his activities. The campaign reached as far back as January 1964, when FBI officers installed microphones in a room at the Willard Hotel in Washington DC, and recorded King having sex with an unnamed woman. A few months later, days before King was to be awarded the Nobel Peace Prize in Oslo, the FBI sent an edited copy of the surveillance tapes from a mailbox in Tampa to his wife, Coretta. The intent was obvious: to ruin King's marriage and undermine his reputation. The anonymous package contained a letter proposing that King should consider suicide rather than risk the humiliation of his sexual secrets being made public.

Early in the spring of 1966, FBI agents learned from local contacts in the religious community that King was scheduled to speak at the Central United Methodist Church overlooking Grand Circus Park in Detroit. Agents mingled conspicuously in the church, suited, nervous and out of place. They had tracked King from his arrival in Michigan to the State University, where he had delivered a short speech, and followed him to Detroit. Information had been leaked to Special Agent Druken that King planned to lead a Freedom Day Rally at Cobo Hall, and although the arrangements were not yet confirmed he was expected to stay in the nearby Pontchartrain Hotel, where a few months later a group of Motown songwriters would famously congregate to write the historic Diana Ross street song 'Love Child'. The acquiescent management cooperated with the FBI, King's hotel room was bugged, and on his arrival he was guided into the trap.

King insisted that the Freedom Day Rally should not become overwhelmed by the Vietnam issue and that it was an opportunity for those in the North to donate funds to drive voter registration in rural Alabama, where discriminatory laws meant that poorer African-Americans rarely voted. The rally was eventually sponsored by a coalition of Michigan groups and raised $100,000, mostly through donations from prominent black businesses in Detroit, including members of the Gordy family and two of the family's favoured organisations – the Booker T. Washington Business Association and the Michigan Association of Elks.

In the weeks before King's Cobo Hall rally, an anonymous telephone call was made to the Detroit police. It came from an unidentified employee of General Motors' Clark Street assembly plant. The caller claimed that 'elements of the Ku Klux Klan' among the 12,000-strong workforce intended to assassinate King. The caller intimated that another Clark Street employee was the local Klan's grand dragon. The information was redirected to the FBI's secret surveillance unit, which established that the most likely culprit was a loose-lipped racist named Jack Davis, a middle-aged autoworker and the grand dragon of the Michigan Ku Klux Klan. He had already been boasting in local bars about his plans to stage a rival rally featuring the Klan's imperial wizard – 'the big man hisself', Bobby Shelton Jr. According to Davis, everyone was welcome to the Klan's Detroit rally to listen to the former tyre salesman, 'except beatniks and niggers'.

Although the FBI had identified as many as 2,000 white supremacists who had threatened to kill King, most of them were in the rural Deep South, and none were known to be based in Detroit. By 1967 the Ku Klux Klan's influence in Detroit was in retreat. They had been a significant force in the car plants in the post-war era, but the soil of the South had always been more fertile ground for their ideology. By 1967 there were only a couple of Klan 'klaverns' in the Detroit metropolitan area. One was in the rented premises of a Slovenian workers' hall on the West Side and another was in Taylor Township, which, due to the southern redneck roots of many of its original inhabitants and the whites-only covenants that underpinned local housing, was seen by many as a haven for Jim Crow values and was nicknamed 'Taylortucky'.

The Klan was by now a dwindling and ineffectual force, and the threat to assassinate King was bar talk and not much else. Nonetheless, the FBI surveillance team and their colleagues at the Detroit police department were frustrated by King's people, who had refused the offer of protection. King had good reason to mistrust the FBI and sensed that any protection they offered would be fatally flawed or designed to compromise him. FBI files from the era describe King as uncooperative: 'While in the Detroit area in connection with his appearance, he was evasive in furnishing the Detroit PD with his itinerary and location of his accommodations' and 'most uncooperative in assisting the Detroit PD in their attempt to afford him maximum protection'.

The campaign to vilify King continued its vicious path until his assassination in Memphis in 1968, but the tangled wires of surveillance and the whispered evidence gathered in covert operations exposed divisions within government. The Washington editor of the *Nation*, David Corn, described wiretapping and the ethics of law enforcement as a 'titanic clash' between US attorney general Robert Kennedy and Hoover, whose distrusting relationship had festered into one of the great power feuds of American politics. According to Corn, it went beyond personality or politics and was 'in a way a fight over the meaning of justice in America'. And the meaning of justice hinged on one very relevant anxiety: the uninvited ear.

Conscious of public anxiety about surveillance, President Johnson committed to a Right of Privacy Bill and issued a directive to all federal agencies to halt bugging that was not 'fully in accord with the law and with a decent regard for the rights of others'. To force the pace on privacy, the president established the Senate Subcommittee on Administrative Practice and Procedure, led by Senator Edward V. Long of Missouri. The subcommittee held its preliminary hearings in Detroit back in April of 1967, and unearthed a wide range of covert practices. Long's committee held public hearings on electronic eavesdropping by the Detroit police department and by officers of the Internal Revenue Service, where one particular case attracted widespread public interest. An IRS tax inspector had agreed to wear a transmitter in one of his cowboy boots, with a battery in the other boot and connecting wires that ran up his trouser legs to a microphone belt buckle. These absurd devices were written about endlessly, contributing to the popular fascination with surveillance.

Leading the Detroit investigation was a bespectacled lawyer named Bernard 'Bud' Fensterwald Jr, who fired a shot across the bow of the police department, telling the press that he was in Detroit to root out the illegal use of wiretapping and that no one was immune. 'When police officers engage in illegal activities, it tends to corrupt their own organization,' he warned. 'Police use paroles, or people on probation, or people they can hang a charge on.'

Often peering at committee documents as if he were partially blind, Fensterwald reminded law enforcement officers that surveillance was often the prequel to corruption, and where there was corruption the fingerprints of organised crime were never far away.

Although she had now officially left the Supremes and had nothing to hide, Florence Ballard was worried about her privacy. Her phone calls increased. She spoke to local friends, to her new lawyer, and made long-distance calls to contacts she had made on tour. She was anxious about whom she could trust and, according to those closest to her, she seemed to lurch from confidence to emotional crisis from one day to the next. On Saturday, 2 September, Ballard made an extraordinary decision. That evening Diana Ross and the Supremes were appearing in concert and were scheduled to play the first of three concerts as part of the Michigan State Fair. The shows were to be held at the Music Shell, an outdoor arena with a cascading seashell backdrop set in the fairgrounds complex at Eight Mile and Woodward. Ballard decided to go to the concert. The Michigan State Fair was a Detroit institution and, for Motown acts, something of an emotional homecoming to a place they remembered from childhood. The Supremes had played there several times before and, in a piece of clumsy political theatre, had once appeared onstage with Governor George Romney. Although the fair tried to reach out to the whole of Detroit, its roots were firmly planted in the agricultural industries and in the white working-class experience. By 1967 a ragtag bunch of every conceivable form of music took to the stage. The headline acts included Sergio Mendes, Buddy Rich, Buddy Greco and the New Vaudeville Band. Only four weeks before, the fairgrounds had housed hundreds of armed soldiers from the US Airborne Division, who had camped there while trying to quell the July rebellions. Tents had been hurriedly erected on the grass, armoured vehicles parked in the entrance, and soldiers had practised anti-sniper fire among the bleachers.

In a promotional interview published in the *Detroit News* on the morning of the first show, Diana Ross hinted heavily at a serious rift between the girls and was more outspoken than ever before, adding fuel to the now widespread view that Florence Ballard had compromised Motown's codes of professionalism. 'We're still good friends,' she said. 'We always had to give Florence a little pull, a little push.' It is not clear if Florence Ballard ever read those brief, niggling words or if they irritated her, but rather than stay away from the concert and maintain an air of professional dignity, Ballard secured tickets for the event and sat prominently in the front row, watching her replacement, Cindy Birdsong, onstage. Backing the Supremes that night was the Jimmy Wilkins Band, a collection of local session musicians whom Ballard had performed with countless times. She periodically attracted their attention and waved to fans in the audience who had spotted her. It is impossible to fathom what Ballard hoped to achieve. Was it a gesture of goodwill, a public statement that she had moved on, an act of defiance? Her sister Maxine believed it was confused fury that drove her to the show: 'They think they can replace me with Cindy Birdsong,' she remembered Flo once saying. 'They have lost their mind.' Whatever her intentions, showing up at a local Supremes concert demeaned Florence Ballard and made her appear a victim, not a superstar. As in many of the decisions she was to make in the months and years to come, telltale signs of self-destruction were surfacing. Maxine described a woman who was not in complete control of her emotions: 'Flo was in constant conflict with herself because she was angry at the thought that Diane and Mary had betrayed her, and even though she said it in public a thousand times, her heart just wouldn't let her believe it.' Most likely it was in a conflicted state that Ballard made the humiliating decision to sit through the show in the uncomfortable eyeline of the performers and in full view of an audience of thousands.

She planned to marry Tommy Chapman, who, with no obvious skills in financial or music management, was now controlling her affairs. The cash she had secured as settlement for her departure from Motown had made her wealthy compared to those she had grown up with, but it was not destined to last long and her career prospects were at serious risk. For now, however, Ballard ostensibly had what she wanted. There was no need to travel, no need to listen to Berry Gordy, and no need to sing the chorus of songs she knew painfully by heart. Most reassuringly of all, there was no longer any need to stand two steps behind Diana Ross and smile as if she meant it.

Her contract with Motown was over and so too were her public commitments, but an uneasiness was about to take over her life. Now at home more than ever before, she discussed her private affairs with a decreasing number of people, mostly her mother and sister and, rarely, old friends from Motown. It was in that context of isolation that her anxieties grew, and she began to suspect that Motown cared a lot more about her affairs than they actually did. Eager to make major labels in New York City aware of her availability, she put out feelers through several contacts, but she had yet to cleanse Motown from her soul. Ballard now planned to question the contractual settlement that had ended her association with the Supremes. Her family felt she had signed too hastily, and other Motown artists goaded her to rip up the agreement. Like many Motown artists before and since, Ballard exaggerated the power and influence of Motown's white executives and came to believe they were watching her closely. The four figures who loomed large in the minds of Motown artists were one-time A&R head Ralph Seltzer, lawyer Harold Noveck, his brother, accountant Sidney Noveck, and, most unsettling of all for Ballard, the corporate vice-president Mike Roshkind. It was Roshkind who had handed her the severance papers at the Northland Inn. All four have been portrayed as sinister, ruthless or austere by numerous Motown artists, but while they might well have been tough negotiators, they were part of the necessary bureaucracy of a burgeoning creative business.

Florence Ballard's anxieties were nonexistent when compared to the experiences of John Sinclair and the MC5. They had been targeted by the Detroit police drug squad for nearly two years and only came to understand the full extent of the covert operations against them more than twenty years later. A secretive group of officers from the city's Red Squad had developed an obsessive interest in Sinclair's movements. The Red Squad was an unregulated unit working on undercover operations from a base at 1300 Beaubien and had existed intermittently for over thirty years, dating back to a wave of industrial action in the car plants in the thirties that had raised fears of Communist infiltration. The Red Squad had played a controversial role in the historic sit-down strike at the General Motors plant in Flint, Michigan, in the thirties and again during the era of McCarthyism. By 1967 the squad had supposedly disbanded, but in reality it had simply shaken off the dated Cold War name and become a well-resourced elite who worked in secret and had access to the latest surveillance technologies, including rifle microphones, pocket cameras and transistorised bugging devices. Their files were kept hidden and their existence officially denied until the eighties, by which time most of them were either dead or retired.

John Sinclair was an easy target for the uninvited ear. The six-foot-six hippie had an unmistakeable electric-shock hairstyle; he wore wire-rimmed John Lennon glasses and often donned blue-collar 'union-made' denims. By 1967 his blue-collar clothes had given way to flamboyant guru-style caftans and Moroccan beads. His bearlike demeanour was deceptive. A journalist at the time described him as 'a large and yet very gentle man whose manner belies his appearance'. Despite the threat hanging over him for previous drug misdemeanours, Sinclair lived recklessly and refused to fade quietly into the background. He had a rock journalist's grasp of hyperbole and found high drama in every living moment. Sinclair drew attention to himself by both word and deed: 'We were rock-and-roll maniac dope-fiend hippies,' he once wrote, 'running around Michigan making the most dynamite rock-and-roll music in the history of our culture and telling all of the kids we played for that all we would have to do was drop out of the American madhouse and do our own thing and everything would be beautiful.'

Sinclair had known the members of MC5 for over a year now. They had played at a homecoming party for his release from jail in the summer of 1966 and had argued with him over the future direction of music. A lifetime lover of the great jazz fiends of the twentieth century, Sinclair advocated the revolutionary power of free jazz, while MC5's lead singer, Rob Tyner, was a vociferous exponent of R&B's journey to rock. Together they coined the phrase 'the new avant rock', and as their friendship grew Sinclair became an increasingly influential figure, first as a mentor and then as the band's manager. Although they never rivalled Motown's record sales or its international reputation, the radicals that congregated around MC5 were vocal and visible. The major Motown acts were frequently out of town, working at hotel residencies or honouring overseas engagements, while MC5 stayed locally, squatting apartments and rehearsing at their favoured spaces – the Artists Workshop, the Grande Ballroom and a cavernous old venue called the Mystic Knights of the Sea Lodge Hall, a vacant movie theatre near Cadillac Square. Most of their business was run from a row of occupied storefront apartments on Warren, which housed MOBE, the Mobilization to End the War in Vietnam, and the offices of a new underground magazine, *The Fifth Estate*. This was the home of the Steering Committee, which, as 1967 wore on, became the theoretical wing of MC5.

By September 1967 MC5 had another venue in their unofficial empire: a bookstore called the 100 Camels, which had opened amid a small hippie enclave on Plum Street. It was managed by a new and charismatic member of the guitar army, Lawrence 'Pun' Plamondon, an Ottawa runaway who had absconded from his home in Traverse City as a teenager. Plamondon was to find national notoriety as an underground rebel a year later when he joined the FBI Ten Most Wanted list for conspiracy to bomb the CIA offices in Ann Arbor, Michigan. He described the area around the commune as being made up 'mostly of students and recent dropouts from Wayne State University, blacks and Chicanos, and a smattering of poor whites. Urban decay was rapidly rotting the neighborhood.' Half a block from the Steering Committee's commune was a house he described as a parent's worst nightmare – 'out-of-work musicians, poets who heard voices, co-ed cuties, dime-bag reefer dealers, speed freaks, and stone junkies'. The area was the home of Detroit's radical underground and periodically came under attack from the far right, regularly targeted by Breakthrough, a proto-fascist group styled in the image of the John Birch Society and led by a right-wing city council employee named Donald Lobsinger. Breakthrough reputedly stoned and firebombed the commune, and the Steering Committee claimed, without providing categorical proof, that Lobsinger was an agent provocateur who enjoyed the tacit support of the Red Squad.

In the autumn of 1967, MC5 were the support band for Grateful Dead at a sold-out concert at the Grande Ballroom. At the time, Sinclair was no more than a valued friend of the young Detroit rebels, but backstage he met Grateful Dead's semi-fried managers Rock Scully and Danny Rifkin. On meeting them, Sinclair immediately understood that management did not need to be stuffy, suited or serious. It was a weird epiphany, but the meeting had a great impact on him, and he agreed to become the MC5's manager. 'When I first saw them, I thought they were incredible. Just totally fucking great,' Sinclair told one interviewer. 'They desperately needed management. They had a couple of relationships with managers who did teenage rock bands in the Detroit area that didn't really lead to anything . . . I was inspired by the managers of the Grateful Dead when they came to Detroit on their first tour in 1967, late summer. I hung out with Rock Scully and Danny Rifkin for a few days. I thought, "Man, these guys are just as nuts as I am . . ." Before, I was always completely mystified by the music business, thinking it was the realm of specialists for which I had no qualifications. I was just a music lover and a cultural activist . . . I was never really hired or anything. We never really had an arrangement. I just leapt into the fray and took charge of the vacuum that existed.'

Sinclair had a galvanising effect on the fortunes of MC5, taking them from the Detroit garage-band subculture to a place at the heart of alternative rock. Within a matter of a year, Kool-Aided by acid, they became one of the most talked-about bands of the sixties, permanently screeching on the margins of the law. 'Everybody got high. So first off, you were on the other side of the police,' Sinclair remembered. 'They didn't want you to get high . . . That was what really drew the line. That's what really politicized us. I think of politics as being involved in actions involving groups of people, not just an outlook. If you have an outlook, you're a philosopher. If you're doing something about it, you're an activist. So we wanted to do something about it. The term I used was that we were LSD-driven total maniacs in the universe . . . We thought that that should all be just blown to smithereens by LSD and electronic instruments. I don't know how to stress enough that we were on acid. We were lunatics. We just didn't give a fuck.'

What he lacked in experience he made up for in utopian energy. Sinclair was a whirlwind of ideas. He grabbed concepts like a magpie, stealing them from the history of jazz, from the San Francisco counterculture, from the peace movement, and from the street soldiers of the Black Power movement. Trans-Love Energies quickly morphed into a production company, and the Steering Committee became its stoned advisory board. A new record, *Looking At You/Borderline*, was released; an official fan club was launched, overseen by Plamondon's wife, Genie; and an unofficial fan army called the Highland Park Stompers was born. Compared to the Motown Record Corporation, it was ramshackle and spaced out, but it had energy on its side, and a generation of young Michigan musicians, including Ted Nugent of the Amboy Dukes and Jim Osterberg Jr – the self-styled Iggy Pop – were drawn into Sinclair's renegade circus tent.

With John Sinclair as their manager, the MC5 were guaranteed two things: attention and trouble. Sinclair's flair for rock rhetoric was unrivalled anywhere in America. He laced his language with acidic anarchy, and by the force of his personality turned the band into a cause célèbre. In the autumn of 1967, he invited public controversy by comparing MC5 to the Viet Cong. 'The MC5 actually function as rock-and-roll guerrillas,' he said, 'building up a popular base among the people of the Michigan youth community, and we followed up our musical successes with written propaganda which attempted to explain what we were doing and what was so far out about it, so our people could become conscious of their role as cultural revolutionaries who were going to inherit the country and reshape it in their own image.'

Guitarist Wayne Kramer attributed much of their success to Sinclair: 'John Sinclair was the only person that we respected and whose direction we could respect. We were not *manageable*. We were barely sane.' Creative insanity took MC5 closer to the desecrations of the day and to one of the grand rock gestures of the era: flag burning. Anti-war protesters had been setting fire to their draft cards in public protest for nearly two years, and burning the Stars and Stripes had become a familiar act at anti-war demonstrations. Although rock history has elevated Jimi Hendrix's iconic performance at Woodstock, when he burned the American flag during an improvised performance of 'The Star-Spangled Banner', the gesture was by then already two years old. MC5 had pioneered it onstage in the spring of 1967, when they risked being banned from the Grande Ballroom and arrested by the Detroit police. The artist Gary Grimshaw, who designed the band's kaleidoscopic posters, had already been arrested for desecrating the flag in July. He had bought an Independence Day kite designed with stars and stripes and had scrawled across it 'Fuck America – Go Fly a Kite'. It hung from a window at the rear of the commune's storefront apartments in Warren Forest and led to his arrest.

After many changes of personnel, the 'barely sane' MC5 were by now settled as a five-piece band: guitarists Michael Davis, Wayne Kramer, Fred 'Sonic' Smith, drummer Dennis 'Machine Gun' Thompson and their hyperactive vocalist, Rob Tyner, whose natural afro and dark shades made him look like a ghetto hippie. Tyner was already a fine R&B singer whose ragged throaty voice owed as much to local blues and soul singers like Singing Sammy Ward and Little Willie John as it did to the new rock. The writer Brett Caldwell said that Tyner's voice 'bled emotion through his raw larynx, but unlike many of the punk vocalists that followed his lead, Tyner could really sing too'. Although MC5 flirted with free jazz and looked enviously across town at the best of the ghetto singers, it was a very different kind of musical style that began to set the band apart. Fortified by their $3,000 Vox Super Beatle amplifiers – the most powerful speakers available on the market at the time – MC5 became the creative ambassadors of feedback and disruptive noise. One of the band's most celebrated songs was a 'midnight-hour' R&B track that sounded as if Wilson Pickett had been electrocuted. The band called it 'Black to Comm', taking the name from the wiring mechanism on their amp.

MC5's national notoriety would reach a spectacular height in the summer of 1968 when violence broke out at the Democratic Convention in Chicago. Many bands had agreed to play live to support demonstrations against the war in Vietnam, but it was the Detroiters that defied the heavy militarised police presence. Sensing he had witnessed rock history, Michigan music critic Don McLeese described the performance with unrestrained wonder: 'This was rock unhinged, guitars gone berserk, molecules spinning haywire, testosterone-crazed knuckleheads bouncing off each other like a human pinball machine . . . They took me by shock (and awe) – that a band could be so manic, so savage, so undeniable in its intensity.' Outside the convention, anti-war demonstrators clashed with the police, the army and the Illinois National Guard. An estimated 1,000 Secret Service agents were in the city on surveillance duties, some filming protesters, and one dedicated unit followed MC5 throughout their stay. The footage they shot on concealed cameras supposedly showed the band stoking the crowd's emotions and inciting rebellion. McLeese went on to describe the towering Sinclair as an 'oversized Ho Chi Minh' and a figure of dangerous creativity.

What was not yet known was that John Sinclair was being watched by a bewildering range of agents twenty-four hours a day. He was being tracked by the Detroit drug squad, whose members were determined to jail him again; he was loathed by the police department for staging the riotous Belle Isle love-in; he was stalked by the Michigan police for encouraging MC5 gigs that lurched from political agitprop to deafening genius; and he was under surveillance by local FBI agents, who regularly monitored the city's political radicals on campuses and in the car plants. The

MC5's live shows routinely attracted a police presence, individual band members were monitored, and when the band left the Detroit area information was shared with state police. Plamondon claimed that arrests and harassment were commonplace and described driving through Detroit with John Sinclair in an Opel car as the two of them distributed underground magazines across town. The police stopped them, searched the vehicle, and subjected them both to a beating. 'They yanked us out, pushed us around some, called us fags, and made us lay face down in the gravel parking lot while they ransacked Sinclair's Opel,' Plamondon wrote. Sinclair remembered the era with caustic pride: 'By this time there was a full-scale suppression campaign underway, and the control addicts who were running it were determined to put an end to this madness by any means necessary. They knew what they were up against even if we didn't understand it ourselves, and they knew that our "revolution", if it were to succeed, would put an end to their rule once and for all.'

Sinclair and Fred 'Sonic' Smith were subsequently arrested by Oakland County police when a dispute between the band and local promoters kicked off at the Loft club in Leonard, Michigan, forty miles from Detroit. They were driven to a police station in nearby Pontiac, followed by a convoy of fans, and charged with 'assault and battery on a police officer'. Sinclair was given thirty days in jail but was later acquitted, and a bond of $2,500 was set. A few days later all five members of the band were arrested at West Park in Ann Arbor and released on a bond of $125 each. A charity gig to be held at the University of Oakland at Auburn Hills, Michigan, in aid of the Assistance to the American Children with Leukaemia charity, was cancelled due to the outstanding arrest warrants. Sinclair remained adamant that these incidents, sparked in part by their high-octane stage shows and by their motherfucker of a signature tune, 'Kick Out The Jams', was part of a wider conspiracy against the band. 'The attack on the rising rainbow culture took two distinct forms, subversion and outright repression,' he once said, 'and while both of them managed to slow us down, they've also brought us to a new stage of development by making us aware what we are up against and what we have to do to get through to the other side of the great American desert.'

The anger of Detroit's counterculture lessened somewhat as it reached West Grand Boulevard, where psychedelia was simply one of a hundred diluted influences. 'Reflections' by Diana Ross and the Supremes had climbed the national charts, and although it had none of the full-blown acid-rock influences of MC5, it was a song of its era and a nod to pop psychedelia. When the album of the same name was released, the accompanying cover art even aped the dreamy graphics and psychedelic collages made famous by Detroit's revolutionary designer Gary Grimshaw. 'Reflections' was one of the last songs to come from the stuttering bandwagon of Holland-Dozier-Holland as they formalised a delay tactic and refused to produce more hits unless an improved offer was made to them. Gordy resisted the pressure, and the misty 'Reflections' was one of the last the trio would compose for Motown with any good grace.

Sometime during September Diana Ross recorded lead vocals for 'Someday My Prince Will Come' and 'Heigh-Ho', two saccharine songs taken from Disney's *Snow White and the Seven Dwarfs*. The recordings were supposedly part of the ill-fated Disney tribute album that Gordy had kick-started on hearing of Disney's death in the last days of 1966. Both songs had been co-written by the tragic film composer Frank Churchill, who had shot himself at his piano at the height of his career. Although it would be many years before they would see the light of day, the songs reflected the creative schizophrenia now driving Motown and emphasised the distance Berry Gordy and Diana Ross had travelled since their early years in Detroit R&B.

Public reaction to the killings at the Algiers Motel worsened throughout September. The failure to take meaningful action against the accused officers encouraged many within Detroit's African-American community to believe that the police department was not only callously racist but also had immunity from murder. The families were still in a state of grief, but a steelier resolve had grown. Three important developments kept the killings at the forefront of public life. First, the victim's families had formed a coalition to appeal against the release of one of the officers; second, two of the white girls who had been partying with the young soul group the Dramatics before the police stormed the motel were in the news again; and third, more court cases were imminent.

Earlier in the month, a Detroit police officer had arrested two white girls who the authorities suspected were working as prostitutes – Karen Malloy and Julie Hysell, both teenage runaways from Columbus, Ohio. Malloy was apprehended by a plain-clothes police officer for soliciting at the rear of a Midtown drive-in motel called the Astor. According to the warrant recommendation:

> At about 1:45 a.m., Patr Samuel Stone assigned to the Vice Bureau was driving North on Woodward....The officer pulled into the curb and observed the Def (Karen Malloy) standing there. The Def motioned the officer to the rear . . . The Def then asked the officer how much he'd spend and he said fifteen dollars. The Def said OK and the officer asked what he'd get for his money and Def stated a Half & Half. At this time the officer identified himself and placed the Def under arrest for Accosting and Soliciting.

Karen Malloy was placed on probation for six months, but the arrest had further consequences for the grieving families and brought more sordid details of the Algiers Motel case into the public domain. A key witness arrested for prostitution had offered a policeman a 'half and half'. It was clear to anyone with even the faintest understanding of Detroit street life that it wasn't milk and cream on offer but oral sex and full vaginal penetration. Malloy's arrest was a body blow to the families, allowing the police and their friendly journalists in the press to construct an image of the slain teenagers as ghetto pimps who had befriended or possibly controlled prostitutes. It was baseless, but the insinuation was there. Worse still, the police knew that the image of African-American teenagers consorting with white girls still provoked visceral reactions in the city and could be used to demean witnesses and the deceased. On 13 September the arrest of another two girls connected to the Algiers killings raised suspicions that the Detroit police were maliciously targeting potential witnesses to undermine their credibility in the event of a full trial. Other witnesses spoke of being apprehended for minor infractions such as traffic misdemeanours or jaywalking. The warrant recommendation against the next two girls, eighteen-year-old Julie Hysell and nineteen-year-old Janet Wright, described how Patrolman Montgomery – again in plain clothes – had been working around the Algiers Motel, which, remarkably, was still open for business and no longer taped off as a crime scene. Hysell had approached him in the lobby area, offering sex, and when they went to a room together she suggested that he could hire two girls for forty dollars. Janet Wright, a prostitute who had not been present on the night of the killings, arrived and a deal was struck. Hysell would give the officer a 'blow job' and Wright would 'fuck him'. The officer then revealed his real identity and placed them both under arrest for soliciting.

On 27 September the two white police officers, Robert Paille and David Senak, and the black security guard, Melvin Dismukes, faced a lesser charge of 'conspiracy to commit a legal act in an illegal manner'. The hearings against them divided public opinion still further. One of the witnesses, Michael Clark, a nineteen-year-old who had been at the motel on the night of the killings, proved to be an insolent witness and was chastised by the judge for his demeanour. Clark had been with the call girls Malloy and Hysell at the time of the killings, and during the lunch recess he was overheard threatening a court lawyer. Clark exuded the kind of swaggering disrespect that many older people feared in their city, and his callousness did the families of the deceased a woeful disservice. In a few short hours, the police leaked the story to compliant journalists, allowing the newspapers to portray the youth at the Algiers Motel as an anti-authoritarian gang of young black men living an immoral life. Many Detroit citizens stubbornly believed that the victims were unworthy of justice and that Clark was a street pimp with no moral compass. For the victims' families, September came to a depressing and deflated end, with justice fading further into the distance.

At Motown the lines were becoming more clearly drawn between management and talent. Holland-Dozier-Holland were no longer willing to write or produce, the Supremes were still adjusting to the fallout of Ballard's emotional departure, and the Hitsville studio was in a constant state of revolt as various members of the Funk Brothers rose up to challenge their second-class status. At the point when he least needed it, Gordy was confronted with yet another warring faction, this time a series of bitter fights within another Motown group, Martha and the Vandellas. Martha Reeves was on a collision course with Motown and with life itself. In September 1967 her single 'Love Bug Leave My Heart Alone' was released internationally, and she worked incessantly at Hitsville, recording 'Forget Me Not' and adding final vocal dubs to the follow-up, 'Honey Chile'. Any spare moments were devoted to her favourite activities – promoting herself by giving interviews, meeting visiting journalists and making international calls to magazines around the world. Reeves knew the phone system and Motown's internal office culture intimately. She had been a secretary there in the early sixties, working for Mickey Stevenson, and in the intensely cramped conditions of the small West Grand studio, she had been a secretarial rival to Diana Ross. Her relationship with the other two members of the Supremes, Ballard and Wilson, flowed deeper. All three had studied at Northeastern High School under the school's influential vocal coach, Mr Abraham Silver, a respected Jewish composer who, when he was not directing synagogue choirs in the Detroit area, gave fatherly training to young ghetto vocalists.

The career of Martha and the Vandellas paralleled the Supremes in two unflattering ways: it was marred by internal disputes, and it ended in personal breakdown. After a torrid personal time involving drug abuse and a failed marriage, Reeves became embroiled in a series of dire relationships with two other members of the Vandellas, Rosalind Ashford and Betty Kelly. Her relationship with Kelly was particularly fraught. Kelly had joined the Vandellas from a rival Motown girl group, the Velvelettes, and although they tried to accommodate each other, their relationship had always been tense. In her autobiography Reeves admits that throughout 1967 their relationship – it was never a friendship – was strained to breaking point: 'My relationship with Betty began to deteriorate very rapidly,' she admitted. 'For whatever reason, Betty clearly began to resent me. She would be sarcastic and sharp with me between shows. Onstage gestures that were once choreographed routines with swinging arm movements had now turned into what looked like karate moves. Instead of concentrating on my performance, I was distracted by her insolence.'

Offstage tension resulted in onstage disputes: 'Our friendship was becoming strained, and the anger that I began to feel toward her nearly spoiled one of my show business high points. We were on a local Philadelphia television show along with the gracious Sammy Davis Jr. I wanted so badly to be at my best when I met Sammy, but Betty chose that show to do everything she could to antagonize me . . . My problems with Betty continued to grow. It had gotten to the point where we barely spoke to each other. There was an icy limousine ride between the Latin Casino in Cherry Hill, New Jersey, into Philadelphia, to appear on the *Mike Douglas Show*,' Reeves said in her autobiography. After the show the mood darkened. In scenes that paralleled the Supremes' vicious disagreements backstage at the Flamingo in Las Vegas, the Vandellas metaphorically tore each other apart: 'I directly confronted Betty,' Reeves wrote. 'I told her that I couldn't put up with her onstage sabotage and her offstage sarcasm. This had to end, and I informed her that it was time she did something else with her life. It was getting impossible to keep up the artificially happy outer appearances.'

Motown was a corporation founded on a contrived surface appearance. Turmoil within the ranks was unwelcome. Betty Kelly was already pregnant by a band member, Tracey Wright, and the time to leave had come. She could have left with quiet pride, but such was the seething animosity between her and Reeves that she went into a towering rage and never spoke to Reeves for many years to come. There is no simple way to describe the layers of vitriol that surrounded the Vandellas. It was fuelled by drug abuse, backstage jealousies and hurtful arguments. The trouble had escalated earlier in 1967, when Martha and the Vandellas were booked to play a week of shows at the appropriately named Trip Club on Sunset Boulevard. Rather than travel with musicians, Motown had arranged for a Watts funk band called Garnell Cooper and the Kinfolks to provide backing. Within the ranks of the band were three outstanding L.A. instrumentalists: lead guitarist David T. Walker, who went on to become one of the great virtuoso guitarists of soul music; his friend Tracey Wright, a bass player; and an organist by the name of Vonzell 'Buzz' Cooper. Walker was a charismatic mixed-race Native American who had grown up in the Watts ghetto, and when the Kinfolks took to the road, travelling extensively with Motown acts, sleeping arrangements became increasingly complicated. Reeves had an affair with Walker, and her fellow singer Kelly fell in love with Wright. It was an emotional minefield that became further strained when the attractive Walker had an affair with the group's hairdresser, Winnie Brown, who was already seeing Paul Williams of the Temptations. To complete this expanding circle of discontent, Brown was the cousin of the disgruntled Florence Ballard, whose brother had once dated Rosalind Ashford of the Vandellas. Almost every group within Detroit had similarly complicated connections, and by the fall of 1967 Motown was a mess of incestuous, corrosive and nasty relationships. Although the company's charm school, under the watchful eye of Maxine Powell, taught decorum, deportment and personal restraint, the love affairs, one-night stands and sexual liaisons had created a toxic atmosphere, and in the case of the warring Vandellas it brought an end to an otherwise brilliant act. Martha once said, 'Lead singers not only do the majority of the work, but their personalities are singled out and taken as the general attitude of the unit.' If that were so, then the Vandellas were lurching between glamour and God.

A few months after 'Honey Chile' was released, Martha Reeves was hospitalised with psychedelic disorientation after taking LSD. She always maintained that the acid was slipped into her champagne by persons unknown, but the drug was freely available in Detroit and commonly taken by Motown stars. Reeves subsequently spent time in a psychiatric unit, and the Vandellas, who were still engaged in their own little civil wars, temporarily ceased to exist. Martha and the Vandellas sang together only sporadically in the final few months of 1967, when Reeves drafted her sister Lois into the line-up during the 'Honey Chile' sessions. As fate and history would have it, the last high-profile concert that featured the definitive Vandellas – Martha Reeves, Betty Kelly and Rosalind Ashford – was the concert at the Fox Theater in July when the riots encroached downtown.

It was a historic time in Florence Ballard's dispute with Motown too. The previous day Motown had handed over $75,869 to a local attorney acting on her behalf. It was not a settlement, nor was it an admission of any wrongdoing; it was the contents of a trust account that Motown had held in Ballard's name and that had been used in part to fund her lifestyle. Ballard never received the money and only heard about the transfer haltingly over the phone – yet another error in the catalogue of mistakes she was to make in the months to come. The deposed member of the Supremes had listened to friends and family and had contracted local lawyers to dispute her hurried settlement with the company. It was clear to Ballard that there was no way back.

On the evening of Tuesday, 26 September, Florence Ballard lay on her couch watching television. The Supremes were performing on a network variety show, and for the first time ever in a television appearance Ballard was missing from their ranks. Cindy Birdsong flickered in the background. Occupying the majority of the small screen was the unmistakeable figure of Diana Ross. She and the Supremes sang 'Reflections' as if the world had moved on and nothing much had changed. But it had changed, and Ballard admitted to a friend that she cried so hard she wanted to die.

Already locked in a legal dispute with Ballard and facing a showdown with his most successful producers, Berry Gordy contemplated a third problem, arguably the most intractable of all. The city that had given Motown its global identity and had been home to the greatest black-owned company in musical history was increasingly associated in the minds of the American public with urban decay, violent crime and social unrest. As autumn darkened, the trees of Detroit shed their leaves and light-brown blemishes lay limply over car bonnets on the streets. Something about Motown had changed; a sense of joyous hope had given way to fear and spiritual dereliction. Berry Gordy had begun to lose patience with one of his greatest romances: he had fallen out of love with Detroit.

United. Marvin Gaye and Tammi Terrell pose for a Motown photo shoot in 1967.

OCTOBER

Collapse

Marvin Gaye shifted dreamily from one ambition to another. He imagined himself as a jazz singer and a Las Vegas crooner, and even talked his way into a trial for the Detroit Lions, convinced he could make it as a pro football player. He saw himself variously as the black Sinatra, a star quarterback, and a masculine Billie Holiday, and although he was passably good at many things, his true greatness was a distinctive soul voice that could make seductive even the most stilted lyrics. Despite the battles within the ranks of Motown that had damaged the Supremes, Martha and the Vandellas and the hit-writing team of Holland-Dozier-Holland, the corporation had enjoyed one substantial creative success with the duo that become the personification of young love in a vastly changing society, Marvin Gaye and Tammi Terrell. But, predictably, it too hid a thousand emotions.

Marvin Gaye had married into the Gordy family, and while it brought him closer to power and influence, it also dragged him further away from emotional stability. His relationship with Anna Gordy was unravelling, and in October 1967 he was to witness one of the genuine tragedies of the Motown era when his co-singer, Tammi Terrell, collapsed with a brain haemorrhage.

The Motown publicity machine always asserted that Marvin Gaye and Anna Gordy were happily married, but it was clear to those closest to them that their happiness was fading. The couple had a relationship strangled by doubt and deepening jealousy; neither could be described as easygoing, and both had a strand of selfishness that made compromise difficult. When they ventured out together, it often ended in public rows. Anna was eighteen years older than Gaye, and the age difference, which had been easier to negotiate when they first met, became a strain. Gordy had put on weight, and while she was still an attractive woman she was often ill at ease around younger slimmer women. Their marriage had become like an unspoken metaphor for Motown itself, a close family damaged by disputes and destined for greater unhappiness. According to his biographer, David Ritz, Gaye had 'fought himself all the way to the top . . . His self-torturing, self-destructive design allowed for only minimal peace of mind.' Sometime in 1967 Gaye tracked his wife to a local motel and found her in bed with a lover. It was not a unique occasion. She had tolerated his many indiscretions and had long suspected that her own brother Berry was an untrustworthy influence on her husband. They were men whose relationship was founded on a love of jazz and sexual infidelity, and they often confided in each other as they played poker, building an immoral camaraderie. Each covered for the other when it came to one-night stands, sexual affairs or dubious excuses, but with every passing month Gordy and Gaye's friendship was put on trial as they negotiated the fierce loyalties of the Gordy family.

The warring couple had recently taken the keys to Berry Gordy's former home on Outer Drive, and Anna moved in with their three-year-old adopted son to what was supposed to become a permanent family home. Gaye tried to make it work, and so did Anna. He posed jauntily in a sailor's hat for photographs by the garage and played football with the neighbourhood kids, but it was a home mired in rumour. The natural mother of their adopted baby boy (also named Marvin) was Gordy's teenage niece Denise Gordy, and one story was that the adopted Marvin was in reality Marvin's natural child and that Denise had agreed to carry the child on behalf of her childless aunt as part of a family pact. It was a rumour that was almost certainly baseless, but such were the jealous tensions around their relationship that even those closest to the couple never probed too much. It was accepted that their son was adopted, and that was where the matter rested.

Berry Gordy always claimed that his relationship with Gaye was more fatherly than boisterous, but that was only his side of the story. 'Marvin had a divided soul,' Gordy wrote. 'He looked upon me as a father figure and friend, but he wanted to have his own independence, and he would disagree with you all the time just for the sake of disagreeing. At the same time, he was a pure, wonderful, spiritual person who was looking for truth, honesty, and love. But I had major fights with Marvin Gaye because he did not think it was legal to have to pay taxes. He was convinced that it was not lawful, and I said, "Well, I don't want to debate that with you, Marvin, but I do know if you don't pay your taxes, you're going to jail."' Eddie Holland described him more succinctly: 'You had to love Marvin – he was like a spoiled child.'

By 1967 he had secured his greatest success not as a soloist but as a co-singer in duets, first with Mary Wells, then briefly with a more obscure singer named Oma Heard (sometimes known by her married name Oma Drake), and then with Mickey Stevenson's sultry wife Kim Weston. Anna Gordy had watched with varying degrees of tolerance for five years as onstage and in the studio her husband declared his undying love to a string of other women. Although she laughed it all off, there were clearly times when her husband's love duets hurt her inside and undermined her self-esteem. Since Kim Weston's departure in January 1967 Motown had paired Gaye with yet another singer, this time the most romantic of all – Tammi Terrell, who at the time was sharing a Detroit apartment with her boyfriend, David Ruffin of the Temptations. Although they were virtually strangers, the bond between Gaye and Terrell grew to be profound. David Ritz wrote: 'The fourth of Marvin's five musical marriages was the most intense – intensely melodic, spectacularly successful, devastatingly tragic.' The professional partnership between Terrell and Gaye exceeded all others and came to represent the creative and spiritual summit of the sixties soul duet. Gaye and Terrell managed to weave two different voices intimately together and conjure images of love, whether the songs were about a first date, a fleeting affair or a deep betrothal. Songs like 'Ain't No Mountain High Enough', 'If I Could Build My World Around You', 'Your Precious Love', 'Ain't Nothing Like The Real Thing' and 'You're All I Need To Get By' came to define true romance in the sixties, and more subtly it shifted the register of how mainstream audiences viewed 'Negro lovers'.

It was a Cleveland camera crew who magically captured the unique chemistry of Marvin Gaye and Tammi Terrell when they were filmed singing together in an unusual setting beneath the Montreal Expo Express, an elevated railway amid the modernist architecture of Montreal's Expo 67. Motown had contracted Gaye and Terrell to appear in an episode of the popular Cleveland-based pop show *Upbeat*, a local derivative of *American Bandstand* and its UK equivalent, *Ready Steady Go*. It was a booking that went deeper than mere publicity. It had been carefully stage-managed by the senior management of Expo 67 to control negative publicity and reverse a widely held perception that the exhibition was a whites-only affair. The organisers of Expo 67 had pursued Motown for weeks, trying to secure a high-profile soul act who could attract network television coverage by performing live at the event. The organisers had been spooked by growing criticism from a civil rights group called the New York Urban League, which had been fronting a campaign promoting concerns about racial discrimination at the Expo. The league's executive director, Dr Eugene Callender, urged the organisers to reach out to 'Negro tourists' and invited President Johnson to use his influence to withdraw African and Asian nations from the Expo if it did not make visible efforts to integrate its attendees. The board of the Expo privately felt that the

Urban League was grandstanding on behalf of civil rights, and the elegant francophone director of Expo 67, Yves Jasmin, emphatically denied racism: 'There is no discrimination at Expo; anyone who says so is out of their mind.' His certainty was not shared, however, by the premier of Quebec, Daniel 'Danny Boy' Johnson, the Irish-French politician who admitted that there was a problem of sorts and used the dispute to underline inconsistencies in the law, pointing out that if Expo 67 were ever formally accused of discrimination, there would be no prospect of a successful prosecution. 'Discrimination law in Quebec is weak in that it only applies to hotels,' he confessed, but, if anything, his intervention only allowed accusations of racism to linger. Determined to attract more tourists from North American cities like New York, Chicago and Detroit, and to make the accusations recede, Expo 67 approached Esther Gordy about staging a Motown show. She immediately understood that it was an opportunity to position Motown as a family-friendly brand, one that floated above race issues, and so discussed the opportunity in a phone conversation with the producer of *Upbeat*, a close ally named Herman Spero. They agreed that if network syndication could be secured, then Marvin Gaye and Tammi Terrell would be available to fly to Montreal.

The show was eventually broadcast as a TV special, *The Swinging Sounds of Expo 67*, and featured Gaye and Terrell singing their recently released hit 'Ain't No Mountain High Enough', interspersed with a storyline of two young lovers out for the day amid the dynamic elegance of Expo 67. Marvin was in a grey silk jacket with a chiffon pocket handkerchief as if he were a doctor or lawyer on vacation, and Tammi was wrapped in a powder-blue checked coat and a Mod cap as if she were his fashion-conscious fiancée. Both appeared as middle-class and aspiring young professionals, with no trace of the ghetto. Expo 67 finally closed in the last days of October, having attracted fifty million visitors. It was deemed a major commercial success, and the clip of Marvin and Tammi was seen as a transformative television moment. Seen in almost every home in America, it cast the Motown singers as the nation's most recognisable African-American couple. Apart from fleeting scenes in feature films, it was still uncommon for young black lovers to be shown together onscreen, especially in the bright glare of primetime television. For many people in middle America, Marvin Gaye and Tammi Terrell became the personification of a new kind of 'Negro love' – likeable, aspirational and devoid of social anger.

The more Gaye and Terrell performed together, the more people began to sense that the relationship was special, heaping speculation onto their private lives. Years later, Terrell's sister Ludie Montgomery described a bond that went deeper than romance and aspiration: 'Tammi and Marvin were each complex individuals. They were bonded at a deep soul level. I think Tammi was an original, and she had her very own style and no one can compare to her . . . She brought Marvin out, and he was just real when she was around him.' Despite their pioneering role as young black lovers, Terrell's sisters insisted they were never lovers and were never sexually attracted to each other. This assertion was confirmed by Gaye himself. He and Terrell ended each night with a polite kiss or a handshake, as if love was an act that only really ignited when the lights came on. 'While we were singing we were in love,' Gaye claimed. 'The vibe was incredible. The emotions were heartfelt and real. But when the music ended . . . we said goodbye.' Gaye also revealed that his singing partner was actually the dominant force. 'Tammi was the kind of chick who couldn't be controlled by men,' he said. 'That can drive a man crazy – trying to deal with a woman who won't be dominated by anyone. I loved that about Tammi. I knew we could be friends, but never lovers. Independent women have held no romantic interest for me.'

Tammi Terrell was born in Philadelphia on 29 April 1945. She had arrived in Detroit with a reputation as a seasoned singer and as a young woman who had seen too much, too young. Her real name was Thomasina Montgomery, and at a precociously young age she had been discovered by producer Luther Dixon and signed to New York's Specter/Wand Records. Her uncle, a decent lightweight boxer named Bobcat Montgomery, had become a minor celebrity in Philadelphia when he fought in the famous War Bond Fight at

Madison Square Garden. The fight raised $35 million for the army. The Montgomerys had moved north to Philly during the Depression, and Bobcat had gravitated to a notorious inner-city gym known as the Slaughterhouse. As his fame grew, he had befriended numerous celebrities in the R&B scene, eventually introducing his niece to James Brown. At only fifteen Montgomery left home and joined the James Brown Revue, touring some of black America's most hardened soul venues, and threw herself into a life that pitted innocence against experience. She signed on with Brown's independent label, Try Me, recording the song 'I Cried', and subsequently came under the Godfather of Soul's demanding, unpredictable and periodically violent influence. Tammi – her nickname since childhood – became involved in a risky, contentious and ultimately brutal love affair with Brown and by all accounts was sexually abused by him. The Montgomery family was so distraught by her reports from a tour of the United States in early 1964 that they instructed their daughter to return home immediately. Close family witnesses have since revealed the horror of her return. Tammi's mother found a kimono soaked in blood in her daughter's suitcase; she had been sexually assaulted by Brown, who'd reportedly ruptured her vagina with an umbrella. Brown told a more saccharine version of events to his biographer: 'She was just a kid really, and I helped her all I could to learn to be a performer. We became very close very quickly, and then I fell in love with her.' It was a version of the truth, but one that fell far short of the whole story.

The James Brown Revue was a disciplined machine onstage and a despotic farce offstage. It had none of the well-managed and chaperoned culture that had protected Motown's teenage female singers, and so Terrell's savage introduction to life on the road was in marked contrast to Diana Ross's, who throughout her early Motown career travelled under the watchful eye of her chaperone, her own mother. While Ross was relatively protected, Terrell was exposed to hard-core funk, frenetic audiences and backstage debauchery. Brown was a predatory and unforgiving leader and a man who treated the young ingénue as a plaything: 'Somewhere during this time, I cut Tammi on my Try Me label,' Brown reminisced. It was 1963 and Tammi was just seventeen. 'I was crazy about her by then, but I think her family wanted her to do something else. They took her away from me because she had a lot of talent. I think they wanted me to groom her, not fall in love with her . . . It was painful for me.' Brown's opaque account of events remains one of the great deceits in the history of soul music and is self-serving nonsense. Montgomery's parents were incandescent with rage, and her powerfully built father, Tom Montgomery, a trainer and subsequently a boxing commissioner in Philadelphia, had to be talked out of taking revenge into his own hands. He bore a grudge against Brown until his dying day.

Montgomery's parents were adamant that Tammi should bring an end to her music career, encouraging her to attend classes at the University of Pennsylvania Medical school. She returned to live at home, but after a few halfhearted attempts at studying she inevitably drifted back to the limelight. Soul was in her bones. At nineteen she relaunched her stalled singing career for a third time when Jerry Butler employed her as a featured vocalist in his Chicago Revue. Sometime in 1965, the Jerry Butler Show – featuring Tammi Montgomery – performed live at the Driftwood Lounge at Detroit's 20 Grand club. Among the audience were Berry Gordy and Harvey Fuqua. Motown was at its acquisitive height, and compared to most independent R&B labels it had cash at the bank. Within a matter of a few days, Gordy offered Montgomery a contract and prised her away from the Chicago soul scene. It was an impulsive decision, underlining one of Motown's many structural flaws: it often secured the services of singers simply because it could afford to, without any great vision of what it would then do with them, or any real understanding that new recruits could undermine and irritate its own underemployed Detroit talent. In the case of Tammi Montgomery, it meant that a roster of strong female soloists was further disadvantaged. Gladys Knight, Barbara McNair, Brenda Holloway, the female leads of Martha and the Vandellas, fading forces like the Marvelettes, the Elgins, and the Velvelettes, and even the Supremes felt challenged. Within a matter of months, Gordy encouraged Tammi to change her surname to Tammi Terrell, and in the following year she racked up three singles. Her debut was 'I Can't Believe You Love Me', followed by 'Come On And See Me' and then a pulsating version of 'This Old Heart Of Mine'. For all her outstanding talent, though, Terrell's solo career at Motown was no more than middle-ranking. It was only when the opportunity of recording duets with Marvin Gaye arose that her reputation soared and her status increased.

Moving to Detroit should have put a distance between Tammi Terrell and her fast-track life, but it didn't. Within a few months of arriving in Detroit, she had divided opinion among her peers. Some immediately warmed to her effervescent personality, but others instinctively mistrusted her and saw her as new competition parachuting into Detroit. Martha Reeves was not a fan. 'Whenever somebody would ask me to say something nice about Tammi Terrell, I couldn't,' she once said. 'Tammi was a very talented girl but everything she did was crazy, wild and not right.' Reeves was not alone. Motown had a plethora of talented female singers on its books, and a cut-throat culture had taken hold – as one insider put it, 'alley cats with nail polish'.

Within weeks of arriving in Detroit, Terrell was dating the lead singer of the Temptations, David Ruffin. She quickly fell in love with him, and it proved to be an affair that defied explanation and was immediately compromised by Ruffin's complex character, reckless private life and troubled upbringing. Ruffin was already married – an inconvenience he hid from Terrell – and as his life unfolded he often appeared to be hiding something from everyone. Ruffin was a serial womaniser, unfaithful to all his many girlfriends, including another Philly-born singer Dee Dee Sharp; his first wife, Sandra, with whom he had three daughters, and his common-law wife, Genna Sapia, who bore him a son, David Ruffin Jr. His love affair with Terrell blossomed in the midst of this already tangled debris and was conducted in the full glare of Detroit nightclubs like the 20 Grand, where Ruffin's pregnant girlfriend, Genna, worked as a dancer. Ruffin's tumultuous love life mirrored his relationships with his fellow vocalists in the Temptations; he had begun to make professional demands that stretched credibility and eventually tore the heart out of the group. Having witnessed the elevation of Diana Ross to lead singer of the Supremes, Ruffin was determined that he too would win a similar status and that the group be rebranded David Ruffin and the Temptations. Although he was a phenomenally gifted singer, arguably one of the greatest soul singers of all time, it was an egotistical demand and one that at the time lacked creative authority. His persistent demands of Gordy, the press and fellow singers alienated him, and what he singularly failed to understand was that he was one talent among many.

Ruffin was the personification of soul music's well-trodden journey from the church to sexual excess. He was an irresponsible character, but in his defence he had not had an easy upbringing. He grew up in extreme deprivation in the small rural village of Whynot, Mississippi, and his mother had died soon after he was born, leaving him in the care of a domineering and fundamentalist father. The Ruffins lived in a shack with no electricity, no indoor plumbing and precious little love. His upbringing owed a lot to the Old Testament and to the fear of eternal damnation. Subsequent stories have suggested that he might have been emotionally, physically and sexually abused. Billy Wilson of the Motown Alumni Association claimed that 'what happened back in Mississippi fucked up David's life. He couldn't live with the shame and guilt. It affected everything he did.' Ruffin's unforgiving father battered his sons into a tight-knit gospel act that toured with the Five Blind Boys of Mississippi, selling God and voices to local villagers. But as soon as he was able, the gangly Ruffin escaped the malign influence of his father and headed for Memphis under the guise of becoming a minister. Gradually and inevitably, he drifted from God to the secular sound of soul music, briefly changing his name to Little David Bush, a name he adopted from his then manager and surrogate father, Eddie Bush. He eventually moved to Detroit, where the burgeoning local scene offered greater potential and where his brother Jimmy, who was also pursuing a career at Motown, had found temporary work at the River Rouge car plant.

David Ruffin recorded several songs for the local Vega label, but they disappeared without trace, and by 1961 he had signed part-time to a Gordy subsidiary, Miracle Records. For a brief spell, he was on the Gordy family payroll as a labourer, and then by chance – or more likely by calculation – he secured a job in the family's print firm. After a part-time job packing records at Anna Records, he finally made it to Motown as a construction apprentice working on repair jobs for Pops Gordy. His first job at Motown was wearing a tool belt and helping to repair wooden frames above the windows at Hitsville.

Ruffin became aware that the Temptations were looking for a tenor vocalist and approached the group's leader, Otis Williams, to offer his services. By January 1964 he had joined the group as a backing singer, but standing in the shadows was never his destiny. Ruffin was a virtuoso whose voice could move effortlessly from sweetness to aggression and from tenderness to threat, and his seemingly fragile pleas could suddenly soar with great power. Smokey Robinson recognised his potential and set out to write a song shaped for Ruffin's voice, which the singer Daryl Hall of Hall and Oates has since described as a voice with 'a certain glorious anguish'. Even those who came to dislike him conceded his brilliance. Melvin Franklin of the Temptations was in no doubt. 'He was probably the most talented individual of anybody . . . He could turn flips. He was very acrobatic and he could use that stuff emotionally and bring it into play when he was delivering a song. He was phenomenal.' The song Smokey Robinson fashioned was 'My Girl', featuring his now trademark lyrical contradictions – 'sunshine on a cloudy day' – and it grew to become one of the great classics of the high Motown era. What Robinson didn't know was that he had unlocked the door to Ruffin's voluminous ego and sown the seeds of future disputes within the Temptations, encouraging the relatively unknown singer to believe that he was the unheralded leader of one of Motown's greatest male groups.

In December 1964 'My Girl' became the Temptations' first

number one hit. With his lanky frame and distinctive horn-rimmed glasses, Ruffin became an increasingly demanding presence at Motown. Childhood deprivation and the extremes of being psychologically goaded and physically lashed had made him a ball of confusion, at once insecure and attention-seeking. Ruffin was a complex man with a young boy's mind, one who equated sex with love and mistook the thrill of narcotics for emotional wellbeing. His brother Jimmy had a habit of talking down to him, and even in adulthood tended to patronise his younger brother as if he were an infant – which, in some respects, he was. But being treated like a child infuriated David Ruffin and led to volcanic flare-ups and lifelong tension. If ever there was a case study in family dysfunction, it was the Ruffin brothers.

Tammi Terrell swore she had no idea David Ruffin was married. A more likely scenario was that withholding truths suited both of them, and so for several months the couple conducted their hectic love affair in clubs, in limousines and at local motels. Although the relationship was supposedly secret, Ruffin's limousine could not have been more conspicuous – it had his trademark glasses emblazoned on the side doors, and he often parked it carelessly at the rear of the Algiers Motel. In early October, with the wheels of justice slowly cranking forward, Prosecutor William Cahalan filed suit number 368, effectively slamming a closure order on the Algiers. It suited everyone. Detroit's religious community saw the Algiers as a totem of vice, the victims' families no longer wanted to see the place where their young boys had died still trading, and the police department, now engaged in a bitter internal war about what had really happened inside the motel, had come to loathe the place too.

Ruffin and Terrell had their first night of sex in the Algiers, in a shabby room in the main building. The intensity of their sexual lives has been exaggerated with time, but they have been variously described as voracious and noisy lovers. Billy Wilson of the Motown Alumni once said, 'When Tammi came to Motown, she was damaged goods mentally and physically, because of James Brown having beaten the shit out of her. She was a hostile firecracker, a hot-tempered girl, a real handful . . . Let me tell you, Tammi Terrell was major pussy.'

A few months earlier, in the spring of 1967, Terrell had unexpectedly announced her engagement to Ruffin onstage at the Uptown Theater in Philadelphia. Martha Reeves claimed it was at Harlem's Apollo Theater, and others said she repeated the announcement at several other East Coast venues. She flashed a diamond engagement ring to the audience in what proved to be a fatefully rash announcement, triggering an intense argument with Ruffin and deep resentments with the other women in his chaotic life. Although the couple reconciled, the incident never really subsided, and fights regularly erupted in public. Pumped up by an unrestrained ego and a worsening cocaine addiction, Ruffin's unreasonableness spiralled. He was adamant that he was single, but he could barely sleep alone and needed the comfort and reassurance of being part of a couple. With a wife and a pregnant girlfriend now pursuing him for money and support, Ruffin reserved the paranoid right to be jealous, often accusing Terrell of being flirtatious and leading men on. Ruffin increasingly came to resent Terrell's relationship with Marvin Gaye, and the couple began to bicker about her onstage 'love affair' too. Terrell's tempestuous private life was becoming complicated. It was true that she had been sexually abused on tour by James Brown and had fallen too quickly into bed with Ruffin, but her energetic approach to life was never wholly promiscuous or callous. Offstage Gaye and Terrell observed a professional distance, but such was their sexual chemistry and captivating onstage presence that they appeared to be in love, deeply in love.

It was a bizarre cast of characters: Ruffin, self-centred, needy and impulsive; Terrell, ambitious and naturally effusive; Marvin Gaye, a talented but introspective misfit; and Gaye's ageing wife, Anna, born into the family that owned Motown and afraid of losing her looks. Anna had no great reason to feel resentment towards Tammi, but she did. Her face, once beautiful and elegantly made-up when she stalked through the Flame Bar in the fifties, had now become lined and jowly. She had always pursued the elixir of permanent youth, and now it was betraying her. It was yet another cloud in the gathering storms at Motown.

On 11 October the Isley Brothers were recording overdubs of 'Take Me In Your Arms', a frenetic cover version of the Kim Weston song from 1965. The following day Smokey Robinson and the Miracles recorded 'I Second That Emotion', a song inspired by a trip Robinson and his friend Al Cleveland made to Hudson's department store on Woodward to buy a string of pearls for Robinson's wife, Claudette, who was recovering from the stillbirth of twins. Smokey supposedly said, 'Beautiful,' and Cleveland, meaning to second a motion, mistakenly replied, 'I second that emotion.' They seized on the unintentional remark and immediately wrote a song that became a million-selling record, reaching number four on the *Billboard* charts and topping the black singles charts. The original version had clocked in at over three minutes – a barrier to airplay on pop radio stations – so Gordy insisted that a verse be dropped.

Another epic Friday night was planned at the Grande Ballroom. This time around the MC5 had returned to their roots as warm-up act for visiting UK supergroup Cream, featuring Jack Bruce, Eric Clapton and Ginger Baker. While Clapton was still completing a sound check and pushing the old warehouse's acoustics to their very limit with improvised guitar solos, Marvin Gaye was being picked up by a Motown driver a few miles away at his home on Outer Drive. It was the first leg of a journey that would take him to Metro Airport, onward to Richmond International Airport, and on a drive through the fiery red autumnal lanes of central Virginia for what would turn out to be the most dramatic and fateful concert of his life.

He and Tammi had been booked on a low-paid college tour to promote their latest song, 'Your Precious Love', which had been released on Tamla a few weeks before. White colleges were part of Motown's strategy to reach audiences who might not otherwise buy black music, and back in July, United Artists in New York had taken a concert booking from a local Virginia agency called Top

Star Productions, which they imagined Motown would turn down. The request had come on behalf of students at Hampden-Sydney College in Virginia. A fee of $4,500 was agreed upon and a contract dispatched from Motown's offices offering a promotional show featuring Marvin Gaye and Tammi Terrell and an accompanying six-piece live band. Hampden-Sydney, an all-male liberal arts college, was celebrating its homecoming, and the students had invited girls from Longwood, a nearby women's college in Farmville, Virginia, to join them on the night. The booking had been made by a student of German literature and language named Bill Carter, president of the college's German Club. Carter later said that the binding contract Motown mailed was unnecessary, because Hampden-Sydney had one of the strictest honour codes in the South, and their students had pledged 'not to lie, cheat, steal, nor tolerate those who do'.

The concert was scheduled after a major college football game in the converted Gammon gymnasium, and the club's vice-president, Bill Selden Jr, had been tasked with meeting the artists on arrival. 'The six-member band got there about three hours early, which is very unusual,' Selden said. He sat with them in the gymnasium locker room playing poker until Gaye and Terrell arrived. 'Tammi wasn't feeling well from the time Marvin and she got there, so she stayed in her dressing room, which was nothing elaborate – just two coaches' offices – with the light out. Terrell said she'd be okay, she just had some headaches.' It was not an uncommon occurrence for the singer to rest before a show or lie down in a darkened room to fight off what had been diagnosed as migraine. Another student, Becky Garland, who worked for the local promoters, remembered the singer acting strangely. 'I was uneasy that evening,' she said, 'because she did have some problems.' Despite worries about Terrell, the organisers were reassured that she would recover and that the show would go on.

An estimated 800 students were crammed into space with no air-conditioning and precious little fresh air. Some were seated on a wall of benches, but most were crowded in front of the singers on the basketball court. Gaye and Terrell performed on a portion of the bleachers tied together by gymnasium ropes. There were numerous witnesses to what happened next. Student Bill Selden Jr described Terrell taking the stage uneasily: 'She did come out and sang two or three songs. The last one was "Ain't No Mountain High Enough" before she collapsed. We thought it was because of the heat. At intermission, Tammi still wasn't feeling well. I didn't see her again. Marvin was real nervous and concerned about her.' Another witness, Elliott Irving, recalled that, contrary to subsequent myth, it was 'not true that she fell into Marvin Gaye's arms. Her knees buckled and she lowered herself to the floor.'

Terrell's local paper, the *Philadelphia Enquirer*, claimed she 'collapsed onstage in Marvin Gaye's arms while the two were singing their latest hit'. Other newspapers followed suit, and so an image was cast of two lovers holding each other in a scene of Shakespearean tragedy. Gaye continued singing solo, improvising a show on his own and trying to cover for Terrell, but nothing he could do could lift the anxiety among those watching. The students of Hampden-Sydney had witnessed the last concert that Tammi Terrell would ever perform. She had suffered a brain haemorrhage and would never sing professionally again.

Believing she could fight through the pain, Terrell made a vain attempt to travel to another college the next day but was eventually admitted to a hospital in Richmond, Virginia, and placed in emergency care. *Jet* magazine, briefed by Motown, reported that she was being treated for 'exhaustion', but this was patently untrue. The next day she was flown back to Detroit and treated at the Henry Ford Hospital, but she returned home to the care of her family in Philadelphia at her father's insistence. There Terrell relapsed again and was rushed to the intensive care unit of Graduate Hospital, where she underwent surgery for the removal of a malignant brain tumour. Her sister Ludie described her lying in the hospital after the first operation, one of eight she would have to endure. 'Here was my once vibrant and beautiful sister partly paralyzed on one side. She could barely move her leg, her arm hung loosely by her side. Her face was distorted and her mouth was twisted. Her eyes were glossy, dark – yet they looked as if there was a frosty, milky film over them. She spoke very slowly and with a slur.' Despite neurological surgery and two years of radiation treatment, Marvin Gaye's greatest onstage lover, Tammi Terrell, died prematurely in 1970, and their great unconsummated love affair was brought to an abrupt end.

Terrell's collapse had dire consequences for Motown. It allowed suspicions about the company's callousness to take root and, unfairly, implicated an already alienated senior management team in manipulative wrongdoing. Many commentators who have since spoken of Terrell's illness were wise after the event and have offered diagnoses with the benefit of hindsight. One major Motown figure claimed she had always felt that Terrell appeared inattentive, as if she were dreaming – an entirely credible side effect of her illness – but this was never said before Terrell collapsed and was almost certainly not reported to Motown. Others claimed she had been put under excessive strain by the demands of her singing career and that the company's culture was one of intolerable work schedules. Worse still, some hinted that the medical explanations for Terrell's illness hid a more sinister explanation, a rumour that Motown's evasive and duplicitous press releases did nothing to dispel. They often talked of recovery and briefed the press about Tammi's irreducible personality to try to reassure fans that all was well. But it was not, and on balance honesty might have been a better policy.

The most virulent rumour was that Terrell had been the victim of sexual violence and that her head injuries were attributable to a tempestuous lifestyle and a violent relationship with her boyfriend, David Ruffin. This gossip had spread from Motown's inner circle of artists, and like many untruths about the company it had only a slight and exaggerated basis in fact. By now Ruffin was a heavy cocaine user. It was a drug that did not suit his personality and brought his ego, impetuousness and strident overconfidence screaming to the surface. He began to miss engagements, dropped out of concerts, and fought daily with his fellow band members. It was against this increasingly chaotic backdrop that he met and fell genuinely in love with Terrell. Theirs proved to be a love affair where temperaments were destined to clash and cocaine would ultimately triumph.

Three months prior to her brain haemorrage, in the week immediately after the Detroit riots, Tammi Terrell and Marvin Gaye were performing at solo engagements. Gaye was on the West Coast while Terrell was honouring a summer residency at the Wonder Gardens in Atlantic City. She stayed in a hotel at K.Y. and the Curb, a decaying area a few blocks from the Atlantic boardwalk. Terrell knew the area well; she had visited Atlantic City as a child on family holidays when boardwalk venues hosted the cream of African-American popular music, including Louis Armstrong, Ella Fitzgerald, Count Basie, Duke Ellington, Billie Holiday and Dinah Washington. By Motown standards, however, playing Atlantic City was a modest engagement, and Terrell's motel overlooked rundown backstreets. David Ruffin had gone missing from a Temptations tour to hang out with her and had moved into her hotel room.

Aware that her father had fond memories of Atlantic City and always keen to win his approval, Terrell invited her family to come and see her in concert. 'Our family made arrangements to go see Tommie [Tammi's childhood nickname], perform during this same week,' her sister reported. 'Mom, Daddy, and I arrived at the hotel about three o'clock. Tommie opened the door and she looked peculiar. She had sort of a faraway, dazed look in her eyes and was very surprised to see us . . . David Ruffin was also there that afternoon in Tommie's room, and to me he seemed quite in a hurry. He shoved his motorcycle helmet on and he climbed over the balcony and scurried down the side of the building out the fire escape. I heard his cycle start and roar off.' Terrell's road manager, Doryce Postles, who had previously travelled with the Supremes as a wardrobe supervisor, was staying in an adjacent room and asked to speak to her parents privately. While Tammi was in the bathroom applying make-up, Postles told the family in confidence that there had been a calamitous row and that she feared that David Ruffin, whom she did not like, had hit Tammi across the face and head. According to Terrell's sister Ludie, 'Apparently, there had been a big argument . . . This had been an ongoing feud between them for months, ever since Tommie announced their engagement to a packed house in another state. Effects of this fiasco were still brewing and it came to a head. David was still angry. He was already married and had a family, and Tommie knew this now.'

To try to calm the warring couple and keep the hotel management away from the room, Mrs Postles had hammered on the motel door and barged in. By then Tammi Terrell was lying on the bed with ice on her head, tending a wound. Ruffin had hit her with his motorcycle helmet and then in an act of contrition gathered ice from a soda machine. As the story swept through the music industry, it grew legs with each retelling. It became an accepted fact that Ruffin had hit her with a weapon, usually said to have been a bottle or a claw hammer, and with Terrell's health deteriorating, the finger of blame was pointed at Ruffin. One of his former girlfriends, Genna Sapia, said that the question she had been most frequently asked over the years was 'Did David really kill Tammi Terrell?'

Motown tried to dampen the controversy, but their efforts were only partly successful, and the exaggerated stories had already reached the most important family of all – Terrell's parents and the Montgomery family in Philadelphia. In the aftermath Terrell's sister carefully put things into context: 'There are so many inaccuracies and misunderstandings as to what really happened in the final breakdown in their relationship . . . You can see where things became misconstrued and how things became twisted over the years.' They were kind words written to draw an end to speculation and exaggeration, but what was left unsaid was the pain and self-doubt that her family endured. Her parents often wondered if they could have done more and what, if anything, had drawn their daughter towards two of the most egotistic soul singers of the sixties – first James Brown and then David Ruffin.

Shelly Berger, the energetic talent manager whom Motown hired in 1966 to manage the Supremes, saw in Ruffin a man who had strayed some distance from his gospel roots. 'I think David dreamed of being a pimp,' Berger once said. 'He loved that whole idea of walking in with a big bankroll, buying drinks for everybody, being the center of attention. The women, the flashy cars, the pinkie rings. That was his personality from the day I met him.' This image of Ruffin is consistent with almost every description by those who knew him. By contrast, Terrell's character is more difficult to capsulate. Since her premature death, some have described her as near saintly, forever romantic, almost an innocent in her victimhood. None of this entirely chimes with someone who had been on the Chitlin' Circuit since the age of fifteen. A few descriptions of Terrell break with Motown propaganda. The president of the Motown Alumni Association, Billy Wilson, described her as 'a hostile firecracker, a hot-tempered girl, a real handful', and in an emotionally bruised book about her life with David Ruffin, Genna Sapia describes Terrell as calculating and possessive and can barely contain her long-held resentment. Terrell was 'not as ditzy as she acted,' Sapia claimed. 'She saw an opportunity and she grabbed . . . Those that wrote she was a promiscuous alcoholic nymphomaniac were too kind.' Whatever version of a love affair David Ruffin and Tammi Terrell were involved in – and many people believed it was real love – it was way too chaotic, reckless and unstable to last.

Motown were left with a pressing diplomatic problem: how to keep the show on the road. Gaye and Terrell's single 'Your Precious Love' was scheduled for release in the UK on the Tamla-Motown label, and long-distance transatlantic telephone interviews had been set up with the press in London. Gaye was encouraged to do them alone, although it suited no one. Two days after Terrell's hospitalisation, she and Gaye were scheduled to appear at a six-night engagement at the legendary Apollo Theater in Harlem. The show had been advertised, billboards printed, and tickets pre-sold. Cancelling was not an option, so Motown was forced into taking emergency action. A replacement singer was the obvious solution. There were several options. Gaye had sung duets with stand-in artists before, including Brenda Holloway, Barbara Randolph and a gifted young singer named Ann Bogan, who by then had joined the Marvelettes. But after hurried internal meetings, Motown decided to hire a New York-based singer named Maxine Brown, an experienced duet singer contracted to the Scepter/Wand label. The call came at a low moment in Brown's life; she was frustratingly losing ground to her friend and label rival Dionne Warwick, who in 1963 to 1964 had released six successive hit records, including the international bestseller 'Walk On By' and had become the latest in a long list of African-American chanteuses to dazzle Paris. When Warwick performed at the Paris Olympia, the critic Jean Monteaux paid homage in ways that only a French aesthete could: 'The play of this voice makes you think sometimes of an eel, of a storm, of a cradle, a knot of seaweed, a dagger,' he wrote. 'It is not a voice so much as an organ. You could write fugues for Warwick's voice.'

With Warwick's international success, Wand Records had allowed Maxine Brown to fade from view. On receiving the call from Detroit, she was quickly seduced by Motown: within a matter of minutes she had agreed to a deal, and began rehearsals later that day. As Tammi Terrell rested in a private room at the Graduate Hospital in Philadelphia, Gaye and Brown acted out their rehearsed love rituals in a dingy gymnasium in Harlem before finally taking to the Apollo stage in New York. Back in Detroit, Motown staff members were desperately trying to shore up Terrell's planned schedule. Singer Brenda Holloway, who at the time was deeply disenchanted with how Motown was handling her career, was drafted to fulfil solo performances. As soon as that was sorted out, Motown was presented with another problem: it had pencilled a commercially lucrative album of love songs into the release schedules but had no obvious female lead. Motown's answer proved to be a mixture of compromise and calculation: a series of songs supposedly featuring Tammi Terrell that were put together layer by layer in the studio. In the suspicious wake of Terrell's illness, these disputed songs, which only partially feature Terrell's real voice, have subsequently become known to Motown fans by their conspiratorial name, 'the ghost tracks'.

Terrell had been taken under the care of Dr Richard Harner, chief of the neurology department at the Graduate Hospital. Although a brain tumour had forced Terrell to retire from live performances, Motown initially downplayed the seriousness of the situation, and not wholly for cynical reasons. Terrell's condition was known to be unstable, but her tests took many months, and the exact details of her illness were not easy to comprehend. Motown's press office was briefed by senior executives to deny any suggestion that Terrell had undergone brain surgery, and the influential music paper *Soul* adamantly denied this was the case. By denying what treatment Terrell was undergoing, the vacuum was once again filled with gossip and innuendo. Such was the uncertainty about her condition that not even Marvin Gaye was particularly well informed about how she was doing. Studio singer Louvain Demps of the Andantes described being driven home one night from Hitsville by Gaye; he sensed that Gaye had slipped into a melancholic mood, one that would soon tip into full-blown depression. 'He and I talked quite a lot back then and we were very close,' Demps said. 'This particular night we sat in front of my house and talked about Tammi for a very long time. He shared his fears that he thought she was never going to make it. You would be surprised by the intuitiveness he had when it came to Tammi. He was hurting deeply and he knew she was not going to make it. He said, "Louvain, I know she's not going to make it and there's nothing I can do." From then on anytime we talked, we talked about him getting himself together.'

Highly protective of their daughter, the Montgomery family closed ranks and blamed the music industry for her troubles. They had no particular complaint against Motown, which they believed had acted professionally, but there was a lingering hatred of James Brown and a deep suspicion about the trustworthiness of her ex, David Ruffin. They were resistant to the idea of Terrell returning to a career in music, but silently, and at times in whispered conference with her sister, Terrell herself was determined that illness would not curtail her career. It was an ambition that was brave and admirable but tragically short-lived.

At the early height of Marvin and Tammi's success, another duo had arrived at Motown: Nickolas Ashford and Valerie Simpson. They had met each other in 1964 at the White Rock Baptist Church in Harlem, married within months, and became lifelong partners. They had majestically perfected the art of swapping lead vocals and descanting to the sound of each other's voices, a choral hallmark that dated back to their gospel roots. Ashford and Simpson were part of a growing roster of artists handpicked by Gordy to strengthen the company's songwriting academy and thereby reduce Motown's dependency on the disillusioned hit machine, Holland-Dozier-Holland. Gordy had sensed for several months now that the pipeline of hit songs was slowing, and Ashford and Simpson proved to be at least a partial solution, delivering four stand-out songs in a matter of only a few months: 'Ain't No Mountain High Enough', 'Your Precious Love', 'If I Could Build My Whole World Around You' and 'If This World Were Mine'. All four songs featured on Gaye and Terrell's first duet album, *United*, which was released in the late summer of 1967.

Bronx-born Valerie Simpson was an explosion of energy and an inspirational musician. She was a gifted soloist in her own right and had the strength of character to make demands of Motown's challenging studio musicians. Without any sense of trepidation or self-doubt, she sat at the piano in the Snake Pit and commanded utter respect by force of her personality. She was one of a very small number of people who could reduce the studio's locker-room banter and customary sexism to silence. And Simpson had another virtue: she could sing in the same register as Tammi Terrell. To an untrained ear, they could easily have been the same singer.

It was with Simpson's skills in mind that Motown supposedly hatched an audacious idea: to construct a series of tracks 'featuring' Tammi Terrell, whether she was well enough to record or not. It was Simpson who was to become the unaccredited talent behind the ghost tracks. Motown pushed ahead with recording a new album with Marvin Gaye. When it was eventually released as *You're All I Need*, the liner notes on the back album seemed to imply that the recordings were at least in part therapeutic: 'Such performances have been temporarily denied us due to Tammi's illness . . . Not only did recording this album contribute to her convalescence, but added a new dimension to the Gaye-Terrell repertoire.'

Meanwhile, Terrell had bravely tried to return to singing. According to *Billboard* magazine, in the autumn of 1967 she was often seen entering the Hitsville studio in her wheelchair, wearing dark glasses. She reportedly worked twelve- and eighteen-hour days for a week, and upon completion of the album told *Billboard*, 'I've got a lot more faith in God.' What is not verifiable is if this report is actually true or was placed by Motown's press team. Significant doubt has always surrounded the album. Some studio regulars say they never saw Terrell again at Motown, while others claimed they worked closely with her through painful and emotionally difficult sessions. Whichever version one believes, one thing was certain: the songs were left incomplete or in a state that Motown did not wish to release. Gordy was left with three options: he could follow medical advice in the hope that Terrell would return and complete unfinished songs; he could get Gaye to overdub songs that Terrell had already recorded as a solo singer and embroider them to the extent that they sounded like duets; or he could bring Valerie Simpson to the studio as a surrogate singer and try to replace Terrell. Perhaps through necessity, they did all three. An album of songs was carefully assembled. While some of the final album can honestly be credited to Tammi Terrell, doubt still surrounds several tracks. One plausible theory is that after a six-week stay at the Graduate, where she had her first operation, Terrell returned in a fragile state to Detroit to record the Marvin Gaye duet 'You're All I Need To Get By'. The lyrics seemed to imbue Gaye with gospel-like powers of being a healer, an image that was to mature with time as he merged soul, sexuality and spiritual wellbeing in his global hit 'Sexual Healing'. Motown was adamant that Terrell travelled to Detroit, but her medical records and family narrative suggest she was very weak and moved between different hospitals, eventually undergoing surgery for 'an acorn-size tumor in the thalamus'.

Terrell's closest friend at the time, Dolores 'Cookie' Thomas, claimed Terrell did return to Detroit but was visibly ill and thinner, and when they were alone together Terrell would take off her wig and show her friend recent post-op scars. Thomas added another piece of convincing detail: she claimed Terrell returned to her own apartment on Holbrook and, despite her illness, the two of them went to a basketball game together. Terrell was a passionate fan of the Philadelphia 76ers and had attended many of their home games since the franchise had moved to Philly in the early sixties. Her father was a close friend of two of the players, Wilt Chamberlain and Olympic gold-medallist Luscious Jackson, and often secured tickets through his local sporting connections. According to Thomas, Terrell went surreptitiously to the Cobo Hall, wearing a wig and dark horn-rimmed sunglasses. Although unsteady and hunched, she hobbled incognito into the arena to watch her beloved 76ers play as aspiring NBA champions. They won the game 115–106.

Another reliable witness, the studio singer Louvain Demps of the Andantes, described a process that was closer to collaboration rather than deceit in terms of the album. In Demps's account, Valerie Simpson literally helped the weakened Terrell with vocals: 'She was working closely with Valerie. She gave her all and she showed up and tried. Her spirit came through. She was weak and a little different from the Tammi I knew, she was more quiet.' Demps was adamant that while the sessions were sad, they were far from sinister: 'She was not in a wheelchair or on crutches.' Producer Johnny Bristol also tried to take the heat out of conspiracy theories. 'As far as the overdubbing goes, it was blown out of proportion over the years. Val helped her vocally to get through sessions. There was nothing to it and everyone agreed that Tammi would complete them one day. It was not a big deal at the time.' And Valerie Simpson claimed that she was determined to finish: 'We knew she was weak.'

The ghost tracks might not have been a big deal at the time, but they became one. Marvin Gaye was adamant that at least two hit songs released in 1969 – 'What You Gave Me' and 'The Onion Song' – were both sung as studio duets with Valerie Simpson and not with Tammi Terrell. Many people, including Gaye and members of the Funk Brothers, have commented on the close similarities between Terrell and Simpson's voices and how easy it was to confuse the two. '[Valerie] amazed me with how faithfully she captured Tammi,' Gaye said. 'I felt strange . . . I suppose I felt guilty.' He went further, claiming that at the time he had been reluctant to record the album, which he felt was predicated on a deception: 'At first I refused to go along with the plan. I saw it as another money-making scheme on B. G.'s [Berry Gordy's] part. I said it was cynical and wrong. I didn't want to deceive the public like that. Then Motown convinced me that it'd be a way for Tammi's family to have additional income.' There is no record of Gaye voicing his reluctance at the time, and those remarks came long after Terrell's premature death. Gaye's version of events also sidestepped another important truth: the couple had frequently recorded duets separately. It was standard Motown practice. During most of the sessions that resulted in the Ashford and Simpson classic 'Ain't No Mountain High Enough', Gaye and Terrell were not in Detroit at the same time, so they recorded separate versions of the song many days apart. It was Motown engineers who eventually remixed the vocals, edited out the once dominant background singers, and gave Gaye and Terrell the clear unadulterated leads. Recording studios are by their nature about layering tracks and simulating the power of voices; in a very obvious creative sense they are always predicated on a deception. It is unlikely that the full granular detail of the ghost songs will ever be known, but they came at a time when Motown's reputation was at its nadir.

In mid October 1967 student protests against the war in Vietnam had focused on one corporation in particular. The Dow Chemical Corporation had become synonymous with chemical warfare and the inhumanity of the war. Dow manufactured napalm, the flammable liquid that burned at temperatures of 1472 Fahrenheit and scalded the skin of unarmed villagers in the combat zones. Dow was also a licensed manufacturer of Agent Orange, the chemical defoliant that destroyed forests and undergrowth, and was used routinely by the military to deprive the Viet Cong jungle guerrillas of cover and camouflage. A damaging and highly emotive slogan, 'Babies Are Not for Burning', was being used by anti-war activists to ram home the message, but Dow refused to back down. Rather than halt production of napalm, the company resolved to fight back, organising highly controversial recruitment seminars on university campuses. On 18 October hundreds of students protested against a Dow recruitment drive at the University of Wisconsin-Madison. The protest turned violent when campus police charged the demonstrators. Dozens of students were beaten to the ground, and nineteen police officers were treated for minor injuries at local hospitals. Protesters had tracked at least part of the manufacturing process back to one of Dow's West Coast plants in Torrance, California. It became a regular target for Students for a Democratic Society, and public fury erupted when more than five tons of napalm bombs fell from a trailer on the Pacific Coast Highway en route to Long Beach Harbor, bound for Vietnam.

At an army recruitment office in Baltimore, a Roman Catholic priest and two laymen were arrested for pouring pints of blood over recruitment records, and at Oberlin College in Ohio students trapped a navy recruiter in his own car, preventing him from drafting students to support the war effort. Earlier in the year, Cornell students had burned their draft cards in full view of the world media, using a Maxwell House coffee can as the protest pyre. Detroit had its own network of draft resistance. The Central Methodist Church had earned a substantial reputation for opposing war in any form and for its quiet resistance to Vietnam. Situated at the intersection of Woodward and Adams, the congregation became known as 'the conscience of the city' and provided a home for a draft counselling centre where young people could go to get advice on how to resist the draft. They offered Christian sanctuary to those conscripts who wished to protest the war and the notice boards were overflowing with advice and stacks of flyers recommending local lawyers, among them Justin Ravitz, the young civil rights lawyer who by now had virtually become the in-house legal attorney for the Steering Committee and the MC5.

The storm clouds of civil disobedience were gathering. On 21 October over 70,000 demonstrators besieged Washington DC in a march to 'confront the war makers' under the banner of MOBE (the National Mobilization Committee to End the War in Vietnam). In reality it was a coalition of many different demonstrations stretching across DC from the Mall, around the White House, and on scattered campuses across the inner city. The students of Howard University invited soul and jazz singers to their Sixth Street campus to attend a soul rally against the war. Stax singer Carla Thomas and jazz musician Donny Hathaway, who were both registered students, took part, as did some of the local Shrine label artists whom Berry Gordy's former wife Raynoma had invested in with her divorce income. They included her nephew Dale Warren, a conservatory-trained violinist from Detroit who had only recently produced Washington's answer to the Supremes: a female soul group called the DC Blossoms.

David Dellinger, a radical pacifist and MOBE coordinator, had circulated information promoting the invasion of Washington to hippie leaders across the country, including the Ohio-born yippie leader Jerry Rubin, John Sinclair and the Detroit Committee to End the War in Vietnam, a city-wide organisation increasingly led by the Socialist Workers Party. The media were simultaneously excited and appalled by the bombastic showmanship of the new left. Jerry Rubin and his radical collaborator Abbie Hoffman had hatched a bizarre plan to invite hippies to sing and chant until the Pentagon 'levitated and turned orange', thus 'driving out evil spirits and ending the war in Vietnam'. *Time* magazine published eyewitness reports that were sceptical, curious and at times poetic. 'The demonstration began under the crystalline noonday sky at the Lincoln Memorial . . . beneath the marbled gaze of Lincoln's statue . . . Speakers caterwauled in competition with blues and rock bands as the demonstrators jostled across the lawns.' Although the Pentagon never actually moved and rationalism won the day, the symbolic act attracted the attention of every major news outlet. Cameras followed a group of hard-core hippies along Pennsylvania Avenue to the White House, where they tried to wake up President

Johnson with Buddhist chants. Back in Detroit, Trans-Love Energies staged a simultaneous protest to help with the levitation. John Sinclair and his friend Jim Semark – no strangers to acts of demonstrative theatre – supported MC5 and were billed as 'performance poets'. Sinclair regaled the audience with lyrical rants about Vietnam, a polemic against napalm, poems about his war with Michigan's drug laws, and tirades against his greatest personal obsession – the corrupt Detroit police.

Although restlessness about Vietnam was at its height and youth counterculture was demanding a new America, the Supremes appeared to be regressing to a more wholesome decade. They were now firmly established as the greatest black pop group of the sixties but seemed increasingly more aligned to the mainstream consumerism of the fifties, when family values, suburban lifestyles and commercial television came of age. As they moved from hotel room to airport to concert hall and on to their next network television studio, many of the major political events of 1967 passed them by. In mid October, they flew south to the central Mexican river resort of Las Estacas to take part in the NBC television series *Tarzan*, in which, incomprehensibly, the Supremes played the role of three nuns in the jungle. They were highly respected performers at supper clubs from New York to Las Vegas; they had recorded a live album at the Copacabana; they were regular guests of Johnny Carson and almost every network talk show; they lent their voices to a Hollywood movie, *The Happening*; they recorded tribute albums to the Beatles, Nashville, Broadway, and a gut-wrenchingly awful one to Walt Disney; they had sung at a fundraiser for the president; and now they were playing opposite Tarzan as Sisters of Mercy. It was a resumé that seemed to be blindly unaware of radical social change and looked backward with nostalgia. For a group whose origins were in the raw ghetto sounds of Detroit R&B, the Supremes had been magically transformed into the greatest girl group ever. For some, it was an audacious achievement and a triumph over racism; for others, it was a shimmering compromise.

The Supremes returned from the Mexican jungle to a period of intensive touring. They performed in cities across the Northwest, with shows at the University of Oregon, the Portland Coliseum, the Arena at Spokane, the Seattle Arena, and then onward to the Oakland Coliseum. Back in Detroit, Ballard was experiencing extremes of emotions. She had bouts of mania and euphoria, followed by depression and feelings of intense loathing. She had been vociferous about needing a rest from the intense demands of being a Supreme, but after a short break at home in Detroit niggling doubt and unexpected yearning began to eat away at her. Ballard was reaching the conclusion that she had been 'constructively dismissed' by Motown and was the victim of a plot. The more she brooded about her disputes with Gordy, the more she sought the opinion of boyfriend Tommy and her brother Jess. Spurred on by the ill-advised encouragement of others, she decided to go to war with the most powerful black-owned corporation in the entertainment industry. It turned out to be a decision that precipitated disaster.

Florence Ballard was never friends with Tammi Terrell. They had known each other at a distance and spoken only in passing, so there was no reason for Ballard to visit Terrell in the hospital or call her parents to enquire about her health. Most of the communication between Detroit and Philadelphia was carried out through the Montgomery family and Berry Gordy's redoubtable sister Esther, who was the de facto head of Motown's International Talent Management Inc. (ITMI), a division known colloquially as 'It-Mee'. For many artists it was a term used dismissively as a focus of discontent for contracts and rates of pay, but ITMI had another important function: overseeing talent management and artists' welfare. It was also the administrative hub of Motown's Blue Cross health insurance, a benefit extended to contracted singers. It controlled the fund that paid for Terrell's medical treatment.

The Montgomery family maintained a round-the-clock vigil by Tammi's bedside and camped out at the Graduate Hospital so that if she woke up, day or night, someone recognisable would be there. Visitors were rationed, fans were graciously turned away, and, given her parents' suspicions about the music world, only a select few from the industry were ever made welcome. A month after her first surgery, Terrell was allowed home to her own bed and to a newly decorated room full of flowers, fan mail and gifts, including a lucky teddy bear from East Orange sent by the New Jersey-based soul singers Dionne Warwick and Cissy Houston, and a shelf full of homecoming presents from neighbours. It was as if Terrell had retreated in time to her childhood bedroom in Germantown, back to an age of innocence before soul. However, after weeks of extreme headaches and heavy periods of sedation it was clear that time at home was not enough. Her doctors worked on plans for a second operation. The timescale was hurriedly moved forward when she was rushed back into emergency care after a build-up of fluid on the brain. The treatment was successful and again she was allowed home, now weighing only ninety-three pounds.

Sometime after Terrell's second operation, Marvin Gaye and road manager Doryce Postles drove from Detroit to visit her. The family knew and trusted both of them and felt that the visit would strengthen their daughter's resolve. According to imprecise accounts, Gaye possibly spent three unrecorded days alone with her, travelling locally from his hotel to her bedside. He claimed they talked about life and music and what they would sing in the future. Although he always had much to say about Motown and his own insecurities, Gaye remained intensely private about his days with the dying Tammi Terrell. The South African trumpeter Hugh Masekela also came to see her, and so did Jimmy Ruffin and his wife, but David Ruffin was conspicuous in his absence. Although Terrell had long since forgiven Ruffin for assaulting her in Atlantic City, and enjoyed his disarming company, the Montgomery family had not forgiven him, and he remained persona non grata.

After an eighth and final brain operation, Tammi Terrell fell into a coma. Immortalised in song and for ever linked with Marvin Gaye, she died on 16 March 1970. Her sister Ludie, who had witnessed her rise to fame and her dramatic demise, arrived at the Graduate Hospital in time to see one of Motown's enduring stars being slid into a body bag. In one final disappointment, Terrell's safe at the hospital had been broken into and some of her personal effects stolen. When news of her death reached Detroit, it came with the terrified disbelief that frequently accompanies young death. Marvin Gaye, who had predicted for many months that it would happen, slid into a long period of self-reflective despair. Smokey Robinson's wife, Claudette Rogers, a singer with the Miracles, said that Gaye's grief was 'noticeable to us, and it was painful to watch. He seemed to want to give up his career and was sad to the point of depression.' Terrell's sister described his feelings as 'being so conflicted no one could reach him or console him . . . Marvin became isolated in a cocoon of pain and the people in his life found it impossible to influence him.' Jackie Hicks, another member of the Andantes, told Terrell's family, 'We were all devastated when she died . . . It ripped Marvin apart.'

Gaye went into what many described as a period of seclusion. He performed less often and avoided the Hitsville studios. 'I was devastated by Tammi's death,' he said later. 'I think maybe what scared me the most was that I was so angered by the senselessness of it all. I had to accept that it was God's will, but it was difficult to understand at the time. I grieved for years, and the fact that deep down inside I hated performing . . . made it easier for me to stop.' His self-imposed exile from Motown was in fact a period of untreated depression worsened by his use of recreational drugs and a marriage that was tearing itself apart. He spent day after day in Gordy's old home on Outer Drive, wandering around barefoot and rarely venturing out. The sharp suits of his earlier career were discarded for slovenly and oversized sweatshirts gifted to him by the Detroit Lions. He confessed that he would stare for hours at the same wall and wander listlessly around the house for hours. His depressive silences further alienated his frustrated wife, Anna Gordy, who had struggled to believe his love for Tammi Terrell had been confined to music. By now both were unfaithful, and a deep chasm had grown at the heart of their marriage.

Many conflicting versions of Tammi Terrell's life have fought for attention since 1967, but by far the most convincing and detailed comes from Terrell's sister, who has written about the illness in ways that are refreshingly free from rancour. There was much misunderstanding to clear up. The normally reliable Smokey Robinson had not helped by trying to shift gossip away from Motown and the much maligned David Ruffin to James Brown. In an interview less than a year after the collapse, Robinson claimed that the real reason for Terrell's illness was that she was injured as a teenager and 'as a result, she had to have a blood clot removed from her brain'. It was a deflection without any truth or merit. Yet Martha Reeves offered a similar rationalisation: 'She was James Brown's woman. That lie they put out about David Ruffin hitting her on the head with that hammer, causing that brain injury to her head, trust me, that happened way before David Ruffin's time. I know for a fact.' But it wasn't a fact, not in any verifiable sense.

Many years later, Terrell's neurologist, Dr Richard Harner, released a formal diagnosis of her condition to the Montgomery family that challenged all the innuendo and finally laid the Motown rumours to rest. 'The kind of tumor she had was a slow-growing tumor,' he said. 'It was malignant and basically terminal all along. We didn't tell her the prognosis because we didn't know for sure; technology was much different then. Some of the symptoms she might have had from the tumor were dizziness, weakness and headaches; these could come on prior to diagnosis and then medications and more pressure could cause hallucinations. Once headaches start, that means there is blockage of fluid. There has never been a case where being hit on the head caused a tumor. Tumors are not caused by trauma.' However compelling it might have been for the gossipmongers of sixties soul, there is no credible evidence whatsoever that either the exploitative James Brown or the self-centred David Ruffin were implicated in the death of Tammi Terrell.

Heavy Eyes, Heavy Heart. An emotionally drained Florence Ballard
at the height of her legal problems.

NOVEMBER

Law

Florence Ballard backed her Eldorado Cadillac into a deserted street. It was a crisp, cold morning in the first days of November, and frost clung to the hedgerows like crystal meth. She sang silently to herself, sometimes anticipating the high notes of the crackling car radio, and her warm breath condensed the inside of the cold window. Tommy was still in bed. Ballard had arranged an early-morning meeting downtown with her lawyer, Leonard Baun, although he had already told her there was not much to report. Motown's legal team had refused to release any details of past record sales; they had not replied to his request for an income and expenditure account that would help detail her life as one of the Supremes; and there was no clarity about what value she could hope to accrue from the future use of the name she had come up with. Baun had persisted vainly, making unanswered calls, sending hand-delivered letters, and threatening court action by courier, but he was stonewalled at every step of the way and would continue to be ignored for many months to come.

Motown had no great need to respond to Ballard's new lawyer. They had Ballard's signature on a settlement agreement and had paid her $75,689, which for a time was held in an interest-bearing escrow account at the Bank of the Commonwealth but had now been moved to a new account under her newly created company Talent Management Inc. (TMI). Baun was designated as president and treasurer; Ballard and Tommy Chapman were joint signatories; and all three had begun to spend the deposits on legal expenses, incidental costs and family gifts. Ballard had booked a winter Caribbean holiday. Motown took those actions as evidence that the settlement had been accepted and life had moved on. Gordy's lawyers had greater resources than Ballard, and they knew it. The odds were stacked against any new agreement being reached, and Baun was left in the wilderness. He had no idea how Motown accounted for record sales or how units sold converted into royalty payments. The music industry employed a murky arithmetic at the best of times, and anyone unfamiliar with the curious alchemy of copyright law was at a massive disadvantage. Motown did not set out to victimise Ballard, nor was there any systematic conspiracy against her, but it was company policy – and a Gordy family trait – to be guarded about earnings. So Baun was reduced to making things up, and in the process he seriously underestimated the singer's true worth.

By November 1967 Motown was the most successful independently owned record company in the world, and yet not a single gold record hung on the walls of Gordy's offices. That was no accident. Gold records were certified by the Recording Industry Association of America (RIAA), and since its first national hits in the early sixties Motown had refused to open its books up to industry audit. So despite the mountain of sales, Motown never received any gold records. Critics have seized on this closed-door policy as proof that Gordy was cheating his artists, but like much to do with Motown it was not as simple as that. Internal audits fell under the managerial gaze of the savvy Esther Gordy, who was Motown's desk sergeant, and she resented any intrusion on the family's affairs, approaching the business as if it were solely their domain. The Gordys had embraced success as a family, but it was not abundantly clear that America had made the same concerted efforts to embrace them. Throughout the post-war period, the wider Gordy family had been signed up to the values of self-help and civil rights and participated in numerous campaigns against racial bias in business. Had auditors from the RIAA turned up unannounced at Motown, Esther Gordy would quite probably have refused them entry. One Motown insider put it less politely – she would have told them 'to U-Haul their asses back to New York'. Motown was convinced the RIAA did not have its best interests at heart. It was a conservative institution hardwired to publishing powerhouses like the Brill Building on Broadway and saw Detroit as an anomalous outpost. Even as late as 1967, it was unclear if the RIAA was comprehensively tracking record sales in the ghetto stores of Chicago and Detroit, let alone the southern soul citadels of Atlanta, Memphis and New Orleans, so throughout the sixties independent soul labels frequently complained that they were underrepresented and fatefully cheated out of chart prominence.

Whatever the reason for Motown's secrecy, it did not help Ballard's lawyers to build a case against the company. Leonard Baun had no connection with the music industry, and at first that made him superficially attractive. Ballard and Chapman had stoked each other's paranoia about Gordy and his pervasive power within the industry. Hiring a lawyer unknown to Motown appeared to be a plus, but Baun's appointment proved catastrophic. Although he did not know it at the time, he had a massive tumour pressing against the frontal lobes of his brain, and those who worked closely with him had begun to detect slight shifts in his personality. Like Tammi Terrell, he was often dizzy and listless, and his casual approach to office life had given way to unpredictable outbursts and flights of arrogance. Colleagues described him acting as if he were influential, and he talked uncharacteristically about leaving conventional law behind for a career in artist representation or music industry law. It was a tragic fallacy. Although it was dull and routine work, Baun was more accustomed to drafting wills, handling divorce papers, and pursuing neighbourhood disputes than to unravelling copyright law. Whatever residual sentiment there was for Ballard among the freelance musicians at Hitsville, the senior management had moved on, and in the ice-cold language of the music industry Florence Ballard was history.

Throughout 1967 Detroit had become an increasingly litigious city. Increased rates of divorce, new civil rights legislation and escalating workplace disputes had made the legal profession a very lucrative business. Newly established law offices had sprung up across Michigan in towns, in the suburbs, in the urban skyscrapers and even in the decaying converted townhouses that lined West Grand Boulevard. For its part, Motown's empire had expanded piecemeal into an incoherent collection of neighbouring houses that had been converted into overflow offices, rehearsal rooms and storage space. Every time a lease became available locally, it was swallowed up by the Gordy family as they struggled to play catch-up with the global scale of their success. It was a grab-as-you-go philosophy that was never likely to accommodate Motown's meteoric growth and was at best a disorganised response to what was now a thriving international corporation. The hunt for new premises began.

As Leonard Baun scuttled around Detroit trying to glean information on the Supremes' earning power, Detroit's most successful songwriting team, Holland-Dozier-Holland, had decided to make their own legal challenge. Eddie Holland's resentment about his share of royalties and company profits had grown like a cancer throughout 1967, and by November it had reached a stage where he felt his suggestions were being either ignored or rebuffed. Despite their past friendship, Gordy and Holland had travelled down different paths. Holland believed he was underpaid and undervalued, while Gordy felt that he had provided a global distribution platform for the trio's significant and growing wealth. One felt cheated, while the other felt he had done everything to help. Gordy had tried to buy off Eddie Holland in January 1967 by promoting him to the crucial role of head of A&R, replacing the departed and much better-suited Mickey Stevenson, but it was a promotion with a toxic consequence. Rather than settling down, the dispute worsened, and although Holland-Dozier-Holland maintained the illusion that they were working on a pipeline of new songs, they effectively turned off the tap and squirrelled their best ideas away for another day. It was already beginning to affect the Four Tops. The group had enjoyed a rich vein of success with 'Standing In The Shadows Of Love', 'Bernadette' and 'Seven Rooms Of Gloom' but were now reduced to covering the Bobby Darin song 'If I Were A Carpenter'.

Chance played a part in what happened next. Eddie Holland was at a private party with Gladys Knight and some other Motown artists when they fell into conversation with a group of prominent Detroit lawyers. They talked about the music industry, how it operated and who had power on their side; Holland took a business card and promised to stay in touch with one of them. After a series of exploratory private meetings, he convinced his brother, Brian, and Lamont Dozier to hire the services of Edward F. Bell. Suddenly the heat was turned up. Bell, a graduate of the University of Michigan Law School, had risen to become one of the most prominent members of a new generation of African-American lawyers and was one of the rising stars of the Detroit court system. Much to the frustration of the Gordy family, Bell was one of their own, an advocate of the Booker T. Washington movement and a prominent civil rights attorney who had participated in the historic civil rights march from Selma to Montgomery in 1965. In a personal letter to Martin Luther King, Bell described it as the 'most gratifying' moment of his life; King returned the compliment, saying that Bell had 'a drum major instinct for justice'.

Edward F. Bell was a passionate careerist who was unashamed of offering his services to the famous. He cultivated relationships not only with King but with the burgeoning Detroit R&B scene and for a time represented Holland-Dozier-Holland, Gladys Knight, Aretha Franklin and later the heavyweight boxer Leon Spinks. Chillingly, he also represented the wayward basketball star Reggie Harding, the serial offender who as a teenager had raped Florence Ballard. But unlike Ballard's lawyer, Bell knew his way around the tough ghettos of litigation and had a measure of self-confidence that was the equal of Gordy's. He was seriously well connected and had an eye for both politics and the law. By 1967 he was already the Freedom Fund chairman of the Detroit branch of the NAACP and a member of the Wolverine Bar, and he was to become a close affiliate of Operation PUSH, the Reverend Jesse Jackson's Chicago-based civil-rights movement. Bell eventually ran for mayor of Detroit, losing out to his close friend Coleman Young. His office was located high in the sky near the top floor of the neo-gothic Cadillac Tower within the offices of local law firm Patmon, Young and Kirk. Prone to big statements, Bell had moved to Cadillac Tower from a smaller practice on Grand River Avenue. When Eddie Holland first met Bell, he was struck by his self-confidence. Bell was not a man of reticence; he enjoyed showing off the range of his clients and the breathtaking panoramic view of Detroit from his office window. Those who tried to call him Eddie were often reminded that his name was Edward F. Bell, and that the 'F' was non-negotiable. On other days he liked to pick up his phone and use his self-proclaimed nickname, Michigan Bell. He wore neat suits and freshly pressed shirts with elegant cuff links and rarely took off his jacket when he strode confidently into the Recorder's Court. Some thought that his dress sense conveyed a weakness for the good life, while others saw it as a bold response to the coded discriminations of the legal system. Bell often joked, 'They will judge neither my race nor the cut of my suit.'

Like so many great lawyers before him, Edward F. Bell relished high-profile cases, even those that seemed like lost causes. He had angered the already rattled Detroit police by defending the notorious 'heroin in the vacuum cleaner case', a dispute that rumbled through the courts for over four years and pitted the fine detail of civil rights against Detroit's criminal underworld. In 1963 Alice James, Charles Moore and seven other petty criminals had been charged in a thirteen-count indictment with 'conspiracy to violate the narcotics law and with the substantive offense of illegal possession and sale of narcotics'. Federal agents and Detroit police officers had busted an upstairs apartment in the crime-infested

Highland Park neighbourhood to arrest Alice James, a suspected drug dealer who, according to arrest sheets, had habitually concealed heroin in her domestic vacuum cleaner. According to the police, it was an open-and-shut case with nothing much to trouble the investigating officers – except, of course, their own bad practices; the police had not bothered to secure a legitimate search warrant.

In an audaciously argued case that came to a successful conclusion at the Sixth Circuit Court of Appeals in the disruptive summer of 1967, Bell won on a technicality. Irrespective of Alice James's guilt and her unquestionable role in trading heroin in Highland Park, the police had made the casually racist assumption that, due to her colour, they did not need to go through the formality of processing a legitimate search warrant. Bell was adamant that the legal pursuit of civil rights was not just about seeking justice for the meek or the righteous but for the law itself, and he had a reputation for gnawing away at what he perceived was the institutional racism of the Detroit police. In the case of the heroin in the vacuum cleaner, Bell argued that 'the mere fact that the articles seized were contraband does not make the evidence admissible where the search was conducted in violation of the Fourth Amendment'. It was an argument that infuriated law enforcement officers and seemed to support their fear that criminal rights were being given preference over due process, and for many in the African-American community it was a deeply uncomfortable case too. Yet again a high-profile case led back to unpalatable vice and ghetto crime, but it was seen by others as a necessary step on the way to equal rights.

Eddie Holland visited Bell's office in November 1967. His resentment towards Motown was not yet volcanic, but he felt increasingly estranged from the label and had tired of being fobbed off with promises of future justice. He had no great appetite for a legal dispute with Gordy, but Bell reassured him. Holland was nearly ten years younger than Bell, but they shared a natural self-confidence, and it became clear that Holland was in the company of a lawyer with a keen mind and a bullish personality. Holland was aware that, as a writing team, Holland-Dozier-Holland 'were in a class of their own' and had found a system that 'resulted in feel-good music, music that grabbed you'. What he had yet to work out was how that translated into dollars and cents. Bell knew enough about copyright law to have realised that they were among Motown's most successful creative employees and an integral part of the world's most recognisable pop music. Together they began to build an argument that Motown's hit machine was underpinned by songwriting and thus dependent on the creativity of Holland-Dozier-Holland. To give substance to that assertion, they did something very simple: they freeze-framed a week in November 1967 and counted up the new releases, the reissues and the greatest hits. The Supremes were touring the West Coast and had a stage act that featured at least eight songs by Holland-Dozier-Holland. They were playing Oakland Coliseum that week and then travelling on to UCLA's Pauley Pavilion, a new basketball arena funded by Richard Nixon's future chief of staff H. R. Haldeman. It was home to a meteoric new star, Lew Alcindor, who was about to join the Nation of Islam and change his name to Kareem Abdul-Jabbar. Bell noted the set list. Over ninety per cent of the songs the Supremes sang at Pauley Pavilion had been written and produced by Holland-Dozier-Holland, and the vast majority of those had been released as hit singles in territories across the world. From memory, Holland recited where records had been released: Japan, Europe and the United Kingdom, and even a couple of releases in Middle Eastern markets via local pressing plants in Lebanon. They kept talking, listing the times that the songs had been used in ad jingles, on movie soundtracks and in television shows, and they tried to estimate the number of times the Supremes, the Four Tops and the Temptations had appeared on network shows at least once a week every week.

As Edward F. Bell worked up his dossier, the less gifted Leonard Baun laboured to assemble a credible case against Motown on behalf of Florence Ballard. Baun made contact with Motown's former publicist Al Abrams. Now on the payroll of Stax Records, Abrams agreed to provide a statement in support of Ballard and suggested a number of people who might also be able to provide testimony that would help the struggling lawyer make reasonable estimates of her true worth. Coincidentally, one of the people Abrams recommended was a New York agent named Lou Zito, a long-time employee of the William Morris agency and manager of blues singer B. B. King. It proved to be another significant coincidence among many. As a young man, Zito had been a drummer with Gene Krupa and subsequently a business manager for Tommy Dorsey, and he encouraged his accountant, Sid Seidenberg, a Jewish war veteran who had been born in Poland, to provide information about industry-wide royalty payments. Zito also chipped in some other advice and unofficially acted as a go-between, introducing Ballard to ABC Records in New York, the label to which B. B. King was signed.

On the evening of Friday, 10 November, B. B. King was scheduled to perform a week of shows in Detroit to celebrate Veterans' Day. Zito travelled with him to Detroit, camped out in a downtown hotel, and attended most of his shows during the week. It was traditionally a big week in the calendar of Detroit soul, with shows scheduled across the city. Martha Reeves and Lou Rawls were performing at the newly secured Cobo Hall, local entrepreneur Le Baron Taylor had hired the Driftwood Lounge at the 20 Grand for a showcase featuring J. J. Barnes and the Parliaments, and B. B. King himself was appearing at UAW Local 212 Hall, a union social club that could trace its legacy back to the militant era of the Great Depression. Local 212 was one of Detroit's most revered union branches. It had played a pioneering role in sit-down strikes and proved to be a thorn in the vulnerable side of America's biggest independent auto-body plant, Briggs Manufacturing, known locally as Briggs Body. It is more than likely that Ballard met Zito either at his hotel or backstage at the UAW Hall, but wherever the meeting took place, they talked about her severance dispute with Motown and the opportunities that might open up for her at ABC in New York.

Zito encouraged Ballard's interest in a solo career and began to influence a sudden shift in her thinking. She had always aspired to a solo career, but having instructed Baun to challenge her July settlement with Motown, she was now urged to give her ineffectual lawyer new and conflicting instructions. Zito told her that ABC would only be likely to sign her if she were free of any legal encumbrances, and that a complicated dispute with Motown would scare them off. After the meeting Ballard, buzzing with different options, began to pursue two rather incompatible outcomes: she wanted a better severance deal from Motown, a clean break with no loose legal threads, and she wanted to go to New York to meet ABC with the knowledge that she could sign a new deal. Although it is largely hearsay, some Motown insiders have claimed that Gordy had also held out an olive branch to Ballard, offering her studio time to record as a solo artist with Motown, but her meeting with Zito galvanised her to look elsewhere and she became determined to sign up with ABC, preferably before the year's end.

Suddenly the clock was ticking faster. Leonard Baun was in the unenviable position of negotiating with dismissive, unconcerned and busy Motown lawyers and demanding that they speed things up. It was a dreadful poker hand and a negotiation he was almost certain to lose. Unknown to anyone within the Detroit scene, B. B. King was having his own bitter fight behind the scenes and had fallen out with Zito over money. Within months of helping Ballard secure a meeting with ABC in New York, Zito was sacked after bitter financial wrangling and was replaced by accountant Sid Seidenberg, who masterminded the next phase of King's career.

As Ballard's legal dispute with Motown entered its fourth acrimonious month, Diana Ross and the Supremes had moved on, both literally and metaphorically. They were now more frequently on the West Coast, much closer to film and network television opportunities. Between 6 and 12 November they were in Los Angeles rehearsing and taping *The Tennessee Ernie Ford Special* for CBS with Andy Griffith and Danny Thomas, a show that was scheduled to air in early December. Back in Detroit the Motown manufacturing plant ground on regardless. On 7 November Junior Walker and the All Stars' 'Come See About Me' was released on the Soul label. It was a raucous throwback to Motown's R&B

origins, a hectic saxophone-led cover version of the 1964 hit by the Supremes that had been primitively recorded the previous summer at Motown's newly acquired Golden World Studios. The final produced version of Junior Walker's cover proved to be a historic release, the last end-to-end production wholly overseen by the Holland-Dozier-Holland production team. A few days later, frustrated by being cold-shouldered in their repeated bids for more money, they downed tools and refused to cooperate with Motown's management. They would now be guided by Edward F. Bell.

Berry Gordy had one overpowering emotional weakness, and it was neither greed nor vanity. He had a deep-seated nostalgia for the early days of Motown when, as a young black songwriter, he had walked down St Antoine with hopes and dreams. He always felt comfortable in the company of those who had been on the journey with him – Smokey Robinson, Janie Bradford, Eddie and Brian Holland and, despite their maddening unpredictability, the studio musicians Earl Van Dyke, James Jamerson and Benny Benjamin. It was a nostalgia that often failed to differentiate between friendship and business, and it meant that Gordy had a bad habit of deflecting difficult conversations to others, often one of his straight-talking sisters. Gordy felt uncomfortable firing artists, especially those who knew him from the days before he had money. The singer Mable John, sister of the incarcerated soul star Little Willie John, once joked that she would still be at Motown if she had not fired herself. As a young woman fresh from high school, Mable John had worked at Friendship Mutual, the pioneering Negro insurance agency operated by Gordy's mother, Bertha. John had driven Gordy around the streets of Detroit in the infancy of Motown when he couldn't afford his own car, and she had been one of a small roster of blues singers who had originally signed to the label. As the Motown Sound commercialised and became the spectacularly popular 'sound of young America', the older gutbucket R&B sound inevitably became obsolete. After John's contract ran out she freelanced as one of Ray Charles's backing singers, the Raelettes, before joining the exodus to Stax Records in Memphis. At no stage in their long friendship – which survived her departure to Motown's southern rival – could Gordy ever admit to her that she was no longer a priority. He simply avoided the issue.

Gordy's tendency to let problems fester had already exacerbated disputes with the singer Mary Wells, producer Mickey Stevenson and Florence Ballard, but it was his dispute with Holland-Dozier-Holland that posed the greatest threat to Motown. Although the dispute never reached the hysterical levels of conspiracy that surrounded Ballard's departure, it threatened to short-circuit the electric power of sixties soul and placed the corporation's future in jeopardy. Gordy had known Eddie and Brian Holland for over a decade, but knowing them had become part of the problem. Of the two brothers, he instinctively preferred the younger, Brian. Gordy had coached him as a hopeful young singer, and a close bond had grown up between them. Brian Holland had been an attentive student and saw Gordy as his music-industry mentor. With characteristic sentimentality, Gordy once said, 'Brian had been with me even before there was a Hitsville. Most of the time he slept on a couch or on the floor, always watching, assisting, learning. He was sensitive, sharp and had a pure heart. I cared about him and we always had great communication.' The same was not true of Eddie Holland. The older brother tended to distrust the entire Gordy clan, and as the years passed his suspicions deepened and he began to openly resent the wealth that Gordy and his family had accumulated. With wildcat strikes in the car plants escalating across the city, Eddie began to take notice of labour politics and often quoted the esteemed leader of the United Automobile Workers, Walter Reuther. His fascination with the politics of the workplace led him to believe that the only way to secure more rewards from Motown was to withdraw his labour. Throughout much of November, Holland stayed at home and did not report for work on West Grand. Most Motown colleagues thought he was on vacation or out of town, but as senior management failed to keep a lid on gossip, it became clear that the Hitsville conveyor belt was being disrupted.

Gordy was in Los Angeles working on new projects from

Motown's West Coast offices, and the geographic distance exacerbated the problem. Eddie talked less about Gordy as a friend and now referred to him only as a boss – a remote and uncaring manager. Gordy had made a big mistake in the first few weeks of 1967 when he replaced the departing head of A&R, Mickey Stevenson, with the restless Eddie Holland. It was intended as a symbolic compromise, a way of giving Holland more status and a salary increase, but Gordy's former wife Raynoma described the promotion as an error of judgement on Gordy's part: 'Eddie's ascent had led to dissent.'

Eddie Holland was born in Detroit in 1939. By the mid fifties, he was an aspiring teenage singer whose angelic looks and slick pomaded hairstyle gave him the look of a matinée idol. Otis Williams of the Temptations described him as 'a hit with the girls . . . He sounded a lot like Jackie Wilson, which drove girls wild with desire.' By day Eddie Holland worked as a demonstration artist for a local Michigan publishing company. His job was to sing songs to customers directly from music sheets and encourage them to buy the sheet music. Some of his demo songs, such as 'To Be Loved' and 'Lonely Teardrops', went on to become famous songs for Jackie Wilson, but it was Eddie Holland who had first brought them to life as an unnamed publishing-house vocalist. Despite a self-confident singing voice, Holland suffered from stage fright, and throughout his adult life he had a deep anxiety about appearing in front of audiences, which effectively ended his performing career. Holland did appear on local talent shows, and provided the vocal lead for a few unspectacular songs such as 'Merry Go Round' and 'Jamie', but he was so comprehensively upstaged by the rampant show-offs of Detroit soul that by the early sixties he had retired from performing and was making a hand-to-mouth living as a full-time writer-producer. One of his last pitches at solo success was the opportunistic 'If Cleopatra Took A Chance', which Gordy rush-released in 1963 in the slipstream of the infamous movie *Cleopatra*, starring celebrity couple Elizabeth Taylor and Richard Burton, which at the time was the most expensive film ever made and, due to chaotic overspending, nearly bankrupted Twentieth Century Fox. Eddie Holland's failure was modest by comparison, but the cash-in single sank without a trace, and his singing career was over.

Eddie's brother, Brian, was even less successful. His first single in 1958 was on a local gospel label, Kudo Records, underwritten by local DJ Joltin' Joe Howard, whose show on WCHB out of Inkseter, Michigan, pioneered radio for black teenagers in the fifties. The flip side was written by Gordy and had all the hallmarks of Detroit's primitive independent music scene. Holland's name was spelled wrong on the label, and the record lay unloved in local stores under the name of 'Briant Holland'. As relationships evolved and Motown professionalised, Brian Holland joined forces with the third member of the writing team, Lamont Dozier. Raynoma Gordy described him as 'a cordial broad-featured fellow with a country drawl'. Dozier had been a singer with several local doo-wop groups, including the Romeos and Ty Hunter and the Voice Masters, before releasing solo records for the Gordy sisters' nascent soul label, Anna Records, under the pseudonym Lamont Anthony. Brian Holland and Lamont Dozier teamed up to release a 1963 single under the joint name of Holland-Dozier, but it was as musical arrangers that the two men were to find fame, first with the Marvelettes and then with Martha and the Vandellas. Although he still harboured fading hopes of overcoming his stage fright and relaunching a solo career, Eddie Holland eventually joined them as a lyricist. One senior Motown source hinted that a failed singing career left a residue of bitterness in Eddie Holland's soul, one that he never fully expunged.

Eddie's career at Motown was prodigious. Between 1962 and 1967, he grew to become one of the greatest composers of popular song, crafting lyrics and vocals for some of the most enduring soul records of all time. In one extraordinary year, 1965, he produced 'Stop In The Name Of Love' for the Supremes, 'Nowhere To Run' for Martha and the Vandellas, and the irrepressible 'Can't Help Myself (Sugar Pie, Honey Bunch)' for the Four Tops.

Gordy always subscribed to the old truism that the entertainment industry was a hits business and that success begat further success.

According to Raynoma Gordy, 'Holland-Dozier-Holland were in an incredible hit-making groove and were benefiting from one of Berry's game rules: if a producer had a hit with an artist, he automatically produced the next release on that artist. This meant that HDH maintained a stranglehold on the Supremes and the Four Tops, even before Eddie was given the job of handing out production assignments.'

Success brought reputation, celebrity and money, but it was the third item that finally drove a wedge between Gordy and his producers. By the autumn of 1967 Gordy had tired of Eddie's persistent demands and had reached a point where he felt manipulated. Gordy once said that 'HDH benefited from my policy that if two records under consideration were equally strong, the release would be given to the producer who had the last hit.' Rewarding success by repeating the conditions of that success had become Motown policy, and it had arguably held back other potentially successful producers. The ambitious Norman Whitfield and, to a lesser extent, the loyal poet Smokey Robinson were further down the company's pecking order and had to accept their songs being delayed or cancelled. But Eddie saw things differently. 'After "Where Did Our Love Go" became a hit,' he claimed, 'the director of sales said, "We have to keep these girls hot. They're the flagship of this company, because they're spreading over to such a wide audience."'

Although Gordy argued he was fair with royalties, he was more defensive about ownership of the company and was adamant that diluting Motown stock was too great a compromise. In his memoirs he spoke of his frustration: 'Eddie's constant requests for added incentives had mounted through the years. They were a team and I knew I had to pay an additional cost to keep them happy. It was part of doing business . . . After a series of generous readjustments to his compensation package, which I had agreed to, there had been the last "request" Eddie had made for a personal, interest-free loan. I had said no. I felt this so-called strike might have something to do with that.' Eddie was planning to buy property and had approached Motown for a loan. Gordy's refusal meant that their relationship irretrievably broke down, and from the autumn onward Eddie refused to produce any more Motown sessions and began to stockpile new songs that he hoped to one day release under his own label. Several years later the Holland brothers and Lamont Dozier set up the Invictus/Hot Wax labels, recording neo-Motown hits by Chairman of the Board, Honey Cone, and Freda Payne. While the music was not identical to Motown, it had the same energetic feel and storytelling lyrics.

Gordy claimed he tried to repair the damage but offered nothing but warm words about the past. 'When Eddie told me about this,' he wrote, 'I went to one of the piano rooms to talk to Brian. I could see he felt awkward and was having as much trouble as I was about the situation.' In their private meeting, reportedly uneasy and embarrassing for both men, Brian supposedly said, 'I hope you understand and have no hard feelings. But that's my brother and you know how it is.' For all of Motown's well-worn myths about being a family, it was a brotherly bond that now posed the greatest threat to the company's future success.

At first Eddie Holland was nervous about taking on Motown. It would almost certainly end his relationship with the Gordy family and force friends to take sides. His younger brother urged caution, but once they had taken Edward F. Bell's advice Eddie's bravado kicked in, and the Holland brothers steeled themselves for a fight. Holland admitted as much: 'Berry Gordy was paying artists, producers, and writers when most companies, including the majors, were not doing so,' he confessed retrospectively. 'We were making more money than our peers were making. By far. But you get lawyers involved, and it took on a life of its own.'

However, Motown was not inclined to roll over. Gordy stuck to his unshakeable principles and said in his affected casual style, 'I love these guys and they love me, but they obviously wanted to get away so bad and do their thing. All my people said, "Just give them a few thousand dollars and the case is over." My legal fees were astronomical, but I said, "No, I cannot settle this for anything" – it [would] mean they were right.' Gordy was not being entirely honest.

He did not call all the shots and was often overruled by Motown's senior legal and financial managers. The power behind the throne lay with the notorious Noveck brothers, who were known for their scrupulous attention to detail and unforgiving financial management. Gordy once admitted as much. 'Harold Noveck was my tax attorney, and his brother Sidney was my accountant,' he wrote in his biography. 'Anytime we got in any trouble we didn't worry about anything, because [the Novecks] would spend a thousand dollars to find a penny. The books had to balance, all the time. So whenever I would sue somebody or someone would say the artist didn't get paid, I'd say, "Hey, you're barking up the wrong tree." In order to protect the legacy, if somebody would tell an outright lie, I would sue them and I would always win, because the truth will win if you can afford to fight for it.' Motown staffer Shelly Berger described the Novecks in darkly gothic terms: 'I used to refer to [them] as the Malach Hamovis – that's Yiddish for the angels of death. They were very, very conservative. Since Motown's fiscal year was on the calendar year, December 31 was the end of the fiscal year, and each year I'd book the Supremes in some great place where we could all go for Christmas and New Year's and bring our families – whether it was Tahoe or Miami. Then the Noveck brothers would show up on December 26 to tell Berry Gordy, "You're going to lose everything and you're insolvent." So . . . for four days we're living in absolute misery, because the Malach Hamovis had come.'

At first Gordy thought that Eddie Holland's sullenness would pass, that it was a tantrum of sorts, but when he stopped coming to the studios it began to affect schedules and eat away at company morale. Holland was not only a member of Motown's most successful writing team, he was the head of A&R and a key member of staff. Gordy described his frustration: 'I would call Brian's office and he was not there . . . I would call Eddie's office about the same thing and he was not there,' he wrote in a retrospective court deposition. 'Then I became pretty alarmed. I thought maybe they were recording things and they weren't becoming hits or weren't good enough. When I was informed that they hadn't recorded in the last couple of months, then I became a little more alarmed.' Gordy instructed the Novecks to review the detail of Eddie Holland's staff contract. There had been no formal communication of his wish to leave the company, no period of notice, no request for vacation or a period of absence, and no indication of long-term illness, so Motown considered Holland to be in breach of contract and planned to issue him a formal warning. A day or two later, Gordy probed other staff members about their views and was told via the Motown grapevine that the Holland brothers and Lamont Dozier were already in secret negotiations with Capitol Records. If it were true – though there was nothing reliable to shore up those claims other than gossip – it was a catastrophic development. Compared with Ballard's negotiations with ABC in New York, this posed a threat to Motown's future profitability. Gordy knew that singers could be replaced, but proven songwriters were thinner on the ground. 'This was really bad news,' Gordy said. 'Not only had they become one of the most prolific writing and producing hit teams of that time, but [they] had risen to such power positions in the company that their leaving could mean disaster in many ways.'

Motown's next move inflamed an already fractious situation, and Gordy has since admitted that he allowed his heart to rule his head, that he felt 'emotionally charged'. Motown threatened to sue Holland for breach of contract, and battle lines were drawn. In one corner was the ambitious black lawyer, Edward F. Bell, and pitted against him were two uncompromising Jewish brothers known as 'the angels of death'. It proved to be a stand-off marked by uncompromising personalities and unspoken racial resentments. This was an era when deep feelings of anti-Semitism, often connected to poor housing and disputes with slum landlords, were alive within the ghettos of urban America. The novelist James Baldwin described it thus: 'In Harlem our . . . landlords were Jewish, and we hated them. We hated them because they were terrible landlords and did not take care of the building. The grocer was a Jew . . . the butcher was a Jew, and, yes, we certainly paid more for bad cuts of meat than other New York citizens, and we very often carried insults home, along with the meat . . . And the pawnbroker was a Jew – perhaps we hated him most of all.' Although the old Hastings Street ghetto was long gone, obliterated by a gigantic freeway, bitter memories of slum landlords lingered. Despite the progressive role that Jewish radicals played in the civil rights movement, surveys of the time showed that black Americans were significantly more likely to hold anti-Semitic views than others. But to portray the encroaching battles at Motown as sectarian would be to misrepresent the story. Deep cross-community friendships were firmly in place too. One of the most creative was the bond between childhood friends Cornelius Grant and Rodger Penzabene, who co-wrote a trilogy of hits for the Temptations: 'You're My Everything', 'I Wish It Would Rain' and 'I Could Never Love Another (After Loving You)'. Grant was a self-taught guitar prodigy from an African-American family in the Deep South who played with Mary Wells's band as a youngster, while Penzabene was a self-effacing Jewish kid with a scholarly grasp of poetry and the written word. They grew up as neighbourhood friends and were classmates at Mumford High, a school that epitomised the shifting patterns of Detroit. Mumford was built in 1949 to accommodate a largely Jewish community on the North Side, but by the sixties many Jewish families had already moved out to wealthier suburbs in Oakland County. The homes they vacated were often snapped up by incoming professionals from the African-American community. All of this gave Mumford High a distinct identity. Its art deco exterior, with distinctive powder-blue and maroon walls, housed a school population that was both Jewish and African-American, allowing teenagers from different communities to study side by side. Cornelius Grant, who grew up to be a Motown stalwart – 'the sixth Temptation' – had studied alongside the Jewish-American film director Jerry Bruckheimer (*Beverly Hills Cop*, *Pirates of the Caribbean*) and in the same era as the shamed Wall Street trader Ivan Boesky. For Grant, that life would be very long and creative indeed; for his quiet and troubled school friend Penzabene, it would last little more than a month.

★

An elderly white woman by the name of Edythe Wayne arrived for a meeting with her lawyers in a skyscraper in downtown Detroit. When she emerged from the elevator she had magically transformed into three self-confident young African-American men. 'Edythe Wayne' was the collective pseudonym that Holland-Dozier-Holland adopted when they wrote new songs. Legally bound to the Motown publishing company Jobete under their own names, Edythe Wayne was a contrivance to put Motown's lawyer off the scent. Lamont Dozier had chosen the name Edythe in honour of his mentor Edith Burke, a white woman who had been his public school teacher at Edgar Allen Poe elementary school, and was the first person to encourage his passion for music. Wayne was for Wayne State. The story goes that when the songwriting triumvirate were trying to settle on a bogus name they looked out onto Woodward and saw signs for Wayne State University. So Edythe Wayne was born. 'She' was soon in productive partnership with another Motown escapee Ron Dunbar, and they went on to write numerous soul hits in the early seventies, including Freda Payne's 'Band Of Gold'.

Eddie Holland later admitted that arguments with Motown had another combustible element: familiarity. 'Think in terms of a family member that you have a disagreement with. It was a molehill turning into a mountain. He's a fighter, I'm a fighter, and so, through the lawyers, we fought for many, many years, and he wouldn't bend and I wouldn't bend. That's what happens when you get two bulls locking horns.' And so the horns locked. With a cold ruthlessness he often showed when he felt betrayed, Berry Gordy lashed out and acted on his threat to sue Holland. 'Though I could not calculate what losing them would cost,' Gordy wrote many years later, 'I sued them for four million dollars for breach of contract. I wanted them back and I figured it was only a matter of time before they would come to their senses.'

Gordy's legal suit was a bizarre way to try to bring everyone to their senses, and predictably it had the opposite effect. With Edward F. Bell prompting their every move, Holland-Dozier-Holland reacted with wounded indignation, triggering one of the fiercest disputes in the history of popular music. They countersued Motown, accusing the company of 'conspiracy, fraud, deceit, overreaching, and breach of fiduciary relationships in the amount of $22 million'. Although Gordy tried to shrug it off as legal posturing, the words 'fraud and deceit' hurt him deeply, and the accusation stayed with him for many decades to come. Even long after the dispute was settled, he could recite the words near verbatim: 'conspiracy, fraud, deceit, overreaching, and breach of fiduciary relationships in the amount of $22 million'. Those words had been shaped by Edward F. Bell to attack the way Motown did business and to question the way it accounted. By citing conspiracy, he implicated a wider group of senior management in the claim. Although the words were principally aimed at Gordy, they were a shot across the bow for Motown's white executive managers – sales director Barney Ales, accountant Sidney Noveck, Gordy's tax attorney Harold Noveck, and the corporation's contract lawyer Ralph Seltzer.

Over thirty-two uncompromising pages, the legal suit claimed that since 1957 Brian Holland had never had a contractual agreement that he could see or study. That since its formation in 1961, the writing team was never issued with a contract or legal agreement that they could see or understand, and that they had no independent legal advice. That since 1961 Berry Gordy had repeatedly promised to transfer ownership of Motown stock to Brian Holland and had made a promise to give Holland $1 million or the equivalent in Motown stock as remuneration. That 'throughout the period of association with the plaintiffs', Gordy was 'their true friend and in effect their father', a man that could be trusted to look after their best interests. That the Motown publishing subsidiary Jobete Music Incorporated underpaid them in royalties, and that the defendants 'fraudulently attempted to, and did, deprive the plaintiffs of proper accounting and legal advice'. On behalf of the writers, Bell further claimed that Motown had assets of $11.5 million and that Jobete had assets of $2 million, most of which, he argued, had been derived from the writing success of the plaintiffs. He attested that such was the level of distrust of Berry Gordy and his management team that the court should prevent Motown from 'transferring earnings, assets, [and] copyrights' and asked that a receiver be appointed to this end. It was a brutal and unprecedented request, and in effect it invited the Detroit Circuit Court to place the city's most famous asset into receivership.

Teenage friends who had become dollar millionaires on the back of their shared love of soul music could not find a way to compromise, and more court papers were filed. Eddie Holland described Gordy's business practices as 'malice, fraud, [and] oppression', and he claimed to be saddened by the loss of contact with a man he described as his 'black father figure'. In response Gordy, no longer trading on the myth of Motown's family image, said disdainfully, 'I doubt if he's ever been my friend.' Each legal missive escalated the dispute, and eventually Edward F. Bell turned up the heat to boiling point by instructing the blue-chip Manhattan law firm Miller, Canfield, Paddock and Stone to act as specialist legal advisers on behalf of the Holland brothers. They had an office in Detroit, but Bell was more interested in expertise from their offices on Fifth Avenue in New York, which was staffed by world-class copyright lawyers and case law experts from the Brill Building.

Mary Wilson of the Supremes, still emotionally bruised from being caught in the war of words between Diana Ross and Florence Ballard, tried to steer a middle path. 'They were an integral part of the Motown machine, and Eddie felt that he knew the business inside out,' she wrote in her memoirs. 'That was one reason they wanted to be more involved on a corporate level, which Berry refused to consider. Their contribution to Motown's success – and the Supremes' – was incalculable, and when it was clear they had stopped working, Berry went into action.' Eddie Holland retaliated with his version of events. 'Not everybody is the type to pick up a sword and crusade,' he told *Vibe* magazine many years later. 'I happen to be one of those people, but at Motown they called me a troublemaker. Because I voiced my opinion – not in a bad way or a loud way, not in a truculent or venomous way, but it was an opinion.' Dozier, the least vocal of the three, has since tried to write off the dispute as a common characteristic of doing business: 'The lawsuit was just our way of taking care of business that needed to be taken care of, just like Berry had to take care of his business. Business is business, love is love.' What he did not go on to say was that any real love was now stone dead.

Gordy's closest lieutenant, Smokey Robinson, erupted when news of the countersuit against the company broke. Smokey had worked in parallel with Holland-Dozier-Holland in the past, but they were in effect his rivals, and when the chips were down he was always destined to side with Motown. Breaking with company protocol, Robinson published his own personal press release denouncing the Holland brothers. It was a small but significant moment in the battle, one that Gordy describes as a spontaneous act of anger taken independently by Robinson, but it is unlikely to have been written or released without Motown's prior approval. Robinson was a writer-producer who had a poetic way with words, but he lacked the network of publicity contacts to send out a national press release. To get it taken up by the music press, he distributed it in the form of an ad. It read as follows:

> Motown was started on the idea of whatever money a person has coming – give it to them. Whether it's a penny or a million dollars – if they have earned it – pay them. 'Honesty is our only policy.' So it gets me angry to hear people who have been a part of our love and family feeling – telling people that Motown has not paid them every penny they had coming.
>
> Each year Motown pays out millions of dollars to its creative people who keep coming up with the product. I've seen royalty checks for people from ninety-eight cents to hundreds of thousands of dollars. I know Motown pays. I've even forgotten some of my royalty checks and been called two days after royalty date and asked to please come and pick up the check. This makes it hard for me to understand how guys like the three well-known writers and producers, who to my knowledge, never had jobs before being made popular at Motown, could ever leave. They were paid millions in royalties and had key positions in the organization. What more could a young man ask for?

Even our not so popular artists are receiving free artists development training courses so they can still work on dates and earn some money. There are many beneficial things happening and going on at Motown on behalf of our artists, producers and writers, which are not even considered at other companies. No brag – just fact.

Smokey Robinson's personal press release found its way into the mailboxes of every significant journalist and music executive in the world and was clearly a proxy for Gordy's own views. It was aimed not simply at the Holland brothers but at the disgruntled and now complaining Florence Ballard, whose lawyer's daily requests for royalty statements were beginning to irritate the head office.

Sometime in the fall of 1967, Berry Gordy's ex-wife Raynoma returned to Detroit after a disastrous period in Washington DC, where her rival indie label, Shrine Records, was failing ignominiously. She wished to negotiate a return to Motown, having worked there in the early days, and came back to Detroit with a rose-tinted view of what life was like in the overstretched properties on West Grand Boulevard. Her views had been shaped in the early sixties when Motown was still a homemade enterprise, and in the years she had been away the culture of the company had noticeably changed. The mood was less hopeful and more cynical. Gordy was frequently away from Detroit, either on tour with the Supremes or working from the Hollywood offices, and his absence had been filled by a new management class. 'The more insulated Berry became and the less available he was on a day-to-day basis . . . the greater the void,' she wrote. 'It left producers bickering among themselves with nowhere to go for valued direction.' There was some truth in her observation. For the first time in his adult life, Gordy had let his grip on Motown slip.

Buoyed by the dispute with the Holland brothers and the departure of Ballard, several more artists began to question their terms and conditions. A new word entered the vocabulary of Motown: 'escrow', the obscure accounting term describing a special-purpose bank account into which Motown diverted money into artists' nominee accounts. It was a well-established practice, but the unfamiliarity of the term provoked suspicion, not reassurance, and when some employees heard the term they suspected a scam. Otis Williams of the Temptations once admitted, 'All that I know is that for years my money and the group's was being held in escrow. Whatever that meant . . . Everybody at that time got the same kind of deal, it was take it or leave it, because no one was in the position to say, "Hey, wait a minute."' Although the Gordy family championed equality and supported many worthy civil rights causes, not everyone was treated equal. The Temptations, for example, had much greater power over their affairs than lesser artists, whereas some freelancers were paid from petty cash.

Otis Williams has since admitted that Motown's payment system simply failed to keep up with success. 'The only thing wrong was that Motown continued dealing with its artists and their money the same way they had when they were kids making a couple of thousand a year,' he wrote. 'The tack Berry took with his artists when it came to money was an extension of his attitude toward them in general: he believed he knew what was best for us.' It was a paternalistic view founded on the belief that young ghetto artists had a tendency to squander wealth, and in that respect Gordy was not entirely wrong.

Shelly Berger, a drama graduate from Boston University who joined Motown in 1966 to become the Los Angeles-based manager of the Supremes, saw the escrow arrangements as a breakthrough in the fortunes of black American music. 'Not one artist at Motown had a tax problem during those years. Their taxes were always paid, and correctly.' Until the mid seventies Gordy was resistant to sharing information with the Recording Industry Association of America (RIAA). The Temptations' hit 'My Girl' was not certified until 1977. Tax returns were normally done by Motown staff on behalf of artists, raising still further the perception that Motown was dishonest. But it was never a one-way street. Many of the artists were happy to be rid of the responsibility of filing IRS forms, while others simply allowed them to pile up behind the door of short-let apartments. Tax was not their forte. Berger went on to claim that the tax and escrow arrangements were protective and not suspicious: 'Mr. Gordy knew firsthand how easy it was for black artists to be taken advantage of, left naked and in the cold. People talk about being ripped off at Motown. They don't know what they're talking about. He was preventing them from being ripped off, they didn't realize how much money he was saving them. He had two accountants, who were very, very conservative, the same people who were handling his own money. And all those acts were making money hand over fist because of that. So I don't want to hear that Berry Gordy ripped off his artists. That's just pure bullshit.' But Otis Williams interpreted the situation differently: 'Motown provided our lawyers, accountants, and managers. Today we'd call this a clear conflict of interest, but Berry's term was "complement of interest."'

Shelly Berger's robust defence of Motown was too little, too late. A lid had been lifted on Motown's affairs, and in the absence of audited facts the vacuum was almost always filled with exaggeration and bad blood. Gordy's most famous song, 'Money (That's What I Want)', which he had co-written back in 1959 with his friend Janie Bradford, had suddenly taken on a tone of scheming avarice. The Beatles had made the song famous globally, and it grew to become one of the most covered songs in the history of Detroit R&B, but by the end of 1967 it was sometimes sung sarcastically behind Gordy's back.

John Sinclair spent much of November 1967 in contact with his lawyer too. He had instructed a tall and athletic Jewish radical with black hair, dark energetic eyebrows and an enthusiastic smile. His name was Justin Ravitz and he was from Omaha, Nebraska. He had arrived in Detroit in 1965, a week before the infamous Kercheval incident, when armed black militants faced off with police officers on Kercheval and McClellan at the so-called 'crossroads of America'. Ravitz – nicknamed 'Chuck' – was one of a small group of visiting law students from Babson College, Massachusetts, who were sent door to door in the ghettos of Detroit on a research scholarship. It was on the streets around Kercheval that Ravitz met another young lawyer, the so-called city slicker Ken Cockrel Sr, a high-school dropout who had attended Northwestern High School with Motown singer Mary Wells and Funk Brother James Jamerson. Ravitz and Cockrel clicked and embarked on a lifetime journey fighting injustice in Detroit public life, gaining substantial reputations as anti-racism lawyers. By the early seventies they had led a sustained campaign to legally dismantle STRESS, a notorious Detroit police undercover unit that by then had murdered twenty people, seventeen of them black. Ravitz bravely called himself the only Marxist judge in the United States, banned the American flag from his courtroom in protest at the Vietnam War, and refused to stand for the Pledge when he was sworn in. He cut a unique figure in court, dressed in black legal robes that hung incongruously above battered and worn-out hippie boots. 'We have built up this bizarre belief in neutrality,' he once said. 'I'm not neutral about rape or murder. Neutrality is not cool at all.'

In November of 1967, Ravitz was still a relatively young attorney who was learning his trade at the side of his mentor, Sheldon Otis, a lawyer about to leave Detroit for California to take up a job with the Legal Aid Society in San Mateo, where he would oversee two of the main trials of counterculture, defending Black Panther activists Angela Davis and Huey Newton. Otis joined the Angela Davis defence team to fight charges of murder, kidnapping and conspiracy, and negotiated Newton's return from self-imposed exile in Cuba to face murder charges stemming from the death of an Oakland prostitute. Even as a young man in Detroit, Otis had a reputation as a 'brilliant and meticulous' lawyer and 'a master of courtroom technique' whose thirst for risk attracted him to challenging and unpopular cases.

By November 1967 Ravitz and Otis were so well known on the Detroit hippie grapevine that they were the preferred attorneys of almost every radical cause in the city. Ravitz had successfully defended the artist Gary Grimshaw from charges of desecrating the American flag; most members of the MC5 had hired his services to oversee minor misdemeanours ranging from noise abatement to assault; and, most notoriously of all, he defended the band's manager, John Sinclair, in his titanic fight with Michigan's draconian drug laws. Sinclair reflected on the era with characteristic passion: 'At the time Michigan still callously misclassified marijuana as a narcotic – against all scientific evidence to the contrary – and punished convicted smokers with up to ten years in prison. My actual crime had been giving the two joints as a gift to an undercover policewoman. I was determined to challenge the constitutionality of the Michigan narcotics statutes from the moment of my arrest on January 24, 1967, about two years after I had founded Detroit LEMAR as an attempt to challenge the marijuana laws in the court of public opinion. By the date of my arrest I had been blessed with legal representation by the great Detroit attorney Sheldon Otis and his associate, Justin "Chuck" Ravitz, then just out of law school. They agreed not only to defend me in Detroit Recorder's Court against this scurrilous charge but also to take up my cause in general.'

Sometime in the third week of November, Sinclair visited Ravitz's office in his suite at 1756 Penobscot, high up in an ornate art deco skyscraper, after he had been banned from speaking to pupils at a local school. The principals of Thurston High School in Redford Township had refused Sinclair permission to speak to the school's current events club, a student-run society encouraging democracy and debate. Although the club had already extended welcomes to a diverse range of viewpoints, including speakers from the John Birch Society, a local Black Power chapter and the white supremacist Breakthrough organisation, somehow Sinclair was seen by education officials as beyond the pale. What lay behind the ban was a series of intemperate statements Sinclair had made onstage as a guest poet opening for MC5.

Sinclair held an unshakeable belief that Detroit was not just another city but had all the characteristics of an 'independent nation' with its own culture and integrity. He had unbridled faith in the teenagers of the Motor City and saw them as the potential vanguard for change, and his analysis, albeit steeped in countercultural romance, was not without merit. Sinclair reasoned that Detroit youth had been the unique witnesses to fundamental change in

American society. They lived in a city transformed by the inward migration of poor African-American families from the South, a city that had survived successive decades of industrial failure and rebirth. A generation that had grown up amid the relentless noise of car plants had seen first hand the pressures of desegregation, the riotous collapse of inner-city life, and a consequential flight to the suburbs. There was no greater polemicist in sixties America than John Sinclair, and he knew what raw nerves to touch. He claimed that the coexistence of different races living side by side had given Detroit its unique tense creativity: 'If we weren't a whole new people by then,' he wrote, 'we were sure a whole lot closer to the forbidden niggers of our parents' nightmares than we were to them.'

Sinclair's polemical love of Detroit and his revulsion for what he saw as the betrayals of the post-war parent generation made the city fathers deeply suspicious, and the thought of Sinclair talking freely at local high schools was enough to scare the horses. In a speech he gave around the time, Sinclair argued that Detroit's rusting manufacturing crisis had its 'roots in the old industrial society, and . . . is shot through with the filth and disease of a dying civilization'. He reckoned that the city's love affair with R&B 'had turned its sons into lust-crazed madmen and fools, breaking down generations and generations of self-denial and de-sensitivity and completely destroying the sanctity of the Euro-American home forever'. Sinclair had no great love for Motown and what he thought was a saccharine and compromised form of soul music, but he remained a tireless advocate of free jazz and urban blues. Sinclair frequently pitched his polemic at suburban schools like Thurston High and, like a high priest of change, welcomed the children of suburbia into the MC5 fold as if they were seeking asylum from the normal world. 'They began pouring out of the suburban concentration camps where they'd been held all of their lives,' he wrote provocatively at the time, 'to take their place in the ranks of the guitar army' where they would turn on to the counter-culture and thus 'draw a clear line of distinction between people like ourselves, between long-haired dope-smoking street-fucking rock-and-roll maniacs and the rest of the world'.

MC5 were honing their noisy destiny, too, and were caught up in a simultaneous controversy when they performed their self-destructive rock improvisation track 'Black To Comm' live on Detroit public television during a culture show called *Conversations in Depth* with Seymour Rickling. The show's vision statement was to 'educate, entertain and inspire – in partnership with our community', but MC5 took culture to the heights of aggression, attacking their equipment, tearing down speakers, and using cacophonous feedback to end their set. Their appearance provoked numerous complaints and sent a shiver of anxiety throughout the public broadcasting community at a highly sensitive time. Earlier in November President Johnson had signed the Public Broadcasting Act, providing a framework for public broadcasting in partnership with the National Educational Television and the philanthropic Ford Foundation. Money was in short supply and political interference at its most fidgety. The very last thing the network needed was a riotous Detroit rock band spreading noisy contagion.

Justin Ravitz discussed the prospect of suing the South Redford School District for inhibiting Sinclair's constitutional right to free speech, but they agreed it was a distraction from their main objective: to overturn Sinclair's drug violations. Ravitz had already lodged a motion to quash information in the Recorder's Court known as file A-134588. It argued that the defendant, John Sinclair, was prosecuted in a manner that was unconstitutional and in violation of 'the equal protection guarantees embodied in the Fourteenth Amendment to the United States Constitution', as well as of article 1, section 2 of the Michigan constitution of 1963, which stated that 'no person shall be denied the equal protection of the laws; nor shall any person be denied the enjoyment of his civil or political rights or be discriminated against in the exercise thereof because of religion, race, color, or national origin'. Ravitz was determined to argue that Sinclair had been denied his civil rights by the Detroit police department and had been a victim of entrapment by undercover police officers while in possession of two cigarettes containing 11.5 grains of cannabis. Ravitz further argued that Michigan narcotics law, in the words of the deposition, inflicted 'cruel and unusual punishments' contrary to the Eighth Amendment to the Constitution, and that Sinclair's conviction was itself unlawful.

With the Ballard case smouldering in the in-trays back at Motown, Diana Ross and Berry Gordy were living in a rented home in Los Angeles, and the centrifugal force of Motown was moving imperceptibly westward from Detroit to Hollywood. But a shift of emphasis had not resolved the pressure on travel and flights when major engagements and network television demanded. On Sunday, 19 November, having endured a delayed flight from Los Angeles, a convoy of limousines took two of Motown's biggest-selling groups, Diana Ross and the Supremes and the Temptations, to CBS's famous Studio 50, home of *The Ed Sullivan Show*. The groups were due to sing a medley of each other's songs in what was supposed to be a celebration of the casual feelgood friendliness of Motown. The studio set was decorated with a brightly coloured op art mosaic of lights, and projected onto the backdrop was a prominent single four-letter word: ROSS. It was a performance layered with significance: the first television appearance of Cindy Birdsong, now the official replacement for Florence Ballard; the last network television performance of the Temptations' 'classic five' line-up of Otis Williams, David Ruffin, Eddie Kendricks, Paul Williams and Melvin Franklin; one of the last songs written for Motown by the warring Holland-Dozier-Holland team; and the first time that Diana Ross was so visibly singled out as a solo artist. Ross took centre stage throughout and during the Motown medley was strategically positioned in front of the others. The Supremes sang the jaunty 'In And Out Of Love', a song that had been Florence Ballard's final recording for Motown – her voice was overdubbed by backing singers as if she were being airbrushed out of Motown history. In an otherwise routine studio session back in April, with the ubiquitous Andantes supporting, Ballard had gone through the motions, not fully aware of how profoundly her life was about to change. It was the penultimate single she would feature on for Motown, and now the song was being performed on network television with the Temptations acting as the backing singers, a role they resented.

Backstage, Ross spent much of her time consorting with the actor Rex Harrison, star of *Doctor Doolittle*. He had completed the delayed film after much posturing and temperamental behaviour on set and was not the source of advice that Ross needed. If there is a moment that crystallised Diana Ross's rise to fame, then this was it. She had been a teenage fashion student at Cass Tech, a peripheral singer in a third-string soul group, and a part-time secretary in the overcrowded office at Motown, and now she was a global superstar. Ross was fascinated by acting and routinely befriended actors and film stars. She had already signed up for acting classes and been on a studio lot in Hollywood to meet Debbie Reynolds. Over the next few years, she would focus her considerable networking skills on the movie industry, and she increasingly required those working around her to call her 'Miss Ross'. It was the culmination of a journey to respect that her formidable mother had demanded since her ghetto infancy.

Gordy returned to Detroit for Thanksgiving and was told wrongly that Aretha Franklin was on life support at a local hospital. Franklin had been forced to cancel her show at the annual Macy's Thanksgiving Day Parade and had been admitted to the Bailey General Hospital on East Ferry, one of the city's few black-owned medical centres, with an undiagnosed illness. The only female artist with four consecutive gold records, she now had an industry-wide reputation for hypochondria. When she fell ill, she insisted on being taken to the Bailey General, a new hospital that had only recently been established by Dr Claud Young, a friend of her father's. Despite the chaotic breakdown of the summer rebellions, a sense of self-improvement had taken hold, and black businesses were springing up across the city, even in the most traditional areas of commerce. By the end of November, the *Michigan Chronicle* published an editorial that predicted sweeping change across Detroit and proposed rebranding the now derelict and shamed Fourteenth Street as Rosa Parks Boulevard. Gordy's return coincided with a television show on WJBK featuring a roster of local acts including the Rationals, the Miracles, Jimmy Ruffin, Martha and the Vandellas, and beat band Mitch Ryder and the Detroit Wheels, but he had an ulterior motive. Gordy was still seeing singer Chris Clark, who was due to leave Detroit for Europe two days later as part of the so-called Motown Messengers Tour, featuring Gladys Knight and the Pips. Knight's original version of 'I Heard It Through The Grapevine' was charting worldwide, and at long last she had something to show for her disgruntled years in the Hitsville shadows. Gordy spent time alone with Chris Clark, and they dined romantically in a Detroit restaurant prior to her transatlantic flight. Unaware of Gordy's love affair, Diana Ross continued a punishing schedule of live shows and studio recording throughout the remainder of 1967. Her career was creeping closer to a form of mania rather than a profession.

Towards the end of November, Motown hurriedly arranged for Diana Ross and the Supremes to record two soft-gospel songs – 'What A Friend We Have In Jesus' and 'Every Time I Feel the Spirit' – for the Christmas market. It was a bizarre choice of material at such a transformative moment in Ross's career, although the session might have been intended as part of a tribute to Gordy's sister Loucye, the managerial head of Motown's publishing arm, Jobete, who had died of a stroke in 1965. The Gordy family had struggled to come to terms with Loucye's death, and a streak of sentimentality always surrounded her anniversary. Gordy and his sister Esther had already hatched plans to commemorate their sister by establishing a scholarship fund in her name to support young black women to learn leadership skills and pursue a career in business administration. Esther, a graduate of Howard University who had married local politician George Edwards, was by now acting as chief executive officer at Motown and poised to join the full board of the Bank of the Commonwealth, Motown's bank. She had become a beacon of the family's passionate commitment to black self-improvement and saw her sister's premature death as a life unfulfilled. Motown's tribute album featured gospel classics by Gladys Knight, the Four Tops, Martha Reeves and Diana Ross, with the support of Detroit's Tabernacle Choir. The result is probably best described as tabernacle soul, a touching religious sentiment but nothing more than a well-intentioned diversion.

Paradoxically, it was the business dealings of the late Loucye Gordy and her management of Jobete that had become the focus of disquiet at Motown. Gordy reacted by rewarding loyalty. He promoted his contract lawyer, Ralph Seltzer, to head of A&R, a role that Mickey Stevenson had vacated in January 1967 and Eddie Holland had inherited. It was a hugely unpopular decision that erected a stone wall between management and musicians. Seltzer did not command respect and had already built up sizeable list of internal enemies. Raynoma Gordy once described him as having an 'aggressive and abrasive style' and claimed that he had used his privileged position as Gordy's personal administrator to revamp systems throughout the company. She referred to him witheringly as a 'special assistant to the president' and insisted he was a bully. For others at Motown, there was unquestionably a racial dynamic. Seltzer was tall, white, and wore the dark suits and conservative ties of middle management. He was not at ease with creatives and might well have been promoted hurriedly into the wrong role. Songwriter Sylvia Moy saw him as 'a company man, a Motown man, and a Berry man. Everything he did was for Motown and Berry.' She went on to claim accurately that throughout his working day Seltzer was simply doing his job, and since one of his jobs was to control costs of recording budgets and make savings within studio engineering, he predictably alienated some artists and producers. Others, including session producer Ivy Hunter, who co-wrote the Martha and the Vandellas hit 'Dancing In The Street', thought Seltzer had a vengeful streak and relished 'just doing his job'. 'Once Berry brought in Ralph Seltzer, the family background was finally destroyed,' he said years later, by which time Hunter had fallen out with Seltzer and felt victimised by Motown. Hunter grew to believe that he suffered reprisals at work for arguing on behalf of freelance producers and standing up for less well-known artists. He believed that Motown saw him as a mouthpiece for the hopefuls, and there were now hundreds of them to help.

Florence Ballard called Leonard Baun every other day throughout November, forcing the pace of a settlement. Meanwhile, in New York, B. B. King's manager, Louis Zito, had pursued his contacts at ABC and broached the possibility of Ballard launching a solo career. As he had predicted, ABC was interested but insistent that Ballard disentangle herself from Motown. ABC turned up the heat, telling Zito that a release form cutting all legal ties with Motown would be a prerequisite of any future deal. This immediately narrowed Baun's negotiating options and left him in an even weaker position. Although he was still recommending a lawsuit against Motown, that was likely to be costly and take time – too much time – to allow Ballard to sign an unencumbered contract with ABC. So with an impending deadline, Baun pursued an urgent face-to-face meeting with a Motown lawyer named George Schiffer, hoping to bring matters to an amicable closure. The two men arranged to meet in the Caucus Club on West Congress, an aristocratic restaurant decorated with stained mahogany and ornate antiques. It had the surface veneer of a gentleman's club and was to become the final resting place of Florence Ballard's career as a member of the Supremes.

The meeting took place in the second week of November, only a few days before Ballard travelled to New York to sign for ABC. Although official history dates her new deal to the spring of 1968, the local press in Detroit was already reporting it as early as 15 November 1967. Leonard Baun arrived at the Caucus Club first and was shown to a discreet table. He was armed with copies of all Ballard's Motown contracts and several pages of vague arithmetic scrawled on yellow ledger paper. The indecipherable scrawls calculated the presumed royalties that Ballard could hope to earn for future sales of Motown songs she had performed on. He had taken the figures down during a meeting with Louis Zito that estimated sales of records since 1965. They were incomplete, fragmentary and hopelessly wrong. Zito reckoned that the popularity of the Supremes would wane over time and stressed that Ballard had never written any of the group's international hits and so had a lesser claim on royalties. Baun was therefore encouraged to make false assumptions about future earnings and concluded that there would be a steep decline in Ballard's lifetime value and that any recoupable income was most likely to come from the accounting years 1965 to 1967. Motown still refused to share information, and those who had spoken to Baun acknowledged that value would be more likely to accrue to either Jobete or to Holland-Dozier-Holland.

Motown's attorney, George Schiffer, arrived slightly late. He was normally based in Motown's new L.A. office but had flown into Detroit to take the meeting and nip the legal wrangle in the bud. Since Baun's demands for more information about Ballard's earnings had strayed into copyright law, Schiffer was also best placed to argue Motown's case. What threw Baun off was Schiffer's approach. He apologised profusely for being late and held out a warm firm hand. Far from being the ruthless and truculent manipulator of Motown myth, Schiffer was a chummy and avuncular man who was personally fond of Florence Ballard and had no great desire to see her cheated. If anything, he preferred creative artists and their unpredictable personalities to the rigidity of senior management. George Schiffer was a story in his own right. A Jewish immigrant whose family had fled the Nazis in the late thirties, he had migrated to America as a schoolboy, studied law at Harvard, and eventually pursued a career as a copyright lawyer with Warner Brothers in their offices at New York's Rockefeller Center. Outside the workplace he had devoted much of his personal energy to supporting the Congress of Racial Equality (CORE), and before his arrival at Motown he had been an integral figure in the mobilisation of the March on Washington in 1963, where Martin Luther King delivered his historic 'I have a dream' speech. Schiffer represented CORE in some of its most ambitious projects – the desegregation of schools in Chicago, the Freedom Riders campaign in which northern liberals journeyed to the Deep South to encourage voter registration, and a high-profile protest against the mayor of New York, Robert F. Wagner Jr, who was accused of squandering public money on the World's Fair pavilion in Flushing Meadows while Harlem fell into public neglect.

Motown had hired Schiffer for his knowledge of copyright law but deeply respected his civil rights credentials. There were many within the ranks of Motown's famous soul singers who admitted Schiffer had done more in the pursuit of civil rights than they had, and by 1967 he had used his skills generously, becoming a mentor to young writers and producers at Motown, often working independently of the corporation to offer advice. It was around this time that he struck up a close relationship with producers Ashford and Simpson, whom he represented for many years to come, often putting their best interests before Motown's. However close he was to Gordy – and they did have a good working relationship – George Schiffer was not motivated by corporate greed, nor was he a puppet of the Motown machine. He was by nature a conciliatory man with no desire to cheat young ghetto artists out of their rightful rewards.

In the toxic atmosphere that was encircling Motown, very few people reported the severance meeting at the Caucus Club as anything but vicious. The truth was somewhat different. It was not a cruel *coup de grâce*, as some have suggested, but a polite encounter in genteel surroundings. Schiffer was helpful in explaining complex areas of copyright to Baun. By the end of the meal, the two men had sketched out an agreement that would allow Florence Ballard to sign for ABC in good faith. Ballard was to receive a one-time payment of $139,804.94 in royalties and earnings, but Motown insisted that she could not compete by using the Supremes in any future publicity, and the agreement closed down the prospect of further royalties after 1967. Although the details of the compromise deal did not leak out for months to come, the parties left the Caucus Club believing they had settled the matter.

Soon thereafter, Ballard inked a short-form Heads of Terms with ABC Records, pending the signature of a full contract early in the new year. Her ties with Motown had been severed – some might argue for the second time in a matter of months – but yet again harmony proved to be short-lived. For Ballard, there were to be many more years of acrimonious dispute ahead, much of it connected to the legal advice she had taken. 'I trusted Leonard

Baun,' Ballard said a few years later. 'I didn't know what the papers meant, I just signed them. So I guess I signed a settlement.' She had. Ballard's naïvety endeared her to many, but in the end it proved to be her fatal flaw. She had made crucial mistakes: setting up a company with her untalented boyfriend, Tommy Chapman, and deferring to him as a manager, listening to her family give erratic and overemotional advice, and, worst of all, hiring the services of an unspectacular lawyer with a brain injury. Baun had in turn become far too close to his client's wealth. His actions lacked transparency, and he did not fully account for the money he was spending or the fees he was deducting for his services. Baun had become bewitched by the music industry and planned to extricate himself from the local partnership of Okrent, Baun and Vulpe, and set up a grander partnership, Baun and Barton, in the swanky suburb of Harper Woods. There were delusions all around.

Ballard was comfortably well-off when she left Motown but not significantly rich. She had $160,000 held in trust by her lawyer, and history has proven that there can be no question that her settlement with Motown fell far short of her true worth. Almost immediately, the savings that Baun had held in trust for her began to evaporate. Legal fees consumed much of it, but so too did travel expenses, marriage plans and an expensive holiday, which she took after Christmas and before recording her songs for ABC. She paid Chapman a salary as a manager, was generous with other family members, and even before her new contract with ABC was signed she was spending at a rate that her savings did not justify. But nor was she kept fully informed by her lawyer. The inevitable outcome was that Ballard was finally informed the well was dry.

Many have characterised Florence Ballard as a luckless innocent duped by calculating men and a manipulative Motown management, but that was not entirely true. She had made successive errors of personal judgement and had placed too much faith in people who lacked real knowledge and ability. She had a new record deal, a voice from the top quartile of sixties soul, and a determined personality. She was not a passive victim, and as soon as she realised that Leonard Baun had failed to protect her resources she retaliated, sacking him and seeking compensation. With her brother Billy in tow, she went to the police, where they were interviewed by Lieutenant Edward V. Boggs, the liaison officer who had consulted with John Sinclair in the violent and ill-fated love-in on Belle Isle in the spring. Boggs left the Ballards believing that he would investigate a case of legal malfeasance, but he also recommended that Ballard hire a more trustworthy lawyer. They never heard from Detective Boggs again, and so Ballard was forced to file a complaint with the Detroit police department, and her original accusations against Baun came to nothing. Finding a new lawyer proved difficult too. Several declined to take on the challenge. The Ballards met with assistant county prosecutor Jay Nolan, a prominent prosecutor in the aftermath of the summer rebellions, but he declared a conflict of interest as he knew Leonard Baun personally. They visited another lawyer's office, this time in the First National Building, and paid a $200 retainer to O. Lee Molette, yet he too ultimately declined to take on the case and was subsequently suspended for misconduct. Ballard paid yet another $200 retainer fee to a third lawyer, one of Detroit's most famous criminal lawyers, Joseph W. Louisell, who was known at the time as 'Michigan's Perry Mason'. Louisell told her he was too busy, and with good reason – he was simultaneously defending Mafia boss Matthew 'Mike the Enforcer' Rubino on tax evasion charges and co-ed serial killer John Norman Collins, who had murdered six women in the eastern Michigan area.

Eventually Ballard found her way to the premises of Patmon, Young and Kirk, whose offices already represented Holland-Dozier-Holland. Senior partner Frederick Patmon filed a ten-point cause of action suit pursuing Ballard's former lawyer. It was bad news for Leonard Baun and disastrous for Motown. Their two biggest disputes were now housed within the same ambitious African-American firm, and in a few years Gladys Knight would join Florence Ballard and Holland–Dozier–Holland in a dizzying legal blitzkrieg on Motown. Ballard's new legal team cut to the chase and served another aggressive missive, lengthier in contention but following the same basic premise as Holland-Dozier-Holland's countersuit and using the same uncompromising language. It covered the period from 1964 to 1967, the creative high point of the Supremes, and significantly it not only named the various corporate and legal entities of Motown and Berry Gordy Jr individually, it extended the complaint to include Diana Ross, Mary Wilson and Cindy Birdsong, accusing them of participation in a fraudulent conspiracy. Among the 238 paragraphs of dispute, the key accusations were as follows:

On or about July of 1967, the Defendants . . . in furtherance of their conspiracy to oust Miss Ballard from the Supremes . . . dispatched Michael Roshkind to Detroit with instructions to contact Miss Ballard and to induce her to sign certain papers allowing the Defendants to remove her from the Supremes . . .

On or about July 28, 1967 . . . Roshkind fraudulently represented that she was not entitled to receive any monies from Berry Gordy Jr, International, Diana Ross or Motown in the form of present monies or future royalties or earnings; he also represented to Miss Ballard that her performances with the Supremes were having adverse effects upon the group's popularity and that it would be in 'everyone's' best interest for her to allow the Defendants to remove her from the Supremes . . .

The Defendants completed their last substantive and substantial act in furtherance of their conspiracy to fraudulently oust Miss Ballard from the Supremes by having her enter into a purported general release agreement removing her from the Supremes and paying her meager and grossly inadequate sums of monies as it related to her various rights . . .

Defendants, their servants and agents repeatedly represented to Miss Ballard that her professional performances were no longer the high caliber of the other two Supremes . . . that Miss Ballard's performances with the Supremes were having and would continue to have an adverse effect upon the general public's acceptance of the group and the sale of phonographic records . . .

Defendant Motown from 1964 to the present time has fraudulently, falsely and excessively overcharged Miss Ballard for the cost of arrangements, accompaniments and other costs relating to each matter recording and embodying Miss Ballard's performance . . .

Defendant Motown fraudulently and falsely and excessively offset said costs . . .

Defendant Motown failed to pay unto Miss Ballard the proper sums of monies that she was entitled to receive pursuant to the services she rendered.

By the time the complaint was served, Ballard had disappeared off Motown's day-to-day radar, and Motown's release schedule continued at an exhausting pace. In mid November, 'If I Could Build My Whole World Around You', by Marvin Gaye and Tammi Terrell was released on Tamla, and the Marvelettes' song 'My Baby Must Be A Magician', recorded earlier in the year at Golden World Studios, was also released nationally. Motown had another stab at the rock market, releasing 'You Haven't Seen My Love' by Michigan garage band the Ones, a white four-piece act from Lansing. The song was already a well-known local hit on the obscure Spirit label, and Gordy reckoned that with Motown's distribution clout they could take it from the local charts to national prominence, but it faltered and faded without trace. Gordy's determined but fruitless attempts to find the next Beatles were conspicuously unsuccessful, but he continued to pour money into the bottomless pit of the rock market, eventually funding a dedicated rock label named Rare Earth, which never recouped the money spent on it.

Detroit now had a worldwide reputation for soul music, and among its top-tier singers were names that would dominate the legacy of black music: Aretha Franklin, Diana Ross, Marvin Gaye, Smokey Robinson, Gladys Knight, David Ruffin and the radiantly gifted lead singer of the Four Tops, Levi Stubbs. But what was less well known was that the city had also simultaneously given voice to a generation of sixties lawyers whose reputations were forged against the restless backdrop of riots, overseas wars and civil rights. Among them were the elegant civil rights lawyer Edward F. Bell, now fighting in the producers' corner at Motown and defending the rights of Holland-Dozier-Holland; Justin 'Chuck' Ravitz, the

Marxist intellectual who had become the attorney of choice for the city's political underground, including the MC5; Ravitz's mentor, Sheldon Otis, a courtroom virtuoso and arguably Detroit's greatest lawyer ever, who was being seduced away from the city to support the California underground; and the Black Power firebrand Ken Cockrel Sr, the son of a Highland Park assembly worker who grew up to become a champion of America's black militants, not least Detroit's emergent new labour revolutionaries in the Dodge Revolutionary Union Movement. Cockrel, a self-described Marxist-Leninist, was a strident advocate for change within the city's legal system and was a lifetime activist against police brutality and racial bias. He was once famously charged with contempt for appearing on a local television show where he called a presiding Recorder's Court judge a 'lawless, racist, rogue bandit, thief, pirate, honky dog fool'.

By the end of November 1967, legal exchanges were polluting day-to-day life at Motown. Many musicians felt pressured into taking sides, and the disputes had decimated the last vestiges of a family atmosphere. Cost became the enemy of creativity and, worse still, perspective was lost. None of those wrapped up in dispute seemed capable of backing down, so legal missives were exchanged like artillery fire and land was lost. It became an all-consuming dispute that was only concluded decades later, by which time Holland-Dozier-Holland's uncompromising lawyer, Edward F. Bell, had already died of cancer.

Escape from Detroit. A family move their meagre belongings out of an
old fire-damaged house to a new home. Detroit's depopulation begins in earnest.

DECEMBER

Flight

James Hassler's dead body was left slumped at the wheel of a black-on-bronze Mustang on the service drive of the John Lodge Freeway. There was no sign of a struggle; he had been shot from behind through the neck, and a live .38 special bullet was left near the front passenger seat of his car. It was clear he knew his killers, and more than likely he had been the victim of a gangland assassination. Hassler's car had been left abandoned half a mile south of West Grand Boulevard at the interchange many Motown staff members drove through to and from work. A police investigation swept the area, and several employees were questioned as potential witnesses. Many more had witnessed the aftermath and had driven past the cordoned-off investigation area on their way home. The Hitsville studios had narrowly survived the July rebellions, but many buildings in the locality had not and remained burned-out shells, like many other areas in inner-city Detroit, and apprehension had taken grip. The murder of James Hassler, with all its connotations of Mob violence, became office gossip for weeks to come in a city now obsessed with personal safety and family security.

By December 1967 anxious conversations could be heard in bars, at workplaces and across dinner tables, and talk of leaving the city for the suburbs was an everyday preoccupation. For over five consecutive decades, Detroit families had been moving outward to the garden cities of Michigan, where new homes with safe play areas promised a leafy escape from the troubled inner city. It was a trend that predated the rebellious events of 1967 by many years. Sociologists called it white flight, but it was considerably more complex than any crude response to race relations. Since the fifties Detroit's population had been in steep decline, and the racial characteristics of the city were transforming. In 1950 Detroit had a total population of 1.8 million people; by 1967 that number had declined to nearer 1.5 million, and as the years unfolded the city desperately tried to cling to its people. The events of 1967 turned what was a growing trend into a virtual stampede. Depopulation was undermining the topography of the city too. There were more vacant lots, an increase in abandoned houses, and homeowners were increasingly defaulting on mortgage debt. By the city's own count, the events of 1967 led to the eventual abandonment of 30,000 houses, some of them decrepit and unloved but others valuable and once-cherished homes that history had victimised. Abandoned buildings and desecrated lots defied every perception of overcrowded urban life: the teeming streets were being replaced with isolated, unloved and eerily quiet neighbourhoods. Although local communities had rallied in support of a clean-up campaign, the battle for hearts and minds had been lost. The last one hundred families made homeless by the July disturbances were found new homes in early December as part of a scheme called Homes for Christmas, but that failed to reassure anyone, and feeling unsafe was now epidemic. Gun sales skyrocketed, and in the twelve months to July 1968 Detroit issued four times as many handgun permits; in the predominately white suburbs, five times as many. Being safe had become a very dangerous game.

Anxiety about inner-city safety affected Motown's administrative staff much more than it did its famous singers. The top performers were rich – in most cases, cash rich. They had bought property, they travelled in limousines, and they had witnessed lifestyles abroad that contrasted with their own. When they spoke of Detroit to the international media, it tended to be with a fond nostalgia. Those who worked at Motown every day were living in the real Detroit, not beneath the doo-wop lampposts of the mythologised past, and the vast majority were low-paid session singers or engineers who had young families and lived in houses within the 'urban prairies' that formed after the rebellions. They too felt nostalgia for a past that seemed safer and more secure. Motown's cramped warren of offices on West Grand Boulevard were no longer suited to the expanding needs of the company, and plans to move to more appropriate corporate headquarters were hatched. Esther Gordy spoke regularly with local real estate agents, looking to find an office space that could accommodate the company's expanding sales force and provide more professional accommodation for accounts, the legal team and senior management. Curiously, this plan to move the corporation unsettled staff even more, and a concern that the pace of change was out of control took hold.

Two factors were in play: first, a growing fear of crime in the neighbourhoods around the old Motown studios, and second, Gordy and Diana Ross's shared vision of expanding into film and television. Esther Gordy agreed with her brother's plan to start selling off the low-rise houses that surrounded Hitsville on West Grand, closing down the rehearsal spaces and charm school that had been a vital part of Motown's performance and decorum academy, and secure bigger, more spacious and safer office premises. The search began in earnest in late 1967 but did not conclude until nearly a year later, when Motown signed documents securing new premises within the Donovan/Sanders Building at 2475 Woodward downtown. The ten-storey Donovan building had been designed in the twenties by renowned architect Albert Khan and was famed for its Tiffany-designed favrile glasswork. The exterior alone was a far cry from the DIY facilities Motown had started out with.

The move had a deeper influence than many imagined. Sixties soul was largely homemade, often produced in relatively primitive lo-fi studios and sometimes even in converted garages or basements. Motown's southern rival Stax had grown up piecemeal in a converted cinema on McLemore Avenue in Memphis; Chicago's Satellite soul label operated out of the backroom of an insurance company; and Washington's Shrine label – in part funded by Gordy's divorce settlement with Raynoma – was run from the kitchen table of a converted townhouse on DC's Thomas Circle. The pressure to professionalise was not unique to Motown, but the company felt it hardest, and the plan to move to new corporate headquarters did not happen in isolation either. The corporation had recurring cash-flow problems and was haemorrhaging funds. Gordy was under pressure from both family advisers and his senior management team to trim the roster of artists from over a hundred acts at its epic height in 1965 to almost half that number in 1967. What many saw as a betrayal of talent was in the eyes of the management about finding an efficient level of staffing. Those who remained lived with the logic and, inevitably, those who left did not. Jimmy Ruffin said many years later, 'The thing people don't realize is, Berry didn't really know what was happening at Motown. See, Berry was obsessed with the Supremes, he had that tunnel vision, he saw only them.'

Throughout December Esther Gordy was in regular contact with the headquarters of the United Services Organization (USO) in Washington DC, the non-profit organisation that provided support and entertainment to American armed forces in Vietnam. Although Motown had a reputation as a patriotic corporation, some of its most prominent staff, including copyright lawyer George Schiffer, were already involved in the anti-war movement. Others shrugged their shoulders, unclear if the war was necessary or not. The USO and its long tail of political connections, which reached all the way to the Oval Office, was determined to secure the services of the Supremes as a headline act. A high-profile tour of Vietnam featuring the most successful female group in the world would have been a propaganda coup for the military, the

White House and the war effort. The benefits to Motown were more questionable. The company would be guaranteed network television exposure, but opposition to the war was growing at such a rate that there was now a very real risk that a tour of the war zone would backfire. Securing the services of the Temptations was proving just as difficult for the officers of the USO. There was disharmony within the ranks of the group, and reaching a consensus was nigh on impossible. The unpredictable David Ruffin was by now frequently missing shows, and his private life was spinning out of control. Several members of the group were listening closely to the anti-war movement and were reluctant to travel to Vietnam, and as the USS *Pueblo* incident was to demonstrate, there was also a fear within the ranks of the Temptations of Southeast Asia's instability. The group allegedly had a show of hands and decided to reject any overtures to visit Vietnam – it was the wrong place and the wrong time. But early in December the USO had a breakthrough of sorts, and a short contract was signed by Motown's Los Angeles office committing solo singer Barbara McNair to join a live tour of Vietnam with Bob Hope on his annual pilgrimage to entertain the troops. Actress and sex symbol Raquel Welch, the star of the mid sixties movie *One Million Years B.C.*, was also signed up for what would prove to be an iconic and much publicised moment in an entrenched and deeply divisive war.

Throughout the mid sixties two substantial music scenes had coexisted in Detroit but never really met. The independent soul scene and the psychedelic rock sound, which found its noisiest expression at the Grande Ballroom, were separated not only by race and social class but by the odd nuances of youth subculture. By the end of 1967, however, a creative seepage had begun to bring them together in a hybrid form of music later known as psychedelic soul. The term was first coined in Chicago when a local taxi-driver and sometime musician named Saxie Russell recorded a haunting drug track simply called 'Psychedelic Soul'. It was a filthy mess of a record but one that had a raw percussive power that turned the saxophone into a base pipe. John Sinclair, MC5 and the nucleus of hippies that congregated at the Grande Ballroom had all but abandoned the summer of flower power for a winter of discontent. By some distance they had the most radical worldview of any of the communes and rock cadres that grew out of the counterculture. By the fall of 1967 hard-core activists pronounced 'the death of the hippie', and rebels argued that the very term 'hippie' had been subsumed by the media and thus had to be put to rest. They burned a grey coffin labelled 'The Summer of Love' on a funeral pyre and declared that love and peace were now to be superseded by darker themes of drug use and revolutionary violence. Many felt the media needed to be scared of counterculture, not entranced by it. Motown had always tiptoed lightly. It was only in the last dwindling weeks of 1967 that Motown delved deeper into psychedelia, a journey led by an unlikely character – a former pool hall hustler and soda fountain attendant named Norman Whitfield.

Gordy first noticed Whitfield cleaning the Motown studios on the weekends and described him as 'tall, broad-shouldered, with a thick head of hair'. At least on first meeting, Whitfield was an intensely shy man who guarded himself with stubbornness and steely dedication. To Motown's management he came off as persistent to the point of obsession, and his dogged pursuit of great music was by all accounts a pest to the system. Despite many informal warnings that his behaviour went beyond enthusiasm, he would not take no for an answer. Motown's musicians had divided opinions about Whitfield, and some avoided being conscripted into his recording sessions, which often ran for hours through the night. Otis Williams of the Temptations claimed: 'He had to hear something he wanted, and if he didn't we could forget about getting out of there, sometimes until the sun went down and came up again.'

Gordy and Whitfield were cut from the same ideological cloth, and it might have been their similarities that drove them to disagree. Both had been raised on the values of personal achievement advocated by Booker T. Washington; Gordy had absorbed the message of self-help from his father and the network of small businesses the Gordys operated across ghetto Detroit, while Whitfield had imbibed the principle of 'reaching for the best' from his uncle, the Detroit pharmacist Sidney Barthwell. At the height of the Depression, Barthwell had used his savings to buy a failing pharmacy and built a business empire by installing soda fountains in all his premises. By 1967 he owned nine drugstores across the Motor City and had risen to become president of the Booker T. Washington Business Association, which counted several members of the Gordy family within its ranks and whose lawyer was one Edward F. Bell. It was in every respect a small and internecine world.

Whatever his personal characteristics, Norman Whitfield had a creative imagination. He embraced innovation with a bear hug and was keener than most other producers to take his influence far from the mainstream. Whitfield had watched the great Detroit groups of the sixties with a sharp eye and was struck by how similar they all were – phenomenal harmonisers, dressed in matching clothes, and capable of highly choreographed stage routines. But it all seemed out of step with the times. The clothes looked dated, the stage routines hopelessly anachronistic, and the fascination with teenage love irrelevant to the major issues of the day. Something about the music felt stuck like a needle on vinyl, repeating the same phrases over and over again.

Whitfield had embarked on a plan to transform the Temptations' image, and by doing so he changed the direction of Motown. The winds of change were now battering Motown from every direction, and shifts in technology, social attitudes and ways of working were now ripping up the rule books. After years of resisting even incremental change and trying to cling to the glamour and respectability of past decades, Motown inevitably buckled beneath the pressure. Whitfield was not alone in his passion for new technology and his fascination with the events of the era. He was joined by a vanguard of others who were brought to innovation for different reasons. Little Stevie Wonder, Motown's child prodigy, was now nearly eighteen years old, had shaken off his legal obligation to be accompanied by tutors and receive civic childcare, and grown into a self-assured young man. From his childhood he had pursued a crude form of 'night writing', a precursor to the Braille system that had been used by soldiers to communicate silently in the dark. Since childhood Wonder had been fascinated by how sound and instrumentation could aid his blindness. On a Motown tour of Europe, he had sat at Louis Braille's desk at the Institut National des Jeunes Aveugles in Paris, a moment that marked his first tentative steps on a creative journey toward a new synthesised form of soul music or 'inner visions', which ultimately became the title of his historic 1973 album. At first Norman Whitfield's bridge to creative change came through an unlikely partnership with Gladys Knight. Unlike most Motown acts drawn from the high schools of inner-city Detroit, Gladys Knight and the Pips were a family act from Atlanta and were not by any stretch of the imagination naïve about the industry. The group included Gladys Knight, her brother Bubba, her sister Brenda, and their cousins William and Eleanor Guest. As raising children took its toll, two of the female members were replaced by still more cousins, Langston George and Edward Patten, with Gladys Knight the consistent link throughout. The group had already enjoyed a decent five-year career before it signed to Motown, and it was less dependent on the label's guardianship than the Supremes, but, frustratingly, this maturity and professionalism was frequently overlooked in favour of younger, rawer and emotionally more unstable groups. They had never managed to force themselves to the front line of Motown's competitive recording queue, nor had they ever won Berry Gordy's undivided attention. Knight has since admitted that a stalled career was predictable: 'From the start it was apparent that we were not going to be one of the boss's priorities. We were relegated to the lower tier of Motown's acts with the Monitors and the Spinners. Some of their members had to do odd jobs around Hitsville in order to keep their paychecks coming. They doubled as chauffeurs and gofers until they scored on a song.'

Knight had become well aware that the cards were stacked against her. Although none of the group were ever expected to take menial jobs, and they were often sent off on small-scale tours, Gladys Knight and the Pips were stuck in Motown's lower classes, halfway up a social hierarchy of soul that had the Supremes and the Temptations at the very top. 'We didn't become anybody's coat-hanger,' Knight said many years later, 'but our status was made clear . . . We'd hear about parties at Berry's house and company picnics *after* they happened, which is usually a clear sign that we weren't on the A-list.' As ever, Gordy saw it differently. He consistently talked about his abiding respect for Gladys Knight and shrugged off talk of discontent: 'There was also a family feeling about them that made me feel close to them from the beginning. Unlike many of our main acts who had been through the artists' development process, Gladys and the Pips were already seasoned before coming to Motown.'

Whatever Gordy's real thoughts, he didn't convey them at the time. Failing in the charts, feeling marginalised, and unable to see any measurable progress, Gladys Knight joined the growing camp of dissenters at Motown. She had shared her thoughts with her brother and cousins on the road, had attended several parties at the home of disengaged producer Clarence Paul, and had been one of several employees to share her grievances about the Motown system. Although nothing more concrete than therapeutic bitching ever came of the meetings, they had become a place where the disaffected could discuss pay rates and learn about Motown's policies.

Knight believed she was being punished by Motown for upstaging the Supremes at a concert in the spring of 1967, after which she was withdrawn from the tour and demoted. It was an incident that may have been embellished over time, but other artists have complained of similar treatment. Motown always insisted that the top-of-the-bill performers had to be respected, and that clearly rankled, particularly in the eyes of those gospel-reared artists whose heavenly voices made them soar above Ross when they sang together. Knight had been a child prodigy gospel singer and, like Aretha Franklin, had been told she was divinely gifted from a very early age. But riches did not follow her talent, and she performed on the R&B circuit over decades, eking out a pitiful living as success eluded her. When her big breakthrough came, it was seismic and unexpected. The group's third Motown single, 'Everybody Needs Love', released earlier in 1967, had barely grazed the top forty before dropping like a stone. It was not good news. Knight has since admitted to nervously looking at *Billboard* magazine and feeling sick to her stomach when she saw the record descending the charts. Failure meant they would drop further down the studio pecking order and become sidelined. Knight felt obliged to perform at ever more demeaning venues, places she had last seen as a child. She shared her fears with Norman Whitfield, who had already registered some success with female-led groups, producing 'Too Many Fish In The Sea' by the Marvelettes and 'Needle In A Haystack', an effusive dance tune recorded by the Velvelettes. As Knight's career stalled, Whitfield's star was in its ascendancy, earning him the right to produce for the Temptations, and in time he would displace Smokey Robinson as the group's producer as Robinson focused on his own recording career.

In 1966 the success of 'Ain't Too Proud To Beg' by the Temptations had given Whitfield a nascent reputation for innovation and he was convinced that he had many more songs in his locker that could help reposition Motown as a creative label again. One particular song was obsessing him: 'I Heard It Through The Grapevine'. He had hawked a demo of the song around Hitsville for months, offering it to at least three different acts until Knight grabbed the opportunity, admitting later in life that she reacted out of a mix of fear and desperation. Knight had come to the realisation that another failure would confine her to the scrap heap and risk bringing her Motown contract to an end, so she took Whitfield's rudimentary demo home to listen to it. She described what followed as close to a personal epiphany. 'We treated the demo tape as if it was the Hope Diamond. It certainly was our hope for the future of our career,' she remembered. 'We "borrowed" a big reel-to-reel tape recorder from Motown and started messing around with different phrasing, adding little licks and grooves. We lived that song for about a month, getting to know it and playing with ways to make it our own . . . We played it in our sleep.'

When Gladys Knight and the Pips met up with Whitfield again, they had taken ownership of his song, and although the lyrics remained intact the song had been deconstructed and rebuilt. 'We didn't have anything to do with writing,' she admitted, 'but the structure is so important in production. We tore it apart . . . we did all the little things.' Such was their shared enthusiasm that Whitfield and Knight pressured Smokey Robinson into freeing up some of his allocated studio time, and, unusually for Motown, the song was completed in a few short takes. It still faced significant hurdles, though. Gladys Knight was by now a peripheral artist and could not count on much support; the song was allocated an infinitesimal marketing budget, and by all accounts it sneaked out into the stores. It had only one hope: word of mouth. 'They released it and stood back,' Gladys Knight said ruefully many years later. 'No full-page ads. No television or concert appearances. The Motown machine had apparently blown a gasket.'

Unexpectedly, 'I Heard It Through The Grapevine' triumphed over adversity and became one of the great pop songs. Knight's version of the song, later covered by Marvin Gaye, became Motown's biggest-selling single in 1967, moving over 2.5 million copies and outstripping the sales of every one of the Supremes' releases that year. Knight quietly relished a small triumph over Diana Ross and the Supremes and felt personally vindicated at having secured what she describes as a 'moral victory' over bias within Motown. There was a further irony to come. Months before Gladys Knight's success, Whitfield had recorded a more plaintive and introspective version of the song with Marvin Gaye, and although his version was recorded first, Knight's more storming gospel rendition was first to market. A year later, Gaye's version resurfaced to become an international soul anthem. It was a salutary lesson for Berry Gordy. He was a musical leader, but his judgement was sometimes flawed, and he was not in tune with the shifting musical moods of this volatile era. From then on he looked more generously upon Whitfield, describing him not so much as a novice but as a 'bold innovator'.

Whitfield had begun to understand that the wider counterculture of hippies, social revolution and anti-war opinion would eventually penetrate the Motown system, but getting it to happen was no easy mission. Gordy had grown up with harmony groups and wanted Motown to break down racial barriers and take slick African-American music to the supper clubs, Las Vegas and network television. He was uneasy with strident political opinion and saw the counterculture, especially drug-inspired lyrics, as a dangerous distraction. He was not alone. Motown's sales director, Barney Ales, had spent a decade transforming attitudes toward black-owned labels in stores across America and did not want the Motown sales force to be dragged back to the ghetto or contaminated by controversy. Both men were instinctively conservative, deeply suspicious of psychedelic soul, and waved away any druggy lyrics or artwork, conscious that several songs by the Beatles and the Rolling Stones had fallen foul of broadcasting bans in Europe, and also conscious that conservative radio networks, particularly in the southern states, still held deep suspicions about black artists and their music.

Whitfield and others often appealed to one of the obvious chinks in Gordy's armour: his long-standing love affair with music technology. Gordy had a chummy familiarity with Motown's engineers and often sat with them to guide tracks to perfection or push for new sounds by experimenting with homemade electronic devices and studio mixing desks. In the autumn of 1967 he held an excited meeting with Whitfield and Stevie Wonder about synthesisers after reading a story in *Billboard* about Micky Dolenz of the Monkees buying one of the first commercially available Moog synthesisers and pioneering its use on the album Pisces, Aquarius, Capricorn & Jones Ltd. A rare unanimity emerged from the meeting. Gordy was quick to adapt to the synthesiser, understanding the new instrument as a natural extension of the piano – where lay his own skills; Whitfield was motivated by the cult of the new; and Wonder was already obsessed with any form of computer-aided communication. As 1967 came to an end, Whitfield felt emboldened enough to encourage musicians to contort sound and had begun to goad reluctant members of the Temptations to think more radically about using synthesised sound in their stage act.

★

Motown had recently released *The Temptations In A Mellow Mood,* an LP of show tunes harvested from their summer residency at Manhattan's Copacabana. It was a feast of easy-listening standards that included 'Ol' Man River', 'Somewhere' and 'Hello Young Lovers', and it reflected the rise of Motown as black America's most mainstream creative company. But it also sounded dated, confusing critics and consumers alike. The album was a journey into the nostalgic mainstream at a time when their current producer was advocating a revolutionary new direction. For the next three years Norman Whitfield took psychedelic soul forward, experimenting with extreme guitar play, estranged lyrics, and expanded consciousness, composing songs like 'Papa Was A Rolling Stone', 'Cloud Nine' and 'Ball Of Confusion' for the Temptations, the Vietnam protest song 'War' for Edwin Starr, and the darkly sarcastic 'Smiling Faces Sometimes' for new protégés the Undisputed Truth. Otis Williams described it as something close to a mission. 'Musically speaking,' he wrote, 'Norman set a mood that was worlds apart: dark, threatening, and even hostile.' It was the antithesis of what Motown had once been.

One of the many paradoxes of Motown was that its musicians often produced greatness at the height of personal breakdown or disharmony. The Supremes bickered endlessly on the road throughout much of 1965 and 1966 while releasing their greatest hits; Martha and the Vandellas were in constant turmoil when their best songs were recorded; and Marvin Gaye's fictional love affair with Tammi Terrell found its greatest expression as she lay dying. The Temptations were about to take that paradox to a new level. From the middle of 1967, during a few intense months, they recorded some of their greatest hits ever, despite an internecine dispute that reached nuclear levels.

Everyone had a view on David Ruffin's confrontational behaviour, and few sided with the bespectacled vocalist. Gordy was adamant that the Temptations would be better off without him. 'He's holding you hostage,' he once told Otis Williams, implying that firing Ruffin and cutting him loose would come with Motown's blessing. The rest of the Temptations had reached breaking point and had wearily arrived at the same conclusion. 'David Ruffin wasn't a monster, he wasn't evil,' Williams said years later. 'I think he was like a scared little boy a lot of the time and fell under the influence of truly evil people, leeches who fed on him.' But his view came with the benefit of hindsight. At the time he blamed Ruffin's selfish arrogance for disputes within the group, and each passing day soured their friendship. Ruffin was by now a promiscuous lover with a string of girlfriends including Dean Martin's daughter Barbara Gail Martin, and he had recklessly surrounded himself with dangerous drug criminals from the hard core of Detroit's ganglands. According to a Motown colloquialism, David Ruffin was on cloud nine – bloated by ego, cocaine addiction and an inability to shut up. He repeatedly demanded to be a named lead singer, and made irrational demands for more money yet often missed shows. On one or two infamous occasions he showed up late, hid among the audience, and then crashed the stage, grabbing the microphone.

Tour manager Don Foster has since said, 'David was a junkie in many ways, a drug junkie but also an attention junkie.' Foster persistently fought off his requests for higher appearance fees and cash handouts on tour, and found himself accused of short-changing the Temptations. 'When I first began traveling with them, they did not trust me. Because Berry had sent me there, which to them automatically meant I was gonna rip off their money,' he once said. Even as time improved their relationship, money remained a source of trouble. The Temptations had a joint account at the Detroit Savings Bank on West Grand Boulevard a few blocks from Hitsville, and according to Joe Williams, brother of Otis Williams, 'they simply cleaned it out'. Motown artists were often quick to spend and only ever saw 'income', never 'expenditure'. Many never comprehended that paying taxes on earnings was a legal requirement and that cheques sent to the IRS were not disappearing into Gordy's back pocket. Over the years many Motown artists fell foul of tax laws, and many, including Norman Whitfield, ended up owing millions on undeclared earnings.

Ruffin's love affair with twenty-two-year-old Barbara Gail

Martin proved to be a major distraction. From July to September 1967, she had been co-hosting a network television show with her father from NBC's colour studio set in Burbank, and Ruffin had periodically disappeared to Hollywood, irrespective of where the Temptations were performing. With handfuls of cash and a stash of cocaine as company, he often vanished for up to a week at a time, infamously in December 1967 while Martin was recording a Christmas special with the Sinatra family, *Christmas with the Martins and the Sinatras*, in which she played second fiddle to rival Rat Pack daughter Nancy Sinatra, whose smash 'These Boots Are Made For Walking' was an international hit. It was while Ruffin was on one of his jaunts with Martin that the rest of the group hatched a plan to replace him with his friend Dennis Edwards of the Contours. At first Edwards was drafted as a substitute, much like Cindy Birdsong was brought in for Florence Ballard. However, Ruffin would periodically turn up at shows unannounced, and at critical moments in songs like 'My Girl' would charge onstage and grab the mic from the compromised Edwards. Foster retaliated by hiring security to guard the front of the stage, but Ruffin broke their lines more than once and at times stealthily appeared from the wings, having conned his way backstage.

Paranoid about being edged out of the group, Ruffin sued Motown, seeking a release from what he considered to be a draconian contract and demanding the immediate accounting of money due to him. For reasons that only Gordy or his inner sanctum could explain, Motown was keen to keep Ruffin on board and so countersued. The ultimate settlement required Ruffin to remain with Motown to fulfil a solo contract, but the legal exchanges did nothing to enhance anyone's reputation.

By late 1967, as the flight to leave inner-city Detroit intensified, Otis Williams joined the many thousands of Detroiters who were looking outward to the suburbs. He bought a ranch-style home in Southfield, Michigan, with his new wife, Anne Cain, making them the first black couple in an exclusively white neighbourhood. Eddie Kendricks of the Temptations registered with real estate agents, too, with plans to move further afield. He eventually compromised and signed a solo deal with Motown in the seventies, but he remained consistently bitter about Detroit. 'Since I was never a part of the Motown family anyway, I never got on the mailing list,' Kendricks once said. 'There was no relationship as far as I was concerned. The company had certain people it liked and that was that.'

The December issue of the *Michigan Chronicle* was traditionally the biggest-selling edition of the year and crucial to the wellbeing of the local soul music industry. Motown took out the most commanding ads, promoting the annual Motortown Review at the Fox Theater on Woodward. Stevie Wonder was scheduled to headline on the first five days of the show (23–27 December), to be replaced by Smokey Robinson and the Miracles (28 December–1 January). Support acts throughout the run were the Marvelettes, Gladys Knight and the Pips, the Contours, Chris Clark, Bobby Taylor and the Vancouvers, and ventriloquist Willie Tyler and Lester. Buried deeper in the pages of the *Chronicle* was another spectacularly untrue article about the Supremes, almost certainly fed to the paper by the corporation: 'Motown Denies Florence Ballard Has Left the Company'. Ballard had already signed her pre-contract agreement with ABC and no longer visited the Hitsville studios.

Sometime in the later months of 1967, Gordy threw a house-warming party at his new mansion on Boston Boulevard, and although Ballard was not invited she was encouraged to attend by Gordy's older brother Fuller, who presumably saw it as a gesture of conciliation. It proved to be yet another mistake. Nervous about being there and frustrated that she had not had a chance to argue her case, Ballard bickered with Diana Ross over a perceived slight and was asked to leave the party. It was another setback in a friendship that had never much hope of being rekindled and further alienated Ballard by casting her as emotionally unstable.

With Christmas approaching and festive cheer in short supply, the music industry woke up to one of the most dramatic moments in the history of sixties soul: the tragic death of twenty-six-year-old Stax legend Otis Redding. Redding drowned in the frozen waters of Lake Monona, near Madison, Wisconsin, after his small twin-engine passenger plane crash-landed, having encountered difficulty in heavy rain and fog. His body was discovered the following day when rescue attempts were mounted, and he was hauled unceremoniously from the freezing lake. Aretha Franklin and her sister Carolyn were at home in Detroit when news of Redding's death reached them, and they spent the remainder of the day on the phone with Redding's wife and executives at Stax Records in Memphis, trying to make sense of the patchy information on local news. Gordy was at Motown's Los Angeles offices and called his old friend Mable John, who was signed to Stax and closer to the Memphis scene. She had toured extensively with Redding and knew him well. But such was the paucity of information that Otis's widow, Zelma Redding, struggled to make sense of events and has since admitted she barely coped with the pain of managing the 'frightened emotions' of her young children. She was advised to delay funeral arrangements until the family was able to function and to allow Redding's body to lie in state at the Macon City Auditorium in Macon, Georgia, where he had grown up. Redding's burial had all the heightened importance of a state funeral, but significantly in a music scene still largely regionalised, Motown's northern-based stars stayed away. It was not a snub, nor was it seen in that light; it was simply not Motown's day. A north–south divide still shaped the R&B scene, and the mourners were drawn from Redding's world – the rural segregated towns of the Deep South. The pallbearers were mostly southern-based singers – Joe Tex, Jo Simon, Johnnie Taylor, Arthur Conley and Solomon Burke – and among the ranks of the mourners were James Brown, Rufus Thomas and Aretha Franklin, one of the few to make the journey south from Detroit.

Redding's death had reached out across the nation. Vice-President Hubert Humphrey delivered his own personal tribute, thanking Redding for supporting the government's ghetto outreach projects. At the time of his death, Redding had been negotiating with the vice-president to go with him on a morale-boosting trip to Vietnam. His simple and emotionally enduring tribute quoted a single prophetic line from Redding's current single, '(Sittin' On) The Dock Of The Bay': 'I roamed two thousand miles from Georgia, never to go back home again'. It was an oft repeated line that captured the tragic futility of the plane crash as well as the loss to the disintegrating world of sixties soul. 'Dock Of The Bay' became the most popular song among Vietnam veterans in the months and years to come, capturing an unspoken realisation of a war already lost.

It was a death much nearer to home that brought 1967 to its sombre conclusion. In the second week of December, Norman Whitfield was at Hitsville overseeing production on a Gladys Knight song called 'The End Of Our Road' and preparing for the release of 'I Wish It Would Rain' by the Temptations. The common denominator was the diffident young lyricist named Rodger Penzabene, and although no one at Motown had made the connection, the titles alone spoke of a depressive temperament and a young man reaching the end of his endurance.

He was Ruffin's polar opposite, a self-reflective man who disliked crowds and preferred the solitary role of the lyrical poet. His high school photograph shows him as a clean-cut Jewish boy with a scrubbed olive complexion. But by 1967 Penzabene's appearance had changed. He had become a restless hippie with long cascading hair and a deep tan that often led people to presume he was black. Otis Williams described him as 'young, nice looking, but kind of quiet and reserved . . . very humble'. Penzabene had grown up in the Palmer Park district of Detroit, the son of a relatively well-heeled family, and was introduced to Motown by his Mumford High School friend Cornelius Grant, whom he had known since childhood. Grant was by now a studio guitarist at Hitsville who had secured work on the road with the Temptations. Sensing that his friend's way with words had the same quiet self-confidence as Motown's poet in residence, Smokey Robinson, Grant introduced Penzabene to Norman Whitfield. Penzabene's darkly romantic love songs were to become some of the most sophisticated songs ever recorded in the maelstrom of Motown.

Penzabene had not been at the corporation long when his first song for the company, 'You're My Everything', featuring Eddie Kendricks as lead vocalist, was included on the 1967 album *The*

Temptations With A Lot O' Soul. Although Ruffin sang the outro, the decision to bring Kendricks to the fore irritated Ruffin immensely, and when the song charted as a single release he grouched endlessly at Whitfield for 'passing him over'.

Although Penzabene's stock was rising, his private life was stacking hopelessly against him. Recently married, his wife had started a love affair with another man and, racked by self-doubt, he turned his melancholy into his songs. Within a matter of a few months, he had composed one of the great trilogies in the history of Detroit soul: 'You're My Everything', 'I Could Never Love Another (After Loving You)' and the final masterpiece, 'I Wish It Would Rain'. All three were about a man profoundly lost without love. What Penzabene's collaborators and friends had failed to grasp was that the songs were desperate reflections on Penzabene's own circumstances and probably a cry for help. In the run-up to Christmas, Penzabene had been invited to a birthday party and puppet show for four-year-old Johnny Whitfield, the young son of Norman Whitfield, but he didn't show up. Several Motown staffers, including Johnny Bristol and the Holland brothers, delivered their kids to the Whitfield home, but Penzabene, who had no children, ducked the invitation. Although his creative star was in its ascendancy, he avoided Motown social events, and on the last night of the year he was home alone in his Detroit apartment, sinking deeper into a hopeless depression. A Motown office party to thank administrative staff for their efforts in 1967 was in full swing in a downtown hotel, and there was a company-wide expectation that production staff would at least show their faces. Some did, but Penzabene was not among them. Unable to come to terms with infidelity or to face the new year with any hope, he shot himself through the head and died instantly. His best song, 'I Wish It Would Rain', with all its emotional images of a tear-stained man alone in his room, was on the cusp of extraordinary commercial success and destined to become one of the greatest soul songs of all time.

Although Motown had been paying the lyricist a modest wage, he had yet to receive any royalty payments for songs that went on to rack up many millions of sales. 'I Wish It Would Rain' was so creatively rich it went on to become the greatest recorded performance of the so-called 'classic five' – David Ruffin, Eddie Kendricks, Melvin Franklin, Paul Williams and Otis Williams. According to Williams, irrespective of their furious infighting, the song captured 'a special magic which can never be recreated'. Ruffin was ultimately fired for unprofessional conduct after he failed to show up for a concert at the Versailles Motor Inn in Cleveland, and Paul Williams's drinking tipped perilously into alcoholism. Fighting sickle-cell anaemia and a series of failed businesses, Williams shot himself in an alleyway only a few blocks from the Motown studios, another victim of the tangled emotions of Hitsville USA.

On the day that 'I Wish It Would Rain' was officially released, churches and synagogues across Detroit were staging an interdenominational vigil to protest against the Vietnam War. Candles flickered in the cold damp air, and hymns rang out through the trees. Unlike the noisier anti-war demonstrations much loved by the countercultural youth, the religious vigil was composed of older citizens and children. Among their number was a small and determined group of Catholics from Detroit's East Side who had hatched an ambitious plan to use the city as a fulcrum for a major inquiry into the conduct of American troops in Vietnam. They had already made contact with several returning Detroit Marines who had agreed to provide a public testimony of war crimes, atrocities and genocide. The idea took three full years to come to fruition and became known as the Winter Soldier Investigation.

Protesting the war was now a daily occupation, and the growing army of dissenters across Detroit found expression in the actions of a determined campaigner, Rebecca Shelley, whose credentials as an anti-war activist dated back to the First World War. She hounded President Johnson wherever he went, and in December she flew to Europe to protest outside American embassies, staging dramatic candle-lit vigils in prominent public places. In Paris Shelley launched a symbolic protest called 'Mourn with Me' in which she dressed up as a village widow shrouded in black clothing and invited Parisians to join with her in a requiem for the war dead. Newspapers across France rushed to report on her protest, and her reputation as a thorn in the side of the American military sharpened. Rebecca Shelley's dedication to pacifism was tireless. She remained in Paris for much of December, denouncing the military and openly questioning America's moral authority to wage war. Her actions stimulated the interest of rioting French Maoist students, but she remained a principled character and a steadfast force amid the noise of 1967.

On Christmas Day, the American military in South Vietnam numbered almost half a million. Uncertainty about the war had begun to seep into even the most patriotic communities. On his annual sortie to entertain the troops, America's ultra loyal comedian Bob Hope sprinkled his stage routine with jokes that questioned the popularity of the war. 'If you guys don't get better ratings,' he told one army audience, 'the networks may cancel the show.' As the laughter faded, he hit them with another – 'Trust me, guys, the country is behind you – fifty per cent.' Hope's stand-up routine came precariously close to political satire when he told troops at a show in Da Nang that Dow Chemical was planning to get even with student protesters: 'They came up with an asbestos draft card.'

Bob Hope's entourage performed at twenty-two bases in fifteen days. Among their ranks were Bing Crosby's singing son, Phil Crosby, the Peruvian beauty queen Madeleine Hartog Bell, who had been crowned Miss World, and the voluptuous actress Raquel Welch. Representing Motown was the songstress Barbara McNair, a compromise booking offered up by Gordy's West Coast office when none of Detroit's superstars stepped forward to fly to Vietnam. Traditionally Bob Hope took to the stage carrying a golf club, but on this occasion he opened the show with a clownish parody of the song that had come to define 1967, Martha and the Vandellas' 'Dancing In The Street'. The biggest single audience was at the army depot at Long Binh, the largest military installation in the world and home to a medical evacuation centre and the notorious prison stockade nicknamed Camp LBJ. A crowd of

28,000 service personnel crammed into a corrugated metal amphitheatre held up by huge wooden supports, hurriedly erected in the midst of the camp on dusty hillsides scattered beneath a brutal sun, where a largely male audience, many stripped to the waist or wearing stained chinos, gazed at the sexy elegance of Raquel Welch in a knitted wool miniskirt and the 'ravishing Barbara McNair, dressed in a shimmering red cocktail dress'. The show ended with triumphant sentimentality. Barbara McNair's poignant rendition of the Christmas hymn 'Silent Night' was broadcast to millions across America on network television, providing Motown the kind of cross-over appeal that her mentor, Berry Gordy, had strived to achieve for more than a decade. For all its mawkish emotions, her performance was a triumph of racial integration, and two years later McNair would become one of the first black women to host her own network television show. Her voice, powerful in its devotion, carried over the parched fields to Silver City, the solitary confinement block of Camp LBJ, where Ronnie Ward, the young Marine facing charges of desertion, lay baking inside a converted shipping container, desperate to be freed from hell and deported home to Detroit.

By Christmas more than sixty per cent of Americans favoured withdrawal from Vietnam, and a high proportion of those expressed concern about the conduct of soldiers in the war. It was in Detroit that the first evidence of war crimes trickled out to a wider public. The Winter Soldier Investigation was conceived in the dying days of 1967, when local Catholics and pacifists tracked down returning veterans and recorded their testimony verbatim. The recordings were designed to publicise military atrocities in Vietnam, and although the public three-day gathering did not actually take place until 1971 much was already known to local activists in 1967, and 109 witnesses had agreed to give public testimony. Most were honourably discharged soldiers, retired civilian contractors or medical personnel, but with no great financial resource to fund the tribunals the interviews took time and ended up in the ignominious surroundings of a windowless room in a downtown Howard Johnson motel; the operational centre was a family home on the industrial East Side. A film of the events was sponsored by celebrity radicals, including film stars Donald Sutherland and Jane Fonda. As the participants testified about war crimes they had witnessed over the previous eight years, they were partly undermined by senior military personnel who rejected 'falsified statements' and were damned with faint praise by the press, which largely boycotted the proceedings. Several Detroit area veterans gave testimony, among them Marine Gordon Stewart of Royal Oak, who accused his battalion of genocide during raids into Laos in the final phase of Operation Dewey Canyon. As more and more incriminating evidence of war crimes leaked, the volume of public outrage increased. During the week of Sergeant Stewart's self-incriminating testimony, Motown released a new single by Marvin Gaye on the Tamla label. It took as its starting point a series of incidents far removed from Detroit and thousands of miles from the jungles of Southeast Asia, but it became one of the true masterpieces of the era.

Renaldo 'Obie' Benson of the Four Tops was travelling between venues on the West Coast when he witnessed police charging a group of students occupying the People's Park in Berkeley, California. Officers in helmets, shields and gas masks laid waste to over 6,000 demonstrators. National Guard troops with fixed bayonets attacked the crowd, and paramilitary officers obscured their badges to avoid being identified. One hundred and fifty-eight students were injured, some with gunshot wounds and head injuries. The incident appeared to have been pre-planned and became known in countercultural circles as 'Bloody Thursday'. The park had long been a contested issue between local residents and the authorities of the University of California, who had plans to develop the area as part of the expansion of the Berkeley campus. The park had become a meeting place for student radicals and local bohemians, and had provoked the conservative governor of California, Ronald Reagan, into a characteristic outburst when he called the Berkeley campus 'a haven for Communist sympathizers, protesters, and sex deviants'. When an otherwise unspectacular student rally about the Arab–Israeli conflict spread to the park, Reagan seized the chance to fulfil an election pledge to curtail student unrest at Berkeley. By sheer chance, as the battle raged, a tour bus carrying the Four Tops was attempting to navigate Dwight Way on the fringes of the park, and like some grotesque tableau the worst of the violence was visible through the windows where Benson was sitting.

On his return to Detroit, Benson recounted the story to songwriter Al Cleveland, who at the time was sharing his apartment. Together they fashioned a song that was eventually to become Marvin Gaye's epic 'What's Going On'. For Gaye and the discontented musicians at Motown, it was a catharsis of sorts, opening a floodgate that breached the dam of caution that Berry Gordy had erected at Motown. Among the flurry of songs that soon followed were Edwin Starr's 'War', Marvin Gaye's 'Abraham, Martin, and John', a tribute to the memory of assassinated leaders Abraham Lincoln, Martin Luther King Jr and John F. Kennedy, and Gaye's state-of-the-nation concept album *What's Going On*.

Although it was not released until 1971 against the backdrop of the Winter Soldier Investigations, Gaye's album had its roots firmly planted in the historic themes of 1967, when Detroit had been caught up in a deadly rebellion and his brother Frankie, a radio operator in Vietnam, had returned home to recount his combat experiences. Marvin and Frankie had exchanged letters between Detroit and Vietnam over the course of three years, and Frankie's first-hand accounts found their way into the lyrics of the album. 'I saw all the things I never wanted to see,' Frankie told Marvin on his return. 'I was in places I never wanted to be . . . You couldn't stand up: you had to crawl through the mud over things that moved when you touched them. It rained so much that everything on the ground rotted and smelled like week-old garbage, from the heat, rain and humidity . . . Once you see people dying, cut up, or being tortured, day after day of that you get desensitized, then paranoid . . . Still you want to believe there's a reason.'

For Gaye, Vietnam was an emotional landmark. His cousin Marvin Edward, nicknamed 'Bay-Bay', a twenty-one-year-old

Marine from Lexington, Kentucky, was killed in Quang Nam Province, South Vietnam. He often waited anxiously for another letter from Frankie, telling friends that he was concerned he might lose his brother too. Whatever political reasons there had been for America's involvement in Vietnam, by the end of 1967 they had begun to disintegrate. Gaye became increasingly fascinated by his private conversations with his brother and the world around him in inner-city Detroit, and although he had once imagined himself as a crooner – and back in 1964 had released the sentimental studio album *Hello Broadway* – Gaye had travelled to a very different place in his mind. He increasingly talked about the scarred surfaces of the inner city, the brutality of the Detroit police, the public failure to provide welfare for children, the trauma of veterans returning from Vietnam, and the troubled anxieties he felt about the role of God and formal religion. Fighting depression, facing a ruined marriage and a daily cocaine habit, Gaye determinedly clung to his vision, stealing studio time, calling in favours, and corralling friends to join him on a series of improvised through-the-night jam sessions, often using Motown's Studio B complex on West Davison. When he finally emerged, Gaye had produced a savage and mournful memoriam to 1967 – and arguably the greatest album in the history of popular music. The opening song, based on Obie Benson's confrontation with police brutality in Berkeley, had itself been transformed. Benson told the writer Dorian Lynskey that Gaye 'added some things that were more ghetto, more natural, which made it seem more like a story than a song . . . We measured him for the suit and he tailored the hell out of it.' The song is narrated through the eyes of a returning Vietnam vet – probably a personification of Gaye's brother Frankie – as he walks the streets of Detroit, bewildered by what he is seeing around him.

Excited by the recordings, Gaye described the song over the telephone to Berry Gordy, who was on vacation in the Bahamas when most of the tracks were laid. Gaye was given a frosty reception, and by the time Gordy returned to Detroit to listen to an early mix, he told his brother-in-law that he hated its strident and undisguised politics: 'I thought it was really meaningful, but he was a pop singer, and I told him, "Marvin, think about your great image that you built up: do you really want to talk about police brutality?"' Gordy tried to counsel him into abandoning the track. 'I could see he had pain and passion and he wanted to awaken the minds of men. He said, "B. G., you gotta let me do this," and I was really hesitant. Not for me, but for him. I didn't want his career to be gone. I said, "OK, Marvin, but if it doesn't work, you'll learn something, and if it does work, I'll learn something." So I learned something.'

An exodus from the inner city was now gathering momentum. Most headed out to the suburbs, but Motown looked further west to Hollywood, where opportunities in film and television were unrivalled. Coincidentally, and for very different reasons, MC5 and their caravan of radical hippies and hangers-on hatched plans to leave Detroit too. Months of police oppression and constant surveillance had weakened their resolve. A series of targeted attacks by right-wing thugs finally encouraged John Sinclair and the countercultural Steering Committee to shut up shop and look for a new base. The final straw came when a firebomb was thrown onto the roof of their office commune in Warren Forest, fire took hold, and the rooms below became uninhabitable. Only a few weeks earlier, the offices of the Detroit Committee to End the War in Vietnam had also been firebombed, and so the closely connected collective of political radicals abandoned the commune, ditched tons of debris, and scrapped piles of soot-streaked files. One of the few pieces of memorabilia that survived was a sign emblazoned with the slogan 'Burn, Baby, Burn', a tribute to the Black Panther Party and to Detroit's July rebellions. The communards bought two dilapidated townhouses in Hill Street, Ann Arbor, the Michigan university town known by the nickname A2.

MC5 used mountains of cheap cladding to convert an old garage into a soundproof rehearsal space and continued their sonic assault on America. Pun Plamondon, who was by then describing himself as Minister of Defense of the White Panther Party, claimed that the relocated Detroit hippies became 'an enclave of cultural assassins right in the heart of the university campus'. John Sinclair's East German wife, photographer Leni Sinclair, described the Hill Street communes as less stressful than Detroit, with a more amenable local police force. 'Except we didn't know that we were infiltrated,' she later claimed. 'They had the goods on us. They had our phone tapped; our lives were an open book to the FBI.' Throughout December 1967 the 'cultural assassins' of MC5 played locally, supporting Moby Grape, Cream and Vanilla Fudge at the Grande Ballroom and headlining at smaller venues across Michigan, including Club Limberlost in Lakeville, the Crow's Nest East on St Clair Shores, and the 5th Dimension in Ann Arbor, a converted bowling alley. By now the group's cacophonous reputation had travelled far from Detroit and they had become a bankable commodity, reaching the cover of *Rolling Stone* and signing an album deal with Elektra Records, who had acquired a hip cachet by being one of the first labels to sign countercultural bands like the Doors, the Paul Butterfield Blues Band and MC5's Detroit acolytes the Stooges, featuring Iggy Pop. MC5's debut with Elektra proved to be as provocative as their early recordings and tested their new label's tolerance to the limit – tracks included the iconoclastic 'Kick Out The Jams' and the riot anthem 'Motor City's Burning'. Hudson's department store in downtown Detroit, where Diana Ross had once worked as a sales clerk, refused to sell the record, considering it too obscene for its customers. MC5 retaliated with an ad in the *Ann Arbor Argus* that said, 'Kick out the jams, motherfuckers! And kick in the door if the store won't sell you the album on Elektra.' The not-so-subtle slogan – 'Fuck Hudson's' – was accompanied by a photo of MC5 and the logo of the commune's trademark, Trans-Love Energies. Unsure about the forces they had let loose on everyday consumerism, Elektra's management panicked and looked at ways of severing MC5's relationships with Sinclair and what they saw as an incendiary and uncontrollable Detroit underground.

It was among the student cafés, head shops and rambling townhouses of Ann Arbor that Detroit's 'counterculture in exile' acted out its next dramatic chapter. In September 1968 a bundle of dynamite was exploded outside an innocuous office at 450 Main Street. According to reports, the device blew a three-inch-deep hole in the sidewalk, shattered windows, overturned furniture, and caused thousands of dollars of damage. A well-informed rumour had circulated around Ann Arbor's left-wing student community that the office on Main Street was a front for the CIA, where Agent John F. Forrester recruited University of Michigan undergraduates to act as informers and join the CIA. Investigations lasted more than a year, and eventually a federal grand jury indicted three members of the recently formed new leftist group the White Panther Party. They were White Panther Minister of Defense Pun Plamondon, who was charged with having set off the bomb, White Panther Minister of Education Jack Forrest, then in the hospital with a shattered leg, who was charged with conspiracy to commit the bombing, and John Sinclair, by then the White Panther Minister of Information and still MC5's manager, who was charged with conspiracy. Plamondon chose to make his escape and went on the run, hidden beneath a tartan travel rug in the rear of an old Buick. He hid for a while in Ohio and then in various communes in California. While on the run he became the counterculture's most wanted man and the first hippie to feature in the FBI's Ten Most Wanted list. As part of Sinclair's counsel's strategy, they insisted that the government turn over any electronic surveillance of the defendants, which they suspected might include a warrantless wiretap of Plamondon, transcripts of a phone call he had made to the Detroit office of the Black Panther Party, and a probable wiretap on the commune on Hill Street. The covert actions were almost certainly attributable to the FBI's COINTELPRO surveillance operations, but Leni Sinclair went on to claim that they had also been victims of an informer inside the commune. 'Paranoia struck deep,' she has since claimed. 'We believed that our house was bugged, and that our phone was tapped. So we started holding our important meetings to plan our defense strategy under a tree in the park, thinking that we were safe from the uninvited ear. Only twenty years later did we learn that there was one among us, living with us at 1520 Hill Street, who regularly wrote reports about us to the FBI. To this day we don't know the identity of that informer.'

Sinclair's indictment on the bombing charges was ultimately overshadowed by the most famous night in the history of the Ann Arbor underground music scene – the Free John Sinclair rally at the Crisler Arena, an eight-hour marathon featuring John Lennon's first concert in America since the break-up of the Beatles. Sinclair was already in Jackson Prison, serving an eight-and-a-half- to ten-year sentence for giving two marijuana cigarettes to undercover Detroit police officer Vahan Kapagian back in January 1967. Lennon and Yoko Ono performed a debut of the specially written protest song 'Free John', and Stevie Wonder joined them onstage, leading a who's who of sixties radicalism, including Allen Ginsberg, Jerry Rubin and Black Panther activist Bobby Seale. Stevie Wonder's shift from Motown child genius to fully-fledged political artist was all but complete. Among the supporting acts were local artist Bob Seger, folk singer Phil Ochs and jazz saxophonist Archie Shepp. But the headline act was Sinclair himself, who joined the concert by phone lines routed over the PA system. Most of his words were drowned out by the noise of the crowd, but the concert had already embarrassed the authorities, and within forty-eight hours Sinclair was released into the arms of his tearful wife and children.

It would have been the perfect radical reunion had it not been for the absence of MC5. Sinclair's relationship with the group had soured. They had become closer to Elektra, which wanted the group to put distance between themselves and Detroit and play down the revolutionary politics espoused by Sinclair and Plamondon. They had not been invited to perform, and even if they had it is not certain that Elektra would have endorsed their appearance. MC5's album, recorded live at the Grande Ballroom over two ghoulish Halloween events in late October 1968, secured their place in garage-rock history. Rob Tyner took to the stage with the band's furious motto: 'And right now . . . right now . . . right now it's time to . . . kick out the jams, motherfucker!'

★

In early December the Supremes appeared on a network television spectacular hosted by Tennessee Ernie Ford. Two years before, it would have been cause for company-wide celebration, but now it passed unnoticed. Divisions within Motown had deepened irrevocably amid a storm of aggressive legal claims and counter-claims. Events were brought to the fore by a memo circulated to all internal staff in early December. The communiqué announced the resignation of Eddie Holland from his role as A&R director. It was sparsely worded to minimise the risk that it could be used in the suit against Motown, and it claimed, in the classic language of corporate understatement, that Holland was leaving 'in order to devote his full time to song-writing and producing efforts'. The brief memo instructed staff that all A&R matters would now revert to the offices of the president, bringing them back full circle under the control of Berry Gordy – or, more controversially, his tight group of senior executives.

Snow returned to the city. It came in flurries at first and then with seasonal vengeance, but it never reached the suffocating intensity of the first few weeks of the year. Berry Gordy had been spending more time in Los Angeles for the best part of eighteen months now and the gravitational pull of Hollywood was strong. He had delegated much of his daily decision making to senior managers and was no longer in day-to-day control of Motown. Gordy assured staff that it was business as usual, but he often undermined these reassuring statements by his own actions. When he wasn't in California working from his tiny office in Hitsville, he would lurch into a frenzy of activity, urging writers and producers to up their game and prodding producers to dust off their back catalogue in the search for hidden hits.

For most of December he tried to remain calm but appeared fidgety and distracted. Gordy knew that the loss of Holland-Dozier-Holland could sink Motown. 'Although I had some serious fears about the situation,' he said, 'my ego would not permit me to think that I couldn't do it without them. After all I had taught them, given them opportunities and driven them not just to be good but to be the best.' He reflected long and hard on why he had allowed the trio to accrue so much power, and he vowed never again to allow Motown to be held captive to the demands of what he called 'background superstars'.

Inevitably, Gordy's survival instincts kicked in, and he met doubt with the full force of retaliation. When he returned to Detroit sometime in the first two weeks of December, Gordy went excitedly to Golden World to record the lead vocals of Bobby Taylor and the Vancouvers' 'Does Your Mama Know About Me'. Speaking enthusiastically to the local press about the superior musicianship available to him in Detroit, he seemed to imply that Motown would never move, as it owed too much to the latent genius of Detroit, and whatever his many justifications for being in Hollywood, he remained genuinely loyal to the musical talent in his hometown and turned a blind eye to the behaviour of the idiosyncratic characters who gathered in Motown's studios. Whatever their faults, which by now included alcohol, drugs and factionalism, he believed they were the cream of the crop and that the disruptive genius of the Funk Brothers only found its true groove when the music started.

It was now six months since the bitter end of Ballard's Motown career, but the matter of her departure was far from finished. Diana Ross and the Supremes were back in Detroit for what proved to be a directionless week. In a series of scattered studio sessions, they recorded a couple of album tracks and some others that failed Motown's demanding quality thresholds. At a time when Gordy needed to be at his strongest, a creative vacuum seemed to have set in, and the final sessions of 1967 were patchy at best. There was an effervescent and but unremarkable song called 'I'm Gonna Make It (I Will Wait For You)', written by Debbie Dean and her guitarist friend Dennis Lussier, featuring Cindy Birdsong singing what would normally have been Ballard's parts. The following day Diana Ross was at Hitsville alone to record a bizarre tribute to African-American history, 'Treat Me Nice John Henry', written by Smokey Robinson. It was a love song about the legendary worker-hero John Henry, a slave who had reputedly worked on the construction of the Coosa Mountain railroad tunnel in Alabama. According to legend, Henry fears for his future when the master introduces a mechanical steel-powered hammer, and a contest is arranged – man versus machine. The exhausted Henry wins the contest but dies with his hammer in his hand. Although the legend of John Henry had been reclaimed by civil rights activists, it was still a bizarre choice of material for a glitzy girl group and a lead singer whose aspirations were already far from the gritty reality of railroad construction. But Motown insiders claimed the song was chosen by Diana Ross and she felt it had a dramatic story that soared above ordinary love songs. While the song's heart was in the right place, it was neither Diana Ross nor Smokey Robinson's finest moment, and the curiously anachronistic track lay buried in the vaults, rejected. A day later Ross laid down lead vocals of a third song, 'Forever Came Today'. Desperate to recapture the old Motown elixir, Gordy had raided an archive of backing tracks produced before the departure of Holland-Dozier-Holland, and Ross's vocals were overlaid. On its eventual release, the song stuttered at only number twenty-eight in the *Billboard* Hot 100.

Outwardly busy, Gordy was staring failure in the face. Rather than capitulate, he set out three different routes back to success. One response was to raid the company's back catalogue for great songs that had been overlooked; another was to ensure that the next generation of writer-producers, such as Norman Whitfield and Ashford and Simpson, were given greater recording opportunities; and the third option was to build a new writing team from scratch. It was the third option that excited him and proved to be one of the most personally satisfying moments in his formidable career, casting him in his favourite role as Motown's demanding mentor.

Although Gordy has been universally portrayed as a man slow to react to the social changes of the sixties, he had one counter-argument: the recording of the Supremes' hit 'Love Child'. He hatched a scheme that was destined to lessen the impact of Holland-Dozier-Holland's departure and mine a new seam of success. He gathered together a nameless collective of writers whose identity would be subsumed into a generic and largely anonymous group that he chose to call 'the Clan'. It was partly a

satire on the racist organisation the Ku Klux Klan and partly a way
of reclaiming the spirit of ancient Scottish clans – a family bound
together by ideals and a shared goal. 'I told them it was a matter of
semantics,' Gordy explained. 'Once again I wanted to take a so-
called negative word and use it positively. I was using the word
"clan" with a "c" for its meaning as a group of friends linked by a
common purpose.'

Gordy wanted the Clan to be virtuously anonymous, to sound
new, unknown and mysterious. He wanted to demonstrate to the
wider music industry that it was business as usual at Motown and
that the corporation's capacity to unearth greatness in Detroit was
undiminished. He handpicked the group carefully, pulling together
writers and musicians who had everything to gain from joining
him, and selecting people who he thought could park their egos at
the door. It proved to be a motley crew who had no obvious
affiliations but shared a passion for musical composition.
Significantly, none of them were identified with any of the warring
tribes at Motown, and all were relatively new to Detroit and keen
to make an impression: Deke Richards, Frank Wilson, R. Dean
Taylor and Pam Sawyer. None of the Clan had powerful positions
at Motown, and none were particularly high up the pecking order.

Deke Richards was in his early twenties, an aspiring young
guitarist with giant white teeth and a gaucho moustache. His real
name was Dennis Lussier, and he had come to Gordy's attention a
few years earlier as a backing musician with Motown's first white
recording artist, the Kentucky-born songstress Reba Smith, who
recorded under the pseudonym Debbie Dean. Lussier had grown
up in a Hollywood family, the son of a failing screenplay writer,
and had a passion for schlock horror movies, often taking days off
from his studio duties to sit transfixed in cinemas across Detroit
watching what a friend described as 'inestimable shit'. R. Dean
Taylor was a Canadian pianist who had moved to Motown to
advance his career as a writer-performer. Frank Wilson was a
twenty-seven-year-old writer-producer from Motown's Hollywood
office who had abandoned a singing career to focus on producing
for Stevie Wonder, Patrice Holloway and Martha and the Vandellas,

and stayed close to Christianity and his gospel roots. Pam Sawyer was the only woman in the Clan. She had striking peroxide-blonde hair, wore dark eyeshadow and skin-tight black polos, and was a first-generation Modernist from Romford near London, who knew more about Motown than most American teenagers and had been brought up on the cult TV show *Ready Steady Go*. She was a fan of R&B who had moved to New York as part of a writing duo with Lori Burton, co-writing for the Young Rascals and the Scottish pop star Lulu, as well as recording her own 'Mod songs' under the name the Whyte Boots. Her obsession with black music took her to Detroit and inevitably to Motown. Gordy had also invited Hank Cosby, the round-faced likeable saxophonist from the Funk Brothers and one of his most trusted lieutenants. Cosby's job was to act as the Clan's foreman and ground any ideas in studio protocol.

Gordy checked the Clan into Detroit's new and ultra cool Ponchartrain Hotel near Cobo Hall. Nicknamed the Pontch, the hotel had once been a historic meeting place for car industry magnates but had been rebuilt earlier in the sixties as a twenty-five-storey luxury hotel with a piano bar, a penthouse restaurant and a nightclub called the Top of the Pontch. The Motown Clan moved casually among them all, talking about songs, swapping lyrics and exchanging hummed melodies in the elevators. Motown had arranged for a piano to be installed in one of the top-floor suites, and at times Gordy himself would colonise the piano in the hotel bar to improvise tunes. As they worked around the clock, grabbing sleep in shifts, they tested potential songs. Many were rejected and others stored to memory in sessions stretching over several days that, according to Gordy, were exhausting. 'On about the second day of coffee and frustration, throwing ideas out in the air that nobody particularly liked,' he wrote, 'I started playing what felt liked Holland-Dozier-Holland-type chords to get in the mood for what I was looking for.' Gordy credits Pam Sawyer as the originator of the song that became 'Love Child' when she suggested a song about teenage pregnancy. At first Gordy was sceptical about such a divisive social issue, but, overruled by the room, he let things run and within less than forty-eight hectic hours, Gordy and Deke

Richards completed the chord structures on piano and guitar, and Diana Ross was summoned to Hitsville to record the lead vocals. The other Supremes were not called and backing vocals were provided by the Andantes. According to Raynoma Gordy, Motown engineer Calvin Harris sat for days taking direction from the boss. 'Berry personally supervised everything about the recording, including the mix. He mixed the hell out of that song . . . and it paid off.'

'Love Child' had not emerged in a vacuum. The ideas that informed the song were regularly talked about at Motown, which counted several unmarried mothers among its most loyal staff, and across the nation, where rates of teenage pregnancy were spiralling. Detroit had among the highest rates in the nation, and the Assistant Secretary of Labor, Daniel Moynihan, had recently published a data-rich report, 'The Negro Family: The Case for National Action', better known as the Moynihan Report. It focused on urban poverty and came to the controversial conclusion that the absence of fathers in urban homes stood in the way of political equality. By then twenty-five per cent of all black births were illegitimate. 'It is the fundamental source of the weakness of the Negro community at the present time,' Moynihan's report said, claiming that 'at the center of the tangle of pathology is the weakness of the family structure. Once or twice removed, it will be found to be the principal source of most of the aberrant, inadequate, or antisocial behavior that did not establish, but now serves to perpetuate the cycle of poverty and deprivation.'

It was the political ramifications of the song that initially worried Gordy and, according to members of the Clan, he was deeply unenthusiastic, fearing it would portray the Supremes and particularly Diana Ross in a bad light. Gordy had grudgingly allowed Stevie Wonder to cover Bob Dylan's iconic protest song 'Blowin' In The Wind' the previous year, but by then the song was widely known, sung in churches across the land, and an official anthem of public marches. It was far from risky.

To try to broker a deal with Gordy and address his reluctance, Sawyer proposed a shift of emphasis and wrote the lyrics of 'Love

Child' in such a way that the girl featured in the song – Diana Ross – rejects sex before marriage for fear that it will produce a 'love child'. Thus a morally contentious subject is turned into a song about 'family values'. It was a shift of emphasis that Gordy could live with and one he could happily promote under the Motown banner. So, having set out to write a hot song that would demonstrate to the wider creative community that there was life after Holland-Dozier-Holland, Motown had overcome another hurdle and written a song that took teenage love in an entirely new direction, one that faced up to sociopolitical issues in the real world. Unintentionally, it became a song that acted as a stepping stone to more stridently political recordings in the months and years ahead. Although Holland-Dozier-Holland had not been magically replaced – and the immediacy of their pop-soul canon never really would be – 'Love Child' was a demonstrable shift in gear for Motown, proving beyond doubt that hits could come from a wider creative community and that nobody was indispensible. Gordy felt vindicated by the song, and at least for a time it rekindled his enormous self-belief.

For all the divisions within Motown, the pace of Detroit soul did not slow. The Four Tops received the Varsity Club Award for Music in Philadelphia, then returned to Detroit to rehearse for their Christmas residency at the Copacabana. Marvin Gaye's 'You' was released, and holiday specials were booked across the city. Chuck Jackson was in concert at the Playland, Buddy Lamp was at Mr. Kelley's Lounge on Chene, the Originals were at the 20 Grand, and Wheelsville Records' biggest draw, the Fabulous Peps, were performing at the Local 876 union hall. Despite all the promises of a more manageable schedule, the Supremes travelled back to Metro Airport to catch a snowbird flight to Florida to begin a two-week residency at the Deauville Hotel on Miami Beach, followed by a tour of Italy, France and the United Kingdom early in the new year. The crippling itinerary that had driven Florence Ballard to exhaustion had not let up.

★

The underlying social themes of 'Love Child' and the new era of creativity it brought to the surface at Motown proved to be one of the lasting legacies of 1967. Disputes between Gordy and his artists unlocked creative tensions that paralleled the wider social disruptions across the city. The year 1967 proved to be fertile soil, and the seeds of two seismic albums were sown in the year of discontent. Marvin Gaye's *What's Going On* and MC5's *Kick Out The Jams* were destined to stand out like cultural beacons. Both expressed political anger in ways that reflected the different musical subcultures of Detroit. *What's Going On* was to become a masterpiece of the inner city, echoing the events of the Algiers Motel killings, the 'trigger-happy policemen', the lives of returning Vietnam vets, the emotionally devastated mothers who had placed their faith in the benevolence of God, and the scattered fragments of a riot-torn city. *Kick Out The Jams* was packed with youthful rage, urban resistance and anti-authoritarian disgust, a noisy polemic against materialism, drug laws and the city's despised police force. They were recorded almost simultaneously but in very different versions of the same city. Despite their difference, they were united in their disgust for late sixties America.

The National Advisory Commission on Civil Disorders – commonly known as the Kerner Commission, after its chairman, Governor Otto Kerner of Illinois – was not due to report until February 1968, but enough of its controversial content had been leaked in advance. Among its most challenging findings was the simple but damning sentence, 'Our nation is moving toward two societies, one black, and one white – separate and unequal.' Although the academic John Hersey had refused to participate in the commission, his book on the Algiers Motel killings unearthed astonishing personal testimony from the families and friends of the dead boys. Hersey had interviewed people that neither the police nor the daily newspapers had gotten close to. But rather than write a one-sided brutal condemnation of the Detroit police, Hersey had also examined the lives of low-ranking police officers. Buried within the pages of the Kerner report was a sentence that Hersey might have authored: 'The role of the ghetto policeman . . .

is already one of the most difficult in our society. He must deal daily with a range of problems and people that test his patience, ingenuity, character and courage in ways that few of us are ever tested.'

Patrolman August admitted shooting nineteen-year-old Aubrey Pollard and was charged with first-degree murder. He claimed self-defence, and an all-white jury sided with his version of the story. After numerous false starts, it was decided that Detroit could no longer host the emotive and deeply divisive trial. To assuage public feelings, a decision was made to move the trial from downtown Detroit to Ingham County Court, a beaux arts courthouse on a tree-shaded street in Mason, Michigan, over ninety miles from the inner city. It was a white farming community with a rural economy and a 'sleepy demeanor', but it proved to be an ill-advised choice of location, and a legal process designed to calm public feelings appeared to the bereaved families as part of an unfolding conspiracy. Forty-eight witnesses lined up at Ingham County Court to accuse the police of ritually beating people in the motel in the vain attempt to locate an imaginary sniper who simply did not exist. According to Prosecutor Avery Weiswasser, the Detroit police were pursuing a policy of 'kill first and investigate later', and in the surrounding chaos August was induced to take Pollard into a motel room, where he was shot. *Time* magazine described August as sitting 'mute and ramrod straight through most of the trial'. He was portrayed by his lawyer as an 'upstanding family man' who admitted shooting Pollard when the teenager 'came at me'. August admitted that he had acted suspiciously when he gave shifting and conflicting statements to senior police officers in the immediate aftermath of the incident, but in his defence he claimed that he feared being 'sacrificed' and blamed for all three killings.

In what was a tense courtroom the equal of any television drama, Judge William Beer took an unusual legal move, ruling out lesser charges of manslaughter or second-degree murder and directing the jury to make a stark choice: either to acquit August or to find him guilty of first-degree murder with a mandatory life sentence. Beer himself was a man of confusing absolutes. At the time of the trial, he was living the most extraordinary double life.

Having refused to divorce his wife, he had fallen in love with his secretary, with whom he cohabited. He had three sons by his wife and nine further children with his secretary and yet claimed to love both women equally. The all-or-nothing choice he left the jury to deliberate upon made conviction even more difficult than it might have been, and after nearly three hours the jury voted for acquittal. The dead boy's mother, Rebecca Pollard, already numbed by the death itself, wept bitterly outside the court and told reporters, 'I didn't look for them to find him guilty. All whites stick together.' August and his two colleagues, David Senak and Robert Paille, were suspended from the force and faced federal conspiracy charges of violating the civil rights of eleven motel occupants, including the three dead teenagers, but the deaths were never satisfactorily explained in court, and the families had to stomach one of the great injustices of 1967.

Although 1967 ended on a note of high hope for Florence Ballard, it was short-lived. She was pregnant and due to give birth in the new year, and Larry Newton, the square-jawed boss of ABC, was at last satisfied that Motown had no legal hold on Ballard and welcomed her into a new home. Newton was more like an ageing football coach than a music magnate, but he had managed to assemble a roster of artists in New York that included some of the very best voices of sixties soul, including Chicago's the Impressions, led by the peerless Curtis Mayfield, blues legend B. B. King and vocalist Della Reese, who had grown up in Detroit's old Black Bottom ghetto and had once sung at the famous Flame Bar, where the Gordy sisters owned the cigarette concession. It is not entirely clear who influenced the direction of Ballard's short career at ABC – the artist or her advisers – but when she came to record, there were numerous nostalgic connections back to Motown. Ballard's first release, the bouncy 'It Doesn't Matter How I Say It (It's What I Say That Matters)', was produced by George Kerr, then an emergent writer-producer who worked with the O'Jays, the High Keys and the late great Linda Jones. He had been one of Raynoma Gordy's first recruits when she set up the Jobete/Motown offices in New York after divorcing Gordy. The song stiffed on release and was not helped by a gagging order placed on Ballard, forbidding her from using the words 'the Supremes' in any publicity. Coyly ABC's official press release said simply that Ballard 'was a member of a popular singing trio for many years'. Her second single, 'Love Ain't Love', was written by Van McCoy and arranged by Bert De Coteaux, both of whom would go on to play a formidable role in the evolution of disco. This time the producer was an old face from Detroit, Robert Bateman. Bateman had been in a short-lived Detroit doo-wop group, the Satintones, with Brian Holland, and both had joined the first-generation Motown backing group the Rayber Voices. Bateman had discovered the Marvelettes at a talent show at Inkster High School and was for a time close to the Gordys; Raynoma once even hinted that they'd had an affair when her marriage to Berry Gordy was collapsing. Hiring Bateman might have been insignificant, or it might have been guided by Ballard's sense of security, since Bateman had been in the room at Hitsville when the Supremes first auditioned for Motown. What is more than coincidental is that both of Ballard's ABC producers were friendly with Raynoma Gordy at a time when she herself was in a legal dispute with Berry Gordy. It might well have been a case of the old adage 'the enemy of my enemy is my friend'.

Ballard had no diagnosed history of mental illness, nor was she someone who lacked resilience in her day-to-day life, but by the end of 1967 it was clear that her self-confidence had been battered, and her brief, under-promoted solo career with ABC never came close to matching the success or fulfilment she had enjoyed at Motown. The cocky belligerence she had once as a teenager had been sapped by legal wrangles, bad relationships and an overwhelming sense of professional betrayal. It all conspired to drive Ballard to a dark place. Her marriage to Tommy was happy for a spell, and she gave birth to twins, but as many had predicted the relationship was doomed from the outset, and although there were periods of reconciliation she lived much of her life as a single mother.

At a low point, Ballard told Peter Benjaminson, then a local journalist with the *Detroit Free Press*, that she had begun to drink even more heavily and had taken to walking the streets of Detroit alone at night. 'It was like I was in a daze, just walking,' Ballard told him. 'It was like I didn't care anymore. I had given up. I began to go into a complete depression, where I would just withdraw from people completely; just stay locked inside and wouldn't come out . . . I just didn't want to be seen or anything.' At the worst point of her breakdown, Ballard inevitably turned to her family and to one of her closest brothers, Billy, who in turn was convinced that Motown and her former lawyer, Leonard Baun, might have been in league against her. It was a nonsensical idea but one that took a damaging grip and left Ballard entertaining yet more conspiracy theories.

When it was clear that her solo career had run out of steam, Ballard's old fears that Motown was watching her escalated. She and her brother Billy grew convinced of a conspiracy against her and she 'felt like so many people were involved in it. I began to think that they were too. Then I began to get scared, scared to go outside. I don't know why I just had fear . . . I got that way because I was out of the group, because I couldn't understand what was going on, because I wanted to find out about my money but couldn't.' Ballard's alcoholism and mental health worsened, and it may well be that she suffered some form of paranoid disorder that went undiagnosed for the few years she had left. With no real income and a family to support, she defaulted on her home on Buena Vista and moved into a low-cost apartment below her sister near Six Mile Road.

Although Florence Ballard had not set eyes on Reggie Harding for several years, she had not forgotten him and never would. On 25 December 1967, Harding sat down at a cheap Formica table, staring at his father and gulping down a TV dinner. It was one of the most pathetic family Christmases imaginable. For all his towering potential and the riches that had been thrown at him as a precocious basketball star, he now lived with his father in a rundown wooden shack on the East Side. Harding's father was a self-proclaimed preacher who lived as if he had never left the rural poverty of the Deep South and was a controlling bully. He could not conceal his disgust at the failures of his son, who, by 1967, was a full-blown heroin addict with the mental age of a child. Harding's gigantic gangly body, which forced him to hunch down to pass through doors, only served to exaggerate his strangeness. Since his teenage years, Harding had hidden an illegal handgun in an old sports sock in his bedroom, and he often lumbered to his room to sit on his bed and play with it as if it were a childhood toy. Although he had no real grasp of other people's emotions, it was clear that Reggie Harding missed his mother profoundly. She had died four weeks before Christmas and at least in part had held her son's damaged life together. The thin and fraying thread of maternal love that had bound father and son together had finally snapped, and now the two men sat staring at each other, unable to communicate except through surly grunts. The father was deeply ashamed of his son and quoted the Old Testament to him as if it were a guide to urban life, and the son was now a serial criminal who despised his father's self-righteousness.

The downward spiral of Harding's life tragically echoed that of his victim. Within a matter of only a few years of signing her failed ABC contract, Florence Ballard's life hit irreversible decline. With no source of income and her money from her time as a Supreme now defrauded and squandered, she was forced to use food stamps and seek welfare support from the Aid to Dependent Children programme (ADC). Although her sister Maxine has since claimed that Ballard's period on welfare was not quite as pathetic a picture as history has painted, it was far from pleasant. As usual she refused to disguise her lot in life and openly admitted that she was on welfare. Florence once told her sister, 'I'm not going to let anyone keep me down, I'm not going to roll over, I'm not going to lay down and die, I'm going to fight to the end.' But by 1976 she had given up fighting and died from a heart attack, aged thirty-two. Her early death is a story of decline so tragic that it has come to personify the cruelty of the music industry and has compelled many to point the finger of blame at Motown. But her life and her death were always much more complicated than that, and she was, at least in part, the author of her own downfall. The naïve trust she placed in the legal profession, her reliance on advice from within her well-intentioned family, and her ruinous decision to allow Tommy Chapman to act as her manager were all factors. Nevertheless, her death attached itself like a stigma to Motown, and for the remainder of his career it pursued Berry Gordy like a dark phantom.

As 1967 faded, the term 'MoWest' began to enter the company's everyday vocabulary. It began as conversational slang, but as the centre of gravity of the Motown Record Corporation moved inexorably from Detroit to Los Angeles, MoWest became a fully-fledged subsidiary label in its own right, with offices on Sunset and Vine and a studio on Romaine Street. By 1971 it had come to symbolise Motown in Hollywood and inevitably espoused a more eclectic and multicultural musical policy than its Detroit parent company. Suzee Ikeda, a Chicago-born singer of Japanese parentage, became the first Asian-American artist to sign for Motown. When her recordings tanked, she took a job with the backroom staff. Frankie Valli and the Four Seasons briefly joined up, and so too did a new generation of hugely promising soul acts, including Thelma Houston, the Commodores, Sisters Love, the Devastating Affair, and a daring experimental funk-rock group from California called Odyssey, who captured the zeitgeist of late sixties counterculture but then disappeared from sight, only to have their name taken by the more famous New York disco group. At worst it was a rag bag of sounds and a sign of how sixties soul music was fragmenting into a thousand different sounds: funk, rock, free jazz, disco, and even back to its roots in gospel and spiritual song.

Diehards in Detroit resented the pull of the West Coast and the talent drain of musicians who moved there. For a while, many Motown lifers felt that those who left the Motor City for Los Angeles were little better than creative traitors. Smokey Robinson, Stevie Wonder and Diana Ross all bought homes on the West Coast and, most remarkably of all, master bassist James Jamerson of the Funk Brothers moved to Los Angeles, lured by Gordy and the promise of a brighter future. But his natural habitat was the late-night soul clubs and semi-legal bars of Detroit, and Los

Angeles proved to be a culture shock. He left Motown in 1973. Others refused to go west. Martha Reeves ended her twelve-year association with the label and stayed in Detroit.

Berry Gordy had not completely fallen out of love with Detroit, and never would, but Los Angeles loomed larger in his ambition. With Shelly Berger opening doors, he began to circulate in movie circles and saw close-up that the Hollywood star system was even more capricious and hierarchal than anything he had experienced in soul music. Gordy's last face-to-face meetings with Florence Ballard became disagreements about the nature of stardom, a subject that hurt her sense of pride. 'He would say, "Flo, you don't know how to be star,"' she told a journalist. 'And maybe I didn't, because as far as I was concerned, I was a person, and I had to be a person. I couldn't be anything else. It's frightening to go all the way to the top, and somebody say that you have to be a star, that you can't mingle with certain people. People, to me, has always meant people, and I've always felt that if I don't have people, then I don't have anything; and I still feel that way.'

What Ballard struggled to articulate was that Motown was unhappy about her closeness to her family and to her old friends back in Detroit, who in Gordy's mind still had ghetto attitudes and were holding her back. That was in marked and fateful contrast to Diana Ross, who was not only born with star potential but came from a family who fed her social aspiration with her milk. By the end of 1967, Motown instructed staff, especially those new to the company, to address Diana Ross as 'Miss Ross'. Throughout the previous twelve months, Miss Ross had gradually distanced herself from daily life at Hitsville and from the other members of the Supremes too as Gordy groomed her for a solo career. Ballard was unambiguous that their different attitudes towards life had driven them apart, claiming that Ross was intensely private and had 'an ego, a big ego, a very big ego'. In the nine years between leaving the Supremes and her premature death, Ballard and Ross only spoke once or twice and never reconciled. But what Ross's many critics rarely concede is that her driving ambition and self-centredness were underpinned by a tireless professionalism and capacity for hard work that was unrivalled by any of her Motown contemporaries. She also had another unique characteristic: the ability to turn weaknesses into strengths. As a teenager her rasping nasal voice had been the subject of ridicule among the big gospel voices of Detroit – Mable John, Aretha Franklin and even Florence Ballard – but it adapted perfectly to the shifting surfaces of sixties pop music. Her stick-thin frame made her an easy target, but it was the perfect frame for fashion, photography and cover photos, and anticipated the rise of heroin chic and size-zero modelling by decades. Her acting skills were limited, but cameras loved her. Her personal idiosyncrasies – being surrounded by designer dogs and personal flunkies – were a blueprint for highly-strung talent, and they secured her legendary status later in life as a gay icon.

Diana Ross was never the most intellectual or politically committed figure at Motown, and the big social narratives of the sixties were at the periphery of her life, but what is rarely acknowledged is that, in her own way, she rewrote the rules of black American music and seized on a widely ignored civil right: the right to pursue fame or, more bluntly, the right to be as famous as any white singer before or since. For all the animosity that surrounded her eventual departure from the Supremes, Ross was destined to become the most famous black woman on the planet and built a career that survived the decades. Her flight to fame inevitably took her away from Detroit and beyond the cultural shackles of soul music into new stratospheres of stardom. She took acting lessons in L.A., read voraciously about acting theory, and set her heart on playing Billie Holiday in *Lady Sings the Blues*. It had become an obsession shared by both Ross and Gordy, who had met Holiday in Detroit's Flame Club in the mid fifties. She won the role, and the film went on to earn five Oscar nominations. Ross subsequently played the romantic and self-reflective role of industrious fashion designer Tracy Chambers in another movie, *Mahogany* (1975), produced by Motown and directed by Gordy. The tag line spoke volumes about her imperious sense of self: 'Mahogany: the woman every woman wants to be and every man wants to have.'

Although Ross and Gordy were to stay linked professionally for much of their lives, the love affair that had flourished first in secret and then publicly across 1967 had reached its natural conclusion. Gordy claimed that 'it just came time when it was best for us to split up. I don't really remember my part in that – I was always objective. The fact that I went with Diana Ross – she never took advantage of that and I never gave her an advantage. She didn't want any favors; she wanted to do what was right. If she got more attention at Motown, it was because she was good; it was all about the work. That's why we broke up . . . I knew she wanted to be a superstar.'

As Rodger Penzabene's body was taken from his West Side apartment to the city's overcrowded morgue, the Temptations were on tour in New Jersey, and his most famous song, 'I Wish It Would Rain', was steadily rising up the *Billboard* charts. The Supremes were onstage at the Deauville Hotel in Florida, and Berry Gordy had travelled with them. Smokey Robinson and the Miracles were still in concert at the Fox Theater, and Detroit's protopunks MC5 were backstage at the Grande Ballroom on Grand River, waiting to play-in the new year. The gun crime that had dogged the city since the turn of the decade – that many local politicians still blamed on the laxer gun laws in nearby Toledo, Ohio – exacted a heavy price on independent soul. Club owner Mike Hanks, a lifetime rival of the Gordy family and owner of the D-Town and Wheelsville labels, was shot in a nightclub dispute. Vocalist Darrel Banks, who recorded for Revilot Records, was shot and killed by an off-duty policeman after a dispute about a mutual girlfriend. And the infamous Diamond Jim Riley – pimp, gangster, and record producer – was shot dead in a fight at the Detroit jazz club Watts Mozambique. In the week of Diamond Jim's death, Detroit was registering ten homicides a week, and its crime-infested inner city was national news. The rebellious summer had laid waste not just to Detroit's inner city but to the small shops, nightclubs and independent studios that had been the lifeblood of sixties soul. Some were destroyed, others so badly damaged they struggled to recover; others simply ran out of steam, uninsured, undercapitalised, and under siege. The artists who had made Detroit the most important musical city in the world faced different fates. Some relocated to Los Angeles, while others stayed loyal to the city and tried to rekindle its greatest moments. Some were drawn deeper into drug dependency, while others faded into obscurity.

The traumatic events of 1967 did not kill Motown, nor did they seriously derail the progress of African-American music. On the contrary, one of its most successful acts, the Jackson Five, who hailed from Gary, Indiana, were yet to be discovered and had years of fame and scandal ahead of them. But by moving the locus of his company first to corporate offices in the Donovan Building downtown, and then to Los Angeles, Gordy unintentionally undermined the creative energy of Detroit soul. Never wholly reliant on Motown, the music soldiered on well into the future, but something unprecedented had happened: soul music had been blown apart by the powerful social events of 1967 and began to fragment into a myriad of new parts. The influence of counterculture led to the rise of a more rock-oriented form of psychedelic soul that was soon reflected in the Temptations' album *Cloud Nine*. The pursuit of meaningful lyrics broke Motown's obsessions with teenage romance and led to the great concept albums of the early 1970s – Marvin Gaye's *What's Going On*, Funkadelic's eccentric *Free Your Mind . . . and Your Ass Will Follow*, and Curtis Mayfield's urban masterpiece *Super Fly*. Elsewhere, the rise of a more orchestral form of soul music emerging from the studios of Philadelphia International and new indie labels in New York such as SalSoul, West End Records, Casablanca and Prelude laid the groundwork for metropolitan disco and then house music and eventually hip-hop.

As the clock struck midnight and 1967 came to a restless end, the snow that had besieged Detroit at the start of the year briefly threatened to return. But when it fell, it was soft sleet. As the bespectacled night workers made their way to the Wayne County morgue on the edges of Greektown, the old mock-Egyptian building was crammed full, bodies lined row upon row in tiled drawers. It was one of those pristine body coolers that would become the penultimate resting place of Rodger Penzabene, the man who had provided the pained lyrics of one of Motown's greatest songs.

Penzabene's death was one of the last to be registered in 1967. Most of his colleagues at Motown were unaware of his suicide and only heard of it when they returned to work in the new year. The Temptations were told of his death backstage at the Latin Casino in Cherry Hill, New Jersey. Among their ranks that night was guitarist Cornelius Grant, who had known the dead man best of all. Grant had known his friend Rodger was down but had not realised how desperate his depression had become; nor did anyone at Motown know that the song Penzabene had written was in some sense a suicide note. His death became an unexpected requiem for 1967, twelve eventful months that had taken Detroit to the very limits of its endurance and brought the music of the Motor City to the verge of collapse. It was not the end of the assembly line, but it was never quite the same again, and in a very real sense it was the end of Detroit's place at the forefront of world music – and the end of sixties soul.

BIBLIOGRAPHY

Primary Sources

Al Abrams Private Papers, the personal papers and memorabilia of Motown publicist Allan Abrams, Bentley Historical Library, University of Michigan, 1150 Beal Ave, Ann Arbor, MI.

Blues and Soul Magazine, London, 1966–72.

Detroit Free Press, 1965–70, Detroit Public Library, Detroit. (*Note*: publication was interrupted in late 1967 due to industrial dispute.)

Detroit News, 1965–70, Detroit Public Library, Detroit. (*Note*: publication was interrupted in late 1967 due to industrial dispute.)

Detroit Police Department Reconnaissance. Photographs and records taken by the Detroit Police Department following the 1967 Detroit riot; views of burned-out and vandalised businesses and offices, including interior and exterior views of drinking clubs. Bentley Historical Library, University of Michigan, 1150 Beal Ave, Ann Arbor, MI.

COINTELPRO Papers, The FBI Education Center, Pennsylvania Avenue, NW Washington, DC.

Gordy Family Archives, 1920–59, Bentley Historical Library, University of Michigan, 1150 Beal Ave, Ann Arbor, MI.

Michigan Chronicle, 1962–72, Detroit Public Library, Detroit.

NAACP Collection, cataloguing the activities of the Detroit branch of the National Association for the Advancement of Colored People and its

related activities, 1909–79, Walter Reuther Library, Wayne State
University, Detroit.

The John and Leni Sinclair Papers, 1957–79, Bentley Historical Library,
University of Michigan, 1150 Beal Ave, Ann Arbor, MI.

Newsweek, vols 68–69, 1967.

The Papers and Correspondence of the Reverend Martin Luther King Jr.,
Martin Luther King, Jr. Center for Nonviolent Social Change ('The King
Center'), Atlanta, Georgia.

Secondary Sources

Blackstock, Nelson, *COINTELPRO: The FBI's Secret War on Political
Freedom*, New York: Pathfinder Press, 1988.

Branch, Taylor, *At Canaan's Edge: America in the King Years 1965–8*, New
York: Simon & Schuster, 2006.

Callwood, Brett, *Sonically Speaking: MC5, A Tale of Revolution and Rock 'n'
Roll*, Church Stretton: Independent Music Press, 2006.

Carpenter, Bill, *Uncloudy Days: The Gospel Encyclopedia*, San Francisco:
Backbeat Books, 2005.

Carson, David A., *Grit Noise and Revolution: The Birth of Detroit Rock 'n'
Roll*, Ann Arbor: University of Michigan Press, 2005.

Donner, Frank J., *The Age of Surveillance*, New York: Alfred A. Knopf, 1980.

Fine, Sidney, *Violence in the Model City: The Cavanagh Administration,
Race Relations, and the Detroit Riot of 1967*, East Lansing: Michigan
State University Press, 2007.

Gentry, Curt, *J. Edgar Hoover: The Man and His Secrets*, New York:
W.W. Norton & Co., 1991.

George, Nelson, *Where Did Our Love Go*, London: Omnibus Press, 1985.

Gordy, Berry, *To Be Loved*, New York: Warner Books, 1994.

Hauser, Thomas, *Muhammad Ali: His Life and Times*, London: Robson
Books, 1991.

Hersey, John, *The Algiers Motel Incident*, Baltimore: Johns Hopkins
University Press, 1968.

Kotz, Mick, *Judgment Days: The Laws That Changed America*, Boston:
Mariner Books, 2006.

McLeese, Don, *The MC5's Kick Out the Jams*, London: Bloomsbury
Academic, 2005.

Posner, Gerald, *Motown: Music, Money, Sex and Power*, New York: Random
House, 2005.

O'Reilly, Kenneth, *The FBI's Secret File on Black America, 1960–1972*, New York: Free Press, 1991.

Rylatt, Keith, *Groovesville USA: The Detroit Soul and R&B Index*, Worthing: Stuart Russell, 2010.

Ritz, David, *Divided Soul: The Life of Marvin Gaye*, New York: McGraw-Hill, 1985.

Shaw, Todd C., *Now Is the Time: Detroit Black Politics and Grassroots Activism*, Durham & London: Duke University Press, 2009.

Salvatore, Nick, *C.L. Franklin, The Back Church and the Transformation of America*, New York: Little Brown & Co., 2005.

Sauter, Van Gordon & Hines, Burleigh, *Nightmare in Detroit: A Rebellion and Its Victims*, Chicago: Henry Regnery Co., 1968.

Sinclair, John, *Guitar Army*, New York: Rainbow Press, 1972.

Singleton, Raynoma Gordy, *Berry, Me and Motown*, Chicago: Contemporary Books, 1990.

Smith, Suzanne, E., *Dancing in the Street: Motown and the Politics of Detroit*, Cambridge: Harvard University Press, 1999.

Sugrue, Thomas, *The Origins of the Urban Crisis: Race and Inequality in Postwar Detroit*, New Jersey: Princeton Studies in American Politics, 2005.

Surkin, Martin & Georgakas, Dan, *Detroit: I Do Mind Dying: A Study in Urban Revolution*, Detroit: South End Press Classics, 2012.

Traborelli, Randy J., *Call Her Miss Ross*, London: Sidgwick & Jackson, 1989.

Wilson, Mary, *Dreamgirl & Supreme Faith*, New York: Cooper Square, 1999.

Wilson, Randall, *Florence Ballard Forever Faithful*, San Francisco: Renaissance, 1990.

Wright, Vicki, *Motown from the Background: The Story of the Andantes*, New Romney: Bank House Books, 2007.

AUTHOR

Stuart Cosgrove is from Perth, Scotland, and was a television executive with the UK broadcaster Channel 4. A professional journalist and broadcaster, he was a staff writer with the black-music paper *Echoes*, media editor with the *NME* and a feature writer for a range of newspapers and magazines.

A graduate of Hull University, he completed a PhD in modern American theatre history and won a UK Academy Award for his post-doctoral essay 'The Zoot Suit and Style Warfare'. He has since studied at Wharton Business School, University of Pennsylvania, and the John F. Kennedy School of Government at Harvard University. Stuart is an Honorary Fellow of John Moores University Liverpool, an Honorary Professor of Stirling University and Honorary Doctor of Arts at Abertay University.

In 2005 he was named Broadcaster of the Year in the Glenfiddich Spirit of Scotland Awards. In 2012 he won numerous awards including a BAFTA and Royal Television Society award for Channel 4's coverage of the London Paralympics 2012. He was also given a BAFTA Scotland Award for Special Achievement and Industry Excellence in television.

Stuart presents BBC Scotland's popular radio show *Off the Ball*, and lives in Glasgow and London.

INDEX